Van Wyck Brooks:
The Early Years

Van Wyck Brooks: The Early Years

A Selection from His Works, 1908–1925

REVISED EDITION

Edited, with an Introduction and Notes, by
Claire Sprague

Northeastern University Press
BOSTON

First edition published in 1968 by Harper & Row, Publishers, Incorporated, New York. Revised edition published in 1993 by Northeastern University Press.

Library of Congress Cataloging-in-Publication Data

Brooks, Van Wyck, 1886–1963.
    [Selections. 1993]
    Van Wyck Brooks, the early years : a selection from his works, 1908–1925 / edited, with an introduction and notes, by Claire Sprague.—Rev. ed.
      p. cm.
    Includes bibliographical references and index.
    ISBN 1-55553-174-1 (hard : alk. paper)—ISBN 1-55553-175-X (pbk. : alk. paper)
    I. Sprague, Claire. II. Title.
PS3503.R7297A6   1993
818'.5409—dc20   93-30710

Printed and bound by Edwards Brothers, Inc., Ann Arbor, Michigan. The paper is Glatfelter Offset, an acid-free sheet.

MANUFACTURED IN THE UNITED STATES OF AMERICA
98 97 96 95 94 93   5 4 3 2 1

For
BEA SUSMAN
and in memory of
FREDERICK J. HOFFMAN
and
WARREN I. SUSMAN

Acknowledgments

My debt, as always, is a very large one, to the many friends, critics, scholars, and family I have learned from and loved. I must single out Fred Hoffman who started—better, startled—me into the study of Van Wyck Brooks and his colleagues. Then there is Warren Susman, who seems always to have been there and to be there still.

Let me single out, with gratitude, those who read and commented on the new foreword with such care and honesty—Casey Blake, Milton Cantor, Christopher Cullity, Leona Egan, Carol Hurd Green, Ann Lane, Irving Schneider, Zola Schneider, Helen Yglesias—and those whose conversation gave me such pleasure and stimulation, Morris Dickstein and Raymond Nelson. My thanks to Nancy Shawcross, who guided me through the Van Wyck Brooks Papers at the Van Pelt Library of the University of Pennsylvania.

My son Jesse was always there to bear with, sometimes enjoy, and above all to survive yet another of my projects.

New York and Provincetown, 1993

Contents

Chronology

1886 Van Wyck Brooks born in Plainfield, New Jersey, February 16, the younger of two sons of Charles Edward Brooks, a stockbroker, and Sarah (Sallie) Bailey (Ames) Brooks.

1891 Enters Plainfield public schools.

1898 Spends the year with his family in Germany, France, Italy, and England.

1904 Enters Harvard University with the class of 1908, following Maxwell Perkins, his childhood friend from Plainfield.

1905 *Verses by Two Undergraduates* privately printed with John Hall Wheelock. Becomes an editor of the *Harvard Advocate*.

1907 Elected to Phi Beta Kappa; graduates a year ahead of his class. Sails for England alone; remains till 1909.

1908 *The Wine of the Puritans* published in London in the fall; writes for London journals; returns to New York the following spring.

1909 In New York, various writing jobs, e.g., with the *Standard Dictionary*, *Collier's Encyclopaedia*, *World's Work* (under Walter H. Page); interviews and writes about writers, including William Dean Howells. Rooms on W. 23 St.; frequents Petitpas's, where he becomes part of a circle that includes John Butler Yeats, John Sloan, and other artists and writers.

1910 Death of Mark Twain.

1911 In Carmel, California, where, on April 26, he marries Eleanor Kenyon Stimson of Plainfield. Completes *The Soul: An Essay Towards a Point of View*, privately printed in San Francisco, dedicated to John Butler Yeats. Teaches English at Stanford University in the fall. Begins biographies of John Addington Symonds and H. G. Wells, and critical studies of Henri Frédéric Amiel, Etienne Pivert de Senancour, and Maurice de Guérin.

1912   Votes for Eugene V. Debs. Thereafter usually for Norman Thomas. Charles Van Wyck Brooks born in February.

1913–14   In England and France. Teaches for the Workers' Educational Association at South Norwood near London; lives on the Isle of Wight, and for a year at Kent. Completes *The Malady of the Ideal*, published in London in an edition of two hundred copies. Followed by *John Addington Symonds*. Meets Walter Lippmann, Frank Harris, Jo Davidson, and others. Completes *The World of H. G. Wells*.

1914   Returns to U.S. after the outbreak of war in Europe. *Symonds* published in New York soon after. Works for the Century Company. Both he and Eleanor translate, together and separately, from the French. Lives in Plainfield, then in New York City.

1915   *The World of H. G. Wells* and *America's Coming-of-Age*. Meets Randolph Bourne. The two are close until Bourne's death in December 1918.

1916   Oliver Kenyon Brooks born in January. The *Seven Arts* begins publication in November. Death of Henry James.

1917   Becomes associate editor of the *Seven Arts*; fellow editors are Waldo Frank, James Oppenheim, and Paul Rosenfeld. The *Seven Arts* ceases publication after its October issue. Resumes Century job after the magazine's demise.

1918   *Letters and Leadership*. "On Creating a Usable Past" published in the April *Dial*. Revisits Carmel; works on his Mark Twain book. Death of Randolph Bourne.

1919   Completes his Twain biography. Returns east.

1920   *The Ordeal of Mark Twain*. Settles in Westport, Connecticut. Begins to translate *Henry Thoreau, Sauvage* (1914); corresponds with the author, Léon Bazalgette. Becomes literary editor for Alfred Jay Nock's weekly,

	the *Freeman*. Undertakes a weekly column, "A Reviewer's Notebook," as well as other essays and reviews until magazine's demise in 1924. Meets Lewis Mumford.
1922	Contributes "The Literary Life in America" to Harold Stearns's *Civilization in the United States*. Death of John Butler Yeats.
1923	Puts aside his biography of James. *Dial* accepts three chapters for publication.
1924	Receives the Dial Award for 1923. Reader for Harcourt, Brace & Co.
1925	*The Pilgrimage of Henry James*. Begins his study of Emerson. Suffers acute melancholia, paranoia, and suicidal bouts.
1926–31	Spends these nervous breakdown years in and out of institutions.
1927	*The American Caravan*, edited with Lewis Mumford, Paul Rosenfeld, and Alfred Kreymborg. Wife and friends arrange for the publication of *Emerson and Others*, which contains chapters of *The Life of Emerson*.
1931	Returns home late in the year and slowly resumes his life. His brother Ames commits suicide at age 48.
1932	*The Life of Emerson*, largely completed in 1926; Literary Guild publication arranged by wife and friends. Collects and publishes *Freeman* essays in *Sketches in Criticism*.
1933	Revised edition of *The Ordeal of Mark Twain*.
1934	*Three Essays on America*, slightly revised collection of *America's Coming-of-Age*, *Letters and Leadership*, and "The Literary Life in America." Eleanor Brooks runs for the Connecticut legislature on the Socialist ticket.
1935	Elected to the National Council of the League of American Writers, an outgrowth of the first American Writers' Congress. Waldo Frank is chairman.
1936	*The Flowering of New England*, the first of five volumes, representing a twenty-year labor and the first wholly new work since his disabling illness. Awarded the Pulitzer Prize for History.

1937	Runs as Socialist candidate in Connecticut. Elected to the American Academy of Arts and Letters, the centenary year of William Dean Howells, the Academy's first president.
1939	Resigns from the League of American Writers.
1940	*New England: Indian Summer, 1865–1925.* "On Literature Today," delivered at the inauguration of Dr. George N. Shuster as president of Hunter College, in New York City, October 10. Moves to Weston, Connecticut.
1941	*Opinions of Oliver Allston,* earlier published serially in the *New Republic* and the *Yale Review;* the book also incorporates "On Literature Today" and "Primary and Coterie Literature." Becomes a contributing editor for the *New Republic.*
1944	*The World of Washington Irving.*
1946	Eleanor Brooks dies in August. Moves to New York City with the John Hall Wheelocks.
1947	*The Times of Melville and Whitman.* Marries Gladys Rice on June 2.
1948	*A Chilmark Miscellany,* a collection of favorite pieces of the last decade.
1949	Settles in Bridgewater, Connecticut.
1952	*The Confident Years, 1885–1915,* the final volume in the series *Makers and Finders: A History of the Writer in America, 1800–1915.* Travels to Ireland.
1953	*The Writer in America.*
1954	*Scenes and Portraits: Memories of Childhood and Youth,* the first of three volumes of memoirs.
1955	*John Sloan: A Painter's Life.* Travels to California.
1956	*Helen Keller: Sketch for a Portrait.* Spends April and May in Rome, preparing study of American writers and artists in Italy between 1760 and 1915 (*The Dream of Arcadia*).
1957	*Days of the Phoenix: The Nineteen Twenties I Remember,* second volume of memoirs.
1958	*From a Writer's Notebook, The Dream of Arcadia.*
1959	*Howells: His Life and World.* Travels to England and Scotland.

1960   Ill with cancer during the last three years of his life.
1961   *From the Shadow of the Mountain: My Post-Meridian Years*, third and final volume of memoirs.
1962   *Fenollosa and His Circle*. Suffers a stroke late in the summer.
1963   After a period of declining health, dies May 2, in Bridgewater, Connecticut.

Foreword to the 1993 Edition

What dinosaur theorists call an extinction event happened to Van Wyck Brooks. He disappeared from sight. But more assiduous digging shows that however fissured or shifting the nature and extent of his reputation came to be, reports of his extinction were premature. As Brooks was suffering a critical eclipse among his cohorts in the twenties and thirties, for example, he was capturing a new, more popular audience, one that made *The Flowering of New England* (1936) a best-seller for 59 weeks (Hyman 106). Another kind of fissure existed between Marxist criticism, which found his work usable, and the developing New Criticism, which found it totally unusable.[1] Something of the same split exists today as post-structuralists ignore Brooks and new historicists and cultural critics find him again worth reading. His reputation was probably at its nadir in the forties and fifties. In the sixties, not Brooks but Randolph Bourne became a cultural icon. By the late sixties and into the seventies a few university critics began to return to his work (Sprague, 1968 [the first edition of this volume]; Vitelli, 1969; Wasserstrom, 1971, 1979; Hoopes, 1977). More recently, in the eighties and nineties, critics are reasserting the judgment of the first two decades of our century that Brooks's works stand "at the beginning of modern criticism of American literature" (Reising, 1986, 13; see also Nelson, 1981; Blake, 1990; Biel, 1992; Dickstein, 1992). These critics have been immensely receptive to Brooks's cultural criticism and are a sign of the renewed interest that occasions this reprint of a collection published twenty-five years ago.

My 1968 introduction stands—as it should, if only for historical reasons. There are, of course, parts small and large I would like to clarify, sharpen, rearrange, but very little I would erase. Surprisingly, I have no essential disagreements with my earlier self. I am now, for example, less hard on later Brooks but without the impulse to change my assessment of early Brooks. And while I continue to speak of "early" and "late" Brooks, as I think we must, I am still impressed by the continuities in Brooksian thought.

The 1968 selections from the work of Van Wyck Brooks, including the headnotes, are as they were. The Chronology has been added. The continuing unavailability of *The Wine of the Puritans*, *America's Coming-of-Age*, the *Seven Arts* essays, in their original or *Letters and Leadership* form, and "On Creating a Usable Past" makes their presence in this collection especially useful to interested new and old readers.[2] The chapters from *The Ordeal of Mark Twain* (1920) and *The Pilgrimage of Henry James* (1925) are newly added. They are included because the works are central to Brooks's corpus, historically important, and now so difficult to come by. The Twain biography has had an extraordinary career; it has shaped Twain scholarship and continues to affect the way we see Twain's life and work even as we approach the seventy-fifth anniversary of its publication. The James biography did not strike an equivalent nerve. It is now more important as a document in the expatriate debates of the twenties, for its genesis at a crisis point in Brooks's life and career, and for its launching of Brooks's later critical method.[3] In these antipodal yet intersecting works, Brooks pursues two cautionary American lives, using his signature dialectic for the last time.

I begin with my conviction that duality and contradiction are ubiquitous in Brooks's life, career, and critical formulations.[4] A young man of privilege who traced his descent back to 1659 when the Van Wycks arrived here, Brooks grew up with financial insecurities that belied his class status. His father's western copper and nickel mining ventures were failures. His "almost pure Anglo Saxonism" (*Autobiography* 244; one Irish great-grandfather diluted his Dutch/English ancestry) did not spare him other painful experiences, like the anti-Americanism he encountered in Dresden (p. xxxviii of the introduction) or his early knowledge of invalidism, from his father whose image pursued him as Henry James's would later—

"Wherever I went, in whatever I read, I seemed to find my father then" (*Autobiography* 71)—and from the many family friends living in darkened rooms trying to recover from breakdowns. In Brooks's world fathers tended to fail and mothers to survive. Brooks's own lifelong battle with manic-depression (today called bipolar disorder) began in high school but did not immobilize him, he claims, until the years 1926 to 1931. These years can and have been taken to divide his life in two, but the division between the two periods, like so many divisions, is not razor sharp. Brooks endured a severe depression as early as 1919, for example, after the completion of *The Ordeal of Mark Twain*. His retreat from the special kind of activism that he and his *Seven Arts* colleagues represented may have begun earlier yet, with the breakup of the *Seven Arts* group in 1917.

All lives were social document—his own,[5] his father's, those of the literary figures he wrote about—and therefore cautionary, for American lives were thwarted, incomplete, or failed lives. Only later did they become exemplary. The earlier concept was eminently usable, its methodology less so. Nonetheless, Brooks managed to create an effective polemical criticism. One reason for the extraordinary success of his early work is his happening upon what F. W. Dupee calls "the music of antinomies" (121). Beginning with the certainty that the acquisitive and the creative life were permanently at war, Brooks found other terms to forward his argument; the transcendental and the commercial in *The Wine of the Puritans* and the Highbrow and the Lowbrow in *America's Coming-of-Age* are his most well-known pairs. He had, of course, ample precedent among nineteenth-century English thinkers for the habit of antithesis, Matthew Arnold's Hebraism and Hellenism (p. 153), for example, as well as American versions like Teddy Roosevelt's mollycoddle and redblood, William James's tenderminded and tough-minded, and Henry Adams's the Virgin and the Dynamo. Brooks refers his readers to two Ur-literary figures, Don Quixote and Sancho Panza (p. 96). Even if, as Dupee judged, Brooks's development of his polarities was thin, their role as powerful slogans was considerable. His "pairs of opposed catchwords," as Brooks called them, served the radical

intellectuals well.[6] Later pairs are of a different order. In oppositions like "primary" vs. "coterie" literature and "life-affirmers" vs. "life-deniers," Brooks chose a language and a content
more suited to the professorial dry-as-dusts he had attacked
earlier in the century.

Some of his great concerns have lost their urgency or have
acquired historical interest only. That would seem to be the
case with the problem of expatriation. But what if the problem
is turned around and framed as one of deracination for ethnic
and racial groups within this country?[7] That's a heady, perhaps
quixotic, although surely occasionally usable shift in perspective.

Deracinated immigrants were unlikely to be welcomed. They
were too many, too poor, and non-English speaking. Their
presence had already exploded and changed American cities.
Henry James complained in 1904 that one hardly heard English
spoken on the streets of New York. Teddy Roosevelt thun-
dered, "There is no room in this country for hyphenated Americans" (in Abrahams 17). John Dewey spoke otherwise: "the
theory of the melting pot always gave me rather a pang" (in
Abrahams 65). William James provided philosophical support
with his preference for "pluralistic" over "monistic" forms (44
and passim). Brooks is closer to Dewey and James than to
melting pot exhorters and theorists. In his introduction to Randolph Bourne's essays, he considers the melting pot ideal an
illusion. Like his gadfly Bourne, Brooks came to accept something like what we call cultural pluralism today. My "something
like" is an important qualifier, for Brooks was not a cultural
pluralist as we understand that term today. However, both
Bourne and Brooks preferred difference to the melting pot
metaphor that other progressives like Herbert Croly and Walter
Lippmann found persuasive.

Bourne developed a fuller response to the new immigrants
than Brooks did.[8] In "Trans-National America," he argued that
"we have needed the new peoples . . . to save us from our
own stagnation" (263–264), wryly pointing out that English
stock came here for freedom, not "to adopt the culture of the
American Indian" (263). From his point of view English-Amer-
icans were as hyphenated as everyone else in the country save

its indigenous peoples. While Brooks shared Bourne's distaste
for the "washed-out . . . tasteless, colorless fluid of uniformity"
(Bourne, 1916, 269) represented by the melting pot ideal, he
can suggest a twinge at his own displacement, even a touch of
nostalgia for the (supposed) homogeneity of an older America,
as he does when he imagines Rip Van Winkle awakening
to the polyglot America of the twentieth century (p. 97).
Brooks learned, as he acknowledges later, that his original title
for *America's Coming-of-Age*, *A Fable for Yankees*,[9] was all
wrong for a country now "as multiracial as the crew of the
Pequod in *Moby-Dick*" (p. 80; *Autobiography* 244) How
characteristic of Brooks to choose a literary allusion to sanctify
the untoward immigrant invasions of his time!

For a long time, historians did not look at the internal
migration of African Americans northward in conjunction with
the immigrant "invasions" of the period. Together these internal
and external migrations/immigrations profoundly altered the
nation. African Americans were not then hyphenated Americans and their unique historical role as an enslaved and therefore without exception forcibly deracinated population was
rarely compared with new immigrant arrivals. They were not
explicitly included in Bourne's trans-national America.[10] Nor
did they enter into the adversarial critical discourse of the
period represented by Brooks and his colleagues, although
W. E. B. Du Bois's *The Souls of Black Folk* (1903) had appeared five years before *The Wine of the Puritans*. Brooks
could, however, given the right triggering event, erupt with
anger at African American exploitation. One such moment
occurs in a *Seven Arts* essay, "The Culture of Industrialism,"
when Brooks cites as "wonderfully symbolic of our society that
the only son of Lincoln should have become the president of
the Pullman Company, that the son of the man who liberated
the slaves politically should have done more than any other,
as *The Nation* pointed out not long ago, to exploit them industrially" (p. 200). Another such moment occurs when
Brooks records his irritation with the endemic appearance in
American humor of "Negroes [who] grin and chuckle from
daylight till dark" (p. 45).

The record suggests that Bourne enjoyed and took difference

further than Brooks. He thought his country could be a model
for a world federation at a time when Europe was already at
war, torn apart by national rivalries and imperial motives. In
his trans-national essay, he charged that events in Europe were
making "patriotism a hollow sham." These events led Bourne
to question the very basis of Brooksian criticism, to doubt
whether it was worth preserving "the search for 'American'
culture" (272).

Bourne is at that moment connecting political and cultural
nationalism. Brooks could see the two nationalisms both separately and together. Indeed, the burden of his early criticism
insists on the intimate and complicated relationship between
the two. The acquisitive instinct is more than economic; it is
political and cultural and literary as well. Of course, Brooks
counterposes his cultural ideal to chauvinistic talk about a
"'place in the sun'" (p. 132) or to "what the rest of the world
at present calls 'Americanism'" (p. 191). In a *Freeman* essay,
he urges the public to "leave nationalism to the politicians" (p.
236). But when he came to focus more exclusively on the
creation of an "American" literature, it was inevitable that he
be perceived as the wrong kind of patriot. He could not understand why. Forty years after America's entry into the Great
War, Brooks chafed under the accusation of "chauvinism when
political nationalism meant to me so little, when I would have
been glad to surrender sovereignty, with all the other nations."
"Cultural identity," he continued, "was all that interested me,
while the actual America of my belief was the nation of its
promise, a nation that too often broke its word" (*Autobiography*
327). Neither the Great War nor subsequent political events of
his time brought Brooks to publicly doubt the dangers atten-
dant upon a theory of American uniqueness (today often called
American exceptionalism).

American promise functions as a kind of escape clause in
Brooksian cultural nationalism. It makes the defective present
bearable. What wasn't would be. And what was could be
altered, Brooks asserted flatly and emphatically, since "the spiritual past has no objective reality." Or, as Bourne put it in an
early essay, "It is only the Past that we really make" ("Seeing"
218). The reconstruction of the past and the shape of the future

became inextricably tied in Brooks's cultural critique. In "On Creating a Usable Past," easily his most influential and provocative essay, Brooks called for a radical reworking of tradition. Most critics have taken that reworking to mean the encyclopedic record of the literary life Brooks accumulated in the five volumes that make up the Makers and Finders series (1936–1952). The "Usable Past" essay had a different set of objectives. It was a polemic, an exhortation to remake the past by a kind of realigning, uncovering, and discovering that includes filling in the canvas but doesn't stop there. Remaking means rejection as well as inclusion. Today's equivalent, canon revision, is in practice less radical.

Brooks accepts the truth that traditions and canons are always selective. Perhaps only in the twentieth century have they been self-consciously chosen. The point, of course, is who is choosing what and how and why the choices are being made. When Brooks was young, figures like Bryant, Longfellow, Whittier, Lowell, and Holmes seemed to have a secure place in the literary canon. Brooks and his generation initiated the process that led to their dethronement and their virtual disappearance from the standard anthologies. Their presence in current surveys of American literature remains slight. In 1918 Brooks's usable past did not mean the reverential, celebratory, cluttered canvas of Makers and Finders. The word *unused*, as Russell Reising aptly uses it (18), is, in fact, the better word for what Brooks excavates in his Makers and Finders series. The series does recover a past. As such it is immensely valuable. But from the perspective of the earlier Brooks, the unused past acquires full power only when it is shaped in terms of a point of view.[11]

The "Usable Past" essay opens boldly, with a provocative distinction between two kinds of anarchy, one fostering, the other inhibiting. The entire essay exudes confidence and power. It champions the young and attacks the old for disparaging "almost everything that comes out of the contemporary mind." It insists that the young discover or remake the past, as a "vital criticism" always does, and so replace the unusable professorial past. Both the Brooks and the T. S. Eliot traditions were efforts to revitalize the past. The sixties' catchword "relevant" is a kindred effort. Indeed, according to Lewis Mumford in *The Golden Day* (xix), every generation needs to undertake a critical revaluation of tradition. Canons are never "loose," to use Gates's witty phrasing, but in a time of revaluation they are certainly loosened.

Anthologies are a useful index to governing academic taste.[12] The 1993 Macmillan *Anthology of American Literature* places "American Renaissance" writers under an enlarged and all too familiar heading called "The Age of Romanticism." Brooks's generation prepared the way for this displacement, which is at once more old fashioned and more inclusive (the latter makes it more usable, although, as Reising points out, the problem of a limited national canon is not merely quantitative [30]). Not every generation will perform radical canonical surgery; more than one generation usually passes before such surgery is performed. The one currently under way resembles the efforts of the 1910s and 1920s. The young in Brooks's day were re-belling against what they called, using George Santayana's term, the genteel tradition. Today New Criticism survives in the way post-structuralist criticism looks at the work of art, while the more historical emphases of the New Americanists are modifying what used to be called a formalist approach. Quite absent today is the presence of independent critics. Once Brooks's targets were inside the university. Today professors dominate our criticism, writing primarily for one another and their advanced students. Brooks's world was different; he was not alone as a highly influential independent critic; he had the company of others like Bourne, Waldo Frank, Paul Rosenfeld, Lewis Mumford, H. L. Mencken, Edmund Wilson.

America's Coming-of-Age and the *Seven Arts* essays had created a public eager for Brooks's next book. When *The Ordeal of Mark Twain* appeared, its impact was immediate. Its continuing influence has been unprecedented (see pp. 245–247). Even hostile critics (like Hyman) praise *Ordeal* for its cogent thesis, one that nearly seventy-five years later still informs Twain criticism—as it must, for in it Brooks defined and spoke for the first time to the overwhelming presence of doubleness in Twain's life and work and fully addressed the unsmiling aspects of Twain's thought.[13] The timing of *Ordeal* was perfect:

Twain's recent death in 1910, the posthumous publication of the pessimistic *Mysterious Stranger* (1916), the publication of Albert Bigelow Paine's three-volume biography in 1912, Paine's edition of Twain's letters (1917), which Brooks reviewed, the deepening fractures and gloom of the war years, and Brooks's professional and personal readiness for the project all conspired to make for a rare meeting of biographer, subject, and time.

Dwight Macdonald's premise, "The quest of Mark Twain is the quest of America" (116), is precisely Brooks's. No other American writer could have so perfectly illustrated the Brooksian thesis about America's split personality. Samuel Clemens/ Mark Twain is both highbrow and lowbrow, artist and businessman, satirist and funny man, rebel and conformist. Clemens gave in to his Twain self, even to disfiguring his fiction to please the public. Bernard Hart and Albert Bigelow Paine are the armatures for the Brooks biography, Hart for new Freudian concepts like repression, sublimation, projection, and dream-work, and Paine for biographical material. In his study of the discrepancy between potential and achievement, Brooks grieves that the man who might have been the American Cervantes or Swift never made it.

Brooks's earlier remarks about the relation of women to culture are scattered and referential. But in *Ordeal*, for the first and only time, Brooks's attack on a feminized nineteenth-century culture is wholly functional. Women are responsible for having remade culture in the image of nineteenth-century gentility (*Ordeal* 68 and passim). These culturally powerful women who "wrote half the books and formed the greater part of the reading public" uncritically accepted "the religious, moral and social taboos of the time" (*Ordeal* 69).[14] These are the kinds of women—Twain's mother and his wife—to whom Twain capitulated on issues of taste and morality. Thus Twain is caught between and impaled by the conflicting demands of a divided mollycoddle and redblood culture, between over-feminine and machismo ideals.

Brooks did not see and probably could not be expected to see women as victims of American cultural polarities. When women are noticed, they are likely to be attacked as having actively trivialized literature. Before *Ordeal*, at the end of

America's Coming-of-Age, for example, Brooks had suggested that a genuine culture might begin to "send forth shoots" only after "the women of America have gathered together all the culture in the world" (p. 158), that is, presumably, that only after women have completed their harvest will men have a chance to sow the seeds of a genuine culture.

Women artists of the 1910s and 1920s did not claim Brooks's critical attention until they acquired historical validity. By 1952, in *The Confident Years: 1880–1915*, for example, which covers Brooks's own coming of age, Brooks allots considerable space to women artists and activists like Gertrude Stein, Willa Cather, Ellen Glasgow, and Mabel Dodge Luhan. He is very positive about the radical political and artistic communal power of prewar Greenwich Village, but less successful in his "scenic" summary of women's role in that movement (488–489). It never occurs to him to talk about patrons like Annette Rankine and Helen Swift Neilsen, who were not artists but who made the *Seven Arts* and the *Freeman* possible.

Praising women writers and activists was not the same as having one at home. Brooks expected his wife to comply with the separate-spheres model that keeps women at home and men in a different workplace, and she in large part did so. Fissures between private and public life are never uncommon. Eleanor Stimson Brooks managed, however, to bring her working life into the home by carving out a considerable professional life as a translator from the French. She and Van Wyck sometimes co-translated in the effort to supplement what was for a long time an inadequate income. She had the energy and the will to capitalize on her privileged education. She was also politically active, especially in the local Socialist party, on whose ticket she ran for the Connecticut legislature in 1934. (In 1937, Brooks was himself a Socialist candidate.)

Under the influence of feminism, historians have begun to try to put together the private and the public in their assessment of Brooks. Hoopes, for example, considers Brooks's association of "America's irrelevant culture with women" an "indirect attack upon Brooks's mother" (105). Blake constructs a more complex bridge between the biographical and the critical, arguing that Brooks was finally more comfortable with "'feminine' idealism than with 'masculine' practice" (letter, Blake to Sprague, 19 May 1993; Blake 40–45). Lears enlarges from another point of view the gendered assumptions of Victorian thought (220) that created a precarious identity for both the idealized Christian Gentleman and the True Woman (221). Biel notes the gendered nature of Brooks's profession. Criticism, "primarily masculine" (8), tended to exclude women, who were more likely to choose forms of social and political activity "that male critics largely shunned" (social work [Jane Addams] and birth control [Margaret Sanger] are examples) (8). These views both collide and co-exist. Brooks was more "feminine" than "masculine" in his critical approach, but he also rejected what he described as feminized culture and implicitly assumed that women do not do theory.[15]

Recent studies make a more accurate historical placement of Brooks's attacks on a feminized culture possible (see Stoneley, Tompkins, Douglas). Any such placement of Brooks must, however, include his far more straightforward, more consistent attacks on hypermasculinity. Terms like redblood and other masculine halves of the polar deficiencies of American culture permeate his work. The redblood phenomenon even roused Brooks to parody, an unlikely form for him. His spirited lampoon of the redblood Jack London as Jack Paris, author of *Call of the Lungs*, attests to an early aversion to machismo ideals that was to be lifelong (p. 35). The lack of a machismo model at home led him to sympathy for his victim father rather than to a reverse model. Teddy Roosevelt repelled him; adversarial politics was more to his taste. Hoopes may exaggerate in believing that Brooks's ideal writer combined both feminine and masculine traits, as Brooks is far from advocating the kind of androgynous hypothesis proposed by Virginia Woolf in *A Room of One's Own* (1929), but he could counterpose his critique of feminine culture with the belief that "feminine traits" were necessary in a writer. He notices their absence in Mencken (*Confident Years* 465) and prefers "sissyness" to Hemingway's "super-male" position (*Autobiography* 544).[16]

The redblood phenomenon characterizes the puritan-pioneer-industrial triad that is American history;[17] it is Brooks's pri-

mary target. Although Brooks never seriously undertook to
examine the place of women in culture, his criticism as a whole
is a reaction against the extreme gender polarities of the nineteenth century. That he introduced into critical discourse a
concept of undesirable gendered extremes is to his credit. The
gendered implications of every one of Brooks's pairs and of his
analyses of American life have yet to be teased out and eval-
uated.[18]

The Pilgrimage of Henry James lacks the bite and vitality of
Ordeal. In it Brooks shows himself less responsive to James's
irony than he was to Twain's humor (see also pp. 285–287).
The two biographies can be construed to mark a painful dead
end, for neither the writer who stayed, Twain, nor the one
who left, James, was successful. The psychological analysis
that had worked for Twain did not work for James. More
accurately, Brooks did not get to a central problem in James's
life or artistry. What is often cited as the source of James's
major themes, his expatriation/deracination, Brooks takes as
the source of his failure. Furthermore, Brooks simplistically
converts fictional characters into stand-ins for James himself—
for example: "What he, like Milly, had in view" (79). The
method is the same for negative characters who are assumed
to represent what James feared in himself. The decision to read
James simplistically into his characters may, in the end, however, be less destructive than the decision to create a pastiche
of James's novels, letters, and essays without attribution and
so to blur both biographer and subject.

Brooks could sometimes undercut his own great longing for
historical patina. One striking example occurs in the James
biography after he cites the famous passage from James's *Hawthorne* that laments all the absences in American life richly
present in Europe, such as "an accumulation of culture, . . .
[and] a complexity of manners and types." James moves on
from his general assault to a long list of particulars that his
country lacks: "No sovereign, no court, no army, no diplomatic
service, no country gentlemen, no palaces, no castles, nor man-
ors, nor old country-houses," and so on and on, including the
lament that America is not even a state, "in the European

sense of the word, and indeed barely a specific national name" (39–40). Commenting in his own voice, Brooks makes the most unexpected comparative judgment that these absences did not "prevent the emergence" in Russia and Scandinavia "of a fiction entirely comparable with that of England and France" (40). The parallel with America is unstated but inescapable.

The contradictions and the limits apparent in Brooks's criticism should not obscure his real contributions. A word about the former. Caught between two extremes, his earlier thwarted figures and his later exemplary ones, between his Jeremiads and his accolades, Brooks was unable to find for himself that "genial middle ground" he so sought amid writers. Brooks was also caught in the view that criticism is preparation for the organic society that would in turn create great literature. This prescriptive equation is in part responsible for Brooks's inability to find the literary present usable, that is, "to see genius at his very elbow" (Cargill 133). He barely noticed that a substantial body of literature was developing within a society that continued to worship "the Goods Life" rather than the good life (Mumford, 1922, 209).

In fact, America's literary coming of age coincided with its new imperial power, but the possible relation between literary and imperial flowerings, a provocative question for cultural criticism, was not one Brooks could entertain. Unlike Bourne, he seems not to have questioned his version of American exceptionalism. He undervalued the dangers of nationalism—as we all have. His belief in the benign nationalism of earlier liberal theorists was not, like Bourne's, shaken by World War I. After the war, nationalism was supposed to have died, displaced forever by more transcendent allegiances like socialism and communism. Now we know that nationalism went underground for most of this century, only to erupt with greater virulence at its end. In thinking about the relationship between cultural criticism and nationalism, we are precisely, in Lionel Trilling's words, "at the dark and bloody crossroads where literature and politics meet" (22). Brooks, once situated at that crossroads, remapped his territory so that art and politics became "two separate universes" (Dupee 120). He no longer chose to "bring the two into a better relation" (Dupee 120); instead he "entered the 1920s convinced of the need to shore up cultural life as an enterprise separate from politics" (Blake 232).

The direct indebtedness and the diffuse indebtedness to Brooks's work is considerable. Figures like Matthew Josephson, Edmund Wilson, Sherwood Anderson, F. O. Matthiessen, Granville Hicks, Newton Arvin, Malcolm Cowley, F. Scott Fitzgerald, Constance Rourke, Hart Crane, to name a few, were affected by his thesis, as were, of course, writers close to him in those years when "Brooks's personal needs and those of his generation were one" (Paul 209): Randolph Bourne, Waldo Frank, Lewis Mumford, Paul Rosenfeld. He played for some the role J. B. Yeats played for him and Alfred Stieglitz played for others. Thornton Wilder addressed him as "Cher Maître" (according to Wasserstrom, 1979, vii).

Brooks himself provides the best example of his diffuse influence when he quotes from and comments on the following passage from *The Green Hills of Africa* (1935): "We do not have great writers. . . . Something happens to our good writers at a certain age. We destroy them in many ways." "This was," he says, claiming his originating connection with the theme of writer failure, "a constant theme of discussion in American criticism for many years. Hemingway took it up in *Green Hills of Africa*" (*Confident Years* 465). Readers in 1952 would have recognized his claim.[19] The paradox is that as Brooks developed an enormous reading public in the thirties coincident with his embrace of affirmation, he lost much of his "high" culture support.

Brooks's accomplishments remain considerable. He created a cultural criticism at a time when the concepts of "culture" and "cultural" were still being shaped (see Williams). The words are now more stable in meaning than they were, although they continue to cover fields as diverse as history, anthropology, biology, and the arts. Brooks dared to take on a wide range of societal ills, including corporate life, education, politics. These ills were the targets of what Biel so aptly calls his "redemptive debunking" (176). His early work has especially large parameters, so much so that our labels don't fit him. Historian isn't quite right; neither is literary critic. He needs a special rubric (as do Bourne, Frank, and Mumford). He has partly found a home, if not a name, "in American Studies and American Civilization Programs" (Thomas 223; see also Dickstein 136–143).

Plural explorations are risky in an era that values overspecialization. They were apparently risky personally for Brooks as well. He narrowed those risks in his later life and work by moving away from his earlier radical explorations toward a more limited focus on literature. That shift had a physical counterpart, for Brooks left New York, the scene of the pressures that had both energized and afflicted him, and took up his long residence in Connecticut.[20] But his shift in focus is more complicated, for though he limited his subject matter, he enlarged the concept of literature. The matter of the Makers and Finders volumes was, for example, anything but narrow. They may embrace the status quo, but their capacious reach contains a unique reconstruction of "an American tradition of independent artistic and intellectual communities" (Biel 186). Nelson suggests that the five volumes invent a genre unknown in this country, one that has greater links with eighteenth-century encyclopedist objectives than with twentieth-century literary histories (291). That is high praise indeed. Still, the man who heard "the music of antinomies"[21] is missing from Makers and Finders. That man's Tolstoyan fervor was infectious. That man and those earlier, riskier, adversarial confrontations are deservedly reclaiming our attention.[22]

NOTES

Page numbers in parentheses in the Foreword refer to pages in this volume.

1. Like Reising, I cannot resist playing with the word *usable*. Reising adds *unused* and *unusable* to Brooks's *usable* and uses all three in his criticism.

2. These early works are occasionally published by reprint houses. In early 1993 two of the works in this collection, *The Ordeal of Mark Twain* (1933 ed., AMS) and *The Pilgrimage of Henry James* (Hippocrene), were available.

3. Scholars and critics date Brooks's change of outlook and methodology differently. Blake, for example, places it in 1920, after *Ordeal* and

with the move to Westport (232); Biel places it as late as the Emerson biography, as does Wilson: "Brooks's work falls into two distinct divisions, with the break point just before his volume on Emerson" (*Classics and Commercials* 10). Most critics place the change about 1926. That seems to me too late. The struggle with both the state of his health and his point of view may have begun as early as 1917 (see Hoopes 125 ff.). In 1925 Brooks wrote Mumford that he was coming out of a two-year breakdown (*Letters* 33). His difficulties with the composition of *Pilgrimage* and *Emerson* fall within this period. The testimony of Brooks's letters adds to other testimony to suggest that his breakdown period begins as early as 1920 or even 1917 rather than 1926 as Brooks claims. See the chapter in his *Autobiograhy* called "A Season in Hell" for the years 1926–1931.

4. The original structure of *The Wine of the Puritans* (1908) is most revealing. The unnamed narrator receives a telegram on June 20, 1906, announcing: "Graeling died early this morning: appoints you executor: come at once" (Van Wyck Brooks Papers). Thus the narrator inherits the job of presenting Charles Graeling's thoughts to the world. Graeling's parents died when he was eight, freeing Graeling of the encumbrances of heritage and class. The structure of the work experiments with "a child set loose in the modern world to develop personally wholly within himself." Brooks could not himself, of course, be so liberated. This self/alter ego structure is much muted in the final version of *Wine*; the split structure recurs in later works (cf. Wickford [see p. liv] and Oliver Allston [*The Opinions of Oliver Allston*; see p. lviii], who are projections of Brooks). Brooks's fascination with division surfaces in different and complicated ways in his choice of biographical subjects and has deep roots in his own psyche.

5. Brooks did not choose the title *An Autobiography* for the three volumes that cover his life; it was chosen for him after his death (Hoopes 287). He did not intend to reveal his inner self. His intentions and his strengths are pictorial. The title of the first volume, *Scenes and Portraits*, reflects the content of all three volumes. Glenway Wescott points out that Brooks discusses the five years of his massive withdrawal in just eight pages (204). That's far more than he devoted to his wife or to his children. Sexuality, an obligatory subject in our time, has no place in *An Autobiography*. Brooks was, however, able to write about his breakdown in his lifetime as T. S. Eliot was not. His literary allusiveness can be embarrassing. Two examples: in one, he refers to his second wife as "the daughter of Mark Twain's doctor" (575); in the other, he says of Mark Twain, "if he was money-mad, so was Balzac" (426).

6. Eddy Dow describes these oppositions as "a provocative reformu-

lation of the old argument between the flesh and the spirit" (242). I think the old opposition between the active and the contemplative life may be more germane. Casting these oppositions into workable contemporary forces was imaginative. Consider another pair: Brooks argues in *America's Coming-of-Age* that Tammany has as much to teach Good Government as vice versa. This simultaneous division and interaction between pairs is what Holbrook Jackson meant by the Yellow Press and the Yellow Book engendering one another. Mencken's Puritan and Philistine was another dyad of the period. Philip Rahv's later Paleface and Redskin are obviously indebted to Brooks, although Rahv omits the credit. Coining "opposed catchwords" isn't always successful; Lippmann struck out with Inventor versus Routineer.

7. Mr. Shimerda's suicide in Willa Cather's *My Ántonia* (1918) is one of the very few examples in American fiction of the destructive side of immigration/expatriation.

8. Hoopes (133) believes Brooks was unable to live with difference and that the Brooksian notion of a "super-culture" (Intro. *History of a Literary Radical* 6) was not the same as Bourne's trans-national culture. Brooks's term, is, of course, unfortunate in itself and especially in the light of later history; still, I believe the two were close in thought at this time. In the same 1920 introduction to Bourne's essays, Brooks uses left-wing terms like "class-struggle" (11) and "proletariat" and hopes for an alliance between intellectuals and proletarians (12).

9. In fact, there were other rejected titles: "The America Myth" and "Neither—Nor—But? A Note on American Society" (Van Wyck Brooks Papers).

10. Abrahams (68) cites a Bourne review of a 1911 Franz Boas book "demonstrating the unscientific basis of racism" and a 1916 letter in which Bourne indicates his desire to write a book about racism. But by 1918, Bourne was dead. In *The Confident Years: 1885–1915* Brooks's attention to the lives of, the work of, and the debate between Booker T. Washington and W. E. B. Du Bois is rare for 1952. So is the attention Brooks gives to the Harlem Renaissance. In 1958 he was among the few who turned up at the New York Public Library for the dedication of the William Zorach bust of Du Bois, who was celebrating his ninetieth birthday (Wasserstrom, 1979, 236). Neither Bourne nor Brooks ignores Jews. They are part of Bourne's trans-national America. Brooks represents Jews as immigrants and as writers and colleagues a number of times in his work.

11. Nelson argues that a Jeffersonian point of view shapes the series (299–300).

12. For useful critical summaries of anthology selections, see Tompkins, "'But Is It Any Good?': The Institutionalization of Literary Value" (Ch. VII), and Reising (22–25).

13. In 1946 Spiller claimed that "no critic of Twain has since been able to ignore [Brooks's] analysis," which provoked others to "rebuttal, exploration and reevaluation" (1140). He was in part referring to De Voto's explosive rebuttal (1932). There were other responses. Kaplan's 1966 title *Mr. Clemens and Mark Twain* clearly suggests the continuing acceptance of Brooks's thesis although Brooks is a background presence. Sometimes he nearly surfaces, as in the following: "But the central drama of [Twain's] mature literary life was his discovery of [his] usable past" (9). Kaplan's concluding paragraph reports that Twain's "last continuous talking was about 'the laws of mentality,' about Jekyll and Hyde and dual personality" (388). In 1988 A. J. Hoffman cites as the originating biographers of Twain both Brooks and De Voto and adds, "Perhaps this biographical history goes back earlier to William Dean Howells' *My Mark Twain*" (xiv). In 1992 Stoneley's most interesting and overdue study of Twain's relation to the feminine aesthetic considers Brooks's thesis as a gendered one. It could not be part of his objective to look at the gendered nature of Brooksian criticism as a whole.

14. Not all women are implicated in reductive civilizing; French women are different: "Ah, it was not women only, not the sort of women who had so often tended the bright light of literature in France!" (*Ordeal* 68). Hoopes postulates that *The Wine of the Puritans* represents "the opening salvo of Brooks's continuing attack on American femininity" (1). He believes that *Wine*, *Ordeal*, and *The Pilgrimage of Henry James* are all "attacks on those he loved" (1).

15. True, some kinds of contemplation were considered passive and feminine (Lears 255). But were women ever assumed to do theory? Not according to an academic commonplace. Gates alters that commonplace when he adds "white" and turns "man" into "people" to say, "Theory is something that white people do" (83). It is possible to associate female idealism, however shallow or perverted, with theory and male red-blooded behavior with actions as Blake does. But Blake also separates the "feminine temple of gentility" from "the pure fire of the feminine ideal" (40). The divisions refuse to stay neat.

16. According to Wasserstrom (1971, 40), Brooks originally conceived of Twain and James as unsatisfactory extremes for which Whitman was to be the satisfactory synthesis. Brooks dropped Whitman and substituted Emerson, "so the story goes," when he discovered Whitman's homosexuality. Wasserstrom claims as his indirect source Malcolm Cowley. Hoopes comments: "I have not found a single source to corroborate William Wasserstrom's statement" (323*n*53). Mumford does not recall

Whitman as the potential synthesizer; Cowley vaguely recalls Whitman's being mentioned but has no memory of Brooks's recoil from the possibility of Whitman's homosexuality. It should also be recalled that Brooks had previously used Whitman as his "precipitant," his "genial middle ground" between writers like Edwards and Franklin, in *America's Coming-of-Age*. Wasserstrom does add, "However that may be," and continues with his narrative. If Wasserstrom can doubt his story, so may we. In any event, Brooks championed Whitman throughout his life. He called him the "tutelary genius" of the *Seven Arts* (*Autobiography* 269). That magical key word, "organic," describes him best, for Whitman is organic, meaning whole and of the earth: "a great vegetable of a man, all of a piece in roots, flavor, substantiality, and succulence" (see p. 128).

17. The middle term in Brooks's puritan-pioneer-industrial triad has received far less attention than his end terms. For Brooks the pioneer is no mythic figure with positive, uniquely American traits. Brooks attacks "the pioneering instinct of economic self-assertion" (p. 99) and "our competitive pioneering past" (p. 170). The body of his work shows no direct awareness of the Frederick Jackson Turner frontier thesis.

18. Only Stoncley (4–5) uses the gendered implications of Brooks's analysis of Twain.

19. In 1922 Edmund Wilson called Brooks "that expert in American failure" as he pondered how Brooks might assess the limits of Ezra Pound's art (*Shores* 48).

20. Blake is the first to suggest that Brooks's move to Westport, Conn., after his return from Carmel and the completion of *Ordeal* conjoins with a secession from the activist pressures of the city. Nelson points out that Brooks's life had a rare stability after 1931 save for a brief period in the 1940s.

21. Brooks could not sustain the ambivalence he best defined and illustrated in *America's Coming-of-Age*; as Lears puts it, he "never again orchestrated his inner tensions so skillfully" (255). The difficulty of adjusting the conflicting claims of nineteenth-century idealized female dependence and male autonomy made the posture of ambivalence "especially severe among those for whom gender identity was most problematic: women who sought 'masculine' careers in public life, men who nurtured 'feminine' aspirations toward literature, art, or the increasingly feminized ministry" (Lears 221). The conflict was one of the causes of the invalidism and breakdowns of the period for both women and men.

22. Krupnick notes: "It would require a book by itself to explain how American graduate schools have produced a generation of students so knowledgeable about Georg Lukács, Antonio Gramsci, and Walter Benjamin and yet so ignorant of Van Wyck Brooks, Edmund Wilson, and Lionel Trilling" (2).

Introduction

by Claire Sprague

I

The generation of Van Wyck Brooks may be the last to have grown up with an acute sense of American cultural inferiority. The smallest fact of daily existence could become for it a symptom of national deficiency. Brooks's mortification at the unromantic, untraditional name of his home town of Plainfield, New Jersey, where he was born in 1886, probably echoes the experience of a generation. The Eliots, the Pounds, the Faulkners, the Hemingways, the Fitzgeralds who were his exact or near-contemporaries had come from equally unromantic places, even though names like St. Louis or Oxford incongruously carried some of the patina of tradition. The mature Brooks was "greatly relieved" when he discovered that Tolstoy's birthplace, Yasnaya Polyana, meant Plainfield in Russian.[1]

That a young man of such impeccably establishment pedigree should have come to feel so uneasy about his place and his heritage was strange, but not uncommon in his generation. Later, when he had come to terms with his Americanism, Brooks was pleased that his antecedents were, like Melville's and Whitman's, "equally English and Dutch." Such antecedents were commonplace in an Episcopalian and Presbyterian environment. Furthermore, although Plainfield was a "Wall

---

[1] Except where otherwise indicated, all biographical material is taken from Van Wyck Brooks, *An Autobiography* (New York, 1965), which contains the three autobiographical volumes: *Scenes and Portraits* (1954), *Days of the Phoenix* (1957), and *From the Shadow of the Mountain* (1961). Other quotations are identified only if their source is unclear or they are not from works contained in this collection. Brooks does not cite the source for his translation.

Street suburb" (the phrase is Brooks's), peopled by men who had earned their fortunes in railroads, mining, and banking, his upbringing shielded him from an awareness of the "savage and lawless epoch of American finance" in which he grew up. His father, uncompetitive by nature, was a broker; his mother, a cultivated and beautiful woman, was an excellent pianist. Apparently even a family of moderate means could enjoy the abundant servants of the period and took for granted the trip to Europe when Van Wyck was twelve, an experience which was "all a bedazzlement, magical" to the boy.

Yet even in his stable, ritualized world, disturbing evidences of other values intruded. Europe was not quite "all a bedazzlement, magical," for in Dresden a group of boys stoned Van Wyck in resentment over the United States victory in the Spanish-American War. A year later Brooks discovered Ruskin, "the favorite author of my whole adolescence, who illuminated economics as well as art for me." After additional trips abroad, one during his Harvard years, one for eighteen months directly after college, and another which began in 1913 and was cut short by the beginning of World War I, Brooks might have said that Europe or, more exactly, England, had illuminated economics as well as art for him. For Brooks learned his socialism from England, from Ruskin and Wells and Morris and Shaw, writers in whom "the aesthetic and the socialistic met." From such influences he developed his characteristic cultural criticism and overthrew, as we shall see, the impeding aestheticism he had acquired during his Harvard years.

His Harvard years and his European sojourns deepened the symbolic impact of the early Dresden stoning and the exposure to Ruskin. That exposure rightly suggests Brooks's central indebtedness to Victorian thought. Ruskin and other Victorian prophets had warned against the contemporary faith in machinery. In the pioneer and business ethic Brooks found powerful American examples of the religion of mechanism and quantity. Against that false religion, Ruskin fiercely upheld the religious nature of all great art and the prophetic function of the artist. Neither Ruskin nor Carlyle nor Matthew Arnold separated art from its moral function. Even Arnold, more sophisticated and less oracular than Ruskin or Carlyle, asked for the grand style in poetry, for heroic figures and noble actions. For Ruskin a literature that supported the Goddess of Getting On was irreligious. The renewal of society depended on exterminating the competitive spirit and freeing its prisoners. Literature was moral if it helped forward this great cause, These broad postulates about literature and society remained Brooks's postulates for his entire career.

Ruskin is probably also the source of Brooks's conception of "the organic society," interchangeable for Brooks with socialist society. Beginning his career solely as an art critic, Ruskin ended as a pioneer in many areas, including city planning, the improvement of working conditions and the treatment of the unemployed and the aged poor. His interest in the future coincided with his devotion to the tradition of the Middle Ages. His admiration for an era more integrated or "organic" than his own included the convictions that the hand-made was superior to the machine-made and even that revivals of Gothic architecture and the medieval guild were necessary. These convictions must be taken, at least partially, as modes of exposing the failures of industrialism. They also explain Ruskin's enchantment with "the golden stain of time" that "connects forgotten ages with each other, and half constitutes the identity, as it concentrates the sympathy of nations."[2] The young Brooks closed his first book with a longing for the magic of time that recalls Ruskin; he hoped that Denver and Sioux City would one day "have a traditional and antique dignity like Damascus and Perugia." Even more important, Brooks did not, in his early work, assume that admiration of the medieval necessarily joined with political conservatism.

Ruskin had also influenced Walter Pater, whose conclusion to the *Renaissance* (1873) had implied the cultivation of experience for its own sake. Pater was a favorite of the Harvard Brooks knew, the Harvard devoted to the *esprit précieux*. That Harvard was excited about the Celtic revival, then at its height, and beginning to follow the young William Butler Yeats avidly. The professors were generally anglophilic; a "semi-serious cult

---

[2] From "The Lamp of Memory" in *The Seven Lamps of Architecture* (1849).

of royalism" even existed. Other particular passions among the student *avant-garde* were Dante, Sanscrit and the symbolist movement. Charles Eliot Norton's famous Dante evenings progressed in a sacramental atmosphere.

There were, however, many Harvards, then as now. Among Brooks's classmates between 1904 and 1907 were T. S. Eliot, Maxwell Perkins (a childhood friend), Walter Lippmann, Heywood Broun and John Reed. Brooks chose T. S. Eliot as the quintessence of the Harvard he knew. Yet Eliot's Harvard was to a great degree also his own Harvard, the Harvard of the *esprit précieux*. Brooks was self-admittedly a mollycoddle among the redbloods. He preferred Charles Eliot Norton to William James as a professor and Dante Rossetti to the popular Rudyard Kipling. The young Brooks was so deep in his "dream of the Middle Ages and of Italy and Catholicism, which somehow seemed to me one and the same" that he erected an altar in his room, complete with Italian crucifix, set himself exercises like translating Newman into Latin, and, like Pater's Marius the Epicurean, "played at priests." Later a lecture by Jack London at Harvard introduced him to the socialist movement; the lecture did not keep Brooks from parodying London in his first book. London's *Call of the Wild* represented a literary version of "the strenuous life" advocated by the major political figure of Brooks's youth, Theodore Roosevelt. By his alignment with the mollycoddles Brooks established his distaste for "efficiency" and the glorification of "the men who do things."

The record of his early intellectual influences shows that the aesthete and the socialist in Brooks did not always meet harmoniously. Out of their collisions almost all of Brooks's positions developed. To the matter of his student days he was to add the psychoanalytic instrument he discovered in 1918 in Bernard Hart's *The Psychology of Insanity* (1912).[3] Even earlier he had discovered and adopted the analytic method of the Hegelian dialectic.

American thinkers since Coleridge were generally introduced

[3] See Robert E. Spiller, preface, *The Malady of the Ideal* (Philadelphia, 1947), unpaged.

to the Hegelian dialectic through Thomas Carlyle or Coleridge himself rather than directly through Hegel or other German philosophers. Carlyle may have introduced Brooks to the dialectic he so conspicuously uses in *America's Coming-of-Age*. Brooks may also have encountered the method through William James or George Santayana who taught at Harvard during Brooks's student days. Brooks confesses that his sympathies then being, to his later sorrow, more precious than pragmatic, he paid little attention to James and Santayana. If, however, as James thought, the Hegelian school "so deeply" influenced both British and American thinking, then the precise source of Brooks's introduction to the dialectic method may not be easily located. The fact of its diffusion may be more important than its source. James describes the two principles of the method as follows: The first of these principles recognizes "that every object which our thought may propose to itself involves the notion of some other object which seems at first to negate the first one. The second principle is that to be conscious of a negation is already virtually to be beyond it."[4] It did not take Brooks very long to demonstrate the utility of this method in his attack on American civilization.

In the years between his graduation and America's entry into World War I, Brooks and other critics of American culture developed and sharpened their criticism. In 1908 when *The Wine of the Puritans* was published, the fiddles were tuning up all over America, as John Butler Yeats had said, and they were tuning up in both politics and the arts. Whether one accepted the program of the International Workers of the World or what Walter Lippmann called "the colossal phenomenon of Roosevelt," the times seemed ripe for change.[5] By 1911 the radical-socialist *Masses* had come out; in 1914 the *New Republic* was founded by independent progressive supporters, Herbert Croly, Walter Lippmann and Walter Weyl. In 1916 *The Seven Arts* appeared, called by one historian the critical intellectuals' "pure distilled essence and also its culmination," with Brooks

---

[4] *The Varieties of Religious Experience* (New York, 1958), p. 342.

[5] *A Preface to Politics* (New York, 1914), p. 78. Theodore Roosevelt became President when Brooks was 15. Even after he left office, when Brooks was 23, Roosevelt continued to dominate American politics.

as a founder and editor.[6] Croly's slogan, "the New National-ism," which appeared in his *The Promise of American Life* (1909) expressed a program of democratic and cultural na-tionalism Brooks could sympathize with if not entirely support. Croly had envisioned American emulation of the glories of Periclean Athens; Lippmann also was struck by "the close alliance of art, science and politics in Athens, in Florence and Venice at their zenith."[7] All three men had touchstone ideals symptomatic of the desire for significant social and cultural change. The new emphases of historians like James Harvey Robinson (*The New History,* 1912) and Charles Beard (*An Economic Interpretation of the Constitution,* 1913) comple-mented their radical agitation.

New publishers like B. W. Huebsch, Mitchell Kennerley, Alfred Knopf, the Boni brothers, and Horace Liveright played an extremely useful role in getting the younger generation into print. In 1908 H. L. Mencken and George Jean Nathan joined the staff of *The Smart Set.* Beginning in 1912 *Poetry* magazine served the new poetry. As its London correspondent from 1912 to 1919, Ezra Pound stung and propagandized American readers. The Armory Show of 1913 is yet another symbol of the era; it marks the first large-scale introduction of modern art into the United States. In 1916 the Diaghileff Ballet came to the country and *Theater Arts* magazine was founded. These events, even baldly recited, suggest that talk of a renaissance was not unfounded. Brooks believed in that renaissance. It was he who gave Yeats's phrase currency.

The pre-war years were productive, frequently harried years for Brooks. By 1917, when he was thirty-one, he had published six books, really seven, since his seventh, although it appeared in 1918, collected *The Seven Arts* essays he wrote during 1916 and 1917. At the same time he was editing and translating books and working at various hack jobs with a popular mag-azine, a dictionary and an encyclopedia. He accepted a teaching position at Stanford (1911-1913) and later, like his early master, Ruskin, one at a workingmen's college near London. He had also married.

[6] Henry F. May, *The End of American Innocence* (New York, 1959), p. 322.
[7] Lippmann, p. 88.

We know he voted Socialist, but we do not know when, for whom, or how frequently. We surmise that his was probably one of the nearly one million votes cast for Debs in the unusually exciting election of 1912 when Roosevelt had defected from the Republican Party to run as the Progressive candidate. Brooks never forgot the impact of seeing and hearing other striking personalities like Henry James, George Bernard Shaw, Georg Brandes and H. G. Wells. In New York he interviewed William Dean Howells who lived on, anachronistically, until 1920, and saw Mark Twain lying, white-suited, in his coffin, an unforgettable experience. The generation just a few years younger than his would have no personal memories of men like Howells and Twain. These involved years, in London, California and New York, had a clamor and an edge his later long residence in Connecticut lacked.

His childhood may have shielded him, but his adolescence and young manhood must have awakened Brooks to the intense political agitation, to the disturbing new immigrations, to the labor struggles, to the panics that accompanied the "savage and lawless epoch of American finance" in which he came to maturity. If English thinkers gave him a means to explain the world he knew, the specifics of that world remained American even if many of the institutions and attitudes he and his colleagues considered "peculiarly Puritan or American" were called Victorian in England. It was a while before Brooks and his contemporaries fully understood that their target might be as "trans-national" as it was national.[8] Brooks later called these pre-war years "confident." His own career suggests they were not.

II

The present collection represents an effort to bring to the earlier works of Van Wyck Brooks the larger public they deserve. Works like *The Wine of the Puritans* (1908) have been out of print for many years. Copies of *The Soul* (1910) are so rare even scholars are likely to be unacquainted with it. The essay that coined the brilliant and frequently used term, "the

[8] The term is Randolph Bourne's. See "Trans-National America," *Atlantic*, CXVIII (July 1916), 89-97.

usable past," has never been reprinted from its original magazine appearance in *The Dial*. The originality of Brooks's
younger years, best known today through *America's Coming-
of-Age* (1915), has been obscured. Brooks is himself partly
responsible for the overemphasis on his later work. He considered the *Makers and Finders* series (1936-1952) his master-
piece, the one by which posterity would grant or refuse him a
place.

Many critics would not agree. They would single out instead
the earlier works already mentioned and add to them the
series of essays he wrote for *The Seven Arts* (1916-1917)
which were somewhat revised and published as *Letters and
Leadership* (1918), the essay "The Literary Life" (1921),
and one other study, *The Ordeal of Mark Twain* (1920),
which caps and completes his early work.

The basic formulations of the early years are the basic ones
of his entire career. They make continuity as striking as re-
versal in Brooks's development. In the terms personality, nationality, tradition, the usable past and the organic society,
Brooks found a serviceable set of interlocking conceptions.
Perhaps the proper expression of personality is his central ideal
to which his other terms are foils. Certainly his fascination with
personality was lifelong; it led him to biography and to his
constant concern with the literary life.

The remaining terms overlap. Out of his conception of nationality (sometimes called "race") and its interaction with the
great personality Brooks developed his conception of cultural
nationalism. When Brooks applied his conception of nationality to politics, it resulted in support for the kind of Fabian
socialism he learned from William Morris and H. G. Wells.
The only examples of the "organic society" available to Brooks
and his colleagues and predecessors were the medieval society,
which no longer existed, and the socialist society which did not
yet exist. The loose metaphor becomes another ideal which
exposes the defective present. Nationalism applied to literature
becomes tradition, and tradition, more pragmatically defined,
becomes the usable past. The usable past would provide a
national literature with "redemptive" and "revelative" powers.

Between 1908 and 1920 Brooks explored the implications of

his key terms. During these years he also developed and perfected his version of the dialectic method. Contradiction became the description of the American past and present. Synthesis became the prognosis for a better future.

The two young men who examine American civilization from Italy in *The Wine of the Puritans* prefigure many expatriate Americans of the 1920s who were certain they understood America better from Europe or even that they were more American in Europe than at home. Written when Brooks was twenty-two, the work opens the long attack on puritans and puritanism that characterizes the 1920s. Its strength lies in two daring suggestions: that puritanism explains the transcendent and commercial extremes that typify America, and that tradition can be consciously, even publicly, created. In fact, the transcendental and the commercial may be more highbrow terms for the famous highbrow-lowbrow categorization presented in *America's Coming-of-Age*. The young Brooks is already defining by extremes although he is more sure of the commercial type which develops from the pioneer, a figure Brooks finds unsympathetic. (He never lamented the closing of the frontier.)[9] The line that develops from puritan to pioneer to businessman realizes itself best in opportunists like Brigham Young, John D. Rockefeller and P. T. Barnum. Brooks has yet to sharpen his extremes into the mystic-Yankee Ur-figures of Jonathan Edwards and Benjamin Franklin.

When his two speakers ingenuously debate the problem of how to create tradition in a country without tradition, one laments:

It's all so vague, so difficult. You can't deliberately *establish* an American tradition. Walt Whitman was on the right track, possibly: but you can't build literally on *cosmos*. Universal comradeship means —nothing. It means just "Yawp."

By the time of *America's Coming-of-Age* Brooks was willing to "build literally on *cosmos*"—with reservations. In 1908 he

[9] See Warren I. Susman's excellent analysis: "The Useless Past: American Intellectuals and the Frontier Thesis: 1910-1930," *Bucknell Review*, XI (March 1962), 1-20.

can only suggest the need for tradition, the need to create it, and the paradoxical need not to be unduly concerned with it. His advice is that we "simply *be American*" and constructive.

His constructive force is here and always the artist who creates out of "the accretion of countless generations of ancestors, trained to one deep, local, indigenous attitude toward life." The artist is at the same time the creator of "racial fibre" and its savior. Brooks's frequent use of terms like "race" and "racial fibre" when he means nationality indicates his subscription to terminology familiar in nineteenth-century critics like Hippolyte Taine and Georg Brandes. His belief that national consciousness or "racial fibre" must precede tradition left Brooks with a rationale for cultural criticism and a prescriptive demand of literature.

Yet in *The Wine of the Puritans* Brooks does not insist that the writer's work be a simple reflection of his racial origins. Choosing his example from his earliest passion, painting, he judges Whistler a better painter than Sargent because of his spiritual conflict about his "race": "His contempt and defiance of race only assert the race he defies." Sargent has no conflict because he has no roots and his paintings reflect a shallower confrontation of self. For these two expatriate American painters the results of expatriation were not in themselves crippling. Brooks retains this view of expatriation for some time. As late as 1920 "expatriation was simply the condition of survival" for Henry James, but by 1925, in *The Pilgrimage of Henry James,* Brooks had decided that flight from one's native soil, from one's "plain primary heritage," was necessarily crippling.

After so fertile a first book, *The Soul* and *The Malady of the Ideal* may represent retreats. They are almost diary entries, so artless and so openly related are they to their author's immediate personal needs. *The Soul* belongs to what Brooks called his Harvard aesthete period when he preferred the medieval outlook to the modern, the Catholic to the Protestant.[10] In

---

[10] In his article on Maurice de Guérin, later included in *The Malady of the Ideal,* Brooks wrote: "There are moments when we turn fully and passionately to Rome, but at no time do we turn more than half-heartedly to Protestantism." See "Maurice de Guérin," *Forum,* XLVII (May 1912), 621-628.

his search for a life ideal he examines, within a sweeping, youthful, forty-page survey of Western civilization, three major souls or personalities: Thomas à Kempis, Martin Luther and Saint Francis. The first represents the contemplative life, the second the active life, and the third, the rare and astonishing union of both. St. Francis, unlike Luther, knew how to participate without becoming an "organization man"; he is "the natural soul in the midst of life." Brooks wants to discover for himself whether action is possible at all for the idealist and, if so, whether it can be genuine. This is the central problem of both *The Soul* and *The Malady of the Ideal*.

The Soul reveals the young person trying to come to terms with his need for idealism as well as for action. He inclines to pure being; he believes in the *fin-de-siècle* purism which sees even literature as ulterior because it implies an audience. Yet he admires Russian literature and especially Tolstoy because Tolstoy, like the other great nineteenth-century Russian novelists, "are not literary men, in the proper sense, at all. They are men who write from the sheer pressure of life." Thus, *The Soul* is at the same time imprisoned by aestheticism and contemptuous of it. The joy and wonder of Russian fiction is that in it "we find literature of the highest order without style in its traditional sense as an independent aspect of the literary art." When, many years later, Brooks believed that modern literature represented a forty-year extension of *fin-de-siècle* theories he continued a point of view he had held as a young man. Then, as later, he had incorrectly assumed that style was suspect and independent of matter. *The Soul* already exhibits a transparent and desperate need to find in literature direct and explicit guidance to the conduct of life.

The Malady of the Ideal (1913) pursues the problem of *The Soul* as it materializes in failure. The soul's job is to correlate the self and the world, the interior and the exterior order. Brooks defines the interior order of literature as "the apprehension of truth" and the exterior order as "the form in which the writer seeks to convey it." In believing that between these two orders "there is a fundamental antagonism, inasmuch as form implies some outward consistency," Brooks perpetuates the impressionist view that expression is a form of compromise to which some natures "have been superior." He has not fully worked out the problem of action yet he craves to do so for his greater end, the full realization of personality. Lives like Plato's, Dante's, Goethe's are fully realized lives. The "records of incomplete personalities," like Sénancour's Obermann, Maurice de Guérin, Amiel, the subjects of his book, are "valuable as precepts." These subjects show characteristics associated with the aesthetes: immense weariness, melancholy, the paralyzed will. Brooks has again chosen three souls but they do not here represent two extremes and a synthesis. They are instead three souls who have not removed the obstructions to the full realization of personality. They have succumbed to "the malady of the ideal" (the phrase is Amiel's). Brooks may have found that writing about the paralyzed personality was a way of exorcising it.

For the first time Brooks had specifically shaped his examination of personality into what can be called biography. Studies of John Addington Symonds (1914) and H. G. Wells (1915) soon followed. They were undoubtedly meant to represent, like Twain and James, a thesis and antithesis. These full-length biographies initiate a lengthy list of biographical studies which remind us of Brooks's primary concern with the conduct of life.

In *America's Coming-of-Age* Brooks pares much of his earlier impressionism in his support of "attached idealism." To this work he brings a new prose style and the brilliant culmination of his thesis that the discrepancy between theory and practice divides and destroys American life. To illustrate, he seizes on two words so new their subsequent intellectual currency, if not their coinage, may be credited to Brooks—highbrow and lowbrow. His seizure of these terms was inspired. They have proved to be more durable than two other analogous sets of extremes created by Theodore Roosevelt and William James: mollycoddle and redblood; tender-minded and tough-minded.

Brooks announces his thesis boldly and cleanly in his first chapter:

Between university ethics and business ethics, between American culture and American humour, between Good Government and

Tammany, between academic pedantry and pavement slang, there is no community, no genial middle ground.

These "equally undesirable" and "incompatible" extremes "divide American life between them." The researches into the American past Brooks inspired probably helped create the middle ground he wanted. If that middle ground has become middlebrow then it is time for a new Brooks to attack and rearrange our image of ourselves and of our past. Or, as other analysts of American culture suggest, the middle ground ideal ought to be abandoned and our contradictions enjoyed as given and characteristic.[11]

When he applies his thesis to American literature, Brooks finds "that those of our writers who have possessed a vivid personal talent have been paralyzed by the want of a social background, while those who have possessed a vivid social talent have been equally unable to develop their personalities." These extremes, more or less rigorously applied, give us Poe and Hawthorne on the one side and Emerson and Lowell on the other. (The later Twain and James studies represent extended examinations of the two deficient extremes.) Brooks's linkage of Poe and Hawthorne as critics of the transcendental ideal was shrewd. Melville had not yet been rediscovered.

Brooks had set up his thesis and antithesis. He needed to posit a synthesis. Whitman is that synthesis, "The Precipitant," the fuser of extremes, the great national voice like Virgil or Mazzini or Bjornson. That Whitman falters, becomes complacent, even exhibits a conventional intellect should not deter the young man in search of a program for America from seeing that Whitman is the "focal center" of his people. For Americans low on the evolutionary ladder—in Brooks's words, "a malleable and still incoherent race to be interpreted to itself"— Whitman provides "the raw materials of a racial norm." Although Brooks was right, "we are not a race, to begin with,"

---

[11] See Richard Chase's interesting discussion on "The Illusion of the Middle Way" in *The Democratic Vista* (New York, 1958), pp. 29-68. The term middle-brow is even newer. Mencken reports in *The American Language: Supplement One* (New York, 1945) that mizzen-brow and mezzobrow have not caught on, pp. 325-326. He had not yet heard of middlebrow.

his dream of making a Europe at home was not entirely useful. As Constance Rourke was to teach him, his country could have a native aesthetic tradition without acquiring a "racial norm."[12]

Brooks could believe with apparently equal force that society needed inner transformation and that "one contagious personality" could trigger social change. He also believed that it is not the artist's business "as such to change society." Although these paradoxes, which needed direct and extended confrontation, remained unexamined and underdeveloped in Brooks's career as a whole, in *America's Coming-of-Age* they exist in muted form. That work is more striking for its liberation from "the malady of the ideal" and its embrace of a polemic critical ideal:

. . . a point of view in criticism, criticism in the genuine sense, is a working-plan, a definition of issues, which at once renders it impossible to make one's peace with the world, at once and permanently sets one at odds with the world, inevitably makes the critic a champion and a man of war.

Expression no longer represents compromise as it did in *The Soul*. In fact, "unattached idealism" has become dangerous. Brooks now believes that "the more deeply and urgently and organically you feel the pressure of society the more deeply and consciously and fruitfully you feel and you become yourself." Conflict between the self and society, the underlying fear of *The Soul* and *The Malady of the Ideal*, is here the condition of selfhood and achievement.

The founding of *The Seven Arts* magazine in 1916 could not have occurred at a more propitious time in Brooks's career. The magazine's concern was precisely with the issues and the program called for in *America's Coming-of-Age*. It brought Brooks to a community of stimulating kindred minds; it brought a naturally diffident man directly to the pressures of the literary marketplace.

Three men actually ran it: James Oppenheim, Waldo Frank,

[12] See Brooks's preface to *The Roots of American Culture* (New York, 1942). Miss Rourke certainly encouraged him to his later belief that minor works make a tradition. *Makers and Finders* could not have been written without that belief.

and Van Wyck Brooks. The supporting "inner circle" members were Randolph Bourne, Louis Untermeyer, Sherwood Anderson, and Paul Rosenfeld. *The Seven Arts* reflected the typical concerns of the little magazine of 1916. It encouraged experimental literature, argued free verse and imagism, derided the moralist heresy in literature, and examined Freud, Nietzsche, and Russian literature. Its contributors included Ezra Pound, Amy Lowell, Robert Frost, Sherwood Anderson, Eugene O'Neill, and D. H. Lawrence. *The Seven Arts* uniquely combined cultural nationalism with experimentalism and a sense of mission which excludes the waxing and waning enthusiasms of *The Little Review* and *The Smart Set* epigrams for flappers and bright young men. The manifesto, a collaborative effort, proclaims the existence of an American Renaissance and believes it expresses "that national self-consciousness which is the beginning of greatness."

In his seven essays and one review written during the magazine's brief life of twelve issues, Brooks pitilessly probes the failures of America's optimism, materialism, literary criticism, puritanism and pragmatism. The seven essays were transposed and edited as *Letters and Leadership* (1918), a title well suited to the burden of all his early work and especially to his essays for *The Seven Arts* and *The Dial*.

Perhaps the magazine's view of the war will best suggest its quality and the kind of intellectual atmosphere Brooks had helped to create. For *The Seven Arts*, World War I focuses the bankruptcy of political nationalism (*The Seven Arts* critics always dissociated political from cultural nationalism) and pragmatism. From April 1917 the lead articles were editorials or essays on current political questions by men like Bourne, Oppenheim, John Dewey ("In a Time of National Hesitation"), John Reed ("This Unpopular War") and Bertrand Russell ("Is Nationalism Moribund?"). Bourne, who had begun as a disciple of Dewey, became one of his foremost critics. Dewey supported the war, the final evidence for Bourne that pragmatism was "scientific method applied to uplift."[13] "Our pragmatic awakeners have really not only failed us but

---

[13] "Twilight of Idols," *Seven Arts*, II (October 1917), 68.

traduced us," Brooks himself charges, because they have ended
in the self-complacency which is the special American hydra.
Brooks believed, as he later put it, that opposing the war was
like opposing an earthquake and thought besides that Pan-
Germanism was "a terrible menace." But, like Bourne, he was
a critic of pragmatism and, like the other *Seven Arts* policy-
makers, he supported Bourne's right to attack the war. Probably only Bourne, who had "that deep, shaking impact of
personality" Brooks hunted for always, could have united *The
Seven Arts* editors behind his anti-war position for as long as
he did.

The Seven Arts may have helped, as Waldo Frank suggests,
to release Brooks from his timidities.[14] Brooks himself confesses that his attempts "to earn a living on *The Seven Arts*
and *The Freeman* were accompanied by a chronic sense of
disaster and defeat." His reader, however, knows that in his
Seven Arts essays there is no disaster and no defeat; there is
a very special kind of triumph: Brooks's militant critical self,
the moment and the means had happily met. The essays remain
to embody that meeting.

For the Martyn Johnson *Dial* (1916-1919) Brooks produced his most influential shorter essay, "On Creating a Usable
Past," and several other articles. If Brooks's only contribution
had been the invention of the term, "the usable past," posterity
would know his name. It fittingly names what critics and historians have always done with the past. They have always
selected. It names what an entire literary generation conceived
of as tradition. T. S. Eliot's selective, discontinuous version of
the English literary tradition is the outstanding contemporary
example. His usable past moved from Shakespeare to Donne,
skipped to Dryden, then leapt to Eliot himself. Eliot's construction of the past was eminently usable for himself and for
a specific conception of poetry.

That the past can show us to ourselves is not a new idea.
What is new is the publicly announced determination to select
consciously from the past in order to serve immediate present

14 Waldo Frank to Sherwood Anderson (May 31, 1918). Unpublished letter
in the Newberry Library, Sherwood Anderson Collection.

ends. Brooks says but does not entirely mean that "the spiritual past has no objective reality." He would certainly not care to take that statement to its ultimate literary and political absurdity. Brooks does, however, entirely mean that he did not care to be impartial and "objective." He forcefully attacks the professorial ideal of objectivity and its apparently endemic desire "to shame the present with the example of the past." He wants to use the past positively and partially in the service of the present.

His usable past is, like Eliot's, primarily literary. Brooks's imperative: "Discover, invent a usable past we certainly can, and that is what a vital criticism always does," had in effect already begun in *America's Coming-of-Age*. Brooks was to call his later biographies of Twain and James "cautionary." Like these biographies his usable past was primarily "cautionary." Not even the example of Whitman was entirely "exemplary," as Brooks later claimed his biography of Emerson to be. Out of the colonial past he salvaged no positive figures. Out of the "classic" past Poe, Thoreau, Emerson, and Whitman survive with reservations. Melville later joins these figures. Figures like Bryant and Longfellow are easily excommunicated. The post-Civil War generation, the generation closest to Brooks, is the generation which fixes and exaggerates the worst elements of the American economy and psychology. Brooks accepts Sidney Lanier's judgment of this era as one in which "pretty much the whole of life has been merely not dying." Between the classic American past and the present *The Seven Arts* critics created a barren interregnum which Lewis Mumford alone, in the *Brown Decades* (1931), was tentatively to people.

Is there a usable literary present? Unfortunately, as Brooks's *Freeman* essays (1920-1924) testify, the usable present turned out to be more cautionary than the past. It functioned more as promise than achievement. This was a wry situation for the critic who had attacked the professors for disparaging "almost everything that comes out of the contemporary mind." Brooks had accepted Sherwood Anderson in a spirit of critical joy; his joy was alloyed but his appreciations of Dreiser and Mencken were even more alloyed. His attention to other current writers is essentially referential. When he notices Ezra Pound he notices Pound, the fellow gadfly and propagandist. His review of *Instigations* (1920), here reprinted, shows what common causes these literary radicals shared. Partisanship has obscured the early similarities between them. Their basic difference in 1920 was clear enough: Pound insisted on the concrete necessities of the new poetry and Brooks on the general sanctity of the literary life.

Brooks's strength, in fact, never lay in specific, detailed criticism of literature. It is also true that by the time the best fiction of the twenties appeared Brooks had already defected from his role as champion of the younger generation. What might he have said, for example, had such works as *The Great Gatsby* (1925) *The Sun Also Rises* (1926) and *The Sound and the Fury* (1929) appeared in 1915? He had, furthermore, never displayed a critical sensibility attuned to poetry; criticism of poetry could no more be expected from him than from Henry James. He makes generalized references to a poet like Edgar Lee Masters whom he predictably uses as text, and, as early as 1921, he believes "the pioneers and the imagists are already of the past, while Lincoln and Whitman are with Goethe, Ibsen, and Tolstoy, of the past, the present, and the future. They voice the great collective effort of humanity."[15]

His equation and dismissal of "the pioneers and the imagists" occurs in his *Freeman* columns where, for the first time, Brooks expresses pettish disappointment with modern literature because it refuses to take on the robes of social prophecy. Experiment has become aesthetic sterility. Although he does not relent in his attack on American inadequacy, his literary ideal seems to have become fixed in nineteenth century humanism. He yearns for the familiar features of a Goethe, a Tolstoy, a William Morris. In these columns Brooks first presents his *persona*, Wickford (he is later transformed into Oliver Allston), through whom he objectifies his disturbed responses to contemporary literature. Brook's nineteenth-century outlook is more appropriate in Wickford, who is an old man, than in himself.

[15] "A Reviewer's Note-book," *The Freeman*, III (June 22, 1921), 359.

III

The critic as champion had in effect become, by 1920 or 1921, an old critic new style. Even the metaphors of promise, once used to rationalize American imperfection, no longer worked very well for Brooks. The past had gotten better, the present worse, the future still happily before us.

The years following *The Ordeal of Mark Twain* (1920) were crisis years. From approximately 1920 to 1930 Brooks struggled with the difficulties of maintaining his earlier radical stance. His next book-length work, *The Pilgrimage of Henry James* (1925), represents an oversimplification of the socio-psychoanalytic method of the *Ordeal* in which Brooks had argued that Twain was a frustrated satirist who accidentally turned to humor and stuck to it for pecuniary and conformist reasons. The James work is more interesting as the embodiment of Brooks's final struggle with his own ambivalence toward America which ended in farewell to the critical method he had been forging since 1908 than for itself. He later believed that although he "appeared to be quarreling with Henry James," he had been quarreling with himself. In going through what he terms his *crise à quarante ans* Brooks once again suggests his Victorian forbears who left an extensive record of exhaustion and collapse. Brook's own first full-length biographical subject, John Addington Symonds, suffered one of the most acute and lengthy breakdowns of the era.[16] Brooks locates the origins of his own "formidable nervous breakdown" in 1926 partly in "the state of irresolution" that attended the composition of the *Pilgrimage*. He was even to feel the "great luminous menacing eyes" of James pursuing him.

[16] Walter Houghton's *The Victorian Frame of Mind* (New Haven, 1957) still lacks an American counterpart. The case of John Jay Chapman, who suffered a breakdown in 1901, is particularly interesting since the burden and the tone of his criticism resembles Brooks's. For example: "The conservatism and timidity of our politics and of our literature today are due in part to that fearful pressure which for sixty years was never lifted from the souls of Americans. That conservatism and timidity may be seen in all our past. They are in the rhetoric of Webster and in the style of Hawthorne. They killed Poe. They created Bryant." From "Emerson," reprinted in Edmund Wilson, ed., *The Shock of Recognition* (New York, 1943), I, p. 654.

The irresolution concerning Henry James was an irresolution about a personal and a critical point of view. The imperfect psychological technique and the imperfect aesthetic insight which saw James as a thwarted Balzac resulted in a biography which failed to realize the best possibilities of Brooksian or cultural criticism. The rejection of James was a rejection of ambivalence as a creative critical posture. It was also a definitive rejection of contemporary literature.

When Brooks emerged in 1931 from his long period of doubt and transition he turned to acceptance and celebration. These are his later characteristics. He turned to Emerson (*The Life of Emerson*, 1932), whom he saw as synthesis to the thesis and antithesis of Twain and James. He turned also to a new critical method, a pastiche form of quotations from the subject's writings which were not enclosed in quotation marks; the effect was an uncritical merging of biographer with subject.

The critic could no longer sustain his characteristic dialectic. Certain of the contraries in cultural criticism, some conscious, some unconscious, were painful or unproductive. Others were not. We may easily accept, for example, loyalty to national and to world literature. We must also recognize the tension, sometimes fruitful, frequently painful, between the personality and the community. Brooks believed that in his version of socialism, "Aristocracy in thought; democracy in economics," the exchange between the person and the community could be creative. Although Bourne was to leave Fabian for revolutionary socialism, his ideal, "the beloved community" where "the good life of personality" can be lived, was the same as Brooks's.[17]

An unconfronted and unproductive paradox relates to the artist whom Brooks finds at once determined by his society and independent of it. He also implicitly assumes that artists should always be in harmonious relationship with society, but surely there are occasions when the artist may profit by being, like the critic, at "sword's points" with society.

More and more painful personally to Brooks was the co-existence of his great need to affirm and his actual lengthy list

---

[17] "Trans-National America," p. 97.

of rejections. Brooks knew that "affirmation, in the most real sense, proceeds to a certain extent through rejection." In finding a large part of the American past and present useless Brooks knew he could well end with nothing usable. Yet this formulation is more accurate than his "nothing endures that is based on rejection." He came to choose affirmation only and deserted the stimulating question of how affirmation and rejection can function together in a vital criticism.

One may judge these polarities—national and world literature, individualism and socialism, the autonomous and the victimized artist, affirmation and rejection—limiting and still recognize their usefulness as a basis for criticism. But when Brooks accepted the proposition that an adequate national literature could not exist until the national psychology and social structure had been altered he accepted a more dubious proposition. Although time has undercut this primary assumption of Brooks's cultural criticism (for an American literature exists and the country has yet to achieve the good or the great society), it might have been a fruitful working promise. Unfortunately, Brooks took it to mean· that the critic must alter society first and write criticism later. Given Brooks's temperament, the formula was constrictive. It was suited for pronouncement. Its ironic result was to remove Brooks, the engaged critic, from engagement to "affirmation."

Brooks's present desert-future garden construction also assumed that literature would take the shape of its nineteenth-century predecessors. This was another dubious and prescriptive assumption. It expected familiar statements about the human condition. When, for example, William Faulkner stated directly in his Nobel Prize acceptance speech that man would not only endure but prevail, Brooks recognized what he had been unable to find in Faulkner's work—Faulkner's humanism.

It is worth noting that men sympathetic to Brooks were to reprimand him for his mode of abdication. One *Seven Arts* colleague criticized Brooks for portraiture distortions that became "rationales of failure."[18] Another *Seven Arts* colleague believed Brooks exhibited the "very want of sympathy for art

18 Waldo Frank, *The Re-Discovery of America* (New York, 1929), p. 321.

and the artistic life of which he accuses society." The same colleague suggests that Randolph Bourne's death "deprived him of a powerful stimulus," for Bourne "was the best of foils for the somewhat diffident scholar."[19]

Brooks's later career was not in criticism but in a special kind of literary history. The major work of that career, the five-volume *Makers and Finders,* representing nearly twenty years of omnivorous research, develops and projects a usable past. At its best it convincingly and fully creates the continuity and tradition Brooks and his nation so hungered for; at its worst it is a pastiche of associational anecdotes, names, and places. It is not interpretative but, like so much nineteenth-century criticism, impressionistic and evocative. Its avowed concern is with the literary life, not the literary work. In *The Opinions of Oliver Allston* (1941), Brooks is his own worst critic. He asks of his *persona,* Oliver Allston, "What was his point of view?" and answers, "I have sometimes wondered if he had one." He could not have had such an exchange with his earlier self. That self knew that "once you have a point of view all history will back you up." The later Brooks, who became, like the Victorian heroes of his youth, increasingly oracular, morally earnest, prophetic and unsympathetic to wit and irony, needs to be balanced by this wittier, self-critical younger self.

Indeed, Brooks's brief plunge as "a champion and a man of war" may have been exceptional in his career. If so, he relinquished his early role without changing his basic commitments, for he believed always in art as therapy and in the artist as national awakener and national conscience. He never abandoned his search for a usable past, although he did alter his method of unearthing and evaluating it. His artists came to be called "life-affirmers" in a battle against "life-deniers." This very broad, very abstract polarity did not speak for a generation as his earlier polarities, more specific and more relevant, seemed to do.

As the critic made his major shifts, therefore—from analysis

---

[19] Paul Rosenfeld, *Port of New York* (New York, 1924), p. 60, p. 52. Brooks himself judges that Lewis Mumford took "the place that Randolph Bourne's death had left vacant." *Autobiography,* p. 406.

lix INTRODUCTION lix

and judgment to description and celebration and from a consideration of the self and society to a consideration of the self
and other critics—his ground became narrower and less compelling. To maintain "the natural soul in the midst of life," as
St. Francis had done, had become a more difficult and distant
ideal.

The extraordinary, highly diffused and as yet untabulated
influence of the earlier Brooks cannot, however, be under-
estimated. His attacks stimulated research in American studies.
The exploration, for example, of Puritan culture and society
was intensive and long-lasting. The efforts to rebut Brooks's
position on Edwards and Franklin or Twain and James were
part of a development that gave to American scholarship and
criticism a density, a specificity and a sophistication it had
lacked. Brooks's role in reclaiming the American past, in map-
ping and shaping that "terra incognita," that "vague foggy
wilderness," is impressive.[20]

Perhaps Brooks had indeed performed something of the
service of a Matthew Arnold. For if Arnold's task was broadly
to educate the new and large nineteenth century middle class,
Brooks's may well have been to educate the twentieth century
American middle class. Whatever their differences, he, like
Arnold, had tried to destroy his country's cultural insularity.[21]
Perhaps the gap between theory and practice bewailed by the
young Brooks has not greatly narrowed. Perhaps the nation
still worships Mammon and the Goddess of Getting On. But
as tradition of self-criticism has been strengthened by the work
of Van Wyck Brooks who had the courage to raise the possibility of a polemically engaged criticism. Certainly *The Wine
of the Puritans* opens American criticism of this century. We
have accepted America's literary coming of age. We are less
certain of her critical coming of age. In that possibly longer
process Brooks is more than a merely historical contributor.

Brooklyn College
The City University of New York

[20] *The Writer in America*, p. 38.
[21] Brooks's assessment of Arnold is ambivalent. For an example of a negative
appraisal see *The Malady of the Ideal*, pp. 39-42 and passim. in this collection.

I

The Wine of the Puritans

(London, 1908)

EDITORIAL NOTE: *The Wine of the Puritans* was written abroad. It embodies a major ambivalence among intellectuals of the period: should the American writer stay or go? For the Brooks of 1908 the American writer could successfully do neither. The question became, therefore, "how to change the whole texture of life at home so that writers and artists might develop there." To this question and others the young Brooks addressed himself "in the unripe little book that I wrote, in the form of a dialogue, in the Sussex farmhouse." Its conversational form was in imitation of G. Lowes Dickinson and represented a revision of its original epistolary form. The speakers have no separate personality; the dialogue is more gesture or aura than form. That gesture and aura perfectly suits the tone reflected in the little book's closing hope that Denver and Sioux City will one day "have a traditional and antique dignity like Damascus and Perugia." For the central preoccupation of the young Brooks was how to create tradition in a country without tradition. His contemporary, T. S. Eliot, having elected to "go," had none-

theless to redefine tradition and his relation to it. The work's
concern with identity and tradition as it connects with rebellion against official America may be said to initiate the
1920s. The stay or go dilemma was not quieted. It was to
reach its fullest, most intense expression in *The Pilgrimage of
Henry James* (1925).

For the original London edition Brooks had paid half the
costs. Mitchell Kennerley brought out the subsequent American edition. Kennerley, who later published the biographies
of Symonds and Wells, was also the publisher of the *Forum*
when Brooks contributed to it. With *The Ordeal of Mark
Twain* (1920) Brooks began his long association with Dutton.

Chapter I

The number of the house—Two sorts of founders—The only virtues
—"The wildest dreams of Boston"—Emerson—A man of some distinction—The first premise—A very odd fellow, indeed—Mr. Rockefeller considered symbolically—Eena, meena, mina, mo—Two childhoods—A bowl of daffodils—"La Patrie"—What we left in Europe.

IT WAS ONE of those Italian midsummer afternoons, when
to be abroad, they say, is the same thing as to be an American. Back from its little blue bay the quiet village of Baja
lay up against a circular slope like a great mossy sea-shell into
which twenty centuries had idly tossed their temples and
dwellings, half-covering them as they crumbled there in flowering glooms of dusty verdure. Here and there a line of yellow
columns stood out from the vines like rich candles among the
silks of a splendid altar. The atmosphere itself seemed to
assume a responsibility in the entire absence of any palpable
sound or movement, for it perceptibly trembled vibrantly
back and forth, murmurous with sparkling insects. It was
possible to imagine that this silence had remained to remind
one that the voice of Virgil had broken it once, somewhere

in the ruins. And in this place it seemed as if civilization had fulfilled itself, as if history had said its last word and closed its book—as if, indeed, the genius of romance had lingered here and grown forgetful of itself and fallen asleep.

I was glad when Graeling[1] broke the silence.

"There is something I don't quite like about this. I feel as if a great many things had suddenly come together to brush me out of existence, I think we had better have a discussion!"

As a little ripple broke along the beach we looked up to see a great black ship moving westward from Naples in the outer bay.

"Another shipload of Italians going to take our places at home," he said. "It's so hard to call it home when you have to stop to recollect the number of the house!"

We could hear the flutter of the American flag irritably tugging away from its pole as the stern withdrew quietly round the point.

"How do you suppose it all came about?"

I think we both determined to have it out then and there.

"Well, to begin with, we have the Pilgrim Fathers."

"The first materialists?" I suggested.

"Quite possibly, but there is something else that comes first. Do you see what I mean when I say that, unlike any other great race, we were founded by full-grown, modern, self-conscious men?"

"How unlike any other race."

"Well," he replied, "the founders of all the great original races—original in the sense of having dwelt in one peculiar section of the world since before they became civilized and historic peoples—were rude specimens of one or other of the prehistoric types of man, marked off at the moment of their first settlement in their future homes by almost imperceptible, if indeed any, distinctions from the other members of the common type. Settling, as they did, some in Germany, some in France, some in England, they became moulded by the special traits of climate, natural elements, and properties of the lands of their choice. And although there were migrations

---

[1] Possibly meant to suggest a lover of things Greek, a Greekling.

and invasions and infinite stirrings back and forth of these half-awakened peoples, each race had so far settled itself and taken the colour of its surroundings as to have developed certain distinct racial traits and to have reached a national type inflexible enough to absorb invading peoples and to force its own traits upon its conquerors: all this before the dawn of its own special historic period. The American type, on the contrary, has evolved in the full daylight of modern history. It was deliberately established by full-grown, intelligent, modern men with a self-conscious purpose, in a definite year."

"But the roots of the old civilization were there."

"Oh, I grant you that the men who landed at Plymouth Rock were Englishmen. Exactly in proportion as the memories of the old tradition grew fainter and fainter, the qualities of a new tradition grew stronger and stronger. The growing American idea displaced the dying English idea. Well, of course the particularly vivid reality of pioneering could hardly find its ideal reflection in the genial traditions they had left behind, and of course they were forced to emphasize for protection the virtues of thrift and industry. And these virtues were for so long the essential virtues for the economical welfare of the new state that everything else appeared unnecessary beside them. In the course of time they came to be considered the only virtues, while the Puritan point of view, cut off from immediate intercourse with riper points of view, more and more inclined to believe that whatever was not in some way economically necessary was in some way wrong."

"But your term 'economically necessary'?" I asked. "Civilization is not merely for the purpose of sustaining life—that is the premise, the thing assumed, upon which civilization is built up."

"But the Puritans were unable for so long to assume this premise, were forced for so long to concentrate all their energies upon establishing this premise that they accustomed themselves to the idea that sustaining the machinery of life was a kind of end in itself. And so they came to feel suspiciously toward ritual, pleasure, light-heartedness—all those things which an established civilization can support, as symbols of opposition to the stern economic need."

"And it all remained as a habit long after the need for this materialism had passed, when there were peace and plenty for more gracious purposes?"

"Exactly. One sees in Whittier, Holmes and the rest that preconception of the supreme virtues of thrift and industry, the note of shrewdness and homely comfort, showing that Puritanism had not yet accustomed itself to prosperity or to allowing the unqualified value of anything not essentially and directly connected with the machinery of life.

"But just then something happened. America suddenly ceased to be New England. Nations of foreigners came to our ports desiring to be called American. Now, although we have not produced a national average type——"

" 'The wildest dreams of Boston are the facts of San Francisco' ! "

"Still the native-born Puritan race is the dominant race everywhere, socially at least, deeply tinged with those Puritan ideals, provincial and material still. The New England idea, adequate for a small province, naturally became inadequate for the expression of a great nation. Adapted as this idea was to the needs of a frugal, intellectual people whose development was strictly intensive rather than extensive, it was unable to meet the needs of great prosperity, imperialism and cosmopolitanism. The New Englander carried his philosophy to California and sought to adjust his great prosperity to it, just as he carried it to Europe and insisted on interpreting history through its medium. In both cases, of course, the large need* could not adapt itself to the small interpretation. Now the philosophically inclined New Englander, finding that he could give no rational explanation of the world in accordance with the New England idea, turned aside into Transcendentalism. It seems to me that Emerson and his following represent the despair of explaining the world in general (which had opened to them) by the rational philosophy they were accustomed to apply to the provincial life of New England in particular. And so they threw aside the hope of any rational explanation

* See Appendix p. 60.

at all and sought to interpret life in arbitrary and purely spiritual terms. Emerson is a lofty and inspired sophist who begs the whole question of life, and whose sophism is the direct result of a provincial training, rational as an explanation of the peculiar life of one corner of the world, but inadequate to explain life in the wider sense."

"You put the old wine into new bottles," I suggested, "and when the explosion results, one may say, the aroma passes into the air and the wine spills on the floor. The aroma, or the ideal, turns into transcendentalism, and the wine, or the real, becomes commercialism. In any case one doesn't preserve a great deal of well-tempered, genial wine. The other day I came across a passage in Mr. Riis's *Theodore Roosevelt the Citizen* suggesting how admirable it was in the latter to have made up his mind to work just the same, although, as a young man, he had means to be idle.[2] This really implies that the average man is almost justified in ceasing to exist, so far as the welfare of the world is concerned, if he has a comfortable income, or at least that if he goes on working just the same, his work is to be taken not as a matter of course but as a distinct credit to him. He is *ipso facto* a man of some distinction. Now it seems to me that to imagine that the ideals and purposes one carries in one's head are dependent upon ups and downs of outer fortune is to be pre-occupied with the material side of the question."

"It means," said Graeling, "that the first attention must still be given to keeping life well-fuelled and well-fed; that, in short, American civilization has not yet learned to accept the machinery of life as a premise. Your business man cannot believe that he has gathered together enough money to support this machinery a hundred times over, but goes on making money in the honest conviction that it is necessary for him to do so. And deeper than this, he really loves his business—which means that he loves the machine for itself more than for

---

[2] Jacob August Riis (1849-1914), Danish born, was a lifelong friend of Theodore Roosevelt, an active journalist and lecturer in the service of social welfare and slum reform. His book on Roosevelt was written in 1914. Other well-known titles by him are: *How the Other Half Lives* (1890) and *The Making of an American* (1901).

what it produces. Now, of course, until you have accepted this premise you cannot accept easily and naturally any of the things that are built on this premise. You cannot, in short, accept the arts of life. You can be enthusiastic and extravagant about them but you cannot accept them as perfectly normal, natural elements of civilized life. Enthusiasm in these matters usually implies strangeness and unfamiliarity. . . . It is all a matter of economics."

"Why, we look upon everything from an economic standpoint! Do we not allow religion and recreation and literature their place in our economic system? Do we not condescend to allow life itself an economic value, the office hour being the real criterion by which we measure these things and to which we accommodate them all? We take our exercise, not primarily because we love exercise but because we can do our work better for it. We read, not primarily because we love reading, but to rest our minds from our work. We are conscious toward art and literature, never accepting them as a perfectly normal part of life, but as things to 'go in for' or to 'blow ourselves to'. Or at least we insist upon their economic or their moral value—those sides of art which appeal to the instinct of the machinery, because we have not the instinct of art itself which is concerned primarily with the aesthetic value. We do not care for these things for their own sakes, but as cogs in the machine."

"Fielding has a remark somewhere," said Graeling, "that 'whenever a philosopher appears among us he is distinguished by the name of an odd fellow.' Now, an American who takes it into his head to think for a few years, and refuses to recognize the mechanical instinct as the most important instinct, is distinguished, heaven knows, by the name of a very odd fellow indeed; or else he is overloaded with ill-advised luxury, and sent over to Europe by a prosperous father who wishes him to have all the advantages which he himself was denied. In no case does he seem to fit in anywhere at home, to be accepted easily and gratefully as if his work were perfectly legitimate and essential to civilized life. We hardly feel that art *is* altogether legitimate—there is something odd about it. We do not feel, for instance, that the artist, the man who creates, is as illegitimate a type as the broker, the man who negotiates. 'Poetry and imagination, the portion of a very small number of idlers'—do you remember in Chateaubriand?[3] —'are regarded in the United States as puerilities appertaining to the first and to the last ages of life. The Americans have had no childhood, and have, as yet, had no old age.' "

"That's it, America has had no childhood—in America. We left our childhood in the old world, and the moral and physical struggle to survive in a new country, left neither time nor heart for the cultivation of those instincts and sensibilities which produce a genial superiority to the hard facts of life. Mr. Rockefeller[4]—there is a parallel to the whole story. Reared in barren hardship among surroundings that allowed no play of the imagination, he grew up to manhood and to middle-age with the one fixed idea that he must conquer his circumstances and make easy the material side of life. He put poverty at defiance and steadfastly willed himself to become rich. Well, he became rich. But there was nothing left in him to expand into something superior to his riches, and the only happiness that he could know was—to become richer."

"I suppose it is beside the point," said Graeling, "to remember that America, unlike Mr. Rockefeller, had had her childhood, a forgotten childhood in the old country, full of all things of the imagination. It seems to me that we Americans come back year after year to the home that we remember with a kind of half-dreaming instinct to revisit with a wistful affection the old villages and the old haunts of our ancestors. There is something affectionate in our curiosity as we speed about in our brazen motors from Stratford to Devonshire, tooting along the quiet lanes. It's not sight-seeing really. We feel as if we had lived there in a dream sometime, as if one of

[3] François René de Chateaubriand (1768-1848), the French romantic writer who visited the United States in 1791 and claimed to have taken the Northwest Passage. His idealization of the American Indian effectively fixed the conception of the noble savage.

[4] John Davison Rockefeller (1839-1937). Son of an upstate New York itinerant moneylender and trader who embodies the American success dream. By 1906 his Standard Oil of New Jersey had net assets of $360,000,000, making it one of the richest corporations in the world.

our great great grandfathers had lived in every little thatched
cottage. We half expect the black sheep to say, 'Yes, sir; yes,
sir; three bags full,' and to see the cow jump over the moon.
And in the still of the evening as we pass by the village crossroads we hear the children scampering together while the
leader counts, 'Eena, meena, mina, mo.' Then something
happens. We suddenly remember that this really wasn't our
childhood at all. We see the big brick house and the polished
lawn where we used to play hide-and-seek, and we hear the
full-throated robins calling among the maples. Once more we
shout, 'last look' as we clatter up the side steps after begging
one more game from good-natured Mary. . . .

"There seem to be two of them and we to have lived them
both. I think all Americans have two childhoods, an American
childhood and an English childhood, a kind of picture-book
childhood that we lived before we were born."

"And do you know our oldest friends are really Englishmen.
We can forget everybody we have ever known sooner than
Jack who climbed up after the giant:

> 'Fee, foe, fum;
> I smell the blood of an Englishman.'

Now if he had been a Spaniard or an Italian it would have
been only a story!"

"And then how we do want to believe that Dr. Johnson
drank his ale at the Cheshire Cheese!"

"I wonder if we are really English in our hearts and American only in our heads? Hearts are older than heads. American
history is so unlovable!"

"Yes, we cannot find consolation in remembering our
American forbears until we are grown-up. Their virtues and
sentiments were those of grown-up, fully awakened men and
women, developed and adapted for a special and temporary
situation. A child must fight and kill a great many giants
and live a very long time in the greenwood before he can have
an appetite for Indians. The founders of the old races were
children themselves, and as children possessed of qualities not
biased and stressed and prejudiced for any special temporary

situation, and so never obsolete or ill-adapted to any situation. The old myths that spring out of the childhood of an ancient race must have their message for every succeeding generation, because they represent general racial traits and ideals, and are wider than any special application of them. And this is because those myths sprang up while the race was determining its traits, and before its historic epoch applied those traits to special episodes of self-conscious life. Any virtue or any myth which sprang out of one of these later episodes, and illustrated the requirements of the special situation as distinguished from the general character of the race in all times and situations, ceased to be illuminating when the episode was past. That is why the most ancient legends of a race survive and seem ripe for all times and situations, while the stories that spring out of particular events so soon become only food for antiquaries."

"I think I see. A child's comments on what one is doing are never harsh—never seem to be irrelevant. They are so delightfully general, there is nothing specialized about them. It is the kind of criticism which one receives from a bowl of daffodils on one's desk or the breeze that rustles in the window curtains. Men and women bring their personalities with them, and in their criticism one has to allow for all their habits, and what they have been doing and thinking themselves. One has to subtract their lives before their criticism can become as fresh as the daffodils—and then the daffodils are faded."

"Well, we are all grown-up in America, we are the most grown-up race in the world. We all know exactly what we are about. Our history is like an open book. We can look back and see the beginnings of it all as if it were only yesterday. We can watch the Puritans at their work and read their minds and understand their perfectly simple motives. It is because the old Puritan days were not the childhood of our race but the first episode of our history. . . . We are the most purely intelligent people in the world."

"How often I have noticed that there is a certain shyness about Europeans which seems to be violated by our American briskness and frankness and noisiness. Frenchmen, with all their vainglorious talk about 'La Patrie' and honour and glory, always seem a good deal like little boys throwing out their chests, quite too serious to laugh at themselves: and Italians shooting each other, without a thought, over some pretty girl or other. Do you think an American would be foolish enough to do any of these things? Not he. He is too sensible. He knows what he is about. He is a grey reality who doesn't believe in visions and such nonsense. He doesn't believe in honesty *because* it's the best policy, but he knows very well that honesty *is* the best policy. He doesn't believe in impulses and intuitions, because they interfere with the silent, regular inexorable grinding of the machine. He is at bedrock and he believes in bedrock."

"Exactly. He has not what one might call racial preoccupations. Our problems are all comparatively new and comparatively simple. We have none of those complex and diseased social problems which have grown old and so embedded themselves in the fibre of European life that they have got beyond the power of rational reform, just as cancer may pass beyond the reach of the surgeon, even when the surgeon can tell exactly what the matter is. There is in European societies an accretion of twenty centuries of experience, bound up with prejudice and instinct incalculably complex, which expresses itself in a silent sense of fatality. A kind of melancholy and sombre reminiscence seems to brood over human life which connects these peoples with the mysteries of evolution, and which revives in them the great sorrows and longings, the struggling desire for expression of that brute creation out of which, through infinite gradations of labour and the action of the elements, they have come forth. Of course there is something inarticulate about them, some intermingling of that instinct which is the intelligence of long dead generations with the intelligence of their own generation, something that restrains them from entire frankness and self-confidence, that makes them shy—"

"—Something that makes and keeps them children."

"But we Americans have no bonds with a remote antiquity, no traditions of the soil old enough as yet to have become instincts. As Chateaubriand expressed it in a marvellous phrase: 'We left our childhood and our youth in Europe.' Our only ancestral memories of the old race are like a dream we dream in our childhood and then forget. In Europeans, unlike ourselves, we find a vivid sense of mystery in life—

> 'Blank misgivings of a creature
> Moving about in worlds not realized'—

a something which prevents them from accurately methodizing all their actions and from solving their problems merely by taking thought. But because most of our problems arose from events easily understood by the modern mind and in the clear noonday of modern life, we can hope, to some considerable extent, to solve those problems by purely rational reform. We are not hampered in our work by any 'echoes of an ante-natal dream.' If we have not the splendour and the grace of Europe nor their converse the pessimism of Europe, if we have not that note of diseased inheritance and social decay—Hauptmann, D'Annunzio and Maeterlinck,[5] if we seem born into the world curiously without instincts, we have at least—reason, rationalism."

Chapter II

What we have kept—The kindling of instinct—Ingenuity—On the surface—Instinct or conviction?—Tones and words—The laboursaving principle—"Just about as good"—whitewashed elephants—Pioneering and turtle-soup—Threadbare—"Recreation from hard work"—Stilted sympathies—Derelict machinery—Two views of Mr. Rockefeller—The correct street—Permanent impermanence—The pastime called "Exposure"—Morning paper conversation—The

---

[5] Gerhart Hauptmann (1862-1946), Gabriele D'Annunzio (1863-1938), Maurice Maeterlinck (1862-1949). Of these three dramatists perhaps only D'Annunzio qualifies as a decadent by his total lack of concern with morality. Since Hauptmann's early naturalism soon gave way to symbolism, the three writers have their anti-naturalism in common.

Simple Life and blue silk—Over the telephone—Louis XI and President Buchanan.

YES," I SAID, "and our American rationalism is a disease."

"Just how a disease?"

"Well, as an example, take our prominent trait of ingenuity. We enjoy putting together the machinery and inventing labour-saving machines for the sheer pleasure of the thing. We devise every possible short-cut toward the finished product because we feel that labour itself has no virtue, and because we are more interested in the cleverness of the machine than in the quality of the article it produces. We feel that if we have invented some ingenious device our ingenuity alone gives it a reason for existence. There are many men who spend their lives devising ways of avoiding labour when true happiness is apt to result from the labour itself. This is an example of rationalism recoiling upon itself and becoming intellectually morbid."

"But what do you mean in saying that this is an example of 'rationalism recoiling upon itself'?"

"Well, you cut away, at least to some very considerable extent, a man's instincts, and what is left?—mind. He thinks. He understands his position as if he had been dropped full-grown out of the clouds. He is a rationalist. He does not feel this and that to be true because tradition has proved them so. He is independent of tradition; he has to think it all out for himself. Now of course reason is only a method, a means to an end. He knows that life ought to consist of instincts and emotions. He knows that while there ought perhaps to be nothing in life which reason cannot explain, there are many things in life whose rationality must be taken for granted, and whose significance depends upon the spiritual or emotional superstructure raised above the rational foundation. He knows that one should think until one has established a true basis for feeling, and that then one should feel. That feeling, that impression is the reaction of the mind upon the heart, the kindling of instinct, and that must be left inviolate as soon as one can feel that it has a logical basis, if it is to produce any emotional reaction. To maintain the rational attitude toward

something which is already rationally established is to prevent
the spiritual superstructure and to uproot the incipient instinct.
Plant your seed rightly and then leave it alone or it will never
come to blossom. Now the American, as it seems to me, is
always asking in regard to politics, art, religion: 'How can
I be sure that I have planted the seed rightly?' Well, and how
can anybody be sure? We must take some things for granted
and have faith, if any instincts are to grow out of our reason.
The American is on his guard against the unexplainable. He
is suspicious of anything for which he cannot find the immediate reason. He drags out his instincts every now and then to
look them over and see if they are thoroughly sensible. He
does not allow them time to melt together and form in him a
background and a reserve. There is a danger that in America
the rational point of view will become an end instead of a
means, an instinct itself instead of an instrument for explanation. One sees signs everywhere of an impatience with the
seeds even when they are—so far as one can judge—rightly
planted, and a feeling that the planting of the seeds and not
the gathering of the blossoms is the chief matter. And the
expression of this morbid rationalism is found in that ingenuity
which produces a sense of pleasure in the very workings of
reason for their own sake rather than for what they accomplish. The American, perpetually driven to explaining the
reasons of things, makes a religion of the mechanism."

"I fancy that it is this insistently rational attitude which
gives to Americans that curious appearance of being always
on the surface, and which suggests a certain transparency in
all our thoughts and acts, as if, indeed, we had behind us no
complex undercurrent of social relations. This transparency
exhibits itself in the facility with which we throw out final
judgments on matters that go back into the most impenetrable
recesses of the human consciousness. It is usually possible, I
have found, for an American to explain in perfectly measured
words why he is of a certain mind in politics or religion. He
is able to discuss these questions intellectually and to tell you
why he laughs at certain things, why he believes or enjoys
certain things. In the keen play of his intelligence one hardly
finds the subtler play of instinct, just as in artistic matters he

has not, what I should call, an instinctive perception, but only an intelligent or rational perception."

"And I think," I added, "that our political parties can hardly be said, except perhaps in the South, to represent traditional instincts in the sense in which the Liberals and Conservatives in England represent traditional instincts. An American who is a Democrat today may vote the Republican ticket tomorrow if he prefers the Republican candidate, and the son of a socialist may become a capitalist if his income so allows him. Even if one is a Republican by conviction, and even if one's family has remained Republican for generations by conviction, Republicanism in America is not old enough as yet to have grown from a conviction into an instinct."

"It all reduces itself," said Graeling, "to one statement—we take nothing for granted. Supposing that the human heart is the treasury in which the mind has stored away its discoveries, one by one, age after age: a little dust has fallen through the chinks, and the thoughts and reasons stored away there have melted together into a gathered mass no longer separable to the eye. So long as that mass is left intact heart remains heart and not mind, and is capable of emotions not readily explained by the mind. Just so it seems to me that a civilization can only become mellow when it has learned to assume that many things capable of logical explanation depend for their value upon not being explained, that the potential explanation must be taken for granted, and one's attention devoted to the emotions built upon it. In order to love or enjoy or believe anything we must forget for the moment what love and enjoyment in themselves really are. We must feel a mystery in these things which cannot be quite explained.

"We are civilized, as it seems to me, in proportion to the amount we are able to presuppose. Highly civilized men who meet for the first time are able to appreciate in a second how much they can infer between themselves. They speak by allusions, and a single ejaculation is so modulated as to convey the essence of ten minutes' talk between less civilized men. A civilized man does not judge so much from words as from tones: one can put an untruth into words so as to simulate truth, while a tone cannot be disguised. Words can be measured and understood and looked at top and bottom and all sides: there is in a tone something of the mystery, the—one hardly knows what. And just as it is with civilized men, so it is with civilized peoples. Even supposing that in the one case psychology may be able to explain the tone, and in the other case the emotion or perception or reverence toward art or religion, it is none the less true that civilization, to a certain degree, seeks the esoteric, the hidden, and veils itself in a reserve. It is not transparent; it is moved by gestures and expressions too fine to be explained, by tones rather than words. It is this forbearance in the presence of spiritual things, this deliberate refusal to analyze which produces reverence and instinctive perception."

"Exactly," I said, "and ingenuity works against the establising of this forbearance and this reserve. Ingenuity is valuable as a means to an end, but whenever we find ourselves enjoying a means we are destroying our appetite for the end. The very idea that any kind of labour-saving device justifies its own existence implies that labour is a thing in all cases to avoid as far as possible—where, indeed, the inventor has any aim ulterior to reducing his own personal expenses as an individual manufacturer. The labour-saving principle simply means that labour is a thing to be short-cut, compressed, and dispensed with as far as possible, and that if individual happiness is the outcome of individual labour—well, then, happiness must be sacrificed more and more to progress."

"And that is precisely what most inventors are prepared to admit. Of course it ignores that indefinable difference between the machine-made and the hand-made, which represents the heart of the individual workman; of course it ignores the element of the unexplainable in hand-made work, that curious product of human ambition and pride called quality. But why is it that in America, where we have produced only one great composer[1] and only one or two great painters,[2] we have produced a dozen ingenious devices for manufacturing music and

[1] Brooks is probably referring to Edward MacDowell (1861-1908) who used Indian and American folk themes in works such as "Indian Suite" and "Woodland Sketches."

[2] See his discussion of Whistler and Sargent in Chapter V.

pictures, which are, as we say, 'just about as good' as the true things? It is because most of us are quite content with the substitute. Nor does this contentment with something 'just about as good' stop at music and pictures and other—machine-made goods. . . . We want everything in the form of a pill, a substitute. We take a pill instead of taking exercise. We want our literature reduced to 'snappy' paragraphs, we want what we call culture in the form of capsules—half-hour readings and lectures between the intervals of our more serious business, because we feel that somehow we ought to have these things, and we want to get through with them in as short order as possible. 'The public wants to be fooled,' said Barnum,[3] when someone remonstrated with him for exhibiting a white elephant which he had whitewashed himself. He was perfectly right. So long as the elephant is white, we are not greatly concerned how he came by his colour."

"And then," I added, "do you remember not long ago when Mr. Roosevelt praised a certain poet[4]—I can't recall his name, everyone took it for granted that he was a very great poet and bought him and admired him? It is one of our curious assumptions that a man who has reached eminence in one field is competent to pass judgment in all fields. If we had learned to discriminate in poetry, if we had cared about poetry, we should probably have surmised that we were as good judges in that particular matter as Mr. Roosevelt. But as a nation we have not trained ourselves to discriminate quality in anything sufficiently to allow us to hold our own judgment in opposition to the judgment of anyone who has a name, though the name were made in pioneering and the subject in question be turtle soup. . . . We walk through an art gallery and admire every

---

[3] Phineas Taylor Barnum (1810-1891). The great American showman, born to a Bethel, Connecticut farmer and tavern keeper. His ventures included the discovery, naming and exhibiting of General Tom Thumb, the sponsorship of Jenny Lind's tour and the purchase of Jumbo the elephant. In 1874 he organized "Barnum's Greatest Show on Earth." The line, "A sucker is born every minute," has been attributed to Barnum. It may, however, derive from the older folk phrase: "A fool is born every minute." His books include: *Humbugs of the World* (1865) and *Money Getting* (1883).

[4] Edwin Arlington Robinson (1869-1935).

picture in it, and then go to a concert and applaud every piece equally, and both pictures and music straightway pass out of our heads. All of which results from our endless search for the means of making better things, endlessly ignoring the things made."

"I suppose in a sense it is a form of idealism, if everything is idealism which is persistently unsatisfied with its results."

"But that begs the whole question of modern life. Looked at in one way life itself is a compromise with reason. Supposing that we are all in search of the highest economy of life. And supposing that that economy accepts every discovery of science as one more stone in a foundation an absolute, upon which we may firmly stand in order to learn what man really is, to understand the relations between men, and little by little to raise the racial average. Well then, every moment that we delay, tasting of the quality of things, allowing the most momentary and the most refined expression of the senses, we are countenancing by just so much a stage of existence only imperfectly true; while reason is revealing more and more of the absolute, in psychology and biology, so long as we sacrifice the happiness of its reactions upon ourselves in a thirsty, unresting pursuit of it. . . . But not one man in a thousand is fitted for this part. The great mass of men must always be preoccupied with life itself and the present. They ought to absorb the quality, the spiritual value of life. If there were no need for the spiritual besides the rational, to what futile end would the rational lead us? We ought to believe that the game is worth the candle, and to make it so. Where a whole race is immersed in mechanics the quality of life and its arts is forgotten, and the national point of view—so far as there can be any—becomes curiously threadbare. That seems to me the danger and in a measure the result of our universal ingenuity."

"In what way would you say that American life is threadbare?"

"That for most of us living means getting a living. We never think what life is—we are continually intent upon what life brings. If we stop and wonder whether life is worth living or not we are quite unable to decide until we recall our social engagements and our business enterprises, and then we probably conclude that life is well enough. But this is because we are thinking of our engagements and enterprises and not of life at all."

"I have often noticed that an American business man, who is forbidden by his doctors to work, ceases to have a place in the universe. I have seen him at his summer hotel of a week-end watching the stock-ticker in the office. As a rule he has not that sense of power which keeps a Morgan[5] or a Rocke-feller from being quite sordid. Perhaps he takes his rest now and then and makes a holiday—which consists of a good cigar, a good hotel, and the best seat in the theatre. Whenever he goes to the theatre he makes the excuse of 'recreation from hard work' to see nothing but vaudeville and light opera, and whenever he reads he makes the excuse of 'recreation from hard work' to read nothing but poor novels and wretched magazines. That kind of hard work has really destroyed his taste for anything better: when his distractions are taken away and he has only himself to enjoy, he can do nothing but light a cigar and be irritable. He has never lived in himself at all. . . . It never occurs to him that the clouds are floating over his head. I am sure there is less happiness in America than in any other country in the civilized world. And it is because we associate happiness with spending money."

"Yes. These Italians come to us to gain prosperity and to lose everything else. They find in our life no freshness, no natural gaiety, no holiday-making, no splendid moments, none of the life they knew at home—a splendid, passionate life of elemental emotions—susceptible to every tremor of the senses. How soon they forget that they were once delighted by a ribbon or a song!"

"It really reduces itself," said Graeling, "to the proposition that if we are to consider poverty and happiness to be in-compatible, to that extent we assume prosperity and happiness to be synonymous. It is hard indeed for us to take the simple present as it stands, and to look at it and think about it, to

[5] John Pierpont Morgan (1837-1913). The scholarly financial genius who organized and incorporated United States Steel in 1901. He was widely criticized for his financial operations, which included the dominant role in the Panic of 1907.

expand, to sympathize, to enjoy, to grow human, deep, genuine, serene.

"Naturally enough we judge of a man by his activity. So long as a man is busy we seldom ask whether he is busy to any distinct and good purpose—we instinctively feel that he is right. This nervous activity, largely for its own sake, gives a curious rustiness to the emotions, and I have noticed that the affections and sympathies of many business men are strangely stilted and selfconscious, not so much from egotism as from that hardening of the nature which follows a long suspension of the exercise and free play of the emotions. And we instinctively feel that a man who is not busy is somehow doing wrong."

"I fancy that we so emphasize the value of activity," I suggested, "because it appears to us the outward and visible sign of a much deeper thing, efficiency."

"Efficiency is the well-oiled machinery by which one seeks a particular purpose. But efficiency is surely a bad thing where it has no purpose, and there is in American life, I think, an immense amount of undisciplined, undirected, clashing, wasted efficiency jarring and vibrating to no purpose whatever—an immense amount of derelict machinery, spinning and tearing at high pressure without the least intention of producing anything. Given the idea that a man must be busy anyway whether he has any purpose in mind or not—in short, that the running of the machinery is the chief matter, it is only natural that efficiency should erect itself from a means into an end. Now it is fair to say, I think, that Mr. Rockefeller is one of the unhappiest of living men. He is efficient. He has been nothing else for fifty years. He has made a large fortune. He has ruined his own life. He has ruined thousands of other lives. And when he dies will anybody miss him? Will anybody be honestly able to deny that the world would have been much better if he had never lived? Will there be anything more than a great crash in Wall Street and a thousand more lives ruined? And yet Mr. Rockefeller is an example of efficiency for the sake of efficiency, efficiency directed and controlled for the purpose of being efficient. The really tragic thing about Mr. Rockefeller is not so much that he has ruined thousands of lives by doing any definitely wrong and wicked things, not by being an out-and-out criminal—for all that can ultimately be corrected by law. The really tragic thing is that he has ruined his own life by simply living as all American business men live, only a little more so. For what law can correct a point of view?"

"That is one side of the matter," interposed Graeling. "The other side everyone knows. He has brought hundreds of millions of dollars into the world which did not exist until he created them, and which will exist when he is forgotten. In his own greed he has unconsciously sacrificed himself to produce the opportunity for thousands of men to labour and find happiness in labour. And, incidentally, I have known five men who have become artists entirely because their fathers, thanks to Mr. Rockefeller, were able to set them free, in the second generation, from this 'habit of the necessary.' This may serve as only a minor illustration, but it is one of an absolutely incalculable number of results, good and bad alike, into which the influence of this man resolves itself. Prosperity in one generation means living in the next."

"Quite possibly, but in this generation it takes a form which is, well, unpleasant. And it is unpleasant, I think, because of our curious democratic assumption that so long as we allow ourselves to feel inferior to nobody, we may feel superior to as many as we choose—an assumption so far removed from any genuine question of superiority or inferiority that it ripens with dangerous quickness, I fear, into the belief that all men are equal who have the money. It becomes a social necessity to maintain the appearance of prosperity when we have not the reality. It becomes necessary, for instance, to live in one of the chosen streets which are a sort of passport to social standing. It creates a tyranny of circumstance so strong that children, born in the accepted street, instinctively look askance at children born in the debarred street round the corner. And people wonder why some Americans, when they come to Europe, give up living in the fashion they have been accustomed to, frequent places whose like they would not frequent at home, and live in mean streets. The very best sort of people in France practice the most grovelling and open economies and

travel in any fashion and live in any place. Yes, and many a
reduced baron and threadbare count have I seen standing up
in the steerage of an ocean steamer, graciously accepting
oranges and apples tossed down from the upper decks, and
lifting their hats in an exquisite spirit of condescension. To
them it was a reason neither for pride nor shame to be seen
in the steerage—it was merely a fact, part of the machinery
of life, and as such to be ignored."

"When a social standard is prosperity (or the appearance
of prosperity), it means, I suppose, that prosperity is still a
little unfamiliar and not quite normal, that we have not ex-
panded ourselves enough to be quite at home in prosperity.
And where we approve of a man for the mere fact that he
is busy—without considering the purpose of his activity, we
really approve of him for keeping his mind distracted, and
for perpetually spurning the present moment. And all this
because we regard activity as a symbol of efficiency, and
efficiency as the holy and inviolate proof that the machinery
of life is running well. And because we like to be continually
reminded of this fact, we show that we do not take the
machinery of life for granted—which takes us back to the old
wine that burst the new bottles!—and to the Puritan days
when it was the absolute necessity for every American to put
his hand to the running of this machinery."

"You are running your logic into the ground with a vengeance! There is one odd thing about this 'spurning of the
present' we are so fond of, and 'saving up for a perpetually
receding future.' We apparently want to distract ourselves
from the present by being always busy, and yet at the same
time we are for ever occupied with the things of the moment.
Our exclusive interests are the immediate interests. Our sensations are the sensations of the morning newspaper—that
hardly outlive the morning newspaper. We do not even allow
ourselves the little solace that our transitory state of mind
might bring by lingering in the quality of the passing moment,
but keep ourselves continually in a state of ineffectual irritation. We take up persons of the moment, authors, sections of
the world with enthusiastic impermanence. When Miss Stone
is captured by brigands and set free again, her story is on

everybody's lips. Our magazines pay her thousands for a single article, our lecture-managers fly to the lucrative opportunity, and engage her to tour the country. Does Miss Stone interest anybody now?—or brigandage? Was it not, after all, the desire to see, to touch, to hear a nine days' wonder? It is the editors and the managers who have learned that the one permanent thing is impermanence, and who reap their harvests by watching for everything that has 'topical' value."

"Even our slang words are more ephemeral than the slang words of other countries!"

"And then how convulsively we exercise ourselves every now and then in exposing some public evil, or what we conceive to be some public evil!—Peruna, Chicago beef—or the early home of Vice-President Fairbanks.[6] We take them up desperately for a week, under the influence of a few magazines which have made themselves popular by these means, and then we drop them. And if we have been in the habit of using patent medicines or tinned meats, in a month we are all forgetfully using them again. And we may be sure that the makers of these goods, after ostentatiously allowing themselves to be investigated, go back under new names to their illicit practices as soon as the 'dread voice is past.' We encourage this kind of investigation just as far as it is amusing in print, but we endure any form of evil which does not lend itself to ridicule or sensationalism."

"Just so our conversation is largely morning-paper conversation, the newest developments in politics or the police-courts,

[6] Current or recent abuses. Peruna, a tonic, and Chicago beef refer to abuses that led to the Pure Food and Drug Act (1906). Upton Sinclair's novel about conditions in the Chicago stockyards, *The Jungle* (1906), led to his invitation to the White House by Theodore Roosevelt. The novel's extraordinary influence gave Roosevelt the power he needed to pass the act which had been previously stopped by the Senate. Charles Warren Fairbanks, Vice-President under Roosevelt, was born in Union County, Ohio, and moved to Indianapolis when he began his law practice. Presumably his home had its share of the widespread civic corruption of the era. A French map of political corruption in the United States showed 25 states as wholly corrupt, 13 as partially corrupt, and 6 as free from corruption. Both Ohio and Indiana belong to the wholly corrupt category. George E. Mowry reprints the map from the *Literary Digest,* XXXI (1905), 795 in his the *Era of Theodore Roosevelt: 1900-1912* (New York, 1958), p. 67.

the latest happenings of our friends, or perhaps the latest book we have been reading or the latest play we have seen. The subject which occupies the longest column-space in the news-paper occupies the mind of America that day: Mr. Rocke-feller in the morning paper gives place to Mr. Morgan in the evening paper. We seldom discuss the theories and principles that lie behind these things, the tendencies rather than the events of politics, the qualities rather than the anecdotes of books and plays."

"And do you remember the poor old Simple Life?"

"One of the latest editions was an *edition de luxe* printed on flowered paper and bound in blue silk. The flowered paper and the blue silk live on in America long after the Simple Life has been laughed away into neglected platitude."

"And who beside Mr. Roosevelt remembers the day of simplified spelling?"

"Then again we hear perhaps over the telephone some mention of an old friend's misfortune, some case of poverty or infirmity or chronic disease; and although we may have known about the case for years, our sympathy is suddenly aroused, and we allow nothing to stand in the way of that most pressing and immediate need, the need of sending, often at the greatest inconvenience, some books or jellies or flowers round the corner. We are really touched. We are really regret-ful of all our former thoughtlessness. We have the kindest motives, and we take no end of pains to do the right thing. But the fact is that all those feelings of sympathy and kind-ness were suggested by a sudden telephone message, and when we have set aside everything else to do this immediate duty, the sympathy flies out of our heads again as quickly as it came in—until the next telephone message."

"Well, of course it is natural that our sympathy should be aroused in this way," said I, "for certainly we cannot in our many duties and interests keep them all constantly before us. I suppose you mean that we ought to have a kind of inter-woven, underlying subconsciousness of them all which is pre-pared for these sudden demands and is not shocked and violated when they arise. As it is, of course, a demand of this sort absorbs everything in life for the moment, and calls out a turbulent and excessive riot of emotions. And the result is that we give the matter a degree of thought quite out of proportion to its deserts, that we express a momentary sympathy far beyond anything normal in the relations between two not particularly intimate friends, that our own self-respect is quite needlessly injured by our mortification, and that, in short, we call out all our reserve, and lavish it upon some poor, dazed creature who only wanted five minutes of moderate attention from week to week."

"Yes," he returned; "and it seems to me that really to understand what it all means one must compare it with quite a different state of mind. Take France, for example. The other day I was glancing through the *Journal des Débats* when I found a full column on the front page devoted to a new anecdote which had come to light about Louis XI. It was not a particularly startling anecdote. The significant thing about it, to my mind, was that a piece of historical news about a man who died some four or five centuries ago should be treated exactly as any other kind of news, and be printed on the front page of a popular morning paper along with motor accidents and murders and the latest dispatches from Morocco. It would certainly not have been printed there if the everyday reader had not been prepared to accept it in exactly the spirit in which he accepted everything else on the front page, that is to say, as a perfectly legitimate and even an exciting piece of news. It meant that the average middle-class Frenchman, however volatile we may think him, is anything but volatile in the sense that he has not deep-rooted intellectual instincts, and that the history and traditions of his race are not ever present to his mind. He has, in short, a background and a reserve. I remember wondering at the time if any popular American morning paper would dare to devote a full column on its front page to some newly-discovered anecdote about, say, President James Buchanan."

Chapter III

Education and other incidents—Background and reserve—Cut flowers—"Educated, by George!"—College men and the "rush"—Household philosophy—A fine country but no hogs—Ideals and regrets—"New Thought"—Intelligence and instinct again—Ingenuity and self-centered optimism. The oldest of all thought—Politics considered as an incident—Mr. Carnegie's reasons—Outside and in.

'BACKGROUND AND RESERVE,' you say—that's just the point: they come from the cultivation of instinct. And you know we've already discussed why Americans are transparent! The oddest way it all works out—this preoccupation with the machinery —is that we regard education, politics, literature, and things of that sort (*sic*) as incidents, incidentals, things considered (beside the very important matter of getting a living) as of distinctly secondary importance, and not merely as unimportant branches of life but as unimportant *objects*, things you can touch and handle and separate one from another and turn your back upon. These things are not mixed into our lives, they are in some way excrescences. It is not because we are insincere in the enthusiasm for, say, religion or politics or art which we undoubtedly feel, but that they are not, in spite of our enthusiasm, the primary concern with us. They are reserved for Sundays or Election days, or the Saturday afternoons we spend at the museum, or the winter evenings we spend over a good book; they certainly do not flavour our moments as they pass, as if they were born and bred in us and somehow seemed always present though we never happened to see any particular picture or read any particular book. And although we are entirely sincere in our religion and politics and in our desire for some ideal of education, we are sincere in only one at a time; we do not look at them all from a single unified point of view,

merely stressed a little on one side to meet the special requirements of religion, or art, or whatever it happens for the
moment to be. I mean that we have not towards them all a
constant and unified attitude, to which, as a criterion, we
submit them all and in which they all mix together to form
a spiritual background.

"We allow ourselves to be absorbed heart and soul in the
thing of the moment, and our absorption is not a stress, an
emphasis of one side of our nature, but a momentary abandon-
ment of all consciousness of the rest of the claims of life in
one claim. We leap from one interest to another, entirely
forgetting the first interest in our enthusiasm for the second.
We pass from the drawing-room to the office and think it
necessary to lay aside our manners. We pass from our holiday
to the office and think it necessary to lay aside recreation. We
pass from the church to the office and think it necessary to
lay aside our finer distinctions between right and wrong. And
there is in all this an illustration as it seems to me, of our
lack of purpose, of fixed ideas, of principles applicable at all
times, in short, of a background, a point of view."

"It seems to me too that education, religion, politics, literature, recreation, humour, art—that all these things in America
are somehow *splits* from life, things we reach for on the shelf
as it were, each when its turn comes. They grow out of life in
a sense, but they are cut flowers that hardly stand in the same
vase. Take education, for example. You know it is noticed
that American children on the whole are more agile thinkers
and better informed than European children? And you know,
from what one gathers, that undergraduates at Oxford are
less mature than, say, undergraduates at Harvard? . . . At
Oxford they mature slowly, possibly, but they mature very
surely, and their education never comes to an end. When they
leave the university their degree does not represent a harsh
breaking-off from one kind of life to begin another, as ours
so often does. I know of a certain American student whose
first act after taking his degree was to telegraph home, 'Educated, by George!' Of course it was meant as a joke, but
wherever there is any humour *in* a thing it always means that
there is a certain measure of truth *behind* it. And the truth

is that we are pretty apt to regard education as education and life as life, and that somehow or other these things appear to be distinctly independent of each other."

"Well, we have both known at college undergraduates— and hundreds of them—who were sincerely interested in history or political economy or literature, and who after graduation have plunged into business and have hardly given a serious thought since to any matter outside the immediate matter of making a living. And plenty of them have had leisure enough too—they have totally forgotten even the inclination. They have perhaps gained a certain superior grasp of affairs, but they have gained no lasting sense of the subordination of buying and selling to great ideas. They are at twenty-two or twenty-three larger-minded men than they will ever be in later years. Their minds do not slowly ripen into fixed ideas. Their education does not, as a rule, build the foundation of a solid and cumulative philosophy of life, which grows deeper and mellower as the years go on."

"Yes; college men sometimes feel that they are forced into the 'rush,' but my experience has been that, on the whole, they go in deliberately. Perhaps in most cases they feel that the first step upward is to support themselves. If they have any independence of mind their independence is expected to take that form. But very often it is their *dependence* which takes that form, their dependence on the convention they have been brought up to. I don't think that a man with imagination always serves his family best by harnessing himself into a pre-ordained point of view, even if his family imagine for the moment that they want him to. And it's natural enough for families to feel as they do. All fathers and mothers like to feel that their children are really unusual, but in their hearts they know that only one child in ten thousand *is*, and from close contact they lose all power of judging whether or not their child is that one. So they instinctively act on the assumption that he is like the rest, knowing that if he is going to fall into mediocrity, he will fall more gracefully if he never attempts to rise out of it. For his own good they train him to the idea of mediocrity, or, at best, of a very safe, pedestrian career. . . . The family council takes no stock in ambitions

and enthusiasms—how can it? Not one of us takes any stock
in other people's ambitions. Ambition is one of those impossible things that every man must prove his right to in the face
of experience. And every man who knows anything about
himself knows more than his family. The better the family
the more individuals it contains who make war on the common
judgment of all the rest. They are not worth pulling together
if they do not, one and all, obstinately, steadfastly pull apart,
each in his own fixed idea. It is almost the worst thing that
can happen to a man whose opportunity depends upon his
imagination to be harried and driven by small realities before
his imagination is mature enough to command those realities.
Poverty does not turn a man's mind to his work, it distracts
his mind from his work. Little necessities grind the edge away
from big ideas—assuming that a man *has* ideas. I am sure
that sad mistakes are made in the cause of 'supporting oneself' too soon. So far as they say that it strengthens a man's
will or purpose, anyone who knows what a true artistic purpose
is knows that it needs no goading from the outside. . . . I read
the *Letters of a Self-made Merchant* with a great deal of
admiration—old Graham is the salt of the earth in his own
way.[1] I easily forgave him for writing 'If you're going to be
a Milton, there's nothing like being a mute, inglorious one'—
that goes with the point of view: and as it turned out he was
exactly the right kind of father for his kind of son. But when,
towards the close of one of his letters, I read (*à propos*, I
think, of Texas), 'This is a fine country we're running through,
but it's a pity that it doesn't raise more hogs,' I came to the
conclusion that he would have been a very wrong kind of
father for some kinds of sons."

"After all, as you say; that kind of son is the one in ten
thousand. But in college one in every two is really enthusiastic
about something larger than buying and selling. And the
enthusiasm comes to an end with college. They seem, every
one, to pass through their moments of undergraduate idealism

---

[1] John Graham, pseudonym of George Horace Lorimer (1868-1937), editor
of *The Saturday Evening Post* from 1899 to 1936. *Letters from a Self-Made
Merchant to His Son* (1902) and *Old Gorgon Graham* (1904) boost the virtues
of rugged individualism.

as if it were all a dream, as if after all the world were shabbily
real and there were no help for them. They lay aside their
books and their ideals together as if ideals were too expensive
to keep, and as if it were a kind of virtue to regard life with
the idea that making a living is more important than making
something of themselves. The really significant thing is that
this temporary idealism is profoundly sincere, and that something which has been profoundly sincere can give place to
something so ignoble—that even their memory of beautiful
thoughts should be, except for a little regret, as if it had not
been, and that regret itself should die so easily. . . . Education
does not seem to mix in. It is indeed a kind of incident, something we pass through or that passes through us, and leaves
us pretty much the same as before."

"And I think," said Graeling, "that religion fares the same
way. The religious spirit in general with us seems to be an
emanation rather of intelligence than of instinct—that is to
say, it has no connection with our ancestors or any roots in
anything. For example, only consider the appalling spread in
the last few years of so-called 'new thought' in its countless
forms. As religions, they appear to have the added value of
appealing to the mind as well as the heart. But why do their
followers drift unsatisfied from one form into another? It is
because these teachings do not really appeal to the heart at
all, which is constant, but solely to the mind, which is in-
quisitive and insatiably variable. They appeal in fact to the
mind only, and they achieve a momentary optimism and a
renewed confidence in life which are the reactions of certain
mental processes that seem to justify our faith because, quite
naturally, they work out correctly. They appeal once more to
our American appetite for the ingenious, for the rational for
its own sake, and they are concerned more with their own
mechanism as an end in itself than with their products in
human conduct."

"And so, naturally enough, the followers of 'new thought'
are self-seekers who lay no store by charity, pity, or renunciation—the great products of real religion. It is all for their
own personal health or luck or peace of mind or success, and
the optimism that they discover is seldom compatible with

humility of heart. It is, on the contrary, an aggressive, self-centered optimism, which makes one feel how much better off one is than the rest of mankind. It is apparently a more complex system than that of devotional religion: but it is intellectually complex and not emotionally complex. And thus when one has got to the bottom of it, one catalogues it, and lays it away, as a mental problem solved, a puzzle that one has unravelled—among the stored experiences of the mind, and turns to something new. It is in the last analysis transparent because it is nothing more or less than psychology, and as such capable, at least mentally, of being analysed Devotional religion is theoretically simple enough, but in practice one can no more see the bottom of it than one can see the bottom of the human heart. It cannot be worn out and seen through and laid aside as a piece of scientific experience is bound to be. . . . Not that religion is to suffer when psychology comes to analyse the heart itself: but it appears to me that 'new thought' is in reality the oldest of all thought—Asiatic thought, and that there has developed through the centuries a distinction between the human and the speculative which this revival ignores. It will be admirable when psychology is able to determine what the heart is—we have discussed this before: but psychology cannot deny that the heart is different from the mind though it be only the dead of all our ancestors glimmering collectedly in us. Or, if you like, reduce all religion to natural laws, and you still have the greatest principle of all over and above—renunciation, which cannot be an echo of them. Whatever philosophy may be and whatever religion may be, it seems to me that all philosophies are, at least potentially, embryo religions—theoretical bases for religions, and that religion is merely thought made personal, transmuted into aspiration, carried out of symbols and syllogisms and turned into conduct and practice. So far as our discussion is concerned, it is in this attitude toward religion—not as a rational attitude for religion like everything else deserves to be treated rationally, but as a method of being rational for the mere amusement of being rational, as an end instead of an explanation—that religion becomes a mere incident (or rather a series of incidents!) in our intellectual life."

"Certainly," said I, "it seems as if religion too were an incident, for these countless isms are far more expressive of American life than any of the older churches, because they are native products. It is for just these reasons that our religion is not a commentary on our education, or *vice versa,* and that neither is a commentary on our attitude toward the State. They are all absolutely separate. And being incidents they do not mix together to form a background from which we look out upon life in general."

"Politics—our attitude towards the State: yes, it's the same with politics. Just as the individual contains warring and clashing elements which develop separately and without harmony one with another, so the State is made up of warring and clashing individuals who put their own development before any considerations of the community. Each man works entirely for his own family and his own interests, with no horizon wider than his own immediate affairs. He does not conceive of his relation to a million other men around him.* He is interested in politics only because politics affect the value of his stocks. He makes every possible excuse to avoid serving on a jury. He is as carelessly irresponsible in the matter of national economy as he is morbidly responsible in the matter of personal economy. And in ignoring that part of his own well-being which depends on the community, he loses to just that degree the advantages which the community creates. He simply doesn't care for any of these things."

"There is a terribly apt little anecdote of the Tweed Days that comes to my mind," I interposed. "I think it was in 1871 that the *New York Times* published a list of cheques amounting to six million and odd dollars which had been paid out for repairs in armouries and county offices alone in the first eight or nine months of Oakey Hall's mayorship.[2] Well, as the

---

* When Mr. Bernard Shaw sums up America and the Americans in one final word, "Idiocy," does he mean the word in its exact or in its apparent sense? The Greek meaning of the word "idiot" is a *person self-occupied, of no direct use to the State:* and in this sense no summing-up could be more entirely just.

[2] Abraham Oakey Hall (1826-1898), the Harvard-educated, Tammany-supported mayor of New York, 1868-1872, who was tried in 1872 for implication in the Tweed ring and exonerated. Boss Tweed did not get off so easily; he was caught in Spain after his escape from jail and returned to the Ludlow Street jail where he died in 1878.

mayor made no reply, some patriotic citizen called a meeting of the voters of two wards of the city. They passed an elaborate series of resolutions demanding either an immediate explanation or the resignation of the mayor. These resolutions were signed by a large number of influential citizens who had presumably been present at the meeting, and were sent to the mayor. In two or three days each signer received a printed letter in reply. Mr. Hall did not consider their communication the sort that a gentleman could receive. Mr. Hall had been reliably informed that not one-tenth of the signers had been present at the meeting, that many of the signers were not residents in the wards represented in the resolutions, and that, since the chairman of the meeting had forgotten to put the negative, the resolutions themselves had not been properly passed. Mr. Hall begged to add something of this kind: 'It is not for any of you to ask me to resign under any circumstances.' He was quite right. At this critical moment not one-tenth of the influential citizens had taken the trouble to be present at the meeting, nor had even taken the trouble to read through the resolutions that were brought to them to sign or they would have seen that their signatures were valueless as representing wards in which they were not residents. Furthermore, the secretary had not taken the trouble to pass the resolutions correctly. So the matter was dropped and Mr. Hall continued to amuse himself unmolested. . . . I should call that an example of politics considered as an incident."

"To justify this preoccupation with the tangible and the immediate, and to justify money-getting in general, we speak of the fortunes given away in charity, in founding hospitals and building libraries, as if these things were in themselves the justification for great fortunes. Mr. Carnegie[3] gives three

---

[3] Andrew Carnegie (1835-1919). Scottish-born son of a master weaver, Carnegie perhaps best embodies the Horatio Alger dream of success. He began as a bobbin boy in a cotton factory in Alleghany City (now Pittsburgh). Later, while a clerk with Pennsylvania Railroad, he promoted George Woodruff's sleeping car idea. The success of this promotion formed the basis for his later fortune in the oil, railroad, telegraph, and iron and steel industries. He was also the philosopher of wealth. In works like *Triumphant Democracy* (1886) and *Wealth* (1886) Carnegie publicized his view that rich men are trustees of the nation's wealth who are bound to administer it for the public. He believed that a man should die poor; his own benefactions totalled about $350,000,000.

reasons why it is every man's duty to make a fortune if he can: (1) To bequeath it to his wife and children—which is a criminally selfish reason; (2) To bequeath it to charity; and (3) To spend it well while he is alive. The last two reasons are the only ones worthy to be considered, since money absorbed from the community is bound in justice sooner or later to go back to it. In Mr. Carnegie's view the millionaire has proved his right to be a sort of trustee of the people's money by the mere fact of his having in one way or another got the money away from them. Surely it is a little difficult to imagine, considering Mr. Rockefeller, that the power of making money and the power of best serving the people are identical."

"It seems to me that we need not so greatly the charitable institutions to repair the wrong from the outside as the cultivation of some sort of inner national life which will more and more enable us to dispense with charitable institutions. It is our hurried preoccupation with tangible, personal affairs which blinds us to theoretical principles and incapacitates us for any great idea, any great cause."

Chapter IV

The literature of apoplexy—"The Call of the Lungs"—Grammar school fallacies—The unhelpful Puritans—Sudden light—A strange doctor—Our first humorist—Extraction and distraction—Two kinds of morality—"Pop goes the weasel"—Q. K. Philander Doesticks & Co.—Mr. Dooley's chances—Lowell on cataracts—"Any old thing" —A dead man—Artemus Ward's reputation—The quality of American fame—Normal fame and Barnum—The main chance—Humanity and Greek accents—"Labour talk"—Orchids.

"You know," I said, "I think one can explain in the same way the most conspicuous school of literature we are suffering

just now in America. You know, for example, that one of our
new popular magazines describes itself in its prospectus as
'leaping with red blood' and incidentally 'alive with all the big,
interesting things in the universe'."

"Yes, I *do* know," said Graeling. "It is what I should call
the Literature of Apoplexy. The chief aim of these writers,
apparently, is to avoid using the same superlative twice. It
reminds me of a friend of mine who told me once that, in his
opinion, there were three great English poets, Shakespeare,
Kipling,[1] and Milton. At the time it seemed to me something
of a compromise to put Shakespeare first, for Shakespeare and
Milton were included in deference to authority while Kipling
came from the heart. I understand that frame of mind, I think.
It is the triumphant cult of the manly and the vital—and
there are many poems of Kipling with such a swing to them
that to do justice to the metre it is necessary to slap one's knee
at the end of each line."

"Well," I said, "here is a little sample of it—a publisher's
view of one of his publications." I drew a little paper from
my pocket and read aloud—

*"The Call of the Lungs.**

"(Jack Paris., pp. 318. $1.50.)[2]

"We have little hesitation in saying that this is a book to be
read. Even more than this world-famous story-teller's other
latest work, trenchant as that is with humour and understanding, *The Call of the Lungs* will be the most talked-of book
of the season. *John Sprod* is a man—a strong, tender, hot-
veined man. He is shooting Indians in Idaho when he meets
Lady Gwendolen Cholmondeley-Colquhoun, who, wholesome
and sweet and human woman that she is, wearing of the inani-
ties of effete society, longs for a vital feeling of the big forces

---

[1] Rudyard Kipling (1865-1936). His stories and poems had a spectacular
success. Their rhythms, their dialect, their emotional impact and attitudes
seemed to speak for an era; they may outlast their politically imperialist point
of view.

* Reprinted from *Punch*.

[2] An obvious parody of Jack London's *The Call of the Wild* (1903).

that are animating the boundless West. She has disguised herself as an old Indian war-chief, and single-handed has held at bay, through the interminable Arctic-like winter, seven regiments of United States troops. When spring breaks she has once more the old tired feeling of her race. Seated among her piles of scalps she has just finished her fifth Manhattan cocktail one evening when she hears a voice calling to her from across the boundless prairie hundreds of miles away. It is strong and tender and vital. It is *John's* voice and it calls 'Gwen.' It is a clash of races, and her deep, vivid, passionate nature responds. In a moment he looms beside her, a real living thing, his big, soft, pulsing arms about her, in all the thrill of rich, tender fiction. The book is big: it burns hot with harsh but hopeful truth. The title is not new, suggesting, as it does, *The Call of the Wild, The Call of the Blood,* etc.; but we do not hesitate to assert that *The Call of the Lungs* will make, if possible, an even bigger sensation than these."

"I know the style," said Graeling, "and it has some connection with our imperial theories. It has been growing more and more apoplectic ever since the Spanish war. But how does any one individual come to write in this fashion? And how does any one individual come to relish the reading of it? Those questions have often puzzled me."

"Well," I replied, "I believe you can find the reason—or one reason—in our grammar schools. With the intent of teaching literature—not patriotism in this case, but literature—the powers of the grammar schools deliberately abet the New England provinciality of nine-tenths of the teachers by offering the most provincial parts of Bryant and Whittier. I should not advocate offering Shelley and Wordsworth instead *because* they are not American, but I think that on the whole the study of literature has much deeper results than either patriotism or the lack of it. I should advocate the offering of Shelley and Wordsworth because they are just as easy to grasp as Bryant and Whittier, and are, at the same time, more universal, and better able to prepare one for the true and great forces of life. It is perfectly true that a boy who has read nothing will *feel* something in Wordsworth that he misses in Bryant, and that three or four years in an American grammar school destroys that sense. It is the instinctive perception in all unspoilt minds of the pure work of beauty: which the peasant folk of every land have given witness of in their country songs before they were spoilt by the cheap sophistication, with all its jangling sentimentality, of the city street-songs. And it is what the peasant folk had before the factories gave them tawdry, betinselled crockery and showy, unsubstantial furniture so cheaply, that they could not afford to give their labour any more to making for themselves the fine, sturdy, simple platters and settees that we search out greedily, and make our proudest ornaments.

"That there is something of the factory-made about Bryant is a little beside the point. Bryant and, to a much greater degree, Whittier, express very fervently the fine, intensive moral culture of New England—a culture which produced a noble chivalry to which provinciality was almost a condition. And this old idea is kept alive through the country largely by the general class of our schoolteachers, most of whom are either New England born or trained, and all of whom drift back at least in spirit from year to year to the head waters of American culture, taking home with them the old traditions and ideals, and thus keeping New England alive in distant parts. Nothing in itself could be more beautiful than this ancestral sentiment carried into new and rougher regions, but no sentiment could on the whole be more fruitless or even dangerous. For the Americans alone among all the races of the world, cannot seek for any interpretation of life in their own remote antiquity, simply because the childhood of America is the childhood of another country. We have no myths, there is nothing childlike in our past, and when we look to our ancestors to help us we find them almost as grown-up and self-conscious as we ourselves. We seek in them virtues to be copied, and we find their virtues negative, necessarily negative; noble for them because adapted to their situation, but obsolete and ill-adapted for ours. We can draw less virtue out of an ancestry than any other race, because the founders of America and their descendants of today, as I think you have suggested, are alike full-grown men facing problems utterly different."

"You're bringing up the theory we've discussed before?"
Graeling asked. "Older races 'draw virtue out of their ancestry' because their founders were children, and because the
comments of children are always apt?"

"Exactly. But this is hardly a theory of sentiment. It is
true in a very practical way. For although we have developed
out of the Puritan type our problems have not developed out
of the Puritan problems. The Negro question, the immigration
question, the problem of imperialism, and greatest of all, the
problem of financial prosperity have been thrust upon us by
circumstances which hardly existed in embryo among the
Pilgrims. They are problems which belong to an advanced
state of cosmopolitan civilization, and to meet them the
modern American requires a preparation in kind. And on the
whole, the more vividly we preserve the Puritan idea—with
all its virtues adapted to a special and temporary situation,
the less prepared we are to meet these problems. For, as we
have said, the virtues of the Pilgrims were not those racial
virtues which are always relevant because they have grown
out of an antiquity which held in embryo all the later problems of the race. They were the virtues, negative and narrow,
of a small colony."

"But just how does this explain our 'Literature of Apoplexy'?"

"Well, literature is an index of public sentiment. The poems
of Bryant and Whittier, formerly adequate for the education
of New England, are no longer adequate for the education of
America. They do not train the perception to large and universal truths. They do not widen the mind. They do not prepare
the mind for the general questions of modern, cosmopolitan
life. You know what Whittier said of himself—

> 'Not mine the seer-like power to show
> The secrets of the heart and mind.'

His message in all its beauty is the message of a section, a
province. It is no more the poetry of the normal American of
today than the poetry of George Herbert. It is minor poetry
of a sectarian kind. And yet it is a symbol of our school-
training.

"But now see how it works out. I emphasize this so much because I believe that if a boy is brought up on second-rate literature—second-rate as literature, no matter how high its moral tone may be—when he grows up he will have gained no taste for first-rate literature. It might still be all very well if he had gained a taste even for second-rate literature. But the second-rate has not won his heart, and when he is free of school, and no longer under compulsion, he throws aside literature altogether, and if he reads at all he reads trashy novels and wretched magazines, with the result that his whole intellectual perception, even, I think, his moral fineness, is blunted. It is only possible to train a love of literature from the very best, and for this reason, only well-trained minds can absorb the second-rate with impunity. We Americans are omnivorous readers, but our taste is indiscriminating precisely because our minds have been vitiated by literature, morally harmless enough but intellectually destructive. . . . Familiar since childhood with a literature intellectually primitive and inadequate to a mature civilization, the American suddenly becomes conscious of the great forces of modern life. He is unaccustomed to the literature of great forces. He is almost unaware that great forces have existed elsewhere or before. He has been carefully trained as a provincial and is thrown into cosmopolitan life. He learns to spell Destiny, Wealth, Power, as if they were new experiences, not to him only but to the whole world. He only knows that he feels and feels tumultuously. Is it remarkable that he should be carried away by this intemperate talk about tenderness and strength, bigness and destiny? Is it remarkable that our popular magazines should be conceived in 'red blood'?"

"But surely," said Graeling, "this apoplectic literature more nearly expresses what is really stirring in America than, for example, those purveyors of an irrelevant 'Sweetness and Light'[3] we still find in the magazines and on little cardboard mottoes hung up on gas-fixtures. They are merely the leavings

---

[3] Matthew Arnold made these terms from Jonathan Swift well known as equivalents of the beauty and intelligence which make up perfection. See *Culture and Anarchy* (1869) in which he defines culture as the study of perfection.

of a past generation in England mixed with a good deal of
lukewarm water and simmering on forever."

"Oh, yes, it is simply an attempt to express the great forces
of which we have suddenly become conscious, but for which
we have not been prepared."

"Well, before long, I think, a strange doctor is coming to
feel the pulse of our system, and insert his knife somewhere
to lower our temperature. That strange doctor is going to be
the first great American satirist. He will laugh so loud at
things American that the whole continent shall hear him. And
when he has got us all into his good-humoured, fatherly confidence he will show us what a big over-grown rowdy we have
been."

"Oh," I said, "I am perfectly sure that we are on the edge
of an age of satire. But I think that the great satirist will
show us that we are nearly as big and strong as we supposed
ourselves. He will simply teach us to be quiet about it."

"I suppose then that he will be the first American humorist?" inquired Graeling.

"Are you sure you are not asking that for effect? We are
supposed, you know, to be a nation of humorists already."

"But our humorists don't carry on the great tradition of
humour. As a general thing they don't depend upon being
true to life, upon creating characters that strike us because
they are so absurdly true, as upon whiling away the time with
puns and conundrums and all sorts of extravagant conceits
(like 'Captain Stormfield's Visit to Heaven')[4] which strike us
because they are so absurdly *untrue*. The great tradition of
humour is to play through life interpreting our days to us. In
our humour we seek not life itself but a refuge from life—
not something that will make our days more fresh and real
to us, but something that will transport us somewhere, anywhere to make us happily forget our days. Not only does the
present moment seem less desirable than any other moment,
but we spurn any kind of thought that will make the present
desirable. So our humour is not the humour of *ex*traction from
life but of *dis*traction from life."

[4] By Mark Twain, 1907.

"Well, certainly the humour of Rabelais, Cervantes, Addison and Thackeray is largely a comment on principles and traits of unchanging human nature. Very often it serves to satirize a temporary over-emphasis of certain human tendencies, or to speak the special humours of a single race. But in the main it seeks to picture man as in all times and places he ought to be, by leading before a kind of high court of genial justice men and measures that stand for what man ought not to be. It cuts away all variations from the normal type."

"And the humorist ought to make people not only see but love what is true and normal."

"Yes, he ought to have a perception of the truth not in the mind merely, with its logical realization that what is normal is also useful to the general good, but that perception of the heart also which is the final blossom of a long evolution of dead minds sadly familiar in their day with the weakness and error that lead men aside. It will convince people not merely because it is just, but because its justice is tempered with an understanding of the ways and the delights of injustice."

"But our humour is a kind which has neither past nor future, but only the moment of its flash, a humour not sprung from genial soil nor reflecting the tears and smiles of dead generations, not the humour of sentiment or pathos—it is a humour of light rather than heat, a humour of the pure intelligence, so harsh that if it expressed an enduring mood it would be cynical. It is often what we call dry humour—the kind which rustles through a man's lips without being tinged with blood from his heart, flaring up electrically for its occasion and subsiding grey and chilly, scintillating out of a sordid background, a humour of shifts and grit, common sense and bitter pluck. It implies nothing, it indicates no philosophy of life. It fits the need of the moment and passes with the moment."

"But of course we have had a Humour, as you say, of Extraction as well as a Humour of Distraction: I suppose it was an academic humour brought from Europe. Washington Irving is to the old traditional humour of England very much what George Washington is to the old traditional English gentleman. In both characters one feels the derivation from a European culture. There is a curious difference from that which we recognize as indigenous with us. Just so with Dr. Holmes and George William Curtis,[5] in a sense. Humour with them, as with Addison, is a kind of morality."

"There is the point, I think. The Puritans had another kind of morality. They distinguished harshly between right and wrong, and fixed themselves to follow the right and to impose their standard without compromise or explanation upon all who joined them. They were able to ignore evil because they had trained themselves inexorably away from any leavings that might have lingered in them from their former life in an old civilization, where men could not so easily separate darkness from light. To do sin even the grace of understanding it seemed to them a sort of compromise with the devil: sympathy with weakness was a kind of temporizing with weakness. They neither asked nor welcomed recruits. They believed their view to be right, and they were not careful of other views. They were not propagandists, and they preferred to take all the consequences of their own sectarianism. Such men outside as were so close to virtue that the merest smile of friendship would have gathered their perplexed hearts into the kingdom of the just—such were still outside. Drunkards and murderers alike lingered only a little while under the cloud of the general doom—'Sinners in the hands of an angry God'![6]

"To this morality of damnation and reward, accurately suited to the life of a parcel of noble sectarians labouring at a special moment in the special circumstances of an untempered province, what message could the greater morality of humour bring, suited, as it is, to the unravelling of perplexities which spring from long-established civilizations—a morality which turns men aside to universal ideals from the bigoted excess which is needful to the establishing of any one civilization? Pioneers have always sacrificed the irrelevant greater to the immediate less. They cannot allow themselves the virtue

[5] George William Curtis (1824-1892). An admirer of Emerson and once a student at Brook Farm, he wrote and spoke for causes like anti-slavery, civil service reform, and women's suffrage and conducted for over forty years the column, "From the Editor's Easy Chair," for *Harper's* magazine.

[6] Title of Jonathan Edwards' sermon delivered July 8, 1741.

of breadth. The men who come after can be serious. The pioneers have to be earnest, and to be earnest is to be serious without a sense of humour. . . . But every man will have his humour. And if humour is discredited as a high court of morality, it will have its fling at the windows of any other court. If we refuse it the title of Reverence, it will shock us by being irreverent. If we begrudge it the right to stand sponsor at baptism with Sir Roger de Coverley,[7] it will play profane hide-and-seek with Petroleum V. Nasby."

"Do you remember these lines?—

> 'Now I lay me down to sleep,
> I pray the Lord my soul to keep:
> If I should die before I wake—
> Pop goes the weasel!' "

"But, you know, in one sense our humour is never irreverent—because it is never actually hostile to religion. Only that as the reaction from that rational Puritan morality in which moral law was a cold and righteous necessity to which symbol and sentiment seemed irrelevant, it has become a thing quite apart from religion and morality, and comments in a spirit of untempered independence upon them as upon everything else in life. It was crowded out from the fertile fields and took root among the rocks and brambles to reach a wild, uncultivated, ephemeral growth all its own. But any kind of imaginative comment on religion that is not essentially reverent is necessarily irreverent. Only unemotional scientific writing can keep a strictly neutral tone. The emotions force one to take a position, and all who are not *for* are *against*."

"Yes, our humour has undoubtedly drifted apart and ceased to be an expression of life. And our humorists are homeless, nameless vagrants."

"Nameless! Yes, that is a very significant thing about them all. They never write under their own names. Mark Twain, Artemus Ward, Josh Billings, Mr. Dooley—they have never

---

[7] This Worcestershire gentleman introduced in the *Spectator* (1711) takes his name from an old English country dance and tune.

spoken through their own lips. Each creates a character to
embody his philosophy as if it were something apart from
himself. There is something very odd about this, for these few
names represent one of our traditions. I should say that nearly
a hundred American wits have spoken through masks of this
sort, concealing their own grim, laborious, and often decidedly
unhumorous personalities behind them. Think of Mozis
Addums and Q. K. Philander Doesticks and Orpheus C. Ker
and Petroleum V. Nasby and Bill Arp. All those and dozens
more must have felt either that there lay in their humour
something unworthy of their own respectable names—David
Ross Locke, Seba Smith, and the like—or else that such
ordinary names were not worthy of their humour. But I think
that humour ought not to be a respecter of names."

"Their humour is in some way apart from themselves. And
then again, they are not attached to any corner of the soil.
They have no homes. They apparently have no ancestors.
They wander about from New York to Ohio and the Mississippi, jesting about anything that comes to their notice as if
they had dropped from the skies. They have no connection
with anything."

"And then again, they never comment on life in general,
but only on the events of the moment that comes and goes—
and when the event passes the humour passes with it. You
would be surprised to open an early Dooley book and find
how many of the essays are totally unintelligible, because in
their day they depended upon the vivid presence of certain
events which are quite forgotten. An almost countless number
of war-time humorists were utterly forgotten thirty years ago
for just this reason. . . . It reminds me of the days when I
read the comedies of Plautus and Terence—whenever I
stumbled on a particularly difficult problem in syntax I knew
it was a joke. But there is a difference, for Terence's jokes
did not depend for their meaning on any local events of the
year 160 B.C.—or whenever it was, but were perfectly intel-
ligible as long as Latin was a familiar spoken language. Our
humorists hinge their wit to short moments of time, never
commenting on life, or even upon American life, as it is permanently. To be read broadcast across one decade they sacri-

fice their chance of being read lengthwise down many decades. Josh Billings and Petroleum V. Nasby will live not as humorists but as minor characters of American fiction. Whatever truth there is in them is the truth of a single decade. They reflect no permanent American traits."

"On the whole, I think we have no very clear standard of humour and imagination. Lowell, for instance, was really humorous a hundred times, but he wrote a great many things which make one doubt for the moment that he had a sense of humour at all. In one of his critical essays he speaks of Milton as 'the only man who ever got much poetry out of a cataract —and that was a cataract in his eye,' which is obviously meant for humour. On the other hand, I remember reading in one of E. P. Whipple's[8] essays on poetry that 'Mrs. Osgood[9] did not appear to feel the fetters of rhyme: she *danced* in them.' If that is meant for a witty compliment, something is wrong somewhere. And Lowell speaks of a Negro, 'so black that charcoal made a chalk mark upon him'—a typical example of all native American humour. It strikes us not because it is a true comment on life—an extraction from life, but because it is entirely untrue and preposterous—a distraction from life. Mark Twain is the apotheosis of all these traditions."

"Well, to go back to our first theory, our humour is largely the result of our taking nothing for granted. To uneducated people and children everything is incongruous. Negroes grin and chuckle from daylight till dark. And do you remember where Hazlitt speaks of three chimney-sweepers meeting three Chinese in Lincoln's Inn Fields who laughed at one another till they were ready to drop down? The more civilized we become, the more we learn to take for granted, until the superficial things no longer amuse us at all, and we find true incongruities only in the deep, underlying facts of life. We

[8] Edwin Percy Whipple (1819-1886). Massachusetts author and lyceum lecturer whose estimates of earlier American writers were relatively generous. He was ranked with Poe and Lowell as a critic.

[9] Frances Sargent Osgood (1811-1850). A poetess whose books include *A Wreath of Wild Flowers from New England, The Flowers of Poetry and the Poetry of Flowers* and *The Floral Offering*.

find no humour in jokes that are merely jugglings with words, double meanings, conundrums, and that spurious kind of Artemus Ward wit which depends upon bad grammar and bad spelling, unless they express some real incongruity in the human situation. . . . Our idea of humour is of something contrary to life, not sprung from life."

"Very often, I fancy, our humorists are facetious, because there was no breadth of outlook in their ancestors to blossom into humour. It is in the fact that their humour is never the inevitable expression of a certain situation that you find the origin of our phrase, 'any old thing.' Artemus Ward chose for his lecture the title 'The Babes in the Wood' in preference to 'My Seven Grandmothers'—or indeed anything else in the universe. 'Any old title,' you see, would have done as well as any other, and the question became not how to find the most fitting title but one that sounded the best. If the idea had sprung out of a background it would have required an inevitable title: being merely a bundle of jokes, *à propos* of nothing in particular, any title with an attractive sound would serve."

"By the way, I have had a couple of curious experiences in regard to these American humorists. I once tried to write a book called 'The American Humorists,' modelled on the plan of Thackeray's 'English Humorists.' That is, I tried to recreate the personalities of Josh Billings, Artemus Ward, Petroleum V. Nasby, Hosea Biglow, and a few others, to make them breathe and live and walk. Do you know they simply *wouldn't* live: the real men who stood behind them—Henry Shaw, Charles Browne, and James Russell Lowell—were such utterly different personalities, where they were personalities at all. The lives of Steele and Goldsmith and Fielding are somehow humorous lives, but there is nothing humorous about the life of the man who created Josh Billings. I mean there are no humorous situations in his life and no evidence of his having actually, so to speak, lived humorously. The character of 'Josh Billings' seemed to have sprung out of his head instead of his heart. It is all intelligence without instinct. There is no pathos, no charm, no tragedy anywhere. He is simply a dead man. And they are all as dead as doornails.

"The other experience seems to me to mean even more. You

have probably noticed that in America we have pretty generally forgotten Artemus Ward, except merely that there *was*
such a man and that he was a funny man: while in England
I find that he is read and remembered vividly. Forty years
ago there was not a more famous character in all America,
—his local sayings and topical hits were quoted everywhere;
he was the Mr. Dooley of the 'sixties. In England where his
topical references were never understood, his reputation has
never waned."

"Fame is a strange thing with us. A man who has the good
luck not to take America by storm has some chance of living
a few years after he dies. Is it because our famous men
generally spring out of nothing, because their fame has no
connection with reality, and because they are really exotics?
In other countries a man seems to win fame precisely because
his talent is the blossom of the very deepest roots of national
life; there is a certain perfectly definite range of human
interests which lead to it—war, art, politics, etc. Fame with
us is a sort of gaudy melon-flower. . . . There is no country
which has produced enormously famous men so utterly distinct
from the causes that normally lead to fame.

"It seems that fame with us may crown any antic, any
extreme that catches our imagination. . . . Brigham Young[10]
fills a theatre with his wives and children, occupying the pit
meanwhile with his own slouch hat and long cigar; Rockefeller
creates out of nothing a fabulous fortune; Mark Twain investi-
gates a comic heaven; Barnum turns the whole universe into
a museum of freaks. Whether or not we imagine that we discriminate between the quality of different kinds of fame, these
names are immortal, and these men in their several ways have
achieved reputations which have remained vivid in the popular
mind so long that they will be associated with America while
the race exists. Barnum is an absolutely colossal figure, one
of the few men who vividly illustrate to foreigners the typical
traits of American character. His career, his ingenuity, his

[10] Brigham Young (1801-1877) led the Mormon migration west in 1846-1847
and controlled the cooperative theocracy in Salt Lake City. The number of his
wives and the amount of his money aroused a great deal of public curiosity.

audacity of insight and humour, his immortality would have been impossible in any other country, and at first glance one would say that such a man sprang out of nothing and fulfilled no deep national need."

"But amusement is a very real need. Men like Garrick and Booth deserve their fame."

"There is a distinction. Garrick and Booth won legitimate fame through their personalities. They were men of great hearts, great instincts. Barnum was a shrewd casuist, like Brigham Young and Mr. Rockefeller. They are able to calculate their returns; their imagination is the projection of intelligence rather than instinct. They are all powers behind thrones. Barnum's fame is neither the result of his personality nor of any great traits inherent in his nature: his work was something outside of himself, a sheer intellectual *tour de force*. If he recognised that his scheme filled a popular need, it was not because he instinctively felt the need and his own destiny to satisfy it—for after all a great man of any kind, whether he knows it or not, is normally a *deus ex machina* to some kind of national situation: it was because he saw the need intellectually and his own chance of turning it to his own advantage. He exploited his own Americanism. He studied the American character, he developed his ingenuity and his audacity, his instincts of 'any old thing' and 'just about as good' until, well, he was able to take and hold the country by storm for half a century. And he pocketed the profits."

"And by that you mean to suggest?"

"In the first place, that these three men sprang out of absolutely nothing: that their fame in each case does not represent the fulfilling of a national need which had developed force in their ancestors and burst forth in them: that, therefore, in each case fame was the result of an indomitable pursuit of the main chance: that every one of them understood the policy of honesty. The first cause, the first impetus of all their careers was a thirst for the main chance, inevitably: they were determined to raise themselves out of nothing into something. That is why fame with us, more than with any other people, is usually the result of a *tour de force,* for a large proportion of our famous men have raised themselves out of nothing. In our poorest classes, unlike those of Europe, there is a sense of moral possibility which produces the will to rise. But in our democratic feelings, and particularly in our desire to be more democratic than we really are, we forget that a man who springs out of nothing has, after all, his limitations, and in the average will never quite catch up. We ought to be neither harsh nor sentimental in these matters. A man who starts at bed-rock and builds up a position is pretty apt, unfortunately, to find that his position is not very secure because it has no foundation *beneath* the rock. And if he starts with nothing but his wits he may build up a reputation colossal for the moment but really superficial and one that will sooner or later collapse, unless he can hold it up by sheer will-power until it actually becomes a part of the popular imagination. Reputation must grow up out of racial instincts if it is to live, normally. And we are very silly sometimes and spoil men who really have no racial instincts and no true right to fame, entirely because they have raised themselves out of nothing."

"There is a passage in Thoreau about John Brown which, in a way, illustrates what you mean, although John Brown had racial instincts indeed. Let me see if I can recollect it: 'He did not go to the college called Harvard, but to the great university of the West, where he sedulously pursued the study of liberty; and having taken many degrees, he finally commenced the public practice of Humanity in Kansas. Such were *his humanities* and not any study of grammar. He would have left a Greek accent slanting the wrong way and righted up a fallen man.' I knew there was something off-colour about the tone of this, but something very difficult to analyze. I quoted it to an English friend of mine. 'Labour talk,' he said. You see it implies that any man who *would* have righted up a Greek accent would necessarily have left a fallen man in the gutter."

"Yes, that's it. . . . I was thinking about the quality of this kind of fame. Talent which is developed entirely by will is bound to be a kind of exotic, having no connection with race or any reality. It is as likely as not to go off on tangents, developing into the most colossal absurdities, so colossal that as with Barnum and Brigham Young we have to take them seriously. . . . If these men are 'cut flowers,' they are orchids with a vengeance!"

Chapter V

Americans abroad—Whistler's butterfly—Sargent on ostrich plumes —The *reductio ad absurdum*—Racial necessities—Too much comparison—"Fleet Street"—Asphodels in reality—"Yawp"—Originality and tradition—Shaw and the non-assertive—Constructive forces —Denver and Damascus.

"THE QUESTION IS, why are *we* abroad—we, I mean, so far as we represent a considerable number? To use the dialect we have taken up, are we not cultivating our distraction from American life rather than our extraction from it?"

"There are plenty of reasons for an artist," returned Graeling. "For instance, that in Europe he finds the premises of an artistic life really taken for granted, that he is not expected to appear more prosperous or practical or conventional than he is, that he finds a civilization at the same time accustomed to his ways and stimulating to his work, not to mention picture galleries, the high standard by which one is judged, the sympathy and co-operation one meets with at every turn, and the absence both of that active hostility and that excessive enthusiasm toward art which are so equally distressing."

"But it seems to me that an artist can produce great and lasting work only out of the materials which exist in him by instinct and which constitute racial fibre, the accretion of countless generations of ancestors, trained to one deep, local, indigenous attitude toward life. A man is more the product of his race than of his art, for a man may supremely express his race without being an artist, while he cannot be a supreme artist without expressing his race. If it were not so the Greek sculptors could as easily have made their works in Sicily, or the Venetian painters theirs in Rome. But when the Venetians went to Rome they took Venice with them. I know of no considerable artist whose work does not vividly represent some trait of the race it sprang from."

"Whistler?"

"Not even Whistler.[1] One hardly dares to look for traits of background in Whistler. His contempt and defiance of race only assert the race he defies. If there had been no consciousness of race there would have been no passionate denial of race. A strange, vain, fanatical creature of No-man's-land, he seems to me the logical outcome and the extreme type toward which all American artists who live abroad inevitably tend. He fashions into works of art the splinters of a derelict fancy because he cannot ripen the more wholesome humanity of his imagination. He is one of the great vagabonds who express everything and nothing, a cut flower in a brilliant vase. That symbol, at once wistful, pathetic, and defiant, with which Whistler signed his pictures—the butterfly—seems to me the cry of the artist cut off, in the face of his possibilities of sane and supreme self-expression, from his own country.

"And it seems to me that Sargent[2] is a lesser man because he has no roots. He is a miraculous technician, without soul, without philosophy. There is no relation between his portraits but the relation of a common craftsmanship. They do not reveal the evolution of an artist's soul, they are merely a series

[1] James Abbott McNeill Whistler (1834-1903). The American expatriate painter who, after his discharge from West Point in 1851, left the country to take up residence in London where his new painting ideas and his verbal wit soon made him a leader of the avant-garde. Ruskin, the entrenched prophet and art critic, attacked Whistler's "Nocturne," saying he "never expected to hear a coxcomb ask two hundred guineas for flinging a pot of paint in the public's face." Whistler won his suit for damages, ruining Ruskin's power in the process and his own financial solvency.

[2] John Singer Sargent (1856-1925). Only technically American, Sargent was born in Florence and did not visit the United States until he was eighteen. He was no more than an occasional visitor thereafter. Recognition of his ability came early and generously in both Paris and London. He departed from his usual subject, portraits of the socially celebrated, to do a series of murals, "The History of Religion," for the Boston Public Library and a series of landscapes of Venice and the Tyrol.

of incidents that have passed before an artist's eyes. They do not reveal the evolution of the soul of the subject, but only the spiritual mood in which for the moment he chances to be. And that spiritual mood is often a vivid consciousness on the sitter's part that Mr. Sargent is painting his portrait. They are studies of costume, of gesture, or, at most, of physiognomy—the apotheosis of an ostrich-plume, a symphony in white satin. The sitter himself does not make these accessories inevitable—they are not characteristics of the dominant soul: the sitter is merely part of the scheme, and the unity of the picture is not the unity of a personality but of a decorative idea.

"Sargent reveals his race in the very fact that only America could produce so brilliant an artist so totally without tradition or philosophy or background. And it seems to me that for the same reason those gorgeous panoramas of Abbey's[3] suggest nothing more than they tell, have no connotations and are entirely without reserve. Any portrait by Velasquez gives evidence of three things, the very soul and spiritual average of the sitter, a distinct stage in the evolution of the soul of the artist, and the racial soul of Spain. I don't mean that these three American painters are equally great, but they are all brilliant, and they all vividly illustrate the effects of ignoring racial tradition."

"But how in the world is an artist to cultivate racial tradition when, as you and I have been trying to show, America has no tradition? You know what American art would have lost if American artists had stayed at home. The American school at the present moment is recognized as one of the most brilliant in the world—there is no question about that. But the American school has been trained abroad."

"And what one trait do you find that these American artists all have in common? Precisely that not one of them could be mistaken essentially for a Frenchman or an Englishman or a Spaniard. Their technique may be the technique of any of these foreign schools, but where anything lies behind the

[3] Edwin Austin Abbey (1852-1911). Philadelphia-born painter and book illustrator whose historical canvasses for the Boston Public Library include "The Quest of the Holy Grail" and "The Apotheosis of Pennsylvania."

technique we know that it must be the American spirit, be-
cause we can see that it is not the French spirit or the English
spirit. By a sort of *reductio ad absurdum* we know them to be
American because we can prove them to be nothing else.
Aside from that common point, they vary in technique as Fra
Angelico varies from Degas."

"But if it is impossible to train oneself in an American
tradition—which doesn't exist, is it not something to achieve
a brilliant technique?"

"It's like cultivating a brilliant complexion without cultivating health. We've been discussing the results of just that
process in the parallel cases of American religion and politics
and literature and humour, and although the results are
widely different, naturally enough, in all these cases, they
represent much the same principle."

"But there are many things beside racial spirit behind
technique. There is insight into the immediate soul of the
subject—in landscape and portrait alike. Whistler had that
to an extraordinary degree."

"A great artist does not merge himself in his subjects, he
merges his subjects in himself. His personality is always
greater than any single manifestation of it. He has a philosophy, a point of view. And his treatment of any subject will
be distinguished by some elemental motive, deeper than personal temperament or any accidents of training and later
surroundings which blends in subtle ways with all the acts
and thoughts of one race in one generation. He must be something more than he knows. He must have some criterion of
instinct to which he submits all aftergrowths of technique and
conscious experience.

"When Monet paints a London bridge at dawn he does not
for the moment become an Englishman: the subject is an
accident—he carries France to London with him. But when
Sargent paints a portrait of the Duke of Connaught he *does*
become for the moment—so far as he becomes or remains anything—an Englishman. And I think it would be well for our
artists to discover how soon the training they gain abroad and
the vitalizing effects of this fellowship with all that beauty
in the past has given to these older civilizations, cease to be

a preparation for their own self-expression and becomes an overmastering impulse leading them hither and thither, and merging them intermittently in the artistic consciousness of Spain and Italy and France, unable to carry them below the technique of any. They cannot graft themselves upon the racial tradition that has produced any of the great masters, and they find themselves indeed in sympathy with many races but curiously outside all. The delight that one feels in Italian towers and French meadows and foreign faces must be alien to the nature if it is to be effectual in American art—objects to be treated by a consciousness not moved by them away from itself. Achievement consists in bending them to oneself rather than in being bended by them."

"But if he is contented with his position, if he is unconscious of this call of race, doesn't it mean that for him race does not exist?"

"*That* is usually the result of having subjected oneself to the surface-sensations and the hollow impressions of too much comparison. Such a man is usually one who seeks a sort of harmony along the entire surface of life, never pressing beauty too practically at any one place, because the reaction is so ugly.

"Life comes to seem so slight a thing that depth at any special place must be sacrificed to a fairness and tranquillity of the whole. A dilettante is an artist without a country, an artist who feels no vital connection with some one spot of soil and the myriad forms of life that have grown out of it. He is unduly concerned with perfection of technique, ignoring the ruder elements of life itself which come to him—more and more rarely—bluntly clamouring to be expressed. He wanders like a butterfly, a gipsy without the traditions of a gipsy. He has begun like all men, desiring the newness and strangeness of beauty, but unlike productive men, he has not learned to desire its humanity. As likely as not he ends by joining that vagrant multitude who are too fond of music ever to write a book, too fond of sculpture ever to paint a picture. The absolutely fatal result of unduly emphasizing the technique of an art is that after a while one hesitates to express anything in any form because it would be crystallizing once for all what one might some day have been capable of expressing better. Every degree of fastidiousness is also a degree of stagnation."

"The same thing, I suppose, happened when Rome awoke one morning, so to speak, and found itself artistic, and went over to Greece. It always happens with young countries."

"And the sad thing is that Cato always gives in and studies Greek with the rest in spite of his seventy Roman years. . . . But after all there is nothing to be gained by it. One can really *secure* nothing in Europe of the life that must lie behind artistic expression beyond a few memories. As a newspaper man one is drawn to London by the vague wish to connect oneself with a tradition which draws us all together from the ends of the earth. It is called 'Fleet Street.' Well, I suppose we are all in search of something. We all feel that somewhere there is a romance, a poetry, a passionate life waiting for us. The vague ideal of every soul that has a thought in every age is for that communion of citizens in some body, some city or state, some Utopia, if you will, which the Greeks meant in their word πολιτεία. Those artificial communities—Brook Farms and East Auroras—are so pathetically suggestive of the situation we all are in! 'We get together' (what an American phrase that is!) because we *aren't* together, because each of us is a voice crying in the wilderness, individuals, one and all, to the end of the chapter, cast inward upon our own insufficient selves. . . . We only destroy ourselves by wandering up and down the world. Fleet Street is dead and gone. There are no traditions that live in reality more vividly than they live in our imagination. And we have real lives to live in harmony with the world about us, just as Dr. Johnson lived in his day, and the reality of Fleet Street is the reality of Broadway. It is our business, I suppose, to make Broadway a tradition to our descendants. We think of Horace and his Sabine farm: but the Sabine farm was only a farm until Horace lived there, and it is only a farm now unless one carries something to it oneself. An asphodel is only lovelier than any common flower because in their day the Greeks who have made it our symbol of high romance vigorously submitted to all the limitations of their age. And in reality the asphodel is a very coarse, terrestrial flower indeed. These two realities have grown together long enough in our imaginations to form one ideal. When Americans are idealists they are, by reaction, such *impossible* idealists!—utterly scorning the real and the useful and the practical."

"Yes, I suppose we can't, so to speak, eat our romance and have it too!"

"Well, that is what I mean in saying that we have reached a point where we must sacrifice ourselves. We must act in such a way that this generation will have its romance and its tradition for those who come after. We have got in the habit of living on our imagination without troubling to replenish it with realities. We are living on our capital.

"It's all so vague, so difficult. You can't deliberately *establish* an American tradition. Walt Whitman was on the right track, possibly: but you can't build literally on *cosmos*. Universal comradeship means a great deal, but for practical purposes it means—nothing. It means just 'Yawp.' "

"That is only because we are self-conscious about it, because we keep thinking about the 'tradition' we are founding. And we gain that self-consciousness by accustoming ourselves to European ways of thought. We accustom ourselves to the pleasant delusion that we can graft ourselves upon ancient, finished, mellow, decaying civilizations. And that is what I mean by sacrifice. What are we really? No amount of taking thought can make us anything but the products of a rude, vigorous race, which has not yet finished laying its material foundations, imperfectly civilized. We have nothing to do with tradition. When we allow ourselves to be civilized beyond the point where civilization is representative of American life at its highest present point, we cut ourselves away from vital contact with American life. We polish our individual instincts until they are out of all proportion with our racial instincts. We simply take wings and fly away. No matter how brilliant we may be individually, if we, as Americans, concern ourselves unduly with tradition we become warped, like Whistler, or hollow, like Sargent. . . . Of course we *want* these things—I wonder if anybody in the world understands the sentiment that lies in crumbled castles and tattered frescoes, ruined colonnades and old churches full of dead incense, if anyone understands the very quality of the picturesque as we Americans understand it! Why, we almost invented that insatiable and infinitely pathetic habit of mind called 'sight-seeing': we have made it a synonym for all that is omnivorous, we are so starved for these things. It is the same impulse in a deeper sense that keeps some of us over here. Why? Simply because our perceptions are a little deeper, because in a sense we are the leaders in such matters.

"We must put aside anything that tends to make us self-conscious in this matter of American tradition and simply *be* American, teach our pulses to beat with American ideas and ideals, absorb American life, until we are able to see that in all its vulgarities and distractions and boastings there lie the elements of a gigantic art. The great fault of educated Americans is that they are hostile to too many things—to the 'trippers,' the 'personally conducted' and all their admirations —'if the throng by chance go right they purposely go wrong' —when it would be so much better to copy their enthusiasm. They shrug their shoulders at the word 'art' used as an adjective—'art-furniture,' 'art-framing,' and the like, instead of learning to see the pathos of this vocabulary. 'Art-furniture' is an expression which tries to go one step further than *beautiful* furniture. Leave the poor word alone—it will die a natural death."

"But the average artist is a refined opportunist, a man concerned with the immediate and the individual, what is called a 'clever' man, quite innocent of racial needs and racial tendencies, quite incapable of sacrifice. Any originality that he may have developed abroad would be utterly thrown away in this programme of yours. You are asking a whole generation of artists to nullify their own achievement for the sake of a more or less Utopian future."

"So far as I can see, the chief use of having cleverness is to have some authority for despising it, and to be thus able to destroy the weapons of those who are cynical. And as for originality, it seems to me that all true originality immediately reconciles itself with tradition, has in itself the elements of tradition, and is really the shadow of tradition thrown across the future. The proof of new ideas is that they become traditional in exact ratio to their vitality. And what tradition can this originality be based upon? Can it be anything deeper than a tradition of technique? An American artist can have no true, same originality, deeper than that of technique, which does not spring from American life."

"It seems to me that what you say about our living on our capital, 'living on our imagination without troubling to replenish it with realities,' is true of the rest of the world also. It is true in a curious way of Bernard Shaw,[4] for example: a great man, a Swift, if you like, a great individualist. Shaw is a pseudo-social reformer, a man who, of all men, ought to be creating something positive out of the present. But he gives us stones for bread, he is irrelevant, he gives people what they foolishly fancy that they desire. If they really desired what he gives they would—I don't say love him or believe him, for plenty of true reformers are neither loved nor believed in their day—but they would find in him some really constructive comment on their own lives, something beside astonishing sparks and flashes. The old idols are shattered: Shaw is merely shattering the fragments of the ruins of the old society into smaller fragments. He is merely in an extremely witty way, hanging, drawing, and quartering what is already dead. And the chief note of English literature today seems to me a pandering to the non-assertive which is the reactionary impulse in the people from the great iconoclasts of thirty years ago. People tired of hearing Ruskin thunder, 'If you don't believe that what I say is entirely true you may as well never have lived,' and even of Darwin asserting mildly, '*This* really *is* true.' And so now they like a man to say, 'This is clever enough to be true, but if you don't care for it I can put the opposite quite as wittily'. . . . No wonder socialism is abroad like a whirlwind with its dazzling dream of impossible Utopias where all shall have a definite place. We fancy that we enjoy

---

[4] George Bernard Shaw (1856-1950). Born of genteel poor Dublin parents, Shaw had by the time of this essay written plays like *Caesar and Cleopatra*, *Man and Superman*, and *Major Barbara*, as well as socialist tracts and music criticism. He joined the Fabian Society in 1884; Sidney Webb followed in 1885. The two men gave to the society its characteristic evolutionary and gradualist socialist stamp and its beginnings as a major influence on the Labour Party.

our bewilderment, but deep down we are all longing for something definite, something absolute, something solid. The heart of the world is so numbered, so vacant that it hardly realizes how hungry it is. We need great constructors, great positive forces, someone to bind together the estranged fragments of society. What is a Swift who is not counteracted by an Addison? And is Hall Caine[5] the best refuge the people can find from Bernard Shaw?"

"As you say, the trouble comes from living on the past or rather on reactions from the past—which is negative. And the need is a constructive force in the present—which is positive. And a constructive force is composed less of mind, like Shaw, than of heart, which feels and which compels. But before one can feel one must understand. We Americans do not feel the inspiration of American life because we shut ourselves off from understanding it. Everything in America is in a state of distraction, of divorce. Our humour is not our life, our politics and religion are outside ourselves, we are intelligent without instinct. And we further divorce ourselves by living abroad. . . . We consider it more honourable to trade than to create, whereas the farmer who produces wheat and barley is nearer the civilized ideal than the broker who negotiates them in Wall Street. By his labour he is actually bringing something into the world, not merely transferring something already produced. And the artist also creates.

"But I think a day will come when the names of Denver and Sioux City will have a traditional and antique dignity like Damascus and Perugia—and when it will not seem to us grotesque that they have."

[5] Hall Caine (1853-1931). His early poverty developed into a belief in Christian Socialism. Brooks knew him best as a novelist; after a journalistic career Caine became an extremely prolific and popular novelist whose sales compared with Marie Corelli's.

Appendix

SINCE writing this I have been struck by an incomparable passage in Vernon Lee's[1] latest volume, a comment on Emerson which links the idea I have expressed more deeply with American life: "This vital energy in Emerson's teaching is, I think, given free play only if we liberate it from notions which belonged not to Emerson's mind, but to his intellectual surroundings. His transcendentalism, horrified at science and *despising utility,* arises in great measure from the old metaphysical and theological habit of *regarding the soul as a readymade, separate entity,* come, Heaven knows whence, *utterly unconnected with the things among which it alights,* and struggling perpetually to be rid of them and return somehow to its unknown place of origin. Had Emerson suspected, as we have reason to suspect that the soul is born of the soul, *its fibre the fibre of every plant and animal,* its breath the breath of every wind, its shape the shape left vacant by other shapes, he would not have been obliged to arrange *a purely intellectual transcendental habitation* for this supposed exile from another sphere. And his intuition of a possible universal life would have been strengthened, not damaged, by the knowledge that our soul is moulded into its form—nay, takes its very quality, from surrounding circumstances; and the probability, therefore, that *between the soul and its surroundings there will be a growing relation and harmony,* as of product and producer, concave and convex." (From *Gospels of Anarchy and other Contemporary Studies.*) I have italicized the words and phrases which bear particularly on various points throughout this book.

---

[1] Vernon Lee, pseudonym of Violet Paget (1856-1935), French-born English essayist and novelist especially noted for her works on aesthetics and Italian art. She settled in Florence and did not visit England until she was twenty-five. Her more than forty works include studies of art in Renaissance and eighteenth-century Italy. Brooks wrote an article about her for the *Forum,* XLV (April 1911), 447-456.

II

THE SOUL: An Essay Towards a Point of View

(San Francisco, 1910)

EDITORIAL NOTE: Dedicated to the man Van Wyck Brooks called "mio maestro," *The Soul* is a youthful, highly personal and lyrical reverie on the nature of existence. Its search through history for great souls "who have shown men how to be true to themselves" was part of its author's lifelong search for guides to self conduct and a reflection of his characteristic tendency to see issues in terms of personality. Beneath the work's impressionism the author shows his need to sort out and adjust the conflicting claims of the private and the social self.

Unacknowledged in his autobiography, *The Soul* was published at the author's expense just prior to his marriage.

O beata solitudo
O sola beatitudo[1]

TO
J. B. YEATS
R. H. A.[2]

Or se'tu quel Virgilio, e quella fonte
Che spande di parlar si largo fiume?
Tu se'lo mio maestro.[3]

I

THE LIFE OF a child is indeed that of a chameleon. Who forbade us then to live many lives which had no resemblance to each other? By what magic was it given us then to see that nothing contradicts anything else? We threw off the solemn weight of consistency and in a winter's afternoon, without stirring from the four walls of a room, experienced all the modes of being. And if in later years we feel that then we were above all natural, can we doubt that the destiny of man is to experience the whole of life? Or shall we conclude that a golden age was given us, not as a vision to which life can be made to conform, but as a consolation for what it cannot be?

II

But in youth a fact confronts us. A man has actually to be something, and therefore he cannot be other things as well.

---

[1] "O happy solitude
O sole happiness"

[2] John Butler Yeats (1839-1922). The Irish painter, father of William Butler and Jack Butler Yeats, who migrated to New York in 1908. He met John Sloan a few months after his arrival and Van Wyck Brooks not much later. Yeats was a great influence on both men. Sloan painted a "Yeats at Petitpas, 1910"; Brooks relates his indebtedness in several places including *Emerson and Others, John Sloan,* and *An Autobiography.*
R.H.A., the Royal Hibernian Academy.

[3] Danto, *Inferno,* Canto I, 79-80, 85. "And are you then that Virgil and that fountain of purest speech?"; "For you are my true master." John Ciardi translation.

And again, to be something implies that one has to do something. The social world opens before us and requires of us an economy of morals, a singleness of aim. We possess qualities that cannot exist together in a human being. What selection is to be made? What is to be kept, encouraged, fostered in ourselves?

* * *

XIV

How does the soul thus become walled about, local, definitely and awkwardly formed? Why should life contain nothing but the *fait accompli* and what is certain in the end to become the *fait accompli?* The social ideal is that of unselfishness. But see the result: hardly a fine thing that is not held to be impracticable. Are we not perhaps too ready to consider ourselves selfish? Do we not permit our passions of social generosity to dispossess the finer intuitions of an ultimate humanity? Are suffering and error without really the corollaries of our own weakness and self-absorption? Is not our eagerness to alleviate these things only the better side of the universal mistake—that of being untrue to one's self? If the individual is the measure of society how can he understand society until he understands himself? Does not the whole of humanity advance in us as we advance in ourselves? And yet everything on earth stands like a flaming sword between a man and the intimacy of his own soul. Is a man fit to renounce himself before he has confirmed himself? Or can he confirm himself by renouncing that which makes him capable of love?

Unselfishness is, roughly, doing what we do not want to do. But really what we want or do not want has nothing to do with the question. The perfect thing in Christ was that he never had to surrender anything: he was perfectly happy because he had no self-will. We approach happiness not by surrendering things, but by tending towards an inward point where we have nothing to surrender. It gives us pain to surrender things because we are secretly convinced that the things we surrender are valuable. But when, without bitterness, we are able to see that these things are without value, we are only made more free by ridding ourselves of them. . . .

Counting over to myself the great souls of history who have shown men how to be true to themselves, I came upon the author of that book, unmentioned where men gather together, which has in solitary hours recalled numberless millions to freedom and peace.

XV

In Thomas à Kempis we see above all the solitary man, absorbed in that self which is the measure of the inmost heart of the world.[4]

His mortal years are ninety and of these more than seventy are passed in a single cloister. In the yellow sun of the convent garden, as I fancy, he sits among the bees and the flowers, the slender shadows of a great lilac bush falling silently upon his lap and his crossed hands. His imagination gathers together only the memories which contribute to a sense of ineffable calm, a mood of resignation, of silence, and of peace.

So little can ever happen along that path bordered by flowering shrubs, among the grasses, and by the marble seat! A lizard's rustle, the murmuring of bees, the coming of spring with its procession of gentle events, the stirring and spreading of the blossoms—sunlight and contemplation.

He hears the voice of a quail interrogating the wind, a solitary locust winding off its wiry coil of sound: everywhere an unceasing monotone of ground insects. These tiny voices calling to him out of the grass, noisy in the naïve gladness of things newly arrived, pathetically assert that little as they are they have yet passed beyond the songless worms and are marching upward to the citadels of society. But he does not rebuke them with his wisdom, even if he has arrived only to discover that silence is better.

Here like rosebuds in this garden the fragile thoughts of

---

[4] Thomas à Kempis (c.1379-1471). German monk who studied at Gerard Groote's community, the Brothers of the Common Life, in the Netherlands, his long accepted authorship of the popular devotional work, the *Imitation of Christ,* is now not so certain. Groote himself may have written it and à Kempis have prepared it for publication.

the *Imitation* disclose themselves and he cries with inward rapture: "How sweet it is to love, to be dissolved, and to swim in love!" In the presence of this soul, dissolved in love, the spirits of moral violence, rebuke, propaganda reveal their limitations and confess that they are transitory almost as the forces they oppose. "Against all evil suspicion of other persons and indignation at wrong-doing," he says, "think of all thy own faults from the day of thy birth, and cease to be angry at others." Humility, Patience, Obedience, Poverty dawn upon us like stars in the twilight, and we begin to understand those ironical words of Pascal: "Caesar was too old, it seems to me, to go about amusing himself by conquering the world. . . . He ought to have been more mature."

XVI

But if this man seems to us wholly

> "pale with weariness
> Of climbing heaven,"[5]

if we ask in what way he faces the fact of existence, we shall find that he has derived a lesson from his dreams. In him we see that intense practicality toward the little intimate things about him and about those with whom he lives which is always the mark of minds luminously aware of the vanity behind the greater institutions of the world.

The task he finds before him is that of transcribing the sacred manuscripts. To this he gives himself with reverence and minute care, as we can see from various works of devotion copied exquisitely by his hand which have come down to our day. This reverence which confers nobility upon labour he sought to inspire in those younger monks who were disposed to be inattentive. Thus in his *Manual Parvulorum*,[6] composed for them, he says with a kind of tender worldliness: "And when thou art dead many shall speak well of thee when they

[5] Shelley, "To the Moon."

[6] *Sermons to Novices.*

read thy volumes, and what was once written by thee with so great care." . . .

This calm, determinate practicality assures the authenticity of his vision and stamps it with that simplicity which is the origin of all miracles and which baffles the conventional mind.

XVII

In the outer world we resort to science as the criterion of truth. Formerly, as in Faust, Paracelsus, and the old alchemists the scientist and the mystic were one. Today they confirm each other and, were the scientist not compelled to be a specialist, they would again unite forces; for it is precisely such laws as those of the indestructibility of matter, the conservation of energy, and the evolution of species, obtained by experiment, which the mystic has always divined through intuition at the roots of life. . . . As I thought of that cry of Thomas à Kempis: "How sweet it is to love, to be dissolved, and to swim in love!", I saw in this very sense of the sweetness of dissolution precisely that which animated St. Francis at the moment of death. By some quick intuition of precisely these laws of science, a passionate love for the elements composing his body and soul become articulate in him at the approach of dissolution. We are told that he stretched forth his hands and cried with joy, "Welcome, Sister Death!" And then he began to sing, and summoning his brothers he bade them join with him and sing the Canticle of the Sun, "who brings us the day and who brings us the light, our sister the moon, our brother the wind, and the air and cloud, our sister water, so humble, precious, and clean, and at last our sister the Death of the body, whom no man may escape." And from this hour until his death the house where he lay rang day and night with his songs. This was he who had been God's jester. . . .

XVIII

As I considered this life passed utterly without solace of comfort, food, money, or esteem, and of this death seraphical in love, I thought of the latter days of another man, in the

eyes of the social world the greatest of the modern age—
Martin Luther.

Surrounded by his abundant German family, comfortable,
the idol of a nation, he said in sober weariness: "The world
for these two hundred years has hated no one as it hates me.
I in turn have no love for the world. I know not that in all
my life I have ever felt real enjoyment. I am well tired of it.
God come soon and take me away."

Here was a contrast of great significance. These two men
were alike of the first order as immense spiritual forces,
affecting the destiny of the whole world; and here they were,
placed in analogous positions in regard to life and death. Here
if anywhere lay the point of departure for a just comparison of
their fundamental attitudes.

And the distinction was approximately this: Luther was a
master of the worldly situation. He was a dominant will. He
had stood upon a firm conviction of the truth and all the world
he cared for had swung round to him with a triumphant
unison of praise, honour, and moral appreciation. As a result
of this he had all worldly solace, a comfortable home, a loving
wife, children, friends. He was the mightiest bourgeois the
world had ever seen. It was the logical result of his great
struggle. In the pulpit, the market-place, the battlefield,
wherever men are gathered together for action, moral or
physical, the whole world shouts with one voice a shout which
has echoed through four centuries, "All praise to Luther!"
And even the Catholic Church, in conclave, when the doors
are closed, registers a silent vote of thanks to this man who
confirmed in the modern world the organization of Christianity. So universal is the gratitude of society to any man who
upholds it: substantial response, moral or material. And such
a man was Luther from the first. When at the opening of his
campaign he sent the Elector a copy of his thundering de-
nunciation of the papacy, the Elector secretly and as a sign
of moral support sent him a basket of game. . . . But he was
a weary man without love.

St. Francis, on the other hand, was a moral failure. His
only grief was that the rule he had established had become
an organization, and had in this measure lost its freshness in

the heart of each of his followers. He had in the worldly sense succeeded to a degree which afflicted him. But even this, to him a sign of his own failure, only served to touch with sadness —to mellow and make more human—the divine joy of that blithe soul.

He lay upon boards and his food was bread and water. The poor body could not contain its love, its happiness, life could not contain it, and he fell into trances, saw visions, dreamed dreams, lived at one time many lives, lived in illusions, in the lives of those who loved him, in the lives of birds and fishes, saw himself existing in water, in the clouds, in the wind—so insatiable was the sense of life within him. And at the moment of death he had so identified himself with the whole life of the universe that his death seemed but another trance. There was no longer anything to be separated. The soul had passed out of the body by its gradual identification with all created things, and only the body was left to contribute its share to the life of the worms and the flowers.

XIX

When I remember him I become suddenly unconventional. And if I think of any man about me or in history as a Catholic, a Protestant, a plebeian, a bourgeois, an aristocrat, it is with a counteracting sense of the fluidity of life. Nor is it helpful to use these categories unless we are continually aware that we are speaking first of humanity and of human beings.

How is it possible, in considering history, to feel that one has a right to like or dislike, approve or disapprove of any character? This indulgence we can permit ourselves only to our contemporaries, whom we see only in action and in whom we perceive only results. But if we look back into history we realize the futility of summary judgments. Every act of every man who figures there has its compensating cause, and we respond prematurely and with injustice to ourselves if we stop short and form an opinion without penetrating to that cause. So that, when all is said, the man we love is merely the fortunate man, whom circumstances in the high sense have favoured. The Greeks understood this and frankly honoured the fortunate man, on the eternal principle that to him that hath shall be given. Thus in their tragedy—of Orestes, I think—a group of exiles honour the hero in the very fact they have reason to congratulate him: "Fortunate man, we honour thee that thou shalt at some time return to thy country."

Keats in his "Ode to a Nightingale" has the same Greek intuition:

> 'Tis not through envy of thy happy lot
> But being too happy in thy happiness.

and again:

> Fade far away, dissolve, and quite forget
> What thou among the leaves hast never known,
> The weariness, the fever, and the fret
> Here, where men sit and hear each other groan.

He honours the nightingale because its life has not been marred by circumstances, and he becomes happy in its happiness.

And because we know that sorrow and misery too often rather bedraggle than enrich us, we revere the pure in heart and those to whom temptation is not temptation. We bless the little children divining that until we have become like them, not by renunciation but by a second birth, we cannot find happiness.

Looking upon them we live in their lives our own better lives and we revere in them the ideal which perpetually evades our own situation.

XX

The facts of his origin contributed to the growth in St. Francis of an exquisite inward and outward grace. He was the son of one of those successful merchants who are pleased, perhaps for their own vanity, to give their sons every chance to adopt the ways of the aristocracy: an aristocracy then still feudal, saturated through and through with the sentiment of *noblesse oblige*. Francis became a gentleman in this ancient and most noble sense and although his morals were no doubt all wrong, he became filled with that benign spirit which is able, when it comes to blossom, to do away with morals and substitute in their place love. We see him in his period of worldly extravagance a courteous and graceful soul, tender in friendship, careless of material things, gay, chivalrous, incapable of dogma. And in him we observe the spectacle of a gentle transition, a transfusion of ideas, a gradual inward illumination. In him the feudal gentleman finally utters himself and is merged with the poor, the outcast, and the unfortunate. Extremes meet; and if we examine history we shall find that the two ends of society have always been one in heart because abundant in human nature, while both have been feared and suspected by the conventional classes between.

* * *

XXIII

Having gone thus far I feel that I am in search of a word. I have been speaking of the natural soul in the midst of life. But what do we mean by the word life? Something, surely, so much like everything that when we follow it into its recesses the senses become transfigured and we return into the daylight of common thought speechless, blind, and with empty hands.

I shall use an illustration, for every least thing life contains is a microcosm of the whole and may be taken as its touchstone. Poetry is the most ancient companion of the human soul and the history of poetry may be taken as a parallel of the soul's history in the midst of life.

* * *

Today society is endeavouring to bind itself together in a moral programme. It assumes that this programme will defeat the rhetoric of civilization by placing more and more individuals in a state where they can become conscious of themselves. Thus it overlooks the everlasting law that institutions exist really not for the sake of those for whom they are organized, but for the sake of those who organize them. The poor, the blind, those who are governed, those who are employed—who understands their lives which are, in the sublime phrase, hidden with God, working out through suffering and weakness the mysterious destiny of the soul? They that govern are they that have arrived at conclusions which are false in the mere fact of being conclusions. Life has brought them nothing but opinion and with opinion failure.

* * *

XXX

I saw that people who lived much in the world spoke little of sorrow, love and joy. But here was Mary Magdalene, who possessed them and gave them forth when the disciples turned away faithless. They who had had no outer life had been familiar with these things, but to her, who had come at the eleventh hour, had been given a greater reward than theirs— the power of being faithful.

She alone divined perfectly the message of Christ and she had nothing but love.

The disciples had in some degree been watching, noting, reasoning, teaching, formulating, propagating this message.

But to her it came so intimately, so utterly, that there was nothing for her to say, nothing for her to do. She had reached an inward point where there was no self to be unselfish. Faith had arrived where it no longer needed works to give it reality. And by thus becoming the very measure of the human heart, she outgrew in one flash all the obligations, the responsibilities, the moralities of society.

Her life we guess: and the more sumptuous it becomes in our imagination the more poignant becomes the reality of her love. The disciples had from the first denied themselves, even where they might have possessed, worldly solace. For years they had received the message and lived it. And yet when the final instant came she had the reward. She was permitted then to be true to nature and they were not.

I was puzzled now when I recalled Luther and St. Francis, for with them the situation appeared to be the reverse. It was Luther who had possessed worldly solace in the outward sense, just as Mary had possessed it: while St. Francis, like the disciples, had lived without comfort and without pleasure.

Again, from the social point of view, I saw that still another puzzling rearrangement had to be made. Luther and the disciples had been unselfish where Mary and Francis had been self-absorbed. Luther and the disciples had been morally consistent, while Mary and Francis had ignored and offended morality.

Moreover, Luther and the disciples had given their lives to the expression, in word and deed, of the truth that was in them: while Mary and Francis had never stepped aside to convince anyone of anything.

Here, then, the reward had been given to those who were self-absorbed, immoral, and socially inactive, and had been denied those who were unselfish, moral, and passionately active. And here, too, were the little children ignorant of all words, of all responsibilities, of every emotion but that of an inarticulate love, whom Jesus took in his arms, and in whom he saw the mirror of the sublime human heart.

XXXI

Here was a force which, except in relation to itself, saw no difference between morality and immorality, the active and the passive, the selfish and the unselfish.

One remnant of the social argument remained. Is it less than nothing that a man for one instant, by one word, departs from himself, if by so doing he can bring millions to the knowledge of love? Then I thought of the parable of Dives in hell, who at the last besought that Lazarus might be sent to his brothers from the dead: and the answer of Abraham, "If they hear not Moses and the prophets, neither will they be persuaded, though one rose from the dead."

In this I saw the pessimism of social philosophy: that the individual, in the last resort, cannot be assisted, cannot be other than a hopeless, lonely, inarticulate atom, utterly crushed by the dead weight of the universe; that above all, the individual is finally responsible for himself and is able to make nothing of this responsibility except in relation to an outer standard. The moment we compare we introduce a scale. The moment we consider the individual from the point of view of an achieved universe, an achieved society, he becomes also a fixed entity and of necessity a very small one, an atom. What, then, is the consolation of his responsibility? What is there but to take him into the fold, warm his feet, smother him into self-forgetfulness, give him the best, the only chance he can have, that of sharing the moral consolations of society?

It is this which makes Christianity appear so inexorable, so defiant, so hard, so oblivious of reason, morality, common sense, of everything except that one little fugitive, inconclusive, inchoate thing, the human heart.

* * *

XXXIII

As I began to see the emptiness of all ways of making the best of things, I realized too that there were moments in which I felt no love, in which I was cold, hard, irritated with everything surrounding me. Here was the final oppression and it sprang out of myself. Now more than ever, when everything was reduced to the self, the self felt its awful want. More than ever I was conscious of the pressure, the narrowness of life which could not be relieved by the distractions of the moral world.

And accordingly since there was nothing but love which could relieve me I felt, in the absence of love, the absence of everything.

If in those moments when the outer world has ceased to mean anything to us, we could only know how near we are to the one great happiness!

For in those moments we have unconsciously prepared ourselves for love.

When everything has lost its meaning, when we have winnowed out of ourselves the capacity for all secondary, all outer consolations, when we have reached the inmost solitude and the heart is utterly starved, then we have cleaned house for the wonderful guest that never deserts us.

Nor is there one instant of waiting. There is a quick at the bottom of desolation. And in a flash we are free again and

> Feel through all this fleshly dress
> Bright shoots of everlastingness.[7]

Then for a moment we love the sparrows in the street and every man and thing we see.

Then we are willing to bear all things, to believe all things, to hope all things, to endure all things.

* * *

XXXVI

In literature I seemed to see a refuge.

These thoughts, these impulses, these desires, too conflicting and inconsistent for life to receive and contain—here I could live them to the uttermost, have them out, have my fling to the uttermost.

Here was a kind of vicarious life which demanded no consistency of me, never demanded that I should be one thing at the expense of another. Here was a life which had no barriers, no moralities, asked no questions, reconciled all modes of being with each other simply because the human heart had dreamed of them.

But even in literature there was a touch of propaganda, inasmuch as expression here too implied an audience. And this audience would necessarily be a haphazard gathering, large or small, of persons who would approach it from the social point of view. Here once more a man by expression committed himself, laid himself open to a new set of influences, all the more dangerous because they attacked his most sacred intentions, because they laid siege to his inmost personality. . . .

* * *

XXXVIII

Literature, then, like life, had its conditions. For what could literature be if it were less than one's whole self, the very

---

[7] Henry Vaughn (1622-1695), "The Retreat."

nerve that quickens in the midst of one's being? It could only be what Verlaine scornfully calls it when he says:

> La nuance, pas la couleur,
> Seulement la nuance—
> Tout le reste est littérature—

all the rest, the cold things, the hard things, the unreal things —in a word, rhetoric.

I saw this all the more clearly when I turned to the literature of our own day. Evidently its chief energies were absorbed in the novel. Where, if not in Russia, had it stretched to the farthest limits the possibilities of what the novel can be? Beside the mighty novels of Tolstoy, Turgenev, Dostoievsky there seemed to be a note of triviality about most of our western fiction, a nervous and finite compactness. Here was above all construction, the weaving and threading and balancing of situations, economies and suppressions, parings off, pushings together—art certainly, but art attained only by stifling that swift cry which expresses the anguish of the human situation.

Beside this I saw the Russian novel brooding on things, moving across life with all the cumulative aimlessness of a human soul, gathering to itself sensations, ideas, memories.

XXXIX

The great fact about the Russian people appeared to me this—that they are the most inarticulate people in the world. These mighty novelists are the voices of the inarticulate, voices themselves not quite articulate, but struggling out of some chaotic depths, dragging their dreams out of the soil. Compared with them we of the western world express ourselves easily and toss ourselves to the wind. But they, who have no rhetoric and who cannot speak, accumulate feelings, emotions, thoughts which turn upon themselves within and grow rich and angry and prophetic until, too urgent for anything to stop them, they burst forth and pour out, turgid and volcanic, carving out of tremendous necessity a language all their own. Silent watchers of the elements, they know the works of the Lord and his wonders in the deep.

And this trait of Russian literature finds also a reflection in everything else that is great in the literature of our day. The mysterious forces of heredity, of sex, of race, of the soil, brooding over the modern mind and made more imminent and more mysterious by the discoveries of science, penetrate the works of Ibsen, of Maeterlinck, of Hauptmann and Sudermann, Zola and the writers of the Low Countries impregnated with the profound Germanic soul. And here for the first time we find literature of the highest order without style in its traditional sense as an independent aspect of the literary art. These are not literary men, in the proper sense, at all. They are men who write from the sheer pressure of life and to whom, as Whitman says, "after absorbing eras, temperaments, races, after knowledge, freedom, crimes, after clarifyings, elevations, and removing obstacles," there has come "the divine power to speak words."

XL

Of all these mighty spirits Tolstoy appeared to me to have gone farthest in the region of literature and to have reached the conclusion of the literary life with a misery deeper than that of any other. More profoundly than they he had felt the pressure of life, and in his gigantic despair he felt the utter inadequacy of literature. . . . In his Confession he tells us with what sensations he finished *Anna Karenina:* "My despair reached such a height that I could do nothing but think, think of the horrible condition in which I found myself. . . . Questions never ceased multiplying and pressing for answers, and like lines converging all to one point, so these unanswerable questions pressed to one black spot, and with horror and a consciousness of my weakness I remained standing before this spot. Bodily, I was able to work at mowing hay as well as a peasant. Mentally, I could work for eighteen hours at a time without feeling any ill consequence. And yet I had come to this, that I could no longer live. . . . I saw only one thing—Death. Everything else was a lie."

The refuge of literature, the refuge of all vicarious forms

of existence was inadequate for this man who desired nothing less than an explanation of life in its own terms. Devious paths had brought him to the first question. He saw that since the beginning of the world millions of human beings had solved the problem of life merely by living it. . . . It is so easy to sympathize with those who wish to reform institutions, so easy to grasp their issues, to surrender ourselves to the most arduous, the most exacting propaganda! So difficult for us to allow a new light to illuminate our own ways!

Once, near the woods of Meudon, I had encamped for the day with a friend, a landscape painter. I observed him stooping over, studying the scene from between his knees. It refreshed his eye, he explained, to see in reverse these objects with which he had grown more than familiar.

That is the way we should look at life when we had lived it through, if in all our wisdom we could for one instant return to it with our first love. . . . Tolstoy found that men were untrue to themselves in order to be true to society, while society returned to men nothing but distractions from life itself. Something like this is the teaching of Maeterlinck, of Ibsen in *Peer Gynt*. It is the teaching of every Odyssey since Homer.

* * *

Life with all its resurrections, life so manifold, so iridescent, floods over one—so sad, so merry, so lovable. The mind has such calm things in it, such green retreats!

Who presumes to give form to the blundering chaos of things?

I commit myself to an outward succession of events, a cast of thought. I am like one who has engaged a sculptor to make a mask of his face. In the course of time the mask will be finished, will be shaken off. What will remain there of the innumerable smiles that crossed my lips and eyes?

Yet under the plaster as it grows gradually cold I am free all the time. At the first moment, at the first contact of the damp material I fix my features with a bold rigidity. I give a strong impression to the mould. Then I leave it to perpetuate itself.

I release my lips. I open my eyes. Oh, the silence! oh, the dark solitude! and all that whirls within me.

> *O pondus immensum;*
> *o pelagus intransnatabile:*
> *ubi nihil de me reperio quam in toto nihil.*
> *Ubi est ergo latebra gloriae;*
> *ubi confidentia de virtute concepta?*
>   Im. Chr. III.[8]

---

[8] "O greatness immeasurable! O sea that none can cross! Now I recognize myself as wholly and only nothing! Where now can pride lurk unseen? Where is now my former confidence in my virtue?" *The Imitation of Christ*, III: 14 Trans. Leo Sherley-Price

III

America's Coming-of-Age

(New York, 1915)

EDITORIAL NOTE: *America's Coming-of-Age,* like *The Wine of the Puritans,* was written in England, "in a rented house in the suburb of Eltham." The friend of his childhood and college years, Maxwell Perkins, a fledgling at Scribner's, naturally hoped Scribner's would accept the manuscript. But William Crary Brownell rejected it, finding it mentally independent but "premature."[1] Brownell was one of a battery of older critics Brooks was soon to charge, in a *Seven Arts* essay, with using the past to shame the present. B. W. Huebsch was wiser; he accepted the manuscript and so secured for his imprint a major literary manifesto of the period. A year later he was also wise enough to publish D. H. Lawrence's *The Rainbow* and James Joyce's *Portrait of the Artist as a Young Man.*

[1] *Editor to Author: The Letters of Maxwell E. Perkins* (New York, 1950), ed. John Hall Wheelock, p. 10.

Huebsch demurred at Brooks's original title, *A Fable for Yankees,* knowing Americans had become, as Brooks was forced to realize, "as multiracial as the crew of the *Pequod.*"[2] Many years later Brooks felt that the American past needed reclaiming, not only from academic critics who ignored or disparaged it, but from younger critics like H. L. Mencken, "with a German-American mind," and the younger generation who were largely immigrant and "detached from an American past or any sense whatever of an American tradition." The influx of non-English-speaking immigrants had destroyed the sense of cultural continuity which existed in New England where the American literary classics had been produced. Randolph Bourne was exhilarated by the prospect of a transnational America; so was another contemporary. As he put it: "The great social adventure of America is no longer the conquest of the wilderness but the absorption of fifty different peoples."[3] Brooks was probably less engaged by this phenomenon as social adventure than as loss of the world he knew. (Henry James was far more disturbed by the changed New York he found during his visit of 1904, one filled with Slavs, Italians, and Jews.) But the writing of literary history was a way to preserve the past while a new cultural amalgam was forming that might even ultimately re-create the lost cultural continuity.

When Brooks looked back at the book he had finished just a few months before the outbreak of World War I, he felt that he had undervalued the American past under the influence of an older *Zeitgeist.* The point of view that prevailed when Brooks was a college student was one shaped by scholars like Barrett Wendell, George Woodberry, and W. C. Brownell. The United States was for them a literary dependency of England that had failed to produce a poet even in the rank of Thomas Gray, much less an indisputably great novelist.

The version of *America's Coming-of-Age* reprinted here is the original 1915 edition. Subsequent editions, the 1934 Dutton edition and the Doubleday-Anchor edition (1958), contain revisions later made by Brooks.

---

[2] *The Writer in America,* p. 42.
[3] Lippmann, p. 145.

"The middle of humanity thou never
knewest, but the extremity of both ends."
TIMON OF ATHENS.

To John Hall Wheelock[1]

I. "Highbrow" and "Lowbrow"

I

AT THE TIME when he was trying to release humanity from the cross of gold on which, as he said, it was crucified, the Apostle of Free Silver—in this matter, at least, representing the old American frame of mind—announced that the opinion of all the professors in the United States would not affect his opinions in the least. Now this, plainly, was a very formidable dilemma. For on the one hand stood a body of supposed experts in economic theory, on the other a man whose profession it was to change and reform economic practice,—the one knowing, the other doing; and not only was there no compatibility between them but an openly avowed and cynical contempt of theory on the part of practice was a principal element in the popularity of a popular hero. Was Mr. Bryan, however, to blame for it? To know anything of the economic theory which is taught in American universities—in many cases compulsorily taught—is to confess that blame is not the right word. For this economic theory is at the least equally cynical. It revolves round and round in its tree-top dream of the economic man; and no matter how much the wind blows political economy never comes down. Incompatibility, mutual

---

[1] John Hall Wheelock (b. 1886). American poet, friend of Brooks since their first day at Harvard, who published anonymously with Brooks the volume, *Verses by Two Undergraduates* (1905).

contempt between theory and practice, is in the very nature of things.

One might extend the illustration to literature, merely substituting one professor for another and putting any typical best-selling novelist in the place of Mr. Bryan. It is a peculiar twist in the academic mind to suppose that a writer belongs to literature only when he is dead; living he is, vaguely, something else; and an habitual remoteness from the creative mood has made American professors quite peculiarly academic. "Literature," as distinguished from excellent writing, is, in the American universities, a thing felt to have been done, and while for all one knows it may continue to be done the quality in it which makes it literature only comes out, like the wines, with age.

Now I suppose that most of the American novelists in our day are university men; they have learned to regard literature as an august compound of Browning, Ben Jonson, and Hesiod; and consequently when they themselves begin to write it is in a spirit of real humility that they set themselves to the composition of richly rewarded trash. I am sure of this: it is modesty that lies behind the "best-seller"; and there is an aspect in which the spectacle of writers regarding themselves as humble tradesfolk has a certain charm. But the conception of literature as something, so to speak, high and dry, gives to the craft of authorship in America a latitude like that of morality in Catholic countries: so long as the heavenly virtues are upheld mundane virtues may shift as they will. In a word, writers are relieved of responsibility, and while their ethical conscience remains quite sound they absolve themselves from any artistic conscience whatsoever. And the worst of it is that precisely these writers of immitigable trash are often the bright vigorous, intuitive souls who *could* make literature out of American life. Has it ever been considered how great a knowledge of men, what psychological gifts of the first order their incomparable achievement of popularity implies?

These two attitudes of mind have been phrased once for all in our vernacular as "Highbrow" and "Lowbrow." I have proposed these terms to a Russian, an Englishman, and a German, asking each in turn whether in his country there was anything to correspond with the conceptions implied in them. In each case they have been returned to me as quite American, authentically our very own, and, I should add, highly suggestive.

What side of American life is not touched by this antithesis? What explanation of American life is more central or more illuminating? In everything one finds this frank acceptance of twin values which are not expected to have anything in common: on the one hand a quite unclouded, quite unhypocritical assumption of transcendent theory ("high ideals"); on the other a simultaneous acceptance of catchpenny realities. Between university ethics and business ethics, between American culture and American humor, between Good Government and Tammany, between academic pedantry and pavement slang, there is no community, no genial middle ground.[2]

The very accent of the words "Highbrow" and "Lowbrow" implies an instinctive perception that this is a very unsatisfactory state of affairs. For both are used in a derogatory sense. The "Highbrow" is the superior person whose virtue is admitted but felt to be an inept unpalatable virtue; while the "Lowbrow" is a good fellow one readily takes to, but with a certain scorn for him and all his works. And what is true of them as personal types is true of what they stand for. They are equally undesirable, and they are incompatible; but they divide American life between them.

II

They always have divided American life between them; and to understand them one has to go back to the beginning of things,—for without doubt the Puritan Theocracy is the all-influential fact in the history of the American mind. It was the Puritan conception of the Deity as not alone all-determining but precisely responsible for the practical affairs of the race, as constituting, in fact, the State itself, which precluded in advance any central bond, any responsibility, any common

2 Compare D. H. Lawrence's description of American discrepancy: "tight mental allegiance to a morality which the passional self repudiates." *Studies in Classic American Literature* (New York, 1923, 1951), p. 184.

feeling in American affairs and which justified the unlimited
centrifugal expediency which has always marked American
life. And the same instinct that made against centrality in
government made against centrality in thought, against common standards of any kind. The imminent eternal issues the
Puritans felt so keenly, the equally imminent practical issues
they experienced so monotonously threw almost no light on
one another; there was no middle ground between to mitigate,
combine, or harmonize them.

So it is that from the beginning we find two main currents
in the American mind running side by side but rarely mingling
—a current of overtones and a current of undertones—and
both equally unsocial: on the one hand, the current of Transcendentalism, originating in the piety of the Puritans, becoming a philosophy in Jonathan Edwards, passing through Emerson, producing the fastidious refinement and aloofness of the
chief American writers, and, as the coherent ideals and beliefs
of Transcendentalism gradually faded out, resulting in the final
unreality of most contemporary American culture; and on
the other hand the current of catchpenny opportunism, originating in the practical shifts of Puritan life, becoming a
philosophy in Franklin, passing through the American humorists, and resulting in the atmosphere of contemporary business
life.

Thus the literature of the seventeenth century in America
is composed in equal parts, one may fairly say, of piety and
advertisement; and the revered chronicles of New England
had the double effect of proving how many pilgrim souls had
been elected to salvation and of populating with hopeful immigrants a land where heaven had proved so indulgent.

For three generations the prevailing American character
was compact in one type, the man of action who was also the
man of God. Not until the eighteenth century did the rift
appear and with it the essential distinction between "Highbrow" and "Lowbrow." It appeared in the two philosophers,
Jonathan Edwards and Benjamin Franklin, who share the
eighteenth century between them. In their amazing purity of
type and in the apparent incompatibility of their aims they
determined the American character as a racial fact, and after

them the Revolution became inevitable. Channing, Lincoln, Emerson, Whitman, Grant, Webster, Garrison, Edison, Mr. Rockefeller, Mrs. Eddy[3] are all, in one way or another, permutations and combinations of these two grand progenitors of the American character.

Strange that at the very outset two men should have arisen so aptly side by side and fixed the poles of our national life! For no one has ever more fully and typically than Jonathan Edwards displayed the infinite inflexibility of the upper levels of the American mind, nor any one more typically than Franklin the infinite flexibility of its lower levels.

The intellect of Jonathan Edwards was like the Matterhorn, steep, icy, and pinnacled. At its base were green slopes and singing valleys filled with all sorts of little tender wild-flowers —for he was the most lovable of men; but as soon as the ground began to rise in good earnest all this verdurous life came to an abrupt end: not one green or living thing could subsist in that frozen soil, on those pale heights. It was the solitude of logic that led him to see in destiny only a wrathful tyrant and a viper's trail in the mischievous ways of little boys and girls.

I confess to an old-time and so to speak aboriginal affection for this man, so gently solicitous to make up in his daily walk and conversation for the ferocious impulsions of that brain of his. He was even the most romantic of men, as I thought once, and I well remember that immense old musty book of his theology covered with mildew, with its desert of tiny print, which I carried out with me into the fields and read, in the intervals of birdnesting, under the hedgerows and along the borders of the wood: the sun fell for the first time on those clammy old pages and the pallid thoughts that lay in them, and the field-sparrows all about were twittering in a language which, to tell the truth, was no more unintelligible to me. But everything that springs from solitude shines by a light of its own, and Manfred among the Alps was not more lonely than

---

[3] Mary Baker Eddy (1821-1910). The founder of the Christian Science Church whose doctrines, published in *Science and Health* (1875), stress mental healing.

this rapt scholar in his parsonage among the Indians.

There are, however, solitudes and solitudes. Great poets and fruitful thinkers live apart themselves, perhaps, but they have society and the ways of men in their blood. They recollect in tranquillity, as it were, gestate, live again, and reveal the last significance of active generations rich in human stuff, in experience, in emotion, in common reason. Nothing like this existed in the background of Jonathan Edwards, no profound and complex race-life. Intellect in him, isolated and not responsible to the other faculties, went on its way unchecked; and he was able to spin those inept sublimities of his by subtracting from his mind every trace of experience, every touch of human nature as it really was among his innocent countryfolk.

Notoriously, of course, our great Dr. Franklin simplified existence in precisely the opposite way; for the opposite of unmitigated theory is unmitigated practice. Who can deny that in *Poor Richard* the "Lowbrow" point of view for the first time took definite shape, stayed itself with axioms, and found a sanction in the idea of "policy"? It emerges there full-fledged, in its classical form, a two-dimensional wisdom, a wisdom shorn of overtones, the most accommodating wisdom in the world.

Were ever two views of life more incompatible than these? What indeed could Poor Richard have in common with an Angry God?

And what can Mr. Bryan have in common with political economy?

III

"Our people," said Emerson, "have their intellectual culture from one country and their duties from another." In how many spheres that phrase can be applied! Desiccated culture at one end and stark utility at the other have created a deadlock in the American mind, and all our life drifts chaotically between the two extremes. Consider, for example, our use of the English language. Literary English in England is naturally a living speech, which occupies the middle of the field and expresses the flesh and blood of an evolving race. Literary English with us is a tradition, just as Anglo-Saxon law with us is a tradition. They persist not as the normal expressions of a race, the essential fibre of which is permanently Anglo-Saxon, but through prestige and precedent and the will and habit of a dominating class largely out of touch with a national fabric unconsciously taking form "out of school." No wonder that our literary style is "pure," that our literary tradition, our tradition especially in oratory and political prose, retains the spirit of the eighteenth century. But at what a cost! At the cost of expressing a popular life which bubbles with energy and spreads and grows and slips away ever more and more from the control of tested ideas, a popular life "with the lid off," which demands an intellectual outlet and finds one in slang, journalism, and unmannerly fiction.

After seventy years Carlyle's well-known appeal to Emerson still applies to the spirit of American culture: "For the rest, I have to object still (what you will call objecting against the Law of Nature) that we find you a speaker indeed, but as it were a *Soliloquizer* on the eternal mountain-tops only, in vast solitudes where men and their affairs lie all hushed in a very dim remoteness; and only *the man* and the stars and the earth are visible—whom, so fine a fellow seems he, we could perpetually punch into, and say, 'Why won't you come and help us then? We have terrible need of one man like you down among us! It is cold and vacant up there; nothing paintable but rainbows and emotions; come down and you shall do life-pictures, passions, facts. . . .' "[4]

And what a comment on the same utterance that at this very moment an amiable New Englander should have been painting in Parson Wilbur and Hosea Biglow,[5] respectively, unconscious of any tragic symbolism of things to come, the unbridgeable chasm between literate and illiterate America!

[4] Letter, Carlyle to Emerson, 3 November 1844, *The Correspondence of Emerson and Carlyle*, ed. Joseph Slater (New York, 1964), pp. 370-371.

[5] Parson Wilbur is the pedant editor of Hosea Biglow's shrewd, homespun Yankee poems. The characters are James Russell Lowell's comic creations in *The Biglow Papers* (1846, 1848) which were provoked by Lowell's opposition to the Mexican War. He saw the war as a political maneuver to extend slave territory.

Morally, no doubt, in Jaalam, they understood one another and got along very well, as Yankees will. But in Chicago?

IV

To pass now from the social to the personal question, since the question is at bottom a personal one, let us figure to ourselves how this divergence comes about and how it is that our educational system instead of creating what President Eliot[6] calls a "serviceable fellowship" between theory and practice, tends to set them apart and to confirm us all either in the one extreme or in the other.

Let us figure to ourselves a typical American who has grown up, as an American typically does grow up, in a sort of orgy of lofty examples, moralized poems, national anthems, and baccalaureate sermons; until he is charged with all manner of ideal purities, ideal honorabilities, ideal femininities, flag-wavings and skyscrapings of every sort;—until he comes to feel in himself the hovering presence of all manner of fine potentialities, remote, vaporous, and evanescent as a rainbow. All this time, it can fairly be said, he has not been taught to associate himself personally with ends even much lower than these, he has not been taught that life is a legitimate progress toward spiritual or intellectual ends at all, his instincts of acquisition, pleasure, enterprise, and desire have in no way been linked and connected with disinterested ends; he has had it very firmly embedded in his mind that the getting of a living is not a necessity incidental to some higher and more disinterested end, but that it is the prime and central end in things, and as a corollary to this he has been encouraged to assume that the world is a stamping-ground for every un-trained, greedy, and aggressive impulse in him, that, in short, society is fair prey for what he can get out of it.

Let us imagine that, having grown up in this way, he is sent to college. And here, in order to keep the case a typical

6 Charles William Eliot (1834-1926). President of Harvard from 1869 to 1909; under his long regime Radcliffe College was established, the elective system introduced and the reputation and influence of Harvard greatly increased.

one, we shall have to exercise a little discrimination in the choice of a university.

It will not be Harvard, because the ideal of Harvard, as I shall point out, is not a typically modern American ideal. Nor will it be one of the modern utilitarian universities, which have no ideal at all. It will be any one of the others; and when I say this I mean that each of the others is in one way or another a development of the old American country college; its ideal, its experience, its tradition spring out of and lead one back to that. Now among these old colleges Harvard might have been figured as an ever-developing, ever-liberaliz ing catholicism, of which they were all sectarian offshoots, established on a principle of progressive theological fragmen- tation, each one defending an orthodoxy its predecessors had outworn or violently setting up in defense of some private orthodoxy of its own. They founded themselves each on a remote dogma or system of dogma as their central and suffi- cient basis, and all their wheels turned in relation to the central theological dynamo. In a sense of course this was true also of Harvard, but with a marked difference. For the theologians who founded Harvard were men of action as well; in the seventeenth century a New England minister was also a poli- tician, and the education of ministers for which Harvard was mainly established implied an education for public affairs as well, an education for society, so far as the word society can be used in connection with the early Puritans at all. Thus at the outset the founders of Harvard drove in the wedge of secularism: Harvard had from the beginning a sort of national basis, at least among New Englanders, and its dogmatic structure consequently reflected and shifted with and accom- modated itself to the currents of national thought. Remaining in touch with society, it educated to a certain extent, relatively to an extraordinary extent, the social function of its students; and it is thus no accident that so large a proportion of the political, the literary, and the scientific life of America has sprung from it. But in the eighteenth century the conditions under which Harvard was established had ceased to be true. The minister was no longer a man of affairs,—he was a stark theologian, and usually of a type which the majority of his flock had outgrown. Yale, Princeton, and virtually all the other typically American colleges were founded by men of this type. Jonathan Edwards may figure for them all; the motive which led him to become the president of Princeton being precisely that his flock in Connecticut could no longer see the anger of God eye to eye with him. Already in his time the fathers and mothers of young America had submitted to the charms of *Poor Richard's Almanac*—they had themselves for the most part become inveterately "Lowbrow"; but they seem to have believed that an Angry God might still be a good influence over young America himself.

To return now to the typical case with whom we began, let us imagine that he makes a typical choice and goes to a typical university. Having arrived there will he be confronted with an Angry God, or any sort of direct theological dogma? By no means. But there will have remained in the air a certain fragrance and vibration, as if an ideal had passed that way and not stayed, there will be intangible whispers and seductions, there will be a certain faint, rarefied, remote, but curiously pervasive and insistent influence—like the sound of an Æolian harp or the recollection of Plato in some uncouth slum; there will be memories and portraits of many an old metaphysician, white, unearthly, fragile. It will all seem very much as if, the significance of these remote dogmas having evaporated, only the remoteness, in a way, had remained.

One would have to be very insensitive not to feel the quite unbalancing charm of this quality—so different from its comparatively robust Oxford parallel—in the old New England colleges, as in Princeton, Yale, and the other universities which have developed out of them; but one cannot help feeling also, I think, something vaguely Circean in it. And in fact, given the preliminary method of bringing up which I have sketched, what will be its effect in the case we are considering? Suddenly confronted during four years with just this remote influence of ideals, out of which the intellectual structure has evaporated and which never possessed a social structure, will he not find them too vague, too intangible, too unprepared for to be incorporated into his nature? Certainly ideals of this kind, in this way presented, in this way prepared for, cannot enrich life, because they are wanting in all the elements of personal contact. Wholly dreamlike and vaporous, they end by breeding nothing but cynicism and chagrin; and in becoming permanently catalogued in the mind as impracticable they lead to a belief in the essential unreality of ideas as well.

Indeed there is nothing so tragic and so ominous as the familiar saying that college is the happiest time of one's life. Yet perhaps a majority of college men think of their college life in this way. They deliberately put their Golden Age behind them—and, as things are, they know it is behind them. But consider what a comment this is on the American university itself,—a place, one can fairly say, where ideals are cherished precisely because they are ineffectual, because they are ineptly and mournfully beautiful, because they make one cynical, because they make life progressively uninteresting, because, practically and in effect, they are illusions and frauds and infinitely charming lies. There surely is the last and the most impenetrable stronghold of Puritanism, refined to the last degree of intangibility, which persists in making the world a world inevitably sordid, basely practical, and whose very definition of the ideal consequently is, that which has no connection with the world!

Thus far then for our typical university graduate. He has been consistently educated in twin values which are incompatible. The theoretical atmosphere in which he has lived is one that bears no relation to society, the practical atmosphere in which he has lived bears no relation to ideals. Theory has become for him permanently a world in itself, a kind of *ding an sich;* practice has become simply a world of dollars.

Now supposing he has already become interested in the study, let us say, of economics, three paths are open to him: either he can give himself once for all to economics, or he can go the way of the flesh, i.e., into business, or he can hesitate between the two, becoming an economist for the time being and eventually going into business.

It is just here, at the moment of choice, that the want of ballast in his education becomes manifest. There is nothing for him but to lurch violently to the one extreme or the other; and this, according as there is in his nature a crude preponderance either of intellect or of the sense of action, he does. If he is preponderantly intellectual he adopts the first course; that is to say, he dedicates himself to the service of a type of economic theory that bears no relation to this wicked world at all, leaving all the good people who are managing the economic practice of society (and, for the want of him, chiefly muddling it)—leaving all these good people to talk nonsense in the wilderness. If he is preponderantly a man of action, he adopts the second course; that is to say, he dedicates himself to the service of a private end which knows nothing of theory, which is most cynically contemptuous of ideals, flatulent or other, and which is precisely as indifferent to the economic life of society as the professor of economics himself.

Well, good riddance to both of them, one might be inclined to say, except that on second thought the professor and the business man between them hold in their hands so great a part of human destiny. It is the third case that is really interesting and really tragic. For just so far as our typical student is a normal man, just so far as he shares the twin elements of intellect and action in equal parts, just so far will he be on the fence. The probability is that in this case he will become a professor for as long as he can stand it and then burst into business and become a first-rate millionaire as quickly as possible. The sense of action in him will rebel against the sense of theory and finding in theory no basis for action, no relation to action, will press him into a fresh life where the theoretical side of his nature will at least be of some slight use in furthering his own aggrandizement, and that alone.

V

Naturally the question of economics is only typical. Any branch of human activity which is represented by professors at all—and which is not?—would serve as well. Human nature itself in America exists on two irreconcilable planes, the plane of stark theory and the plane of stark business; and in the back of its mind is heaven knows what world of poetry, hidden away, too inaccessible, too intangible, too unreal in fact ever to be brought into the open, or to serve, as the poetry of life rightly should serve, in harnessing thought and action together, turning life into a distinterested adventure.

Argue which way you will, from the individual to society or from society to the individual, it is the same. Just as the American attitude toward the State has been the attitude of an oratorical and vague patriotism which has not based itself on a concrete interest in public affairs; just as, in consequence of this, the "invisible government" of business has swept in and taken possession of the field and become the actual government under which we live, overgrowing and supplanting the government we recognize: so also in the case of the individual; the cherishing of ideals that are simply unmapped regions to which nobody has the least intention of building roads, the baccalaureate sermons that are no just, organic comment on the educational system that precedes them—precisely these themselves strengthen the forces from below; the invisible government of self-interest, built up carefully from the beginning by maxim and example, fills the vacuum a disinterested purpose ought to have occupied.

Twenty, even ten years, ago, it would have been universally assumed that the only hope for American society lay in somehow lifting the "Lowbrow" elements in it to the level of the "Highbrow" elements. But that quickening realism which belongs to contemporary thought makes it plain on the one hand that the mere idealism of university ethics, the mere loftiness of what is called culture, the mere purity of so-called Good Government left to themselves, not only produce a glassy inflexible priggishness on the upper levels which paralyzes life; but that the lower levels have a certain humanity, flexibility, tangibility which are indispensable in any programme: that Tammany has quite as much to teach Good Government as Good Government has to teach Tammany, that slang has quite as much in store for so-called culture as culture has for slang—that the universities, while emphatically not becoming more "practical," must base their disinterestedness on human, moral, social, artistic, and personal needs, impulses, and experience.

But society cannot become humane of itself; and it is for

this reason that the movements of Reform are so external and so superficial. The will to reform springs from a conviction *ex post facto,* and is strictly analogous to the frame of mind of business men who retire at sixty and collect pictures. Nothing so exemplifies it as the spectacle of Mr. Carnegie spending three quarters of his life in providing steel for battleships and the last quarter of it in trying to abolish war. He himself surely has not been conscious of any inward revolution; plainly with him as with others the will to create disorder and the will to reform it spring from the same inner condition of mind. The impetus of Reform is evidently derived from the hope that a sufficient number of reformers can be trained and brought into the field to match the forces of business—the one group cancelling the other group. The ideal of Reform, in short, is the attainment of zero.

Nothing is more absurd than to attack business as such. But the motives and circumstances of business vary from age to age, and there is a world of difference between industry conceived as a social process and trade conceived as a private end. A familiar distinction between the nineteenth century and the twentieth is that the problem of civilization is no longer the problem of want but the problem of surplus. Roughly speaking, the hereditary American class—the prevailing class, I mean—is faced with the problem not of making money but of spending it; the prevailing American class is in a position of relative, but relatively great, economic freedom, and under these conditions it is plain that in them economic self-assertion ("enterprise") has become to a large extent a vicious anachronism. But force of habit, the sheer impetus and groundswell of an antiquated pioneering spirit find them with no means of personal outlet except a continued economic self-assertion on the one hand, and on the other a reckless and essentially impersonal overflow of surplus wealth which takes the form of doing what everybody else does, and doing it as much more so as possible.

Because it was for so long the law of the tribe economic self-assertion still remains to most Americans a sort of moral obligation; while self-fulfillment still looks like a pretty word for selfishness. Yet self-fulfillment through science, or literature, or mechanics, or industry itself—the working out of one's own personality, one's own inventiveness through forms of activity that are directly social, as all these activities *are* directly social, gives a man, through his very sociality, through the feeling he has that as a good workman he is cooperating with all other good workman, a life-interest apart from his rewards. And just as this principle becomes generally diffused and understood the incentive is withdrawn from economic self-assertion, a relative competence being notoriously satisfying to the man whose prime end is the fulfilling of his own creative instincts; and the wealth of the world is already socialized.

You cannot have personality, you cannot have the expressions of personality so long as the end of society is an impersonal end like the accumulation of money. For the individual whose personal end varies too greatly from the end of the mass of men about him not only suffers acutely and becomes abnormal, he actually cannot accomplish anything healthily fine at all. The best and most disinterested individual can only express the better intuitions and desires of his age and place;—there must be some sympathetic touch between him and some visible or invisible host about him, since the mind is a flower that has an organic connection with the soil it springs from.

The only serious approach to society is the personal approach, and what I have called the quickening realism of contemporary social thought is at bottom simply a restatement for the mass of commercialized men, and in relation to issues which directly concern the mass of men as a whole, of those personal instincts that have been the essence of art, religion, literature—the essence of personality itself—since the beginning of things. It will remain of the least importance to patch up politics, to become infected with social consciousness, or to do any of the other easy popular contemporary things unless, in some way, personality can be made to release itself on a middle plane between vaporous idealism and self-interested practicality; unless, in short, self-fulfillment as an ideal can be substituted for self-assertion as an ideal. On the economic plane that implies socialism; on every other plane it implies something which a majority of Americans in our day certainly do not possess—an object in living.

VI

It is perhaps just as well that Cervantes lived and died in Spain three hundred years ago. Had he been born an American of the twentieth century he might have found the task of satire an all too overwhelming one. Yet his fable, which has its personal bearing in all men always, has in America a social bearing that is perhaps unique. Don Quixote is the eternal "Highbrow" under a polite name, just as Sancho Panza is the eternal "Lowbrow"; and if the adorable Dulcinea is not a vision of the night and a daily goal in the mind of our professors, then there is no money in Wall Street. One admits the charm of both extremes, the one so fantastically above, the other so fantastically below the level of right reason; to have any kind of relish for muddled humanity is necessarily to feel the charm of both extremes. But where is all that is real, where is personality and all its works, if it is not essentially somewhere, somehow, in some not very vague way, between?

II. "Our Poets"

I

It is a principle that shines impartially on the just and on the unjust that once you have a point of view all history will back you up. Everything no doubt depends upon evidence; and considering the case which has been outlined in the last chapter, an appeal to American literature, if literature really does record the spirit of a people, is an appeal that leads, I think, to evidence of a material sort.

Something, in American literature, has always been wanting—everyone, I think, feels that. Aside from the question of talent, there is not, excepting Walt Whitman, one American writer who comes home to a modern American with that deep, moving, shaking impact of personality for which one turns to the abiding poets and writers of the world. A certain density, weight, and richness, a certain poignancy, a "something far more deeply interfused," simply is not there.

Above all, the Americanism of our old writers appears to have had no faculty of development and adaptation. With the death of Emerson, Lowell, Holmes and their group something in the American mind really did come to an end. The generation which has gone by since then is a generation which has produced no indisputable leader of thought and letters, which has destroyed the coherence of the old American circle of ideas, and left us at the height of the second immigration among the chaotic raw materials of a perhaps altogether new attitude of mind.

It is, in fact, the plain, fresh, homely, impertinent, essentially innocent old America that has passed; and in its passing the allegory of Rip Van Winkle has been filled with a new meaning. Henry Hudson and his men, we see, have begun another game of bowls, and the reverberations are heard in many a summer thunderstorm; but they have been miraculously changed into Jews, Lithuanians, Magyars, and German socialists. Rip is that old innocent America which has fallen asleep and which hears and sees in a dream the movement of peoples, the thunder of alien wants. And when after twenty years he awakens again, stretches his cold rheumatic limbs, and discovers the long white beard, he will once more set out for home; but when he arrives will he be recognized?

What emotions pass through an hereditary American when he calls to mind the worthies who figured in that ubiquitous long paneled group of "Our Poets" which occupied once so prominent a place in so many domestic interiors? Our Poets were commonly six in number, kindly, gray-bearded, or otherwise grizzled old men. One recalls a prevailing six, with variations. Sometimes a venerable historian was included, a novelist or so, and even Bayard Taylor.[1]

---

[1] Bayard Taylor (1825-1878). Poet, parodist, travel writer and journalist; his translation of Goethe's *Faust* (1870-1871) brought him academic recognition and, in 1878, the post of minister to Germany.

Nothing could make one feel so like a prodigal son as to look at that picture. So much for the first glance, the first quick impression after one has come home to it from the far wanderings of an ordinary profane existence. But more complicated emotions supervene. What a world within a world that picture summons up! Frankly, we feel in ourselves, we are no longer so fortunate as in those days. It could really have been said of us then, as it cannot now be said at all, that as a folk we had won a certain coherence, a certain sort of ripeness in the better part of ourselves, which was reflected in the coherence of our men of letters. Whittier, for example, was a common basis, and a very sweet and elevating basis, for a national programme of emotions the like of which no poet since his time has been able to compass. One recalls that fact, so full of meaning; and then, deep down, a forgotten world sweeps back over one, a world of memory, sentiment, and association, a world of influences the most benign—like a mournful autumn wind stirring in forsaken places. . . . But sooner or later the ordinary profane existence reasserts itself; and we have to put it to ourselves with equal frankness—has any one of these men, or any one of these influences, the power at bottom to make it any less profane? The most beautiful and benign sentiment in the world will not do so unless it has in it that which grips in some way at the root of personality. . . . Then it is we feel how inadequate, faded, and out of touch they are.

It is of no use to go off into a corner with American literature, as most of the historians have done,—in a sulky, private sort of way, taking it for granted that if we give up world values we are entitled to our own little domestic rights and wrongs, criticism being out of place by the fireside. "But oh, wherever else I am accounted dull," wrote Cowper in one of his letters, "let me pass for a genius at Olney." This is the method of the old-fashioned camp in American criticism, just as the method of the contemporary camp is the method of depreciative comparison with better folk than our own.

The only fruitful approach is the personal approach, and to me at least Thoreau, Emerson, Poe, and Hawthorne are possessions forever. This does not alter the fact that if my soul were set on the accumulation of dollars not one of them would have the power to move me from it. And this I take to be a suggestive fact. Not one of them, not all of them, have had the power to move the soul of America from the accumulation of dollars; and when one has said this one has arrived at some sort of basis for literary criticism.

Plainly enough, during what has been called the classical period of American literature, the soul of America did not want to be moved from the accumulation of dollars; plainly enough the pioneering instinct of economic self-assertion was the law of the tribe. And if the New England writers were homogeneous with the American people as no other group, scarcely any other individual, has been since, it is equally plain that they themselves and all their works must have accorded with the law of the tribe. The immense, vague cloud-canopy of idealism which hung over the American people during the nineteenth century was never permitted, in fact, to interfere with the practical conduct of life.

Never permitted, I say, though it is a more accurate explanation that, being essentially impersonal itself, the essence of this idealism lay in the very fact that it had and could have no connection with the practical conduct of life. The most successful and famous writers, Bryant and Longfellow, for example, promoted this idealism, being, so far as one can see, generally satisfied with the ordinary practices of society: they tacitly accepted the peculiar dualism that lies at the root of our national point of view. Emerson's really equivocal individualism on the one hand asserted the freedom and self-reliance of the spirit and on the other justified the unlimited private expediency of the business man. And as a suggestive corollary to all this, the two principal artists in American literature, Poe and Hawthorne, were out of touch with society as few other artists in the world had been before: to their contemporaries they seemed spectral and aloof, scarcely human, and it could easily be shown that the reaction upon their work of a world to them essentially unreal is equally marked.

Granting these facts, and granting the still more significant fact of the absence from our literature of that deep, moving, shaking impact of personality which would have brought it into more permanent touch with American life, I do not see how we can escape the general axiom: that a society whose end is impersonal and anti-social cannot produce an ideal reflex in literature which is personal and social, and conversely, that the ideal reflex in literature produced by such a society will be unable to educate its own personal and social instincts. In effect, an examination of American literature will show, I think, that those of our writers who have possessed a vivid personal genius have been paralyzed by the want of a social background, while those who have possessed a vivid social genius have been equally unable to develop their own personalities.

II

And here at the outset a distinction must be drawn between what may be called the literature of necessity and absolute literature. It is perfectly plain that in one aspect literature is a simple cog in the machinery of life. The first generation of American writers were like prudent women who, having moved into a new house, energetically set to work laying down carpets, papering the walls, cutting and hanging the most appropriate window-curtains, and pruning the garden— making it, in short, a place of reasonable charm and contentment.

Than Washington Irving, for example, no one was ever more satisfied with things as they are; prosperity in others aroused in him the most benignant emotions, and there is a description by him of a smiling river farm with its fat hens and waddling pigs which rises to a sort of placid ecstasy—in recollection one confuses the pigs with little cherubim, and as to the farm itself one wonders why (or indeed whether) angels have not settled there.

The effect of this idyllic treatment is precisely that of the first warm blaze in a newly constructed hearth. It takes away the sense of chill; the room becomes at once cozy and cheerful, and we enjoy the prospect of spending an evening in it.

That is at least a principal element in the work of Irving,

Cooper, Bryant, and Longfellow. When these men ceased writing the towns, the woods, the wild-flowers, even the bare and meagre history of America were clothed with memories and associations. It was possible to feel them all, and even to muse upon them. The characters of Cooper lighted up a little fringe of the black uncut forest; they linked the wilderness with our own immemorial human world, just as the little figures Piranesi put in his engravings not only give the scale of his Roman ruins and relate them to the observer's eye but also arouse the sense of historical connections, the sense of pathos and of man's destiny.

When they wrote of Europe their essential motive was the same as when they wrote of America. Irving's English essays at bottom, as he himself declares, were deliberately intended to place England and America on a basis of mutual good will—a motive, in the proper sense, political. Longfellow never forgot in Europe that he was on leave of absence, and that in gathering speciments he was to bear in mind the soil to which they were to be transplanted. There was nothing in heaven or earth he was not able to prune and fertilize into harmony with the New England temperature; and who will deny that he in turn altered that temperature, warmed and gladdened it,—that he came back as a kind of gulf stream to our frost-bitten civilization, which has been kindlier ever since?

III

But out of this essential motive of the first generation of American writers a second motive arises. They were moralists, they were shot through and through with all manner of baccalaureate ideals; and this fact opens them to a different sort of treatment. For this let Longfellow and Bryant suffice, for they are typical.

Longfellow is to poetry what the barrel-organ is to music; approached critically he simply runs on, and there is an end to the matter. But nobody dreams of criticizing Longfellow from the point of view of "mere literature": the human head and the human heart alike revolt from that. His personal sanction is rightly a traditional one, and the important thing is to see him as a beautifully typical figure and to see just what he typifies.

To Longfellow the world was a German picture-book, never detaching itself from the softly colored pages. He was a man of one continuous mood: it was that of a flaxenhaired German student on his *wanderjahr* along the Rhine, under the autumn sun—a sort of expurgated German student—ambling among ruined castles and reddening vines, and summoning up a thousand bright remnants of an always musical past. His was an eminently Teutonic nature of the old school, a pale-blue melting nature; and white hair and grandchildren still found him with all the confused emotion, the charming sadness, the indefinite high proposals of seventeen;—perhaps it was because they had never been opposed, never put to the test in that so innocently successful existence of his that they persisted without one touch of disillusion, one moment of chagrin.

But frankly what preparation is a life like this for the poet whose work it is to revivify a people? The most telling thing I know about Longfellow is that, having remarked that "Carlyle was one of those men who sacrifice their happiness to their work," he himself was well content in later life to surrender the greater part of his time and energies to writing autographs and entertaining children. Here certainly the personal sanction oversteps the mark, just as it does in the case of indulgent politicians who exhibit their gratitude and warmheartedness by feathering the nests of all their friends and cousins. Though Longfellow had an unerring eye for the "practical application" that lurks in every shred of romance, totally unable to elude the agile moralist, the value of his moral promptings is just in proportion to the pressure behind them—and where was the pressure? His morals and ideals were, in fact, simply a part of the pretty picture-book, just as they are at seventeen: if they had not been so they would never have been laid on the shelf.

But the "practical application" cannot be dismissed in this way; and if the personal sanction is disarming in relation to Longfellow, the case is otherwise with Bryant, a virile, hardheaded man, whose memory can afford many a blow. To

Bryant the moral ending was no half absent-minded flourish of the color brush—it was a tough Puritan reality; and Bryant's use of the moral ending is emblematic not merely, as in Longfellow's case, of the vacuity and impermanence of so much American idealism, but also of the corollary of these —the failure of Americans in general to develop and express their personality in and through their work.

Bluntly, the use of a moral ending means that the poet is unwilling to leave his effect to the emotion conveyed in the poem itself; he must needs intellectualize this emotion at the close, and show you that this emotion is only used, like cheese in a mouse-trap, to entice the reader into a usually disagreeable fact, for which the whole exists. Now this procedure is full of meaning. For not the emotion, not the expression of personality, but the ulterior object is the essential issue in the mind of the poet: not life, but success, or salvation. And the same principle operates here, and renders the result equally barren, as in work which is done mainly for the ulterior object of making money, in relation which exists for the ulterior object of saving one's soul, in thought which exists merely for the ulterior object of proving something. The excellence and fruitfulness of anything consists in our loving and enjoying it. Real poetry springs from the assumption that the spectacle is its own reward, that feeling, happy or unhappy, is final: it is concerned, as Shelley pointed out, not with effects and applications, which are temporary, but with causes, which are permanent. The moral ending is simply a rigid and impersonal intellectualization of life, which is, consequently, out of touch with the motives that really retermine men.

For this reason Bryant was never a personality; he was, to be exact, a somewhat eminent personage. After his eighteenth year he was miraculously changed, not into stone, but into wood,—he was as bald, as plain, as immovable, so to say, as an old settee. He had no elasticity, no sense of play either in words, ideas, or emotions; two or three poetic forms sufficed him; even as a journalist he was abstract. One sees him during sixty years perambulating Broadway with that old blue cotton umbrella of his, the very picture of a spare old

Puritan patriarch, with his big muscular joints, a hardy perennial. And all about him one sees that spry, flimsy New York of the forties and fifties and sixties—the New York of "Nothing to Wear" and N. P. Willis.[2] It is these gulfs of contrast which let one into the secret of American humor.

Yes, this old man with his palsied gift, who had for two generations been pursued by glimpses of the grave but who had embalmed within him an incomparable vigor and who, past eighty, put Homer into English—this old man is himself Homeric (with a difference) amid that spawn of decadent Byronism which made up the so-called Knickerbocker school. New York has never possessed dignity—one loves the many-headed beast for a thousand other reasons than that; but it has achieved a sort of Napoleonic right to despise dignity, and it has come to possess its secrets. In the thirties and forties it possessed no secrets at all—it was the centre of an ingenuous America which had only just learned to be worldly, which the lightest zephyr from London or Paris set fluttering, over which every ripple of fashion broke into a spray of tinsel.

IV

So much is necessary to give Poe what he badly needs, a naturalistic setting: Poe himself, who emerges from this New York of his time like a wreck at sea with its black spars etched against a sort of theatrical sunset. Ironical and sinister as he is, he is by no means "out of space, out of time," if by space we mean New York and by time the second quarter of the nineteenth century. The little imitation Byrons who swarmed about him write of haunted Gothic castles, Poe wrote the *House of Usher;* Bianca, Giordano, Ermengarde, Elfrida, Asthene, Zophiel were the human properties of their prose and verse, scarcely to be distinguished from the Madeleines and Eleanores, the Eulalies and Annabels, the Israfels and Al Aaraafs of Poe; they also lived in a world of moan and a world of moonlight; madness, irreparable farewells, dun-

---

[2] Nathaniel Parker Willis (1806-1867). Popular editor and journalist, associated with the *American Monthly Magazine,* the *Mirror,* the *Home Journal* and other similar publications.

geons, assignations, premature burials, hidden treasures, exotic musical instruments, prophetic night birds—these things were of the time and very particularly, since New York provided them with an additional unreality, of the place.

Poe took this bric-à-brac seriously—that is always a distinction and it is Poe's distinction. The tacit conventionalities of the romantic epoch became in him objects of a fierce intellectual concentration. In the comfortable safety of good and abundant food, friendly talk, substantial occupation, his contemporaries amused themselves with spectres, Oriental mysteries, hasheesh, and madness: Poe was the delirium which followed. He was a Byron without scope of action and without purging emotions.

Superficially at least he was not conscious of being out of his element. In those critical essays in which he is so accessible and so honest and has so many disagreeable things to say about his contemporaries it is never the false taste, never the epoch which displeases him. He likes *The Dying Rosebud's Lament* by Mrs. Fanny Osgood; what irritates him is bad grammar, bad rhymes, and plagiarism. Nor is there the least indication that he thought America provincial, or bourgeois, or depressing to a man of talent. That indeed is an element in the strength of all the American writers of the old school; an instinct of self-preservation kept them at home in spirit; so much of the missionary element was of the texture of what they had to say that a tinge of the cosmopolitan would have neutralized their best effects, would have rendered them personally, as it has certainly rendered Lowell, a little characterless, a little indistinct. But it is a rather disconcerting fact in relation to the theory that Poe is a kind of supersensual enigma, who might have lived with equal results in Babylon or Sioux City. At his second-best, in prose and verse, he is precisely at one both in tone and execution with his intellectual surroundings. At his best it is this outworn bric-à-brac which is transfigured, just as the suburban bibliolatry of England is transfigured in the drawings of Blake. The important thing is to consider what this bric-à-brac is transfigured into, and why, and what it means.

Since the days of the alchemists no one has produced more

than Poe the effects of damnation, no one has been more conscious of being damned. In his pages the breath of life never stirs: crimes occur which do not reverberate in the human conscience, there is laughter which has no sound, there is weeping without tears, there is beauty without love, there is love without children, trees grow which bear no fruit, flowers which have no fragrance,—it is a silent world, cold, blasted, moon-struck, sterile, a devil's heath. Only a sensation of intolerable remorse pervades it.

Poe is commonly called unreal; it is justly said of him that he never touches the general heart of man, that perhaps of all writers who have lived he has the least connection with human experience. Nothing is more sinister about Poe, for instance, than his tacit acceptance of common morals; you might even say that he is rigidly conventional, if you did not feel that he is conventional merely because the moral world no more exists for him than it exists for a black stone. If you could prove a vicious motive in him, as from certain points of view you can prove a vicious motive in Baudelaire, you might, even in that, establish some fusion between him and the common reason of humankind. Orchids are as much a part of the vegetable kingdom as potatoes, but Poe is an orchid made out of chemicals. Magic is always so; it has the sinister quality of a force operating outside nature, without any relation to human values.

No European can exist without a thousand subterranean relationships; but Americans can so exist, Americans do so exist. Edison, for example, resembles Poe as a purely inventive mathematical intellect and with Edison, as with Poe, you feel that some electric fluid takes the place of blood; you feel that the greatest of inventors cannot be called a scientist at all, that his amazing powers over nature are not based in any philosophical grasp of the laws of nature, that he is in temperament a mechanic rather than a philosopher. His faculty is to that of Darwin, for example, what fish is to flesh,—to the philosophical animal man he is more incomprehensible; and for all the beneficence of his faculty he is himself a kind of prodigious salamander. Poe is a mechanic of the same sort. He has discovered in literature the chemical secret of life. He has produced chemical men, chemical emotions, chemical land-scapes; in *Eureka* he has produced even a chemical philosophy so much like real philosophy that until you try to feel it you will never guess it the most sterile of illusions. For this reason the highly colored effects that light up his tales and his poems are lurid and metallic. The sinister greens and reds and yellows are not, you feel, the flames of honest wood and coal.

To explain all this it is not enough to say that he had a spectral nature, that Emerson and Jonathan Edwards and Hawthorne had spectral natures, that theosophy and Christian Science suggest that this quality is a typical American quality. So much is probably true, but more is required; and to approach Poe is to approach those mysteriously fascinating thaumaturgic elements in nature which are responsible for most of the fraudulent science in the world. One treads warily on the outer edges of psychology, and I suppose it is not accurately known what forces of the mind were involved in medieval witchcraft, in alchemy, in the conception of Mephistopheles. But certainly to the Middle Ages the intelligence in and for itself was felt to be a maleficent force: Mephistopheles himself in the old legends is nothing other than pure intellect, irresponsible and operating independently of life. Necessarily therefore to him faith, love and hope are illusions, and he is the negation of the soul. Above all, it is the secret of creating life for which in the medieval imagination souls were bartered to the devil: one obtained the power of competing with God at the price of a perpetual consciousness of one's own damnation. These are dark ways; but one emerges into the region of knowledge when one affirms that, by their mental twist, witches and alchemists were not convicted by society any more than they were convicted in themselves of having done the unpardonable and the irreparable. And certain it is that Poe experienced in his own imagination this power and this damnation. His haunted face, his driven life, the barren world which he has built and peopled, the horror of his accustomed mood, the inextinguishable obscure remorse that broods in him unite in this fact.

The power he still exerts is an hysterical rather than a literary power, and who can say what it signifies? But one thing seems true, with regard alike to witchcraft, alchemy, and Poe, that the mind can work healthily only when it is essentially in touch with the society of its own age. No matter into what unknown region it presses, it must have a point of relativity in the common reason of its time and place. Poe, having nothing in common with the world that produced him, constructed a little parallel world of his own, withered at the core, a silent comment. It is this that makes him so sterile and so inhuman; and he is himself, conversely, the most menacing indictment of a society which is not also an all-embracing organism.

V

Poe and Hawthorne, certainly, were much more of a common stock in temperament than the New York and New England of their time: the temperament which in Poe is at once vulgarized by vulgar circumstances and pressed up into the intellect is diffused in the character and work of Hawthorne; the harsher lights are neutralized, the familiar world reappears again—but is it the familiar world? Hawthorne's talent is like a phosphorescent pool; you touch it, you move your hand there and a thousand subdued elusive lights dance through it, but before you can fix your eye upon one it has retreated through the clear water, the still depths that in effect are so impenetrable.

No other talent is of so shining a purity as Hawthorne's,—scarcely one other so light, so inevitable, so refined, so much a perfectly achieved intention. He models in mist as the Greeks modeled in marble; his beings take shape in the imagination with a sunlit perfection, but only for a moment; they melt and pass; the air is filled with a phantasmagorical movement of shapes, grouping themselves, putting on corporeality as a garment and at the same time dissolving into the nebulous background. It is a cloud pageant and the clouds are of opal dust. The Puritan conscience in Hawthorne is like some useful but inartistic Roman vessel of glass which has been buried for centuries in the earth and which comes forth at last fragile as a dragonfly's wing, shot through with all the most exquisite colors. He is the most opalescent of writers, and each of his books is an opal of a different type: crimson, purple and emerald cross and recross *The Marble Faun,* and all the most fleeting tints of pale yellow, pale green, and pearly white shimmer through *The Blithedale Romance,* with a single strain of tragic red passing athwart it in the character of Zenobia. A hundred times the world of Hawthorne seems the familiar world, but just as we imagine we have gained a foothold there a wand passes over it, a wall is removed behind it,—it has become a world within a world.

This leads one almost to forget that Hawthorne's range is limited, that his gift is meagre and a little anaemic, that his poetry is not quite the same thing as wisdom. For if like the greatest poets he sees life as a fable, with a fable's infinitely multiplied correspondences, he feels it rather as a phantom than as a man. This being who passed twelve years of his youth in a solitary, close-curtained room, walking abroad only in the twilight or after the sun had set, was himself a phantom in a phantom world. Observe how he treats any one of his typical characters, the elfish little Priscilla, for example. He is describing the rumors current among her neighbors and how they believed that "the sun, at midday, would shine through her; in the first gray of the twilight, she lost all the distinctness of her outline; and, if you followed the dim thing into a dark corner, behold, she was not there." And he goes on in his own person: "There was a lack of human substance in her; it seemed as if, were she to stand up in a sunbeam, it would pass right through her figure, and trace out the cracked and dusty window-panes upon the naked floor." Could anything be more exquisite? Could anything more entirely fail to connect with reality in a practical Yankee world?

It is the natural corollary of all this that Hawthorne himself, as a social being (in his opinions especially—for he did not abstain from opinions), was more than commonly conventional. It is natural that this most deeply planted of American writers, who indicates more than any other the subterranean history of the American character, should have recoiled from every attempt to change, rectify, or spiritualize society; that he should have been incurious of every forward-

looking impulse, a rather more than indifferent anti-abolition-
ist, a much more than indifferent anti-Transcendentalist, and
though actively concerned with politics in one way or another
through his middle and later years always on the uninteresting
side. His talent was a kind of Prospero's isle quite outside
the world he lived in. It was *kept* outside that world by his
own infallible instinct of artistic self-preservation. The comment he puts into the mouth of Miles Coverdale *à propos* of
the "philanthropist" Hollingsworth is really his own comment
on the society in which he found himself: "The moral which
presents itself to my reflections, as drawn from Hollingsworth's
character and errors, is simply this,—that admitting what is
called philanthropy, when adopted as a profession, to be often
useful by its energetic impulse to society at large, it is perilous
to the individual whose ruling passion, in one exclusive channel, it thus becomes. It ruins, or is fearfully apt to ruin, the
heart, the rich juices of which God never meant should be
pressed violently out, and distilled into alcoholic liquor, by an
unnatural process, but should render life sweet, bland, and
gently beneficent, and insensibly influence other hearts and
other lives to the same blessed end."

Hawthorne was right with regard to the society of his
day, but consider what he lost and what we have lost by it.
It is not the business of an artist as such to change society,
and if Hawthorne held aloof from everything that stood for
movement in his time that was the price of being sensitively
organized in an age of rude vague boisterous, dyspeptic,
incoherent causes. The fact that Hawthorne and Poe were the
only two eminent minds of their age to which Transcendentalism was profoundly repugnant is the surest proof that they
alone possessed the full and the right artistic instinct. They
had to do what they could in society as it was—and what
happened? Outwardly accepting it, but having nothing in
common with it, they neither enriched society nor were enriched by it; they were driven to create and inhabit worlds
of their own,—diaphanous private worlds of mist and twilight.

VI

I find it impossible to approach the question of Transcendentalism—the thing itself, and Emerson, Margaret Fuller, *The Dial*, Brook Farm, and all the other permutations and combinations of it—without first of all expelling a persistent spleen, and then submitting myself to long explanations. So much truth, so much talent, so much of the American character is involved in that queer miasmatical group of lunar phenomena, in which philosophy, self-culture, politics, art, social reform, and religion were all mixed up and all felt to be, in some vague way, the same thing. One angel no doubt can stand quite comfortably on the point of a pin, but when a whole battalion of angels attempt to occupy this identical space there is war in heaven.

It is plain enough that the Transcendentalists had no sense of the relationship that exists between theory and practice, between the abstract and the concrete. The world they lived in was an excessively concrete world—a world of isolated facts. The white wooden houses, the farms, the patches of wood, the self-contained villages, each with its town-meeting, the politician, the minister, the lawyer, the merchant were, in fact, very much what Emerson called his own sentences, "infinitely repellent particles;" they had, relatively speaking, nothing in common but the Yankee temperament—and the quality of this common temperament was to be as *un*-common, as individual and as different, as possible. There was no fusion, no operative background of social forces, no unwritten laws. The experience of New England was an experience of two extremes—bare facts and metaphysics: the machinery of self-preservation and the mystery of life. Experience of the world, of society, of art, the genial middle ground of human tradition existed only as an appetite. Painting, sculpture, architecture were represented by engravings; history, travel, world politics, great affairs in general were represented by books. The habit of looking at things in the abstract, native to the old Calvinistic temper, was extended over the range of social and intellectual interests, partly as a result of isolation, partly because of the highly tenuous connection between these interests and the primitive actualities of life as New Englanders knew it.

German philosophy when it was released over the world inevitably came to port in this society, for above everything

else it apeared to let one into the secret of universal experience. If, under the influence of this philosophy, you sat up
late enough at night you could be an Alexander, a Plato, a
Raphael or (in Boston) a Washington Allston, without moving
out of your chair. It is true you gained no territory and
painted no pictures by this method, but you at least placed
yourself at the seat of operations where all these wonderful
things occur.

This accounts for the peculiar flavor of that old New
England culture, so dry, so crisp, so dogmatic, so irritating.
Having entered wholly through the brain in the form of
general propositions, without any checking from observation
or experience, it seems curiously inverted, curiously unreal.
Witness for example that strange far-away tone in which
Emerson so often and so characteristically refers to "Plato
and Paul and Plutarch, Augustine, Spinoza, Chapman, Beau-
mont and Fletcher," or "the remains of Phidias, the Apollo,
the Jove, the paintings and statues of Michael Angelo, the
works of Canova." There would be something quite ludicrous
in this glimpse of St. Paul, Fletcher, Phidias and Spinoza
arm in arm if you felt that Emerson had ever realistically
pictured to himself these men as they individually were. To
him they were all thrice-purified ghosts, ghosts of the printed
page; the associations of the tavern, the synagogue, the drawing-room had fallen from their spirits in the mind of Emerson
as utterly as from their bodies in the grave. To him they were
exceptionally fine manifestations of the Over-Soul; philosophy
like death had leveled them and had, as entirely, removed
them from the region of terrestrial society, literature, and art.
So also in effect when Margaret Fuller comes to the conclusion
that "color is consecrated to passion and sculpture to thought."
Having thus as it were removed the whole question to another
planet, she is able to present us further with a jewel of
criticism like this: "The Prophets and Sibyls are for the
Michael Angelos. The Beautiful is Mr. Allston's dominion"
(statements which make one feel a thousand years old). Yet
this result is inevitable when works of art are approached not
through the eye but through the mind: the element of taste,
the perceptions of sense, once laid aside, there is no gulf

between Phidias and Canova, between Michael Angelo and Washington Allston.

And then consider Emerson's style,—that strange fine ventriloquism, that attenuated voice coming from a great distance, which so often strikes one as a continual falsetto. If it is extremely irritating—and I have known amiable and well-disposed persons to be exasperated by it,—if it is filled with assertions that fairly insist upon being contradicated, it is because so often Emerson is abstract at the wrong times and concrete at the wrong times, because he has so little natural sense of the relation between the abstract and the concrete. Take, for instance, a typical sentence like this: "Archimedes will look through your Connecticut machine, at a glance, and judge of its fitness"—to which the inevitable reply is, that Archimedes will do nothing of the kind: I no more possess a Connecticut machine than Archimedes will put on mortality again to look through it. Is it unfair to literalize these meta-phorical affirmations of Emerson? Of course I understand that to him "Archimedes" is merely a name for that particular aspect of the Over-Soul which broods over machinery, while my "Connecticut machine" means any human device that will serve to exhibit its powers of divination. But a prose which violates the actual overmuch, a prose in which the poetic effect is more than a heightened version of the actual is, I think, a prose one is entitled to find irritating. And furthermore his method of simply announcing as axiomatic what is in his mind is justified only by the possession of a faculty which Emerson does not possess, the faculty of hitting the nail inevitably on the head. Let one example suffice: "Shelley, though a poetic mind, is never a poet. His muse is uniformly imitative; all his poems composite. A good English scholar he is, with ear, taste, and memory; much more, he is a character full of noble and prophetic traits; but imagination, the original, authentic fire of the bard, he has not." Does this really suggest Shelley?

Emerson's artistic impressions are always of this hit-or-miss character; he can write page after page about a painter or a poet without one intelligibly apt utterance. Much the same is true of Carlyle and Ruskin, and for the same reason, that alike they all refer art to an extra-artistic standard. But Carlyle and Ruskin are concrete enough in their own wilful ways, while Emerson is persistently abstract. He never lingers in the bodily world, he is always busy to be off again; and if he takes two or three paces on the earth they only serve to warm him for a fresh aërial adventure. Thus the essay on *Illusions* opens with an account of a day spent in the Mammoth Cave in Kentucky, and after the second sentence he continues in this way: "I lost the light of one day. I saw high domes, and bottomless pits; heard the voice of unseen waterfalls," etc. That is not the tone of descriptive writing; a glamour like that of oratory has fallen over it; phrase by phrase the effect is heightened and generalized under the reader's eye; we see how impatient he is to get to the real business and that the experience is already dimmed and evaporated by the approaching application.

The truth is that Emerson was not interested in human life; he cared nothing for experience or emotion, possessing so little himself. "He generally addressed me as if I were wholly impersonal," writes one of his disciples, who records an observation of Emerson that he "could never turn a dozen pages of *Don Quixote* or Dickens without a yawn." This accounts for the way in which his thoughts inevitably flew for refuge to capital letters, emerging as Demonology, Creeds, Prudence, the Ideal, abstractions all. His point of view was formed very early; all his later books are sprouts from the first one, and there is no indication of growth, imbibition, or excursiveness beyond his original boundaries. If he remained open he was open only as it were at the top; and before he was thirty-five he seems to have acquired that fixed, benignant, musing smile which implies the consciousness of having solved one's own problem and which is usually accompanied by a closure of the five senses.

I say all this without prejudice to Emerson's position in the world of the spirit. There he truly lived and lives, and of all American writers he alone appears to me to have proved the reality of that world and to have given some kind of basis to American idealism.

But Emerson's idealism was double-edged: it was concerned not merely with the spiritual life of the individual, but also with the individual in society, with the "conduct of life." This latter aspect of his teaching was in fact the secret of his contemporary influence. For if the logical result of a thorough-going, self-reliant individualism in the world of the spirit is to become a saint, it is no less true that the logical result of a thorough-going, self-reliant individualism in the world of the flesh is to become a millionaire. And in fact it would be hard to say whether Emerson more keenly relished saintliness or shrewdness. Both qualities he himself possessed in a high degree, as only an American can; and if on one side of his nature he was a most lonely and beautiful seer, the records of his life prove that he lacked none of the sagacity and caution of the true Yankee husbandman. He perfectly combined the temperaments of Jonathan Edwards and Benjamin Franklin;—the upper and lower levels of the American mind are fused in him and each becomes the sanction of the other.

In the long run there is a world of difference between individualism on the spiritual plane and individualism on the economic plane. Were it not so there would be no meaning in the phrase "Stone walls do not a prison make," there would be no meaning in Christianity. And therein consists the beauty and the permanence of Emersonianism. For as the scope of enterprise and self-reliance becomes with every generation more limited, as the generality of men are caught with both feet in the net of economic necessity and are led thereby to seek scope for their initiative in disinterested activity, just so the Emersonian doctrine comes into its own, the Emersonian virtues mount upward and create a self-reliance in the spirit itself. Emersonianism, in short, can only begin to be itself when it has taken its final place on the plane of poetry. In the nineteenth century it was economic as well; it was the voice of just those forces which moved, enlarged, created the American scene; it corresponded to a real freedom of movement and opportunity; pioneers, inventors, men of business, engineers, seekers of adventure found themselves expressed and justified in it. Emerson presided over and gave its tone to this world of infinite social fragmentation and unlimited free will, a world in which—as the presupposition was—everyone started fresh, as if dropped from the sky, where entanglements of heredity and disposition, foreclosures of opportunity, desires and aims which require an already fertilized field for their development, where the whole welter of human history and social complexity had not yet as it were obscured the morning of time.

In all this Emerson was essentially passive. He was the child of his age, and what he did was to give his Yankee instincts free play under the sanction of his Transcendental idealism. He never dreamed of moulding society, and he was incapable of an effective social ideal. Compare him in this respect with Carlyle. The social ideal of Carlyle was the Hero, and what Carlyle meant by the Hero was a particular kind of being whom all Englishmen understand: a creature of flesh and blood who leads men. No doubt Carlyle was absurd enough; but what made him nevertheless a mighty man was that he had the faculty of devising and making intensely real and contagious a social ideal the rudiments of which actually existed in the people he was addressing. The English admire heroism; Carlyle made the Hero a conscious and palpable objective; and his countrymen were stirred through and through. Carlyle counts his disciples from generation to generation; strong men and leaders of men, they go out conquering and ruling creation, and there is hardly a British governor who does not feel the apostolic hands of Carlyle upon his head. Preposterous no doubt they are, having so little of the science and humility that are proper to our late-sprung arboreal species. But who will deny that the doctrine itself has served to make them good human material—for a better doctrine?

What can Emerson show as a social ideal? *Representative Men.* Emerson has chosen six names, five of which are the names of writers, the sixth that of a man of action, Napoleon, whom, let us hope, Young America will not too closely emulate. The social ideal of Emerson, as Froude[3] pointed out, is a sort

---

[3] James Anthony Froude (1818-1894). English historian and editor who moved from involvement with the Oxford Movement to a position of skepticism; his *The Nemesis of Faith* (1849) records this development. A close friend of Carlyle and of Charles Kingsley, he became Carlyle's literary executor and biographer. In 1872-1873 he made a lecture tour of the United States; like most Victorians, his productivity was voluminous.

of composite of the philosopher, the mystic, the sceptic, the poet, the writer, and the man of the world. I wonder what passed through the mind of the American business man of Emerson's day when he heard all these phrases, phrases so unrelated to the springs of action within himself? Did he feel that his profound instincts had been touched and unified, did he see opening before him the line of a disinterested career, lighted up by a sudden dramatization of his own finest latent possibilities, did he not rather, with a degree of reason, say to himself: "These papers will serve very well to improve my mind. I shall read them when I have time"? And did he not thereupon set to work accumulating all the more dollars in order that he might have the more time to cultivate his mind —in legal phrase—after the event?

Looked at from this side Emerson has all the qualities of the typical baccalaureate sermon; and the baccalaureate sermon, as we know, beautiful as it often is, has never been found inconveniently inconsistent with the facts and requirements of business life. A glance at Young America after so many generations of being talked to might well convince one that something is wrong with the baccalaureate sermon. Since the day of Emerson's address on "The American Scholar" the whole of American literature has had the semblance of one vast, all-embracing baccalaureate sermon, addressed to the private virtues of young men. It has been one shining deluge of righteousness, purity, practical mysticism, the conduct of life, and at the end of ninety years the highest ambition of Young America is to be—do I exaggerate?—the owner of a shoe factory. As a result of this exclusive approach through the personal conscience (a conscience by no means connected with disinterested ends and the real development of personality), society in America has permanently stood for two things: in its private aspect as an immense preserve for the exercise of personal virtues like thrift, self-assertion, family provision, nest-feathering in general; in its public aspect as a thing to be coddled with rich gifts (Philanthropy) or scrubbed back to the political intentions of 1776 (Reform).

Emerson is the patron saint of every one of these diverse, chaotic impulses—the gentle, chime-like Emerson who in days to come will sound and shine over a better world.

VII

But since I have spoken of the disciples of Carlyle as arguing the force if not the validity of his social ideal I must add something about the disciples of Emerson, and the personal and social effects of Transcendentalism in American society.

George William Curtis I take to have been the typical Emersonian young man, and I am probably the only person of this generation who has read all his writings. This was the result of having taken a furnished house in California, very new and clean, with little idealistic mottoes hanging from every bracket. Great care had been given to the selection of artistic doorknobs and grass-plaited mats; the cupboards were stuffed with albums of wildflowers and with notebooks filled with nature poems of the minor sort and penciled observations always unfinished and in a vague, wavering hand. An aroma of delicate futility spread from this house, and while gradually becoming conscious of this I discovered everywhere, on the shelves, in the closets, under the albums, the works of George William Curtis: lives, letters, essays, sketches, eulogies, orations. He was plainly the favorite author of the establishment and wherever one sat down for a moment there was George William Curtis at one's elbow.

A dozen or so types exhaust the range of a people, and I have known several duplicates of our milder American Addison. In action he was admirable as a driver out of money-changers—the virginal candor of his type assured that. But he had that pale, earnest cast of mind which always comes from thinking more about what Sir Galahad didn't do than about the object of his quest; and in fact the philosophy of George William Curtis is the most mournful exhibition I know of the inner workings of the Reformer's mind. It is in his social criticism that he betrays the incurable boyishness, the superannuated boyishness of the Emersonian tradition in its main line of influence, and the quantity and quality of his

understanding of society is fairly well summed up in his
energetic though perfectly well-mannered invective against
smoking cigarettes in the presence of ladies.

If Transcendentalism ran to seed in George William Curtis,
what were its personal and social effects at the source? He
would be an ungentle soul who did not feel a certain tenderness
for the Brook Farmers, who did not wish that a really wicked
world had been provided expressly for them to make over.
New England was not wicked: it was only a very just expression of the Yankee temperament, and the reformers showed no
disposition whatever to de-Yankeeize themselves. Their instincts were perfectly right; they rebelled against the sordid-
ness of a world given over to economic self-assertion; but they
did not recognize that in their day economic self-assertion was
the law of the tribe, and that under those conditions the petti-
est communism imaginable could be nothing better than group-
assertion or moonshine. They approached society through the
abstract impulsion of German and French philosophy; having
received this impulsion and being practical themselves they
had to "do something," and what they did was Brook Farm.
Abolition was the one strictly social cause they supported,
and the South had reason to know how abstract was the New
England prosecution of that cause. Half the grotesque, pathetic, and charming futility of men like Bronson Alcott is due
to the extraordinary amount of intellectual and moral machinery they set running, without real pressure and without
real purpose. They were like high-minded weather-cocks on
a windless day.

To Margaret Fuller one turns for the personal bearings of
this malady. She sums up the whole story of Transcendentalism—its cause and its cure. For she was eminently caused by
Transcendentalism and her unique distinction lies in having
been cured of it. In her position as priestess of Boston, Margaret was a fount of this universal experience, engendered
backwards as it were in the unadulterated brain. At sixteen
we find her asking a correspondent whether she would rather
be "the brilliant de Staël or the useful Edgeworth." She sleeps
five hours and masters six languages. She reads herself sallow,
blinks, and speaks through her nose. She is morbid, sarcastic,

and suffers from incessant headache. Emerson, at first setting eyes on her, says to himself, "We shall never get far." At twenty-nine she begins her celebrated "Conversations," choosing the Greek mythology as her theme because it is "playful as well as deep." One member of her class demurring at the idea that a Christian people can have anything to learn from the religion of a heathen one, Margaret finds it very easy to dispose of this objection. At last in a perfect ecstasy of wrong-headedness she devotes four conversations to the subject of Venus considered as the type of Instinctive Womanhood: one fancies how she must have demolished that lady.

But what happened then? It has been the tradition in America to laugh at the first half of Margaret's story; it would have been wiser to pay more attention to the second half, which is a moral to every American idealist.

Margaret, who had always been conscious of possessing what she called the European mind, finally went to Europe. No sooner had she set foot on foreign soil than she began to thaw. Among statesmen, revolutions, sieges, human causes, in hospitals and prisons, this fantastic New England prodigy became serene, capable, commanding. And when, from the Roman military hospital of which she was superintendent during the siege of 1849 she writes home to Emerson, it is Emerson who appears the stiff and limited provincial and she the one that has known men and cities. And this is equally true of her writings. Hysterical in everything she had said of German philosophy, she writes of Cromwell like the wife of an ambassador, with justice, point, and sense, and she is equally just and pointed in her views of Mazzini, Carlyle, George Sand, and Garibaldi, once she has seen them, so to speak, in action. Along with all this she had the good sense to acquire a husband and a baby, two things which always have the most salutary effect on Transcendental women.

What is the moral of all this? It is the moral and the nemesis of all unattached idealism: that the more deeply and urgently and organically you feel the pressure of society the more deeply and consciously and fruitfully you feel and you become yourself.

VIII

This moral is reënforced quite specially by the case of James Russell Lowell.

Very little, it seems to me, is left of Lowell except the size of him. He was a sizable man, he remains a sizable figure, but one that has curiously gone blank. He occupied a considerable space in the world, he became that interesting psychological fact, a Standard Poet, he has been used by the American people to stop the gap where a great critic ought to have been. What is wrong with him, what is missing in him, what has happened to him?

No American writer appears to have been so naturally gifted as Lowell. In his youth he was all animal spirits and impressionability, a sunny, easy nature with a local tang at bottom which gave edge to an otherwise too mellifluous talent. He rose easily and at once out of the provincial atmosphere which constrained all his contemporaries. The Transcendentalists, having sprung from Calvinism, were unable to approach art unless they could in some way justify themselves by making it an organ of religion; they sanctified it by placing it at arm's length and rendering it abstract. Lowell, singularly, was born without scruples of this kind; he read and wrote in a natural secular spirit, and his poems range pleasantly over the ranges of other poets, without effort and without missionary zeal, in a substantial and cultivated way. His critical essays are similar: what distinguishes them is a quality that belongs not to the better sort of criticism in his own age but to that of the age preceding it, the quality which Hazlitt called *gusto*—a spontaneous new-found relish in relishable things. He liked best the placid, unsuggestive, agreeably bovine writers like Dryden, and he called Shakespeare master. Why is it that Shakespeare is never the master of originating minds? Plato may be, or Dante, or Tolstoi, or one's uncle, or the village postmaster, but not Shakespeare. Conceive the discomfort of Shakespeare living had any one proclaimed himself a disciple. The ten-millionth Hindu is a more inevitable master; and certainly anyone who requires a lesson of Shakespeare comes away with nothing but grace and good humor.

Yet one persists in feeling that Lowell's mental framework was on a large scale, that the framework was simply not filled in. Superficially he appears the most complete, the most perfectly fused American literary personality; in reality he suffered more than any other from the want of a suitable background and is the most unfulfilled of all. That is because his culture is European without the corresponding pressure and responsibility of the European mind. He was the contemporary of Matthew Arnold, of Ruskin, of Taine,[4] in his representative character, in his vitality, he is of a stature equal to any of these; but where they have ideas and passions he remains the genial ambassador. The truth is that Lowell had no ideas, or rather what he had were dummy ideas like democracy and patriotism, which in common usage mean nothing but which enable the mind to go round and round in a large kind of way without involving the difficult intellectual act of clinching something. He paid the penalty of detaching himself from the ethical idea, which alone in its various ramifications has been able to make the New England temperament an interesting one, by being unable to arrive at any other.

For this he was not by any means to blame. The individual responds to the pressure exerted upon him; his epoch, his race, his social background determine the character of this pressure. Ideas rarely exist, and when they exist they never come to fruition, except as representative of forces lying behind the individual which press and focus the individual and make him the mouthpiece of something greater, deeper, wider than himself. The real forces of American life during the nineteenth century were forces to which Lowell was not fitted to respond; they were individualistic, ethical, and spiritual—they were, in a word, Emersonian. The strength of Emersonianism in its own time lay in its being a genuine response to an economic situation, an answering pressure, a justification of universally experienced needs and impulses. And what is true of Emerson is true of other writers in their kind and degree. Thoreau, for

4 Hippolyte Taine (1828-1893). French critic and historian; particularly known for his application of the hereditary and environmental approach to literary criticism.

example, was a man of far less native intellectual power than
Lowell, a smaller man all round; but precisely because he was
individualistic and spiritualistic, because, inadequate as his
background was, he was a natural response to it, his talent
became intense, and that vivid little genius of his, that pungent
and confined personality, remains a most positive possession.
All American thought of any eminence (and most of no eminence) has had the nature of a private message; and we have
scarcely produced an even second-rate publicist. For deep
responds to deep.

Now it is equally plain that Lowell was deficient in the
typical traits of effective American thought as that he was
naturally endowed with the traits of a social thinker. He had
no interest either in his ego or in the cosmos; he was not at
home in high latitudes, could not abide Shelley, philologizes
over the loftier passages of Spenser, never speaks of Goethe
without vaguely insinuating a grudge against him; he was not
concerned in pointing morals. On the other hand, he had a gift
for satire, a quite genuine scholarship, a definite good taste in
literature as such (in distinction from the Emersonian view of
literature as a reservoir of examples, morals, phrases, allusions
with which to dress out one's own philosophy), a wide experience of men and manners.

These are two altogether distinct sets of qualities: the point
is, that while the first set, which Lowell did not possess, arrived in Emerson and Thoreau at a quite eminent fulfillment,
the second set, which Lowell did possess, were scarcely fulfilled at all. Emerson and Thoreau achieved their individualistic philosophy, and in that philosophy their individualistic
traits were fused and intensified; but Lowell never achieved
a social philosophy, and as a result his social traits were
scattered and frittered away. His gift for satire was scarcely
developed beyond the clever doggerel of the *Fable for Critics,*
his wide experience of men and manners served only to make
him personally gracious and attractive, his scholarship instead
of serving to unearth and elucidate large conceptions and
general ideas served merely to exhibit a thousand unassociated
verbal ingenuities, his taste in literature found expression in a
series of critical essays every one of which is a *cul-de-sac,*

with twinkling lights all along the way, but leading nowhither and ending with itself.

You run through his poems with a quite astounding sense of talent wasted, prettified, conventionalized for the want of animating issues. Give him an adequate issue and you find his whole manner changes. Witness the *Commemoration Ode,* witness *The Biglow Papers.* Slavery and the Mexican war receive in *The Biglow Papers,* it seems to me, just the right measure of literary attention; and this is a felicity which, in the light of his general exuberance, powers of expression, strength and solidity, makes one feel that he could have risen aptly to issues of a more strictly social type had they existed in his background.

The poems of Lowell, in fact, exhibit something which no other body of American poems exhibit, a constant sense of the want of worthy material, a constant suspension of the best faculties. He marks time, rhymes because the rhymes insist upon coming, because of a sheer exuberance which cannot be gainsaid, aware all the while that his words are far more than adequate to anything they actually convey. Of no other American poet is this true: certainly not of Whitman, who, on the contrary, labors for language equal to his idea, nor of Longfellow in his gentle complacency, nor of Whittier, whose narrow but real talent was precisely modulated to the two or three things he had to say, nor of Emerson, whose words are a chime, choice and serene. And Lowell, on the other hand, as constantly seems to be on the point of rising to great issues, to be waiting for them, to be as it were making bids for them. Whenever his heart is fully engaged in his work (which is not often), whenever his emotion is really vented, the quality of his emotion is thoroughly social; its quality is far denser and of wider scope than that of any other American poet save Whitman. What it almost entirely wants is intellectual structure, intellectual contact, ideas. Consider, for example, *The Present Crisis.* The emotional effect of such a passage as that beginning "For Humanity sweeps onward—" is very nearly a magnificent effect: the emotion of almost any poetry written merely to further a cause (and virtually all American poetry which has any claim to the epithet "social" has been written to further a cause) is thin and shrill beside it; it *has* density, it *has* scope, it *has* some of the splendor which goes with anything massive that has found a voice. But when you try to discover the intellectual structure of it, the intellectual contact of it, the ideas in it, when you inquire what Humanity is and what it is sweeping onward *to* you find that Lowell is as vague and flatulent as Tom Paine and Mr. Bryan. No social pressure, no defined issues, no discipline lies behind him. He is simply being magnificently and generously emotional in a social and intellectual vacuum.

Now, Tennyson is not a poet from whom one expects ideas; he is conspicuously, among English poets, one who shunned ideas, shunned issues of every kind, and would have avoided them altogether if he could. *Locksley Hall,* aside from its curiously antiquated personal sentiment, also contains a picture of the onward sweep of humanity. It has none of the social passion of Lowell's poem, it presents no sort of coherent vision, the ideas in it, like the ideas in *Maud* and *In Memoriam,* once you disentangle them from their poetical glamour, emerge merely as part of the general intellectual bric-à-brac of the Victorian age, owing nothing to the personal experience of Tennyson himself. But the ideas are there; if they are dim and confused it is not because Tennyson was ignorant of them but because he was on the whole not interested in them; he employs them, not for the sake of the ideas, but because he regarded his own poetical function as a representative function and had somehow, if he was to make his particular faith prevail, to make it prevail among these ideas and over them. He was surrounded on all sides by men like Darwin, Mill, Carlyle, Newman, pressed on all sides by conflicting ideas and issues, and with no native inclination for it he was forced into the position of a fighter.

Such is the effect of a social background upon a writer with no native capacity for being a social force. Such is the effect of the want of a social background upon a writer with great native capacity for being a social force. For if the background of Lowell was, in its individual aspect, a spectacle of enterprise and pluck, socially it was arbitrary, undisciplined, windy, bare, and almost infinitely trivial. And there is no doubt that if

Lowell had been produced by any European people he would have been something like a great man. Bred in New England, he was like a born general whose country persists in remaining at peace: such a man skirmishes about in his youth, picks petty quarrels, adopts a commanding attitude, thinks in regiments; and gradually settles down a little fatuously among other military men, talks tactics, tells war stories, reads the reminiscences of dead soldiers, and writes negligible books on armament. In Europe, where the warfare of ideas, of social philosophies, is always an instant close-pressed warfare in which everyone is engaged, Lowell would have had the opportunity to bring his artillery into play. In America, where no warfare of ideas has ever existed, where ideas have always been acutely individual and ethical, and where public and social affairs, disjointed, vague, and bare, have always met with the yawning indifference that springs from a relative want of pressure behind, he inevitably became indifferent. His was the indifference of a simple and confirmed man of letters,—that is to say, a poet who has made his peace with the world.

Lowell, in a word, never arrived at a comprehensive attitude toward the inner forces of which books, men, and affairs are symptomatic. Now a point of view in criticism, criticism in the genuine sense, is a workingplan, a definition of issues, which at once renders it impossible to make one's peace with the world, at once and permanently sets one at odds with the world, inevitably makes the critic a champion and a man of war. Generous impulses and enthusiasms, which Lowell had abundantly in his youth, are not enough, unless they are reënforced and in a way solidified into some sort of personal programme; the sort of programme which, to take instances from among Lowell's contemporaries, Carlyle had in his hero-worship, Ruskin in his central idea of the interaction of harmonious art and harmonious life, Mazzini in his brotherhood of peoples, Taine in his theory of the *milieu*, Nietzsche in his supermorality. To have such a programme is not a limitation; it corresponds on the plane of ideas to style on the plane of letters; it is not merely the mark of intense individuality, not merely the trait which makes men significant and interesting: it is the condition of life in the intellectual and moral world.

III. The Precipitant

I HAVE BEEN trying to show in what way a survey of American literature would inevitably lead us to certain general facts about American life. I opened the survey with a statement which I think no one will contradict, that in American literature something has always been wanting, that a certain density, weight, and richness, a certain poignancy, a "something far more deeply interfused," simply is not there. Beginning with this clue and reaching an axiom to which it seemed to me inevitably to lead, I suggested a certain practical conclusion as the result of our inquiry: that those of our writers who have possessed a vivid personal talent have been paralyzed by the want of a social background, while those who have possessed a vivid social talent have been equally unable to develop their personalities.

There is, I think, something in some not very vague way unsatisfactory about each of the writers we have been examining. Taken as a whole the most characteristic fact about them is a certain delicacy which arrives in literature almost in the degree to which it stands remote from life, achieves its own salvation (after the Puritan fashion) by avoiding contact with actuality. Almost all the greater American writers, placed beside their English contemporaries, have a certain all too unworldly refinement. Purity of style and delicacy of touch at once distinguish Emerson from Carlyle and Hawthorne from any Victorian novelist; but the abyss between their writings and the world in which they lived is immeasurably greater. The American character speaks through them, of course, but it is the American character only in its most sublimated form, carefully cleansed as it were and highly rarefied. Nothing is more marked than their disinclination to take a plunge, reckless and complete, as Carlyle and Dickens did, into the rudest and grossest actualities. The poet Camoëns on his deathbed observed that his whole life had been spent in trying to keep himself afloat in a stormy sea, and his only care had been to exercise his left hand with double energy so that his right hand might be free to hold his *Luciad* aloft, uncontaminated by the waves. This is the whole story of American literature: in a more than usually difficult and sordid world it has applied its principal energies to being uncontaminated itself. It has held aloof, as a consciously better part, like all American idealism. The talent is there, high and dry; and if it is not always too high, it is very often a great deal too dry.

In fact, we have in America two publics, the cultivated public and the business public, the public of theory and the public of action, the public that reads Maeterlinck and the public that accumulates money: the one largely feminine, the other largely masculine. Wholly incompatible in their ideals they still pull together, as the ass and the ox must. But the ass shows no disposition to convert the ox, nor the ox the ass. They do not mitigate one another;—they are, in biological phrase, infertile with one another.

But it happens that we have the rudiments of a middle tradition, a tradition which effectively combines theory and action, a tradition which is just as fundamentally American as either flag-waving or money-grabbing, one which is visibly growing but which has already been grossly abused; and this is the tradition which begins with Walt Whitman. The real significance of Walt Whitman is that he, for the first time, gave us the sense of something organic in American life.

Whitman was himself a great vegetable of a man, all of a piece in roots, flavor, substantiality, and succulence, well-ripened in the common sunshine. In him the hitherto incompatible extremes of the American temperament were fused. The exquisite refinement of the Puritan tradition, summed up as an original type in Jonathan Edwards, able to make nothing of a life so rude in its actuality, turned for its outlet to a perfectly disembodied world, the shadow-world of Emerson, Hawthorne, and Poe, a world fastidiously intellectual in which only two colors exist, white and black. Whitman was the Antaeus of this tradition who touched earth with it and gave it hands and feet. For having all the ideas of New England, being himself saturated with Emersonianism, he came up from the other side with everything New England did not possess: quantities of rude emotion and a faculty of gathering humane experience almost as great as that of the hero of the Odyssey. Living habitually among world ideas, world emotions, world impulses and having experienced life on a truly grand scale, this extraordinary person, innocent as a pioneer of what is called urbanity, became nevertheless a man of the world in a sense in which ambassadors are not; and there is every reason to suppose that he would have been perfectly at home in the company of Achilles, or Erasmus, or Louis XIV.

This fact is full of meaning, and if anyone doubts it let him dwell on the following record in *Specimen Days*. Whitman is describing what he did in the military hospitals at Washington during the war:

For reading I generally have some old pictorial magazines or story papers—they are always acceptable. . . . In these wards, or on the field, as I thus continue to go round, I have come to adapt myself to each emergency, after its kind or call, however trivial, however solemn, every one justified and made real under its circumstances— not only visits and cheering talk and little gifts—not only washing and dressing wounds . . . but passages from the Bible, expounding them, . . . etc. (I think I see my friends smiling at this confession, but I was never more in earnest in my life.) In camp and elsewhere, I was in the habit of reading or giving recitations to the men. They were very fond of it, and liked declamatory pieces. We would gather in a large group by ourselves after supper, and spend the time in such readings, or in talking, and occasionally by an amusing game called the game of twenty questions.

This passage will serve very well to mark the distinction between Whitman and all the other American men of letters of his time. Could Emerson have recited "declamatory pieces," even if it was at the moment the one tactful thing to do? Could Bryant have led a game of twenty questions? Could Edgar Allan Poe have expounded the Bible? Could Whittier have juggled with oranges? Could Lowell have pointed out the felicities that lurk in the pictorial adventures of Nick Carter and the Wharf Rats?[1] Could any one of them, in short, have

---

[1] Nick Carter is the famous dime novel detective of the 1880s, probably created by J. J. Coryell, and the Wharf Rats are presumably a popular comic strip gang.

entered so fully and many-sidedly into the spirit of a great human situation? But allowing for certain inevitable differences in the milieu (orange-juggling and the adventures of Nick Carter being peculiarly democratic and modern), I am sure that Achilles, or Erasmus, or Louis XIV could have done so; and this is why I have called Whitman a man of the world.

It was in these ways that he gained his experience, in these ways that he shared it. And it is the more remarkable since he had sprung from the most provincial, inadaptable, homespun stock, his aspect being, as Edmund Gosse[2] remembers it, like that of a plain old deal table, scrubbed and scrubbed and scrubbed. He let in the air of a wider world on those inadequate decencies; he came home to his own traditions like a prodigal son, visiting for a while, mingling an element of indulgent pity in his new sense of the limited old ways, aware of a few confidences that could not be shared any more and of so many things, human, too, which could find no place there. To compare the particular homeliness of Whitman with the homeliness, for example, of *Snow-Bound* is at once to recall his line "There was a child went forth."

And he challenged the abnormal dignity of American letters. The dignity of letters! It is a question how much dignity letters can afford to have. No doubt in the perennial indignity of our world a considerable emphasis on that becomes all too easily the price of self-preservation. The possession of culture with us has always been rather a jealous possession, it has the nature of a right which has been earned, an investment which might have been a yacht, a country-house, or a collection of Rembrandts instead.

All this was especially true of the New York men of letters who formed the background of Whitman: Stedman, Stoddard, and their group. The eighteenth century was never so meticu-

---

[2] Edmund Gosse (1849-1928). English poet, critic, librarian and translator, especially noted for introducing Ibsen and other modern Scandinavian writers to English readers. He was a friend and supporter of most of the well known writers of the day; they included Swinburne, Stevenson, James, Hardy, Kipling, and Shaw. His essay on Whitman (1893), collected in *Critical Kit-Kats* (New York, 1896), judged that Whitman missed greatness; Stevenson, Swinburne and Symonds were more ecstatic about the American poet.

lous about form, style, presentableness as were these men. Style to them was a quite sacred thing, bought and paid for, as it were; and for them the essence of literature lay in its remoteness from Wall Street. Witness the poem in which Stedman, in order to lift the scene of his daily avocations to the level of literature, achieved the incredible ineptitude of getting the god Pan into it. They had the temperament of collectors, viveurs, connoisseurs of one generation; they understood and they emulated the fragile and the far-sought; and Whitman came in upon them thundering and with his coat off, like an inconvenient country uncle, puddling their artistic expecta tions. Could anything have been more disconcerting than his Olympian summary of what he calls the "endless supply of small coin . . . the dandies and ennuyées who flood us with their thin sentiment of parlors, parasols, pianosongs, tinkling rhymes, the five-hundredth importation—or whimpering and crying about something, chasing one aborted conceit after another, and forever occupied in dyspeptic amours with dyspeptic women"—when, faced with this, he dwells only on a certain substantial grandeur in the mountains of white paper and the crashing, ten-cylinder presses which turn them out?

Whitman—how else can I express it?—precipitated the American character. All those things which had been separate, self-sufficient, incoördinate—action, theory, idealism, business —he cast into a crucible; and they emerged, harmonious and molten, in a fresh democratic ideal, which is based upon the whole personality. Every strong personal impulse, every coöperating and unifying impulse, everything that enriches the social background, everything that enriches the individual, everything that impels and clarifies in the modern world owes something to Whitman. And especially of those American writers who have written preëminently for young men—and which has not?—Whitman alone, it seems to me, has pitched his tone to the real spring of action in them.

All this indicates a function quite different from that of a poet in any but the most radical and primitive sense of the word (the sense in which it was held by Whitman himself), a man, that is to say, who first gives to a nation a certain focal centre in the consciousness of its own character. Virgil did this, Mazzini did this,[3] Björnson[4] did this; and it was the main work of Whitman to make fast what he called "the idea and fact of American Totality," an idea and fact summed up with singular completeness in his own character and way of life. Emerson before him had provided a kind of skeleton outline; but what Emerson drew in black and white Whitman filled in with color and set in three dimensions.

A *focal centre*—that is the first requisite of a great people. And by this I do not mean the sense of national or imperial destiny which has consolidated the great temporal Powers of history. I mean that national "point of rest," to adopt a phrase in which Coleridge indicated that upon which the harmony of a work of art is founded and to which everything in the composition is more or less unconsciously referred; that secure and unobtrusive element of national character, taken for granted, and providing a certain underlying coherence and background of mutual understanding which Rome, for example, had in everything the name of Cato called up, or England in her great remembered worthies, or the elder Germany in Martin Luther. "National culture," to speak in the dialect of our own time, is only the perhaps too-conscious equivalent of this element in which everything admirably characteristic of a people sums itself up, which creates everywhere a kind of spiritual teamwork, which radiates outward and articulates the entire living fabric of a race.

For us, it seems to me, Whitman laid the cornerstone of a national ideal capable in this way of releasing personality and of retrieving for our civilization, originally deficient in the richer juices of human nature, and still further bled and flattened out by the Machine Process, the only sort of "place in the sun" really worth having.

But at this point one has to discriminate. The social ideal of Whitman is essentially a collection of raw materials, molten and malleable, which take shape only in an emotional form.

[3] Giuseppe Mazzini (1805-1872). The outstanding figure of Italy's Risorgimento; his nationalist-revolutionary theories were particularly attractive to Brooks.

[4] Björnstjerne Björnson (1832-1910). Norwegian writer particularly noted for his peasant novels; also a manager-director of the national theater into which he carried his interest in Norwegian history and legend.

This emotional attitude is at bottom the attitude of a perfectly free personality, naturally affirmative, naturally creative; the rude material of right personal instinct, which is, however, antecedent to the direction personality is to adopt and to the ideas that are to inform it.

To ignore this distinction, as most of the direct disciples of Whitman have done, is to go wrong utterly. And in fact Whitman himself ignored the distinction, and himself went wrong. Perfectly right in all his instincts, perfectly right so long as he kept to the plane of instinct, he was lost on the plane of ideas. He lacked a sure sense of his own province and limitations. Influenced no doubt by his disciples, he began in later years to assume functions not properly his own, and the greatness and sweetness of his character were increasingly marred by much pomposity and fatuousness. He was led to speak not as a poet but as an authority, the painful results of which may be seen in his newspaper interviews.

All this was probably inevitable. Whitman's instinct was to affirm everything, to accept everything, to relish the personal and human elements in everything. For himself he accepted "sustenance, clothing, shelter, and continuity." As regards the world he was equally catholic and passive. Soldiers being the strapping upright animals they are he accepts armies because armies breed them. He enjoys an old restauranteur because he knows how to select champagne, likes to look at nursemaids because they are so trim and wholesome and at fashionable women because they are so pretty and gay, likes money because of a certain strength it implies and business because it is so active, nimble, and adventurous. On the plane of instinct where he properly belongs he is right in each case: on the plane of ideas the practical effect is that, in accepting everything, he accepts the confusion of things and the *fait accompli*.

It is, in fact, the simple corollary of his thorough-going mood of affirmation on the personal, instinctive, emotional plane, that his ideas should be perfectly conventional. In ideas he is just an old-fashioned Jacksonian democrat. Except for a certain amount of uncommonly vigorous criticism, of the stock type, on American abuses, he never questions the old institutions. He takes for granted "the unform'd and nebulous state of many things, not yet permanently settled, but agreed on all

hands to be the preparations of an infinitely greater future."
He talks the greatest amount of nonsense about the "feudal-
ism" of a contemporary Europe whose principal artists have
been men like Tolstoi, Dostoievski, Millet, Thomas Hardy.
He is never able to release himself from the vicious comparative; he is morbid about geography. Not being satisfied by the
greatness of anything as a positive fact he has to prove its
greatness by belittling something else. A fertile plain strikes
him at once as more fertile than any other plain on earth, a
grand scene "outvies all the historic places of note," an American general is more of a general than Napoleon, an American
poem has to be better than any poem hitherto.

All this is just what Mr. Bryan says,—it is just our fun.
And the funniest thing of all, from this point of view, is to
find Whitman solemnly posed, as he records it, before a vast
canvas twenty feet by twelve, representing "Custer's Last
Rally," the work of one John Mulvany,[5] finding its "physiognomy realistic and Western," with an "almost entire absence
of the stock traits of European war pictures," and recommend-
ing that it be sent to Paris "to show Messieur Crapeau [*sic*][6]
that some things can be done in America as well as others."
Perhaps one has to be an American to feel the lovableness of
that scene. But if it demonstrates once for all any one thing
it is that Whitman was never intended to be an authority,
even on democracy.

An opportunity and in certain respects also a faculty Whitman had, in his own time and place, very similar to those of
Montaigne. I mean by this, on the one hand, a malleable and
still incoherent race to be interpreted to itself, to be articulated,
to be brought into focus, and on the other a temperament
archetypical of that race, a range of sympathy coincidental
with it, and a power of revealing and in a sense fixing the
racial norm. "I look within myself, I am only concerned with

[5] John Mulvany (or Mulvaney) (1844-1906). Irish-born American painter
who came to specialize in scenes based on Western, Indian and army life, he is
best known for the painting Brooks refers to.

[6] The spelling ought to read Crapaud. Crapaud or Johnny Crapaud to describe a Frenchman occurs in Guilliam's *Display of Heraldry* (1611); it derives
from the ancient device of French kings, three toads erect *(trois crapauds
saltant)*.

myself, I reflect on myself, I examine myself, I take pleasure
in myself," said Montaigne; and all France for the first time
saw itself in a looking-glass and fell together in a common
discipline.

The raw materials of a racial norm Whitman provided; but
—and in this he resembled Emerson—he was too passive to
go further. He assembled in himself and his writings the characteristics of America,—with him originated the most contagious, the most liberating, the most unifying of native impulses;
but he failed to react upon them, to mould them, and to drive
them home. He had no ideas and he was satisfied to have none.
He wanted, above all, intensity. He was too complacent. He
was incapable of discipline and he did not see that discipline
is, for Americans, the condition of all forward movement.

But the conventionality of Whitman's intellectual equipment
is not, for us, a necessary part of the personal attitude which
he originated. History is filled with instances of men who,
having been called upon to originate fresh points of view, have
had, in order to establish these points of view, to adopt a
severely conventional position toward most of the phenomena
of their time. Each of these men has had his disciples in the
letter and his disciples in the spirit,—Martin Luther, for example, especially in questions economic and social. The direct
and immediate children of Luther, those who have laid apostolic hands on one another from generation to generation, are
simply the bourgeoisie of the world; but the true Lutherans
are those who, in every age, have thought keenly and honestly
and independently and have, in so doing, contributed stone by
stone to the great catholicism of the future. So also with Whitman and the children of Whitman. It was inevitable, in the
America of his time, that he should have been so much of an
outrageous egoist (consider the provocation!), inevitable that
he should, in Emerson's phrase, have swallowed the universe
like a cake, inevitable that he should have been indiscriminating, confused, and a little fatuous. To affirm sufficiently, he
had to affirm everything.

We are in a different position, and we have different responsibilities. On the philosophical side, the simple doctrine of
evolution, in its crude form the last word in Whitman's cosmos,

has been refined and ripened. Above all, we have no excuse not to see that affirmation, in the most real sense, proceeds to a certain extent through rejection, by merely dropping off most of the old clothes that Whitman found quite good enough. To keep these old clothes, to affirm that since everything is good they must be good also, to embroider them and make them over and stalk about in them, loudly affirming one's own ego and the indiscriminate grandeur of all creation, with particular reference to the Whole Crowd of Good Americans—all this is not to continue and to reaffirm the right Whitmanian tradition; but it is, in a way, to have the sanction of Whitman's own character and experience, and it is above all to do what the typical contemporary Whitmanian does.

In some way—and primarily by returning upon Whitman as Whitman returned upon Emerson, not, as in that case, by adding emotion to intellect, but by adding intellect to emotion— the social ideal the raw materials of which have been provided by Whitman must be formulated and driven home.

The Whitmanians, meanwhile, have made haste to formulate out of these materials a certain number of spurious social ideals, the more dangerous the more plausible, and even the more "American," they are. Of these the one that seems to me most typical will have to be examined.

IV. Apotheosis of the "Lowbrow"

I

THE PARTICULAR WHITMANIAN I have in mind is Mr. Gerald Stanley Lee; and the particular social ideal is Mr. Lee's "Inspired Millionaire."[1]

---

[1] Gerald Stanley Lee (1862-1944). American Congregational clergyman who wrote works like *The Lost Art of Reading* (1903), *The Air-Line to Liberty* (1918) and *Crowds: A Moving-Picture of Democracy* (1913). In his *Inspired Millionaires: A Forecast* (1908), he believes his era has to choose between "the socialized millionaire and socialism."

Now it must be admitted at the outset that if the social ideal which Mr. Lee has set up is in reality a spurious one, its plausibility is largely due to the fact that in certain ways it seems to be precisely the social ideal that is most needed. It is an ideal which touches reality, it involves the American character as we really know it, it throws into relief certain quite fundamental issues, it attempts to create an outlet through which the American character can express itself in a disinterested way; and finally it is based on that conception of a nonchalant individual, "superbly aplomb and mutual," which Whitman once for all invented as the democratic type. Just as Carlyle's Hero can be taken as a projection of what the typical Englishman, possibly, aspires to be, a sort of Lord Cromer[2] with a halo, just as Nietzsche's Superman is a projection of what the typical modern German seems to be struggling to be, a sort of Bismarck with a halo, so Mr. Lee's Inspired Millionaire is a projection of what the typical American apparently struggles to be, a sort of Marshall Field with a halo.[3] It is the type toward which the personal forces of the generality of Americans appear to be directed, heightened and justified as an ideal.

In all these respects, then, Mr. Lee seems to have done just the one preliminary thing that has to be done. Why then, really, has he entirely failed to do it? How, as I believe, has he made it more difficult than ever for any one to do it?

The idealization of business, to begin with, has, in America, a certain apparent rightness which elsewhere it could not have. For business in America is not merely more engaging than elsewhere, it is even perhaps the most engaging activity in American life. You cannot compare the American commercial type with the commercial type which England has evolved without feeling in the latter a certain fatty degeneration, a solemn fatality, a sanctified, legalized self-satisfaction, which our agile, free, open, though sometimes indefinitely more unholy type, is quite without; for even in his unholiness the unholy business man in America is engagingly crooked rather

[2] Evelyn Baring Cromer (1841-1917). British administrator in Egypt and virtual ruler of the country.

[3] Marshall Field (1834-1906). Chicago merchant and philanthropist who made his great private fortune in retailing.

than ponderously corrupt. Beside the English business man as one figures him at those portentous Guildhall banquets which array themselves like a Chinese wall of roast beef against every impulse in human life that moves and breathes, beside the English business man as he is apotheosized in the Lord Mayor of London (led by that symbolic coachman of his as a winged victory), with his chains and decorations, the liveries that fortify him, the legalities and charters of private liberty that sanction him, the immemorial precedents that fix him foursquare and firm in his encumbered world—beside him the American business man is a gay, sprightly, childlike being, moved and movable, the player of a game, a sportsman essentially, though with a frequently dim perception of the rules. You have only to compare the Bank of England, that squat impregnable mass which grips a score of London acres, with, for example, the Woolworth Tower, which has in it so much of the impulse that has built cathedrals, to feel this divergence in the quality of English and American business.

What is the natural history of this divergence? Why, precisely that the world of trade in England has always been an underworld, precisely that everything which is light, gay, disinterested, personal, artistic has held aloof from it, has been able to form a self-subsisting world which is beyond it, while trade itself is only a dull residuum. The cream has risen to the top, and the world of business is perfectly conscious that it is only skimmed milk; and if the aldermen wax fat and reach for money it is in a spirit that Americans would call defiance and despair. For in America there has been no such separation of the cream and the milk. Business has traditionally absorbed the best elements of the American character, it has been cowed by no sense of subjection, it has thriven in a free air, it has received all the leaven, it has occupied the centre of the field. Just those elements which in other countries produce art and literature, formulate the ideals and methods of philosophy and sociology, think and act for those disinterested ends which make up the meaning of life; just that free, disinterested, athletic sense of play which is precisely the same in dialectic, in art, in religion, in sociology, in sport—just these, relatively speaking, have in America been absorbed in trade. It is not remarkable that, on the one hand, thought and literature are so perfunctory and so barren; while on the other business is so seductive, so charming, so gay an adventure,—not remarkable, for instance, that Mr. Lee is really able to imagine "a million dollars having a good time, i.e., a million dollars full of creative imagination."

Yet though trade may have all the grace and charm of sportsmanship, and all the fervor of a religion, though it may express itself in the most beautiful buildings, though it may stimulate the imagination, though it may turn a factory into an earthly paradise, can it really have the essential quality of religion, sport, and art, can it be at bottom, that is to say, disinterested? So long as the impulse which underlies trade is not that of an exchange of equivalent values, but of an exchange which gets more than it gives and gets as much more as it can, just so long trade cannot be disinterested, and the problem of private subsistence in trade is inevitably bound up with the problem of arbitrary self-interest all the way up and down the scale. Mr. Lee wants his Inspired Millionaire to be an artist, and he defines an artist as one who "loves making a perfect thing more than making money." He wants his Inspired Millionaire to be an inventive man and he says that "inventive men are apt to be dreamers and they are given to being disinterested and to not defending themselves, and they are whimsical and reckless"—statements in which Mr. Lee is very careless of reason; for although it may be possible to be disinterested after one has become a millionaire, it is quite impossible, except through inheritance (which is outside the present question), to be disinterested during the process of becoming one.

This want of logic is very damaging to Mr. Lee when he sets up his Inspired Millionaire as what he calls the only alternative to socialism, for in the second part of his book, "which considers ways and means," he unconsciously reverses his position and gives his whole scheme away. He there shows that in actually bringing about the ideal industrial system he hopes for, it is not the monopolist who conceives "a million dollars as an art form" and who, like every artist, must have a free hand in working out his conception, it is not the millionaire that will have to be inspired, but the salaried superintendent:

The practical difficulty in many cases is not in the condition of the men, nor of the man, who might be superintendent, but in the millionaire. The millionaire finds, as a matter of experience, that the kind of man he would really like for the position of manager is a man who cannot quite be managed. Then he tries to manage him. The real trouble is with the millionaire. He has had it proved to him, over and over again, that the men that can be managed cannot manage any one else. And when it comes to making an actual choice between a second-rate superintendent who can be controlled by money, and the man of the highest order of gifts who is controlled by his own gifts, the millionaire chooses the second-rate superintendent. . . . The man who sees things cannot be had except by men who will let him do them. . . . He has the spirit and the attitude of the artist and the only kind of money that in the long run controls him is the money that buys the whole of him, buys the man and his ideas together, on the condition that he shall carry them out. . . . The time is not far off when it will be generally taken for granted by all concerned that the controlling factor, the strategic position in industry, instead of belonging to the man who has the money, or to the man who does the work, belongs to the superintendent, the man who has the ideas, the great faiths of the business—who is the soul of the business, who holds the owners, and the men, and the plant in his hands, and is putting them together.

One reads this fairly intelligent description of socialism with some perplexity as to what Mr. Lee is going to do about it: certainly from the point of view of the private monopolist he is preaching the starkest anarchism all along the line. For if, as he says, the strategic position belongs to the superintendent whose income, however, large, remains a salary, and if the only way in which the millionaire can get his ideas expressed is by giving free rein to the ideas of the superintendent (who, in turn, as Mr. Lee urges, can only get *his* ideas expressed by giving free rein to the ideas of all his men), how in the first place can the millionaire behind the superintendent remain an "artist" whose own free will is all-determining, and why may not the superintendent as readily accept his salary from the State? And then, too, in a society where the real industrial inventors have only by accident gained fortunes by their invention, where many fortunes are made by the wholly uninventive methods of the Stock Exchange, where the real owners are the innumerable anonymous owners of stock and drawers of dividend whose capital is, as Mr. Lee says, "huge, pulpy, helpless, unmanned"—in such a society how can the increased economic individualism which Mr. Lee proposes discern the millionaires that *are* inventive and assure them fortunes (or rather the superintendents who hold the strategic position and whose ideas the millionaires must give free rein to), how can it suppress and repudiate the millionaires that are uninventive, how can it create inventiveness in the innumerable army of anonymous owners? Having given his account of socialism, Mr. Lee has merely summoned out of it a vast, vaporous, irrelevant Somebody, who has no connection with anything and who would really be very much left out in the cold if there were not so many hospitable people to take him in, "regardless."

But the force of a book like this does not rest in its intellectual structure; as Mr. Lee observes in his appendix, the book is a conception and the point in it cannot be proved by an argument. Argument, I grant, is quite as irrelevant to the conception of an Inspired Millionaire as it is to the conception of a Superman. But then Mr. Lee has opened himself to it, he has used an argument, he has deliberately devoted five chapters to considering ways and means; and his argument is precisely counter to his main conception. His Millionaire is a sort of silly Goliath struck down by the pebble of his own logic. Just because Nietzsche was a poet he never opened himself to an argument, he never dreamed of considering ways and means; that is why the Superman, however questionable on other grounds, is a conceivable and a permanent ideal. The fact that Mr. Lee has had to resort to argument is the first thing that leads one to suspect the validity of the conception itself.

If the conception is a true one, says Mr. Lee, the world will soon find a body for it. When was the world ever so particular about truth? It is the big battalions that find a body for notions of this kind, and these Mr. Lee has already captured.

Now it is no more an argument against Mr. Lee's philosophy that business men are flattered by it than it is an argument against Carlyle that the English aristocracy of his day were flattered by him or against Nietzsche that the Bismarckians and militarists and little supermen of modern Germany have been flattered by him. Every social ideal has formed itself out of the stuff of some nation, has grown up as the reflex and better half of its dominant moral type, and has apparently justified the type on its lower levels. The real question with any social ideal is not whether it seems to be embodied and debased in any existing class, but whether or not it provides a possible moral programme for the individual, a way of looking at life, a point of view.

One may find the Superman a very objectionable ideal, but one has to admit that the Superman's unmorality is itself a moral attitude, a moral programme, a point of view; one may find Carlyle's Hero a ludicrously unscientific and unhistorical ideal, but one has to admit that the Hero considered as the interpreter of a reality which lies behind phenomena constitutes a moral attitude, a moral programme, a point of view. Making every allowance for a possible absurdity in genius, they are both conceivable social ideals. Is the Inspired Millionaire, who has failed so unhappily to establish himself by logic, a conceivable social ideal? Is there, as Mr. Lee says, "no difference between making a fortune and making a book or a picture"?

The one reply is simply that millionairism is itself one a moral entity like heroism or superhumanity: it is a situation, and a situation moreover which is not the inevitable result of any kind of activity, even the activity of a genius for acquisition.

What remains? Everything, unhappily, since the Ass's Head of business to which Mr. Lee plays the part of Titania is interested neither in the truth of logic nor in the truth of poetry. What remains is the very evident new life which Mr. Lee's Apotheosis of the "Lowbrow" has infused into everything that makes honest thinking in America so nearly impossible. Idealism is the most dangerous thing in the world when, having no basis in reason or in pressure, it serves merely to give a transcendental *cachet* to the established fact. And Mr. Lee's flattery is really very subtle; he is keen enough to say all manner of disagreeable things about Mr. Rockefeller, clever enough to make fine distinctions about the futility of Mr. Carnegie, leaving the anonymous "morally beautiful grocer" (who is in fact simply the universal business man, only too glad to feel himself more beautifully moral than the captains of his type) in possession of a philosophy which enables him to patronize St. Paul, St. Francis of Assisi, and all the art, thought, and literature of the world, as he was only too well prepared to do before. In a world where everything is relative it is probably too much to expect that sincerity should be absolute. When Mr. Lee says that not failure or martyrdom or military glory any longer but "success of any kind at any price is what we really worship, and as we are convinced just now that money, instead of being a possible accompaniment or accident of success, is the way to get it, we are worshiping money. We are all idealists"—when he says this, we remind ourselves that Mr. Lee is himself a disinterested thinker, we admit that his definition of a new idealism has the charm of surprise, we hesitate long enough to ask ourselves whether it is really possible in this way to "carry the war into the enemy's country," before we are suddenly overcome by this base ignorance of economic facts, this base perversion of economic issues, this base misuse of the elements of surprise and exaltation, this deliberate sophistication of the one universally diffused point of view which has paralyzed American life and poisoned the wells of all disinterested thought.

To be a prophet in America it is not enough to be totally uninformed; one must also have a bland smile.

II

But now I feel that I owe a certain explanation for making so much of a book which, after all, so few can have read or taken seriously as a social document. (How really tragic it is to consider that even if it had been all that some of the slightly less inspired millionaires have thought it, it could still, since there is in America no criterion by which to test the validity of ideas, have penetrated only an inch deep and must quickly have been forgotten!)

Inspired Millionaires, for all that, seems to me a landmark and a touchstone. For it is in the direct line of the American tradition, it is the climax of our old Transcendental individualism, and bringing as it does this Transcendentalism into line with contemporary life it enables us to see just how far our American blood has played us false. And then too if, owing to his having uncritically accepted this false philosophical basis (owing to his familiar assumption that "America" is an altogether special and abstract thing, with a divine right and divine instincts all its own)—if, owing to all this, Mr. Lee, as I think, has gone wrong from the outset, he has at least attempted something which scarcely any one else has attempted, something which is almost a prerequisite of any further progress, the examination of American society in the light of a social ideal which is itself really American in its traits and in its origin. For the Inspired Millionaire springs, like the flower of the century plant, right out of the apparent heart, right out of the apparent centre, of American society.

The *apparent* centre, I say, because although business is plainly the centre of attraction, I think it could easily be shown so to be only through the want of such an animating motive as a genuine social ideal provides. For if, in the first place, millionairism is not a moral entity and the Inspired Millionaire consequently is not a conceivable social ideal, if moreover trade itself cannot be in essence a disinterested thing, only consider what is involved in the very plausibility of Mr. Lee's theme, in the sportsmanship, the fervor, the charm that actually exist in American business! Only consider the meaning of such a paradox as that the mind of a nation is given over, in a potentially disinterested mood, to an essentially self-interested activity! Only consider that the Will to Reform, negative as it is, has sprung spontaneously out of the welter of business itself! Only consider how much disinterestedness all this, at bottom, amounts to! Who can say what would happen in America if some direct and positive outlet, some outlet normal to the disinterested mood, as the Will to Reform is not, were provided for all this energy that has taken the wrong switch? Who can say what would happen if some one were to appear with a social ideal just as concrete as Mr. Lee's and

just as much an answer to the experience of the American
people, only genuine, central, honestly thought, honestly felt?

More generally Mr. Lee is to be taken as one of a large
group of Windy Philosophers who have swarmed all over the
twentieth century. Scratch any one of them and you will find
an ex-parson or an ex-professor: they include perhaps a
majority of those Americans who, having some capacity for
general ideas, have detached themselves from the universities,
the professions, the parties, and the conventional life of the
time. It is this general class of minds which forms the leaven
of thought in other countries; even with us almost every one
of them is a man of insight associated (equivocally for the
most part) with the best current ideas; but every one of them
rides his broomstick through the intense inane, sublimely
irresponsible, expansively fraternal, infinitely futile.

Consider Mr. Lee in this light. Consider what it means to
American society that a man should win even the position he
has who thinks on three or four levels at once, who is at one
moment fifty years ahead of his time and at the next four
hundred years behind it, who imagines one thing and thinks
another and says a third! Consider what it means that a man
of even Mr. Lee's degree of prominence, who sees eye to eye
with socialism the chaos of the industrial world and the need
of just that free inventiveness in all grades which is paralyzed
by the pressure of profit and dividend, who suggests some of
the most interesting, stimulating, indispensable problems of
socialism, who, being intelligent enough for this, simply because he is isolated and ill-informed and out of touch with
contemporary thought, because he is immensely hindered by
his abstract notion of America and his Yankee instincts of any
sort of individualism at any price, because he is enormously
sentimental, should repudiate socialism, in an unintelligent
formula, as "a machine from the outside"! If Mr. Lee's logic
and imagination bring him directly into the socialist camp
while his Inspired Millionaire is merely a very noisy, windy,
raucous, Popular Æolian attachment, it is not so much socialism that is in danger as the very possibility in America of any
sort of clear, just, intelligent, well-informed thinking.

How much talent goes to waste every day, it seems, simply

because there is no criticism, no standard, no authority to trip it up and shake it and make it think! On the one hand we have the unwillingness and the incapacity of the self-interested financialized brain to extend itself to general ideas; on the other a soft, undisciplined emotionality face to face with crowds, millionaires, prairies, and skyscrapers—an open sea with plenty of wind for the great American balloon.

III

Since, in the matter which immediately concerns the most and the best Americans (for anyone in his five senses must agree with Mr. Lee that most of the really first-rate forces in America have been and still are absorbed in business), since in this matter, and in consequence of this fact, America is so palpably superior to England, perhaps it may be pointed out how in the matter of ideas, and especially in the half-unconscious machinery that makes ideas tell, England is equally superior to America—and why, as a result of this, the problem of England is in certain fundamental respects more hopeful than the problem of America. For certainly the main work of society is to build that garden in the cosmic wilderness, as Huxley[4] (best and brightest of the Philistines) described it; conceiving society deliberately as a work of art which is at war with nature, fertilizing the soil, cultivating and protecting the most beautiful and the greatest variety of plants, aware all the time that every moment we lay aside our tools or lose sight of our ever-developing design the weeds will pour back again and the wilderness will by so much have gained on us.

The only education which can forward this plan is the education which teaches us what a weed is and what a flower is. And the only superiority which England has over America—a relative but a great superiority—is that England really has the rudiments of a sort of botanical laboratory of this kind. It has a few men who are skilled in recognizing weeds and in

---

[4] Thomas Henry Huxley (1825-1895). English biologist and popular defender of Darwin's theory of evolution.

appreciating flowers and who are gradually building up a comprehensive design. While, just because (unlike political economists) they know they are dealing with human material, they are far too sensible to confuse their study with an exact science, they have, I insist, most of the advantages of an exact science; that is to say, standing on a common level, they know where they are, their common rejections correspond roughly to rejections by evidence, they build on rejections, and they keep their minds open toward the front. Having in mind the people as a whole, and every cross-section of the mind of the people (not merely the cross-section that has to do with them as "producers" or "consumers"), they feel each beat of the pulse; they know what Methodism stands for, or the appearance of a new poet, or a Welsh festival, or an Irish Theatre, or a General Strike, or the statistics of unemployment, or a new book on political theory.

This open, ventilated, sceptical, sympathetic centrality of theirs articulates the whole life of the people, and incidentally as a matter of course expresses itself through legislation. More than one English book by an unknown writer has, within two years and owing to this diffused sense of the hierarchy of ideas, penetrated Parliament, convinced it, and been at once and universally translated into action. Utopian event, which an innocent person might suppose the natural course of things in the most rudimentary legislature!

Of course nobody dreams of expecting anything like that with us; and then too, as Mr. Lee observes, "we do not want to take time ourselves to be always climbing up to the Senate. We do not even want to watch it, and the last thing we would enjoy as live busy people would be standing there on the height or on the look-off, day after day, seeing for everybody. We have our own special things to do that we like to do best, and what a democracy is for is to let us do them." I am sure that every true American heart beats to that sentiment; I am sure that every true American only longs to be allowed to go on being live and busy and not seeing for everybody and letting his governors get inspired mysteriously by the still small voice, while the Stars and Stripes do all the rest.

England, to be sure, is just as much the wilderness as

America. All I am urging is that while England has at least a handful of trained gardeners, we have nothing but cowboys and a flag.

V. The Sargasso Sea

I

"THE FIDDLES ARE tuning as it were all over America." This is a remark of the best, the youngest, and the most Irish of all good Americans, Mr. J. B. Yeats. It is true that under the glassy, brassy surface of American jocosity and business there is a pulp and a quick, and this pulpy quick, this nervous and acutely self-critical vitality, is in our day in a strange ferment. A fresh and more sensitive emotion seems to be running up and down even the old Yankee backbone—that unblossoming stalk.

I am speaking myself as a thorough-going Yankee to other thorough-going Yankees,—as a "little American" (to adopt a phrase which, as time goes on, will prove more and more useful). For to find this ferment in the immigrant folk of one, two, or three generations is in itself only natural and the effect of a more vivid, instinctive, and vital civilization in their own past. The importation of radical ideas and the ferment of radical ideas which have been imported scarcely touch, it seems to me, the centre of the American problem. So far as we are concerned, the sea-crossing, to begin with, has a very dampening effect on the gunpowder contained in them. Transplanted they have at once the pleasing remoteness of literature and the stir of an only half-apprehended actuality; they become admirably safe, they become even delightful. In the American mind Nietzsche and A. C. Benson[1]—the lion

---

[1] Arthur Christopher Benson (1862-1925). English essayist and critic who spent nearly the whole of his life in an academic atmosphere, first as the son of a headmaster and then as a fellow and master of Magdalen College, Cambridge. He wrote almost one hundred volumes, among them biographies of Ruskin, Rossetti, Pater, and Fitzgerald.

and the lamb—lie down quite peacefully together, chewing the cud of culture. To get civilization out of the Yankee stock —*ex forte dulcitudo*[2]—is the more arduous and the more inspiriting enterprise. Is it possible? Is it in process? The signs are anything but obvious: one has to keep quite still and hold one's ear close to the ground to hear the sap stirring and the little half-inconsequential voices that whisper and breathe in the intervals of bombast and business. For there is nothing so shy and so puzzled as the fine Puritan temperament face to face with a free world.

If something vibrates in the air it is without doubt the expectation of a social ideal that shall act upon us as the sun acts upon a photographic plate, that shall work as a magnet upon all these energies which are on the point of being released. But the formulation of a social ideal can only be the work of a wiser head and a riper heart than we have yet seen; and we have had, meanwhile, quite enough of the egoism which, with foolish head and unripe heart, has undertaken this intoxicating function.

If it is for the State to weed out the incentives to private gain, it is for us meanwhile simultaneously to build up other incentives to replace them. These incentives must be personal. They must not spring from floating, evanescent ideals, political, spiritualistic, or other; they must touch the primitive instincts which are touched by the incentives they replace. Emerson gave us the Over-Soul; Catholicism gave us the Madonna and the Bambino;—which has really touched the religious sense of mankind?

II

America is like a vast Sargasso Sea—a prodigious welter of unconscious life, swept by ground-swells of half-conscious emotion. All manner of living things are drifting in it, phosphorescent, gayly colored, gathered into knots and clotted masses, gelatinous, unformed, flimsy, tangled, rising and falling, floating and merging, here an immense distended belly, there a

---

[2] Sweetness out of harshness.

tiny rudimentary brain (the gross devouring the fine)—everywhere an unchecked, uncharted, unorganized vitality like that
of the first chaos. It is a welter of life which has not been
worked into an organism, into which fruitful values and standards of humane economy have not been introduced, innocent
of those laws of social gravitation which, rightly understood
and pursued with a keen faith, produce a fine temper in the
human animal.

Now as everybody knows there was a time when the actual
Sargasso Seas were, to the consciousness of science, just in
this uncharted state. The creatures they contain, instead of
being studied with reference to an organic unity of which they
were all modifications, were divided into certain fixed sub-
kingdoms according as they superficially resembled one another; here a group with soft bodies, there a group whose
organs were disposed about a centre, and the like. It was, I
think, Huxley who first exposed the superficiality of this
method and who began the grouping of creatures according to
real identity in structure.

American society, so to speak, is in this pre-Darwinian
state. It is filled with "groups" which have long ceased to
mean anything, which do not stand for living issues, which do
not engage personal energies. A Democrat is no more a genuine
type than one of the pre-Darwinian Mollusca, so called because
they had soft bodies; a Republican is no more a genuine type
than the Radiata, so called because their organs were disposed
about a centre. The superficial characteristics of the types
remain—that is to say, Democrats generally *have* soft bodies,
and Republicans *do* believe in centralization—but the fruitful
elements of a group have departed from them: they no longer
touch personal instincts, they no longer possess the life which
impels to personal action.

The recognized divisions of opinion, the recognized issues,
the recognized causes in American society are extinct. And
although Patriotism, Democracy, the Future, Liberty are still
the undefined, unexamined, unapplied catchwords over which
the generality of our public men dilate, enlarge themselves,
and float (careful thought and intellectual contact still remaining on the level of engineering, finance, advertising, and

trade)—while this remains true, every one feels that the issues represented by them are no longer genuine or adequate.

The most striking American spectacle today is a fumbling about after new issues which no one as yet has been able to throw into relief. We have seen one President advocating a "New Nationalism," another President advocating a "New Freedom," a well-known novelist talking about a "New Patriotism"—phrases which illustrate just this vague fumbling, this acute consciousness of the inadequacy of the habitual issues, this total inability to divine and formulate new issues that really are issues. With us the recognized way of pinning down something that is felt to be in the air is to adopt some cast-off phrase and tack the word "New" before it. A pleasant thrill then runs over the country, something which is vaguely felt to be new having been recognized and labeled as new, and the issue itself is quietly smothered (or springs forth divinely haloed as a Currency Bill).

The truth is that it signifies nothing for politicians to import social issues into the plane of politics, even if they import the whole of socialism into politics, so long as they and we fail to recognize that the centre of gravity in American affairs has shifted wholly from the plane of politics to the plane of psychology and morals. So long as we fail to recognize this, politics can only continue the old endless unfruitful seesaw of corruption and reform. That is why catchwords like the "New Nationalism" and the "New Freedom" are really so much farther from the centre of gravity than catchwords like "Highbrow" and "Lowbrow," or "Bromide" and "Sulphite." The latter lead nowhither, but they at least explain things. "Are you a Bromide?" may be a silly vulgar question, but it is by no means a silly vulgar fact that a whole population should go about putting that question. It is a fact that grows in meaning when you consider that not so much as a remnant of the American people can go about *thinking* any question that stands for a social and psychological issue which cuts deeper than that.

It is pathetic, it is very nearly tragic. How much hunger is represented by all these "New" things which give the American public such a quality of gaseated water to stay their

appetites? How much of a real psychological curiosity mis-
carries at the outset in questions like "Are you a Bromide?"
American slang in general, alive with psychological interest in
a rudimentary state, is the most mournful tribute to a vitality
in the American people, missing fire in a million trivialities,
because it has not been engaged by issues which really touch
home in the personality, because—to put it the other way
round—the catchwords of American society are not themselves
personal.

For it may as well be understood that the human race will
have catchwords and will not budge without them. Consequently it makes all the difference to a people and an age
whether its catchwords really do or do not correspond with
convictions, and whether these convictions really do or do
not reach down among the real problems of personal and
social life—whether they really *catch* at the bottom of things,
like a dredging machine, or whether they merely scrape along
the bottom or stir up the water or ruffle the surface. Home
Rule, No Taxation without Representation, the Right of
Private Judgment, the Three Unities, are catchwords which
have played an immense part in the world of thought and
action, because they have stood for genuine causes, genuine
issues in religion, in politics, in art. The rank and file who
grasp the idea behind them incompletely and in varying degrees and who, if they depended on their understanding of the
idea, would be at sixes and sevens, grasp the catchword and
unite on a common platform which, if the catchword is a
worthy one, educates them through action. Every leader will
have his catchword: his philosophy will be a "Synthetic"
philosophy, his ideal will be the "Superman," his *bête noire* will
be the "Servile" state, and the generality of men will fall in
line according to whether the connotations of these catchwords
do or do not strike home to their own personal preferences.
For generations the test of a living society, a living philosophy
or art, will be whether or not the catchwords it flings forth
really correspond with profound divisions of type, deeply felt
issues, genuine convictions, in whichever field, between—I was
going to say—some good and some evil. But these words are
so unfashionable that if I use them I shall certainly alienate

any Advanced Person who honors these pages with a glance.

But it makes no difference how many games of pea-and-thimble philosophy may play, wherever the thimble is put down the problem of good and evil is the pea that lies under it; and the happiest excitement in life is to be convinced that one is fighting for all one is worth on behalf of some clearly seen and deeply felt good and against some greatly scorned evil. To quicken and exhilarate the life of one's own people— as Heine and Nietzsche did in Germany, as Matthew Arnold, William Morris,[3] and H. G. Wells[4] have done in England—is to bring, not peace, but a sword. With Heine the warfare was between philistinism and enlightenment, with Nietzsche between master-morality and slave-morality, with Matthew Arnold between Hebraism and Hellenism, with Morris between machinery and handicraft, with Wells between muddleheadedness and fine thinking. There are five distinct conceptions of good and five distinct conceptions of evil. And each of these pairs of opposed catchwords stands for a conceivable interpretation of society, a cleavage in things like the cleavage of the Red Sea. Accept them or not as you choose, they go down so deep that you can walk with dry feet between them.

To this happy excitement of urgent issues is due the happy excitement of European thought, the muscular and earthy sense of opposition under which personality becames aware of itself and grows with a certain richness. I do not know how much dull pain, poverty, and chagrin are responsible for these manifestations of high pressure: but certainly it is a pressure of this kind which forces the European to define his position, to form his own microcosm, and by virtue of which the catchwords that correspond with issues defined really represent

[3] William Morris (1834-1896). His many activities may derive from his intense commitment to the designer-craftsman ideal. As poet, artist, decorator, manufacturer, printer, and socialist, Morris tried to bring an organic conception of life and taste to his contemporaries. He helped found the decorating firm which involved so many pre-Raphaelites. In 1890 he founded the Kelmscott Press, famous for its edition of Chaucer. In 1883 he joined the Social Democratic Federation which, largely under his influence, developed into a socialist league.

[4] Herbert George Wells (1866-1946). Influential social prophet who wrote extensively in the cause of socialism.

something and are apt, relatively speaking, to cut deep. And certain it is that while European literature grows ever closer and denser and grapples to life more and more, American literature grows only windier and windier. You will find in H. G. Wells, for example, what seems at times as irresponsible a mysticism as that of any American. But while the American tendency is to begin in the air and remain in the air, you will scarcely find a European thinker who has not earned his right to fly by serving an apprenticeship with both feet on the ground;—if he leaves the earth it is because he has been pressed from it and he carries flesh and blood and clods of earth with him. You cannot have too much mysticism; but on the other hand you cannot have enough good human mud for ballast. The pressure which actuates the European mind is due no doubt to a vast deal of dull pain, poverty, and chagrin. But are we Americans very much happier? In America, I think, pain, poverty, and chagrin are at last very nearly as imminent as elsewhere, and so far we have devised no compensation for them.

Self-fulfillment is the immemorial compensation for having eaten of the fruit of good and evil, and under the conditions of modern life self-fulfillment has to be a somewhat artificial thing. In a world of instincts blunted by trade, system, and machinery, the sweat of the brow, the resurgence of the seasons, the charm of perfect color and of pure form are not for the generality of men sufficient. The exhilarating sense of conflict and of rest from conflict which together make up the meaning of life, no longer universally possible on the plane of instinct, have largely come to exist in the more contagious, the more gregarious, the more interdependent world of the intelligence. In that world the majority are lost and astray unless the tune has been set for them, the key given them, the lever and the fulcrum put before them, the spring of their own personalities touched from the outside.

In the midst of the machine age, as everybody knows, it was the contagious personality of William Morris which opposed the ideal of craftsmanship to the ideal of cheapest work and largest money and substituted for the inhumane stimulus of competition the humane stimulus of fellowship.

No doubt this was only a drop in the bucket. But, speaking relatively, picture to yourself what might have been the inner mind of the average artisan—to adopt the method of patent-medicine advertising—Before and After the William Morris treatment. One contagious personality, one clear shadowing forth of opposed issues—a good and an evil, a humane and an inhumane—touched the spring of personality in how many workingmen! and gave them how rich and how adequate a reason to turn over this world of ours, as a spade turns over a clod of earth. It is of no use to talk about Reform. Society will be very obedient when the myriad personalities that compose it have, and are aware that they have, an object in living.

How can one speak of progress in a people like our own that so sends up to heaven the stench of atrophied personality? How can one speak of progress in a people whose main object is to climb, peg by peg, up a ladder which leads to the impersonal ideal of private wealth? How can the workingman have any reality or honesty of outlook when he regards his class merely as an accidental, temporary group of potential capitalists? And the university man—the man, that is to say, who has had the fullest opportunity to seek and find a disinterested end in living, an end to which the machinery of self-preservation however compelling remains yet in subservience—the man who has within him a world of ineffectual dreams and impotent ideals—what has he to actuate him but a confused and moralized instinct that somehow he must make a lot of money?

It is not a question of blame. You cannot blame the individual, even as a citizen, though as a citizen he overtly upholds the conception of society which is responsible for his helplessness as an individual. His personality, his latent energies go to waste just as the personalities of so many artisans would have gone to waste if there had been no William Morris. The way has not been made straight for him, the waters of the sea of good and evil have not been divided for him; he flounders in the mud and the waves, until at last, if he is exceptionally fortunate, he drowns in a million dollars. It is the economic individualist himself who blames people; socialism has the charity of science.

III

Issues which really make the life of a society do not spring spontaneously out of the mass. They exist in it—a thousand potential currents and cross-currents; but they have to be discovered like principles of science, they have almost to be created like works of art. A people is like a ciphered parchment which has to be held up to the fire before its hidden significances come out. Once the divisions that have ripened in a people have been discerned and articulated, its beliefs and convictions are brought into play, the real evils that have been vaguely surmised spring into the light, the real strength of what is intelligent and sound becomes a measurable entity. To cleanse politics is of the least importance if the real forces of the people cannot be engaged in politics; and they cannot be so engaged while the issues behind politics remain inarticulate.

In spite of their frequent show of strength and boldness no ideas in America are really strong or bold,—not because the talents are wanting but because the talents and the mass have not been brought into conflict. No serious attempt has been made to bring about the necessary contraposition of forces, to divine them, to detach them, to throw them into relief; the real goats and the real sheep have not been set apart. There has not in fact been one thinker strong enough to create a resisting background in the vague element of American life.

To create this resisting background must be the first work for our thinkers. It is incomparably difficult, for it is like standing on clouds and attempting to gain purchase for a lever. The vast, vague movements of sentiment in the democracy directly produce the conventionality of our ideas, for there is no clinch in things, nothing to brace the feet against, no substance against which ideas can assume a bold relief. "To preserve the freedom of the will in such expansion," says Victor Hugo (who had reason to know), "is to be great;" and certainly the man who can throw American life into relief will be a man out of ninety million.

But how shall we know him when he comes?—we who have invented the phrase "any old thing," we whose watchword has always been "just about as good," we who delight in plausible mediocrity and are always ready with tinkling cymbals to greet the sounding brass? To leave behind the old Yankee self-assertion and self-sufficiency, to work together, think together, feel together, to believe so fervently in the quality of standards that we delight in prostrating our work and our thoughts before them—all that is certainly in the right direction. "My belief becomes indefinitely[5] more certain to me as soon as another shares it" is the true catholic observation of a German poet, which all good Americans ought to ponder; for intimate feeling, intimate intellectual contact, even humor —that rich, warm, robust and all-dissolving geniality which never, I think, quite reached the heart of Mark Twain—it is these we chiefly lack. These are the enemies of that base privateness which holds the string of what we call publicity; these promote that right, free, disinterested publicity which the real gentleman, the real craftsman, the real civil servant has always had in his blood.

Socialism flows from this as light flows from the sun. And socialism is based on those three things in the world which, of all things, have the most dignity—hunger, science, and good will. Is it "against human nature"? The foolish socialist laughs in his sleeve when he hears this, convinced as he is that human nature is the sport of circumstances and that when the time is right human nature will fall in line as the trees fall in line through the process of the seasons. Only the foolish socialist stops there. To be a sheer determinist is in all probability to have behind one the authority of the intellect. But human nature is an elusive magical thing which has the faculty of submitting its intellect to all manner of sea-changes. Determinism, which at one moment appears to enslave man, may at the next become the slave of man. There is a free will within determinism by which, as it were, men can cheat nature, convincing themselves—and with a whole heart—that what nature wills is what they will: and if they will it enough, which is master of the situation? We Americans ought to know, for we have produced one of the greatest of determinists, and one of

---

[5] Probably a misprint for "infinitely."

the greatest of all transmuters of determinism:

My foot is tenoned and mortised in granite,
I laugh at what you call dissolution,
And I know the amplitude of time.

All forces have been steadily employed to complete and delight me;
Now on this spot I stand with my robust soul.

IV

All Americans are good—this to me is an axiom; but we are good as the Germans used to be a hundred years ago, as good, that is, as bread which is baked without yeast. We are good and we are humble. We have so schooled ourselves in humility that nobody in the world more carefully, more steadily (and more unjustly) takes down our pretensions than the educated American. In the end it may be our humility that saves us. But the acquisition of culture and the acquisition of money—"Highbrow" and "Lowbrow"—are equally imper- sonal, equally extraneous to the real matter, equally incapable of arousing the one thing needful. When the women of America have gathered together all the culture in the world there is— who knows?—perhaps the dry old Yankee stalk will begin to stir and send forth shoots and burst into a storm of blos- soms. Strange things happen. I have heard of seeds which, either planted too deep or covered with accretions of rubble, have kept themselves alive for generations until by chance they have been turned up once more to the friendly sun. And after all humanity is older than Puritanism.

IV

The Seven Arts Essays

(1916-1917)

EDITORIAL NOTE: With minor revisions, Brooks regrouped his *Seven Arts* essays to form *Letters and Leadership* (1918) essentially as follows:

The essays, "Enterprise," "The Splinter of Ice" and "Toward A National Culture" became Chapter I under the title, "Old America."

"The Culture of Industrialism," "Young America," "Our Critics" and "Our Awakeners" became respectively Chapters II, III, IV and V.

For a brief discussion of *The Seven Arts,* its leaders and its policies, see the Introduction, pages xx-xxii. The essay here omitted is "Our Critics."

1. Enterprise

THERE IS A certain spot in New York where I love to go and ruminate in the summer noontime, a lonely, sunny, windy plaza surrounded by ramshackle hoardings and warehouses unfinished and already half in ruin. It is the fag end of a great cross-town thoroughfare, a far-thrown tentacle, as it were, of the immense monster one hears roaring not so far away, a tentacle that lies there sluggish and prone in the dust, overtaken by a sort of palsy. To the right and left stretches one of those interminable sun-swept avenues that flank the city on east and west, wide, silent, and forsaken, perpetually vibrating in the blue haze that ascends from its hot cobblestones, bordered on one side by rickety wharves, on the other by a succession of tumble-down tenements left there like the sea-wrack at the ebb of the tide. For scarcely a living thing lingers here about the frayed edges of the town, and so overwhelming is the sensation of an utter lapse in its exuberant vitality that one feels as if one had been suddenly set down in the outskirts of some pioneer city on the plains of the Southwest, one of those half-built cities that sprawl out over the prairie, their long streets hectically alive in the centre but gradually shedding their population and the few poor trees that mitigate the sun's glare till at last, all but obliterated in alkali dust and marked only by the chaotic litter of old out-buildings and broken-down fences that straggle beside them, they lose themselves in the sand and the silence.

All our towns and cities, I think, have this family likeness and share this alternating aspect of life and death—New York as much as the merest contraption of corrugated iron and clapboards thrown together beside a Western railway to fulfill some fierce evanescent impulse of pioneering enterprise. Like

SOURCE: I (November 1916), 37-60.

a field given over to fireworks, they have their points of light and heat, a district, a street, a group of streets where excitement gathers and life is tense and everything spins and whirls; and round about lie heaps of ashes, burnt-out frames, seared enclosures, abandoned machinery, and all the tokens of a prodigal and long-spent energy.

But it is the American village that most betrays the impulse of our civilization, a civilization that perpetually overreaches itself only to be obliged to surrender again and again to nature everything it has gained. How many thousand villages, frostbitten, palsied, full of a morbid, bloodless death-in-life, villages that have lost, if they ever possessed, the secret of self-perpetuation, lie scattered across the continent! Even in California I used to find them on long cross-country walks, villages often enough not half a century old but in a state of essential decay. Communities that have come into being on the flood-tide of an enterprise too rapidly worked out, they all signify some lost cause of a material kind that has left humanity high and dry; like the neutral areas in an old painting where the color, incompetently mixed and of perishable quality, has evaporated with time.

I suppose it is only natural in the West, these decayed settlements where time has taken so seriously, as it were, mankind's deliberate challenge to permanence. What shocks one is to realize that our Eastern villages are themselves scarcely anything but the waste and ashes of pioneering, and that no inner fire has taken possession of the hearth where that original flame so long since burnt itself out.

Off and on during the summers I have stayed in one of those ancient Long Island villages that still seem to preserve unbroken the atmosphere of the early Republic, and it has been for me not so much a visible scene as a strange and disconcerting experience. The crazy, weatherbeaten houses that hold themselves up among their unkempt acres with a kind of angular dignity, the rotting porches and the stench of decay that hangs about their walls, the weed-choked gardens, the insect-ridden fruit trees, the rusty litter along the roads, the gaunt, silent farmers that stalk by in the dusk—how overwhelmingly they seem to betray a losing fight against the

wilderness! For generations every man has gone his own way
and sought his own luck. Nature has been robbed and despoiled and wasted for the sake of private and temporary
gains, and now having no more easy rewards to offer, it is
taking its revenge on a race that has been too impatient and
self-seeking to master its inner secrets. Incapable of cooperating with nature, of lying fallow, of merging themselves as
it were in the great current of life, they have accumulated no
buoyant fund of instinct and experience, and each generation,
a little more spiritually impoverished than the last, runs out
the ever-shortening tether of self-reliance. Still pioneers, pioneers or nothing, they have lost the sap of adventure without
developing beyond the stage of improvisation.

It is all so familiar, so intensely American, and yet the
warm ancestral bond eludes one so! One looks out over a
landscape everywhere abundant and propitious, but still in
some way, after so many years of tillage, unimpregnated by
human destiny, almost wholly wanting in that subtle fusion
of natural and human elements which everywhere the European landscape suggests. For Europe is alive in all its members; in its loneliest and most isolated corner there is hardly
a hamlet where life does not still persist, as green and warm
and ruddy as the heart of an old olive tree. Some profound
inertia, some imperturbable tenacity of the spirit, has prevented it from quite surrendering to nature anything, a bit of
ground, a house, a road, that has once passed into the keeping
of the race. And thus it is that while the conquest has been
slow and laborious, invention tardy, ideas few, means inadequate, something cumulative survives.

Old American things are old as nothing else anywhere in
the world is old, old without majesty, old without mellow-
ness, old without pathos, just shabby and bloodless and worn
out. That is the feeling that comes over once in villages like
this, capable only of being galvanized by some fresh current
of enterprise into a semblance of animation. Inhabited as
they have always been by a race that has never cultivated life
for its own sake, a race that has lived and built and worked
always conscious of the possibility of a greater advantage to be
found elsewhere, there is no principle of life working in them,

three hundred years of effort having bred none of the in-dwelling spirit of continuity.

How little of an ample, fostering bosom the traditional scene holds to us Americans, how all but irrevocably it com-mits us to a sharply individual, experimental existence!

2. Young America

SHORTLY AFTER THE outset of the nineteenth century there passed into the intellectual currency of almost every European people a certain phrase which everywhere stood for one sub-stantial, common impulse: a resurgence of national purpose working consciously against a played-out national background. It was the watchword of the new generation—Young Germany, Young Italy, Young Ireland, I mean, to mention a few in-stances; and in each case it represented a warm, humane, concerted and more or less revolutionary protest against what-ever incubus of crabbed age, paralysis, tyranny, stupidity, sloth, commercialism, lay most heavily upon the people's life, checking the free development of personality, retarding the circulation of generous ideas. A little later the phrase and its informing impulse passed beyond the European Turks and finally in Young China and Young India, until within the space of a century the entire Eastern Hemisphere had passed under its rejuvenating touch.

A similar phrase became current at about the same time in our own social history. Who does not remember "Young America," a phrase that served, and continues to serve, though it has long since passed into cant, as a sort of touchstone of American juvenility? Young America blossomed out originally on the covers of innumerable magazines and storybooks, the text of which set forth his ingenious and enterprising career. He was the typical farmer's boy of our national epos, who sought adventure and found success. By shifts and devices

SOURCE: I (December 1916), 144-151.

that all his contemporaries understood, he came back home from time to time, his pockets bulging with greenbacks acquired somewhere on the other side of the horizon, just in time to save his mother from dispossession or a painful death; and in the end, automatically and by easy stages, he arrived at the White House. The story always stopped just at the point where Young America became the arbiter of our national destinies. He had got his particular plum, that was the climax. How the rest of us fared with regard to the plum, how he himself digested it—everything of that sort was manifestly beside the question.

Now, superficially, of course, there is no basis of comparison between such a conception as this and one so far less easily personified as that of Young Italy, for example, or Young China. But, really, I think, Young America stood for the essential impulse of our post-revolutionary history in exactly the same way that the corresponding phrases have stood for the essential post-revolutionary impulse in every other country. As in China, as in Turkey, as in Italy, as in Germany, it stood for the force that overtoppled the old regime—the colonial regime in our case, the aristocratic, or bureaucratic, or despotic, or alien regime elsewhere, as the case might be, and set up the ferment of modern society. In function it was identical, in quality alone it was fundamentally different, just as the American revolution was fundamentally different from all the revolutions of Europe and Asia.

It was fundamentally different, it was unique, of course, in striking the note of a country where, to reverse the proverb, nothing was to be endured, everything was to be done, where the programme was necessarily one, not of reaction through the mass, but of expansion through the individual. Moral and kindly, bold, callous, and simple, Young America had to do with immense, external, impersonal, wholesale tasks like "developing the West"; it had to fence in lands it had never tilled, filch gold out of mountains it had never lived among, and cover the continent with a sound, rudimentary population. The contest lay all along not between man and society, not between youth and age, as it lay in the Old World, but between the human and the non-human, and it called into play so great

an over-plus of will and energy, of self-reliance and self-assertion, that nature, else intractable, was in the end borne under.

That was the quality of our essential historic impulse, the
tune to which every loyal American heart in the old days beat
high, an impulse that was determined not by the pressure of
personality from within, but by the existence, the allure, and
the eventual decay of material opportunities outside. For there
came a time when the tune began to lag, when the pioneer
passed over into the business man and the giants and empire-
builders began to lie back among their dividends, spilling right
and left in public works the millions they had had a clear title
to in the days when everyone felt that their enterprise and
prowess were blazing a trail for the race. Well before 1900
Young America gave up dreaming of the White House, not
because the White House had become less attainable by everyone at once, but because it had ceased to be in the general
regard the merely natural and legitimate prize of the good
boy who had made his way best in the world. The hour of the
epos had struck.

It had struck, bequeathing to us only one human tradition,
by virtue of which we are all "infinitely repellant particles,"
all too rich in the technique of material enterprise, impoverished and without experience in the technique of society and
the intellect. Primitive competition, the competition of the
jungle itself, the only mode of life our fathers knew, had left
us cold and dumb in spirit, incoherent and uncohesive as between man and man, given to many devices, without community in aim or purpose.

Thus it is that the fierce rudimentary mind of America, like
that of some inchoate primeval monster, relentlessly concentrated in the appetite of the moment, knows nothing of its own
vast, inert, nerveless body, encrusted with parasites and half
indistinguishable from the slime in which it moves. One looks
out today over the immense vista of our society, stretching
westward in a succession of dreary steppes, a universe of
talent and thwarted personality evaporating in stale culture,
and one sees the inevitable result of possessing no tradition to
fill in the interstices of energy and maintain a steady current
of life over and above the ebb and flow of individual impulses,

of individual destinies. Is it strange that while the spiritual
life of the Old World, deep-rooted and all-embracing organism
that it is, perpetually blossoms afresh, the spiritual life of
America is at the mercy of everything that passes in the air,
and that any fresh breeze from a new direction can bowl it
over, like a plant sprung up in a sand-waste?

For we are indeed, as Turgenev said of Russia, *grande et
riche, mais désordonnée*. Who can estimate the latent force
that inexhaustibly spends itself in the trivialities of our popular fiction and makeshift art, in the search for successful
formulas, in aimless theorizing and senseless ingenuity, in advertising and ragtime, in rhetoric, jocosity, and vague sentiment, in half-apprehended culture, and the bogs and fens of
theosophy? Our life is like a badly motivated novel, full of
genius but written with an eye to quick returns; a novel that
possesses no leading theme, in which the style alternates between journalese and purple patches, and every character goes
its own arbitrary way, failing of its full effect. So undeveloped
we are, save in the little private role we set ourselves, so
unhabituated in the more comprehensive relationships of life,
that it is as if we lived in relief, as it were, only half cut out.
Encircle most Americans and you will encounter nothing but
a rough block, plainly not intended to be seen.

Now, I assume that we are all quite aware of these things,
that we are all heartily sick and tired both of our own old
ways and the old ways of the life about us, quite aware that
something fundamental in our national background his played
itself out and gone threadbare. To the remotest corners of the
country the new generation is putting to itself the question,
"What is coming next?" Well, I have spoken of Russian
society as at one time, in the one sense at least of possessing
no consciously organic life, comparable with ours. And this,
not to push the comparison too far, is what happened in
Russia at the turn of the tide. The quotation is from Stepniak,[1]

---

[1] Stepniak, pseudonym of Sergey M. Kravchinsky (1852-1895). Many West-
erners acquired their conceptions of the Russian revolutionary movements from
this terrorist. Works like *Underground Russia: Revolutionary Profiles* (1883) and
The Career of a Nihilist (1889), thrilling and vivid, are almost without value
as documentary evidence.

on the revolutionary movement of 1873-1874.

It was a revelation rather than a propaganda. At first the book, or the individual, that had impelled this or that person to join the movement could be traced out; but after a while this became impossible. It was a powerful cry which arose, no one knew where and whence, and which summoned the zealous to the great work of the redemption of country and humanity. And the zealous, heeding this cry, arose, overwhelmed with sorrow and indignation over their past life, and abandoning home and family, wealth and honors, threw themselves into the movement with a joy, an enthusiasm, a faith, such as are experienced only once in a lifetime, and which when lost are never found again.

I will not speak of the many young men and young women of the highest aristocratic families who labored fifteen hours a day in the factories, in the workshops, in the fields. Youth is proverbially generous and ready for sacrifice. The most characteristic feature of the movement was that the contagion spread even to the people, advanced in years, who had already a future clearly worked out and a position won by the sweat of their brows—judges, physicians, officers, officials,—and these were not among the least zealous.

Yes, it was not a political movement; it rather resembled a religious movement in its contagious and absorbing elements. People not only sought to obtain a distinct practical object, but also to satisfy an inward sentiment of duty, an inspiration, so to speak, leading them toward their own moral perfection.

One can see at a glance, of course, how characteristically Russian all that is, how little it bears, in any specific way, upon anything either existent or potential in the American make-up, in which for one thing the religious impulse has for so long ceased to be organic. I quote it simply as the most perfect example of a psychological phenomenon that appears again and again at appointed moments, in one form or another—the sudden fusion of a race, by which all its elements are miraculously set beating together at the highest pitch. Differing in style and degree, according to the peculiar genius, in response to the peculiar need of the race in question, now literary, now political, now agricultural, now religious, or a

combination of two or all of these, it has appeared in all the
national movements of Young Europe and Young Asia, from
the days of Mazzini to the days of Sun Yat Sen,[2] in the
awakening of Ireland, in the re-birth of the submerged nationalities of Eastern Europe, in the sudden tensity of a score
of "national cultures" at the outbreak of the war. It is exactly
as in the opening and the development of a symphony; a lull
succeeds the chaotic din of instruments not yet in tune; in the
presentiment of unison, the general dawn of a leading theme,
an immense calm descends over all, and then slowly, faintly,
at the dropping of the wand, the orchestration begins, weaving
its way hither and thither till at last every mind and hand,
every thought and sense, every nerve and muscle is aflame, and
a whole population is caught up in some supreme system of
ideas.

It is vain to look for anything quite like this in America,
even if it is this alone, or the less ecstatic and more habitual
equivalent of this, which makes a race great and an age great.
For we are not a race, to begin with; we are incongruous at
once in blood and in culture. Unlike the nations of the Old
World, we possess neither a dormant, subconscious multitude
existing on a common level and capable of responding to a
common watchword, nor a student class united in the discipline
of common ideals and capable of arousing them. There are
centers of our civilization where nothing is real but the future,
immense areas of mentality keyed at the Tennysonian pitch,
villages in the interior of Virginia, where, they say, Matthew
Prior, prince of poets in the age of Anne, is still the reigning
favorite in letters, tenacious outposts of culture in Tennessee
and Kentucky where the speech of the people remains un-
changed from the time of Queen Elizabeth. And this is the
tale of the Anglo-Saxon tradition alone. We are a population
at sixes and sevens, holding among all classes and at all stages
of development scarcely any common conviction save one,

[2] Sun Yat-sen (1866-1925). Chinese revolutionary under whose leadership
the Ch'ing dynasty was overthrown and the Chinese republic formed in 1911.
He was the republic's first president.

that "the essential preoccupation of youth," as one of our novelists put it the other day, "is organizing a living."

And yet there is one indisputable new fact that has been gradually coming to light these last years, a sort of epilogue to the Young America myth which may in the end put a new face on things, new in a different sense from that of all the other "newnesses" that have befooled and befuddled us from the days of the Transcendentalists down. And this new fact is that material enterprise no longer possesses the infinite horizon and the spiritual *élan* that once justified it in the eyes of all and could alone continue to justify it in the eyes of a "proverbially generous" youth. One stands on perfectly safe psychological ground in asserting that young men will not for long go on committing themselves to a mode of life that has lost its leaven of spiritual conflict and adventure, a mode of life that no longer calls the poetic faculties into play, and offers nothing to the soul; "organizing a living," without that, is altogether too tepid an affair. One sees how the wind blows in business itself, in the dissatisfaction, so to say, of business with being merely business, in its tendency to pass over its own borders and become a means of expression, an "art-form," as Mr. Gerald Stanley Lee says. But far more significantly one sees it in the tired, baffled expression on the faces of so many middle-aged Americans, bewildered men like Mr. Henry Ford,[3] men who have discovered the inadequacy of business to fulfill their spiritual needs and who, reaching out from it, find themselves lost in a maze of wider relationships with which no technique that they possess enables them to cope.

This is the real disposition of things, and it gives meaning to the painful, insistent, blundering, inarticulate will to exist on a higher plane than that of the domestic animals which manifests itself the country over in so many thousand isolated lives. The poems that all but reach their intention, the novels

[3] Henry Ford (1863-1947). The pioneer automobile manufacturer who, like Carnegie, had many social schemes. In 1914 Ford paid his workers $5 a day (a high rate) and initiated a profit-sharing plan. In 1915 he sent a privately sponsored peace ship to try to end the war. These are examples of the "wider relationships" Brooks refers to. Two years after this essay was written Ford ran unsuccessfully for senator on the democratic ticket.

that never come to market, the religious emotions that never crystalize, the speculations that never quite achieve their master-thought, the political ideas that lose themselves in sentimentality, who can estimate their number, or question the reality of the experience that lies behind them? All this confused, thwarted, multitudinous welter of spiritual impulse is, I believe, the certain visible sign of some prodigious organism that lies undelivered in the midst of our society, an immense brotherhood of talents and capacities coming to a single birth. For we have learned one lesson from our competitive pioneering past—that we human beings are all pretty much, as Balzac said, like the figure O; when another is set beside it we acquire ten times our value.

3. The Splinter of Ice

Ce n'est pas les ténèbres, c'est seulement l'absence de jour.

I

WHEN THE IDEA of *The Seven Arts* first became known and it was said that we were to have a new magazine to focus the new movement in our literature, many people, I think, whose hope and faith are wrapped up in the artistic future of America, experienced a shock of delight and expectation. They felt that a propitious moment had come, that multitudinous forces were pressing together toward this one point, and that in short an enterprise of this kind, inaugurated at this time and with these aims, had every chance of succeeding that wind and wave could offer it; and yet, the first flush over, they must to a degree temper their confidence, as they recall how many are the lights that have misled our dawn. Without

SOURCE: I (January 1917), 270-280.

consciousness of the failures of the past, their enthusiasm cannot build on a real basis.

In any other country than America one's instinctive impulse to welcome what is new would not have been so immediately checked. For the newness of new movements in Europe, the enterprise of enterprises, are the very elements that most excite enthusiasm. And very naturally; for new movements, new schools of thought, new magazines have on such countless occasions proved to be points of departure in the intellectual life of society. Think of the European magazines, think of the European groups and brotherhoods that have been inaugurated on lines approximating those of *The Seven Arts* or that have come together in a spirit similar to the spirit that actuates the contributors to *The Seven Arts!* To name them is almost to tell the story of English, French, German, Russian literature during the last hundred years. Where literature has a tradition, where it is bound up with society, where society is itself an organism, a new movement, in order to get on its feet at all, has to overcome the inertia of the established fact; and thus by the time it has reached the point of articulation it has been fined and rarified, it has passed through a pre-natal process of maturation, and it emerges not only fully conscious of itself but saturated with the under-currents of the racial life.

How different it is in America! Our society has never been an organism and in consequence our social history presents none of the phenomena of development. For a hundred and fifty years we have been called, and have called ourselves, a "young" people, and we are just as "young" now as we were in the days of Washington. Youth is our convention as age is the convention of other countries, and it is the newness of new things and the enterprise of enterprises that have ever been the hallmarks of this convention. That is why they cannot thrill us now.

The history of our literature alone would be enough to explain our disillusionment, for it chronicles an endless succession of impulses that have spent themselves without being able to grapple, or to be grappled by, the soul of the race. If you read those of the historians who are ignorant of what literature has meant in the life of other peoples, you will be surprised to find that our literature has gone through all the motions of a complete historic evolution—although not perhaps in the right order. We have had our age of chronicles (Cotton Mather), our classical age (Benjamin Franklin), our *Sturm und Drang* (Brockden Brown[1]), our Renaissance (in New England), and at last, though sadly transposed from a chronological point of view, our Homer (Walt Whitman). All of these epithets can be found in one or another of the histories turned out by our industrious professors; and at the end of it all we feel that we have not yet, artistically speaking, begun to exist. It is not difficult to see why this is so; the very use of these epithets explains it. That our Homer came at the end instead of at the beginning of what is called our standard literature, that he rings down the curtain in all the orthodox histories, illustrates as clearly as anything could that our standard literature in the mass was created out of whole cloth and that it had an integrity as distinct from the multifarious chaotic life of the American people as the crust of a pie has from the less decorative contents it serves to conceal.

Consequently none of the sincere and repeated innovations of American writers have been able to incorporate themselves in a tradition. Evolving from their studies in European literature not only an artistic technique but a technique of social expression, they have never been able to find in our society a fulcrum upon which to base the lever they hold in their hands. Priceless talents have passed across our horizon, fluttering into sight only to flutter out again. To name only the classic examples: there was Poe, whose work, thanks to the law that to him that hath shall be given, has enriched the literature of Europe only to leave ours the more barren by contrast. There were the Transcendentalists, apostles of the first "Newness" whose aim it was to dethrone the dollar, minds many of them at least of the second or third order that lost their edge in the fogs of their own bewilderment. There were Emerson and Thoreau, who have found their true liter-

[1] Charles Brockden Brown (1771-1810). America's Gothic novelist, deeply interested in psychoses.

ary fruition not among their own countrypeople but in Nietzsche and Maeterlinck and the nature writers of England. And there is Whitman, our own authentic Whitman, who, for one poet that he has leavened in America, has leavened three poets, three novelists, three thinkers in the Old World. And if our superior talents have in this way been lost in the quicksand of our life, what shall we say of our lesser talents? The former have sown their seed in alien soil, the latter have sown no seed whatever, although England has found room amid her fertile acres even for Ambrose Bierce and Stephen Crane.

First steps, in short, have been taken, times without number. The spirit of initiative has never been wanting; but it has never been able to initiate anything permanent, it has never been able to set the ball rolling. The American mind revolves round and round in a sphere as it were miraculously proof against the attacks and incursions of experience, as if, like the hero of Hans Andersen's story, it had a splinter of ice buried in the midst of it, a splinter of ice that literature has never been able to melt.[2]

II

It is a commonplace that immigration from without and migration within the Republic have prevented the formation of any structure in our society for literature to build a nest in. No sooner has the nucleus of a living culture begun to take shape than the tides of enterprise and material opportunity have swept away its foundations. But the point for us is that long before this material opportunity had fully revealed itself—in the great pioneering epoch of the nineteenth century—our society had spontaneously generated a frame of mind favorable to its pursuit, a frame of mind that the pursuit itself inevitably rendered chronic. For there is only one thing that retards the pursuit of material success; a sceptical attitude with regard to the importance of its attainment. And there is only one thing that can give birth to this sceptical attitude; a richly matured emotional experience that endows life with a value and a significance in and of itself. Certainly if our forbears had not previously undergone a systematic

[2] See *The Snow Queen.*

course of emotional starvation they could never have leaped forth, like famished hounds, at the call of the wilderness. Nor, having done so, and having found in adventure a substitute for all they had forgone, could they admit the value of anything that stood between them and the rewards of their sacrifice. The literature they knew, the literature they produced, corroborated them. Emerson told them that the arts and traditions of the past, the tragic discoveries of social man, were vapors in a world that knew no reality but the self-reliant individual. And Mark Twain, the innocent abroad, the Yankee at the court of King Arthur, established the pioneer mind once for all in the sentiment of its own sufficiency.

They did not realize, those old prophets of self-reliant individualism, that it is one thing to be self-reliant as against an alien outworn culture and another thing to maintain that self-reliance in a world that possesses no culture at all but only an over-plus of "things." Full of the old Puritan contempt for human nature and the sensuous and imaginative experience that seasons it and gives it meaning, the American mind was gradually subdued to what it worked in. For possessing as it did a minimum of emotional equipment, it had no barriers to throw up against the overwhelming material forces that beleaguered it, and it gradually went out of itself as it were and assumed the values of its environment.

This is the root of the peculiar optimism, the so-called systematic optimism, that can be fairly taken as what psychologists call the "total reaction upon life" of the American mind in our day. Mr. Horace Fletcher[3] has defined this optimism in terms that leave no doubt of its being at once the effect and the cause of our spiritual impotence: "Optimism can be prescribed and applied as a medicine. Is there anything new and practical in this, or is it but a continuation of the endless discussion of the philosophy of life, morals, medicine, etc? Is it something that a busy person may put into practice, take with him to his business, without interfering with his business, and profit by; and, finally, what does it cost? Does adoption

---

[3] Horace Fletcher (1849-1919). American writer on nutrition who evolved a system called Fletcherism, chiefly concerned with the slow mastication of food.

of it involve discharging one's doctor-friend, displeasing one's pastor, alienating one's social companions, or shocking the sacred traditions that were dear to father and mother? It is ameliorative, preventive, and harmonizing; and also it is easy, agreeable, ever available, and altogether profitable. By these hall-marks of Truth we know that it is true."

Grotesque as this may seem, you will search in vain for a more accurate presentation of the workaday point of view of our tumbling American world. This is the way Americans think, and what they think, whether they profess the religion of mind cure, uplift, sunshine, popular pragmatism, the gospel of advertising, or plain business; and they mean exactly what the beauty experts mean when they say, "Avoid strong emotions if you wish to retain a youthful complexion." Systematic optimism, in other words, effects a complete revaluation of values and enthrones truth upon a conception of animal success the prerequisite of which is a thorough-going denial and evasion of emotional experience. In this latter respect it resembles the systematic pessimism of India. For just as the pessimism of India is undoubtedly the chronic result of contact with a pitiless and monstrous tropical nature, an immemorial subjection to the jungle, to the burning sun, to famine, conditions in which in order to maintain one's equilibrium one's only course is to deny the value of everything the possession of which demands so impossible a price, so also this optimism of ours is the chronic result of contact with a prodigal nature too easily borne under by a too great excess of will, with opportunities so abundant and so alluring that we have been led to reverse the situation, traditionally unaware as we are of the mature faculties, the potentialities, the justifications of human nature, and establish our scale of values in the incomparably rich material territory that surrounds us. Each of these conditions of life has resulted in its own peculiar mysticism; each of these types of mysticism is grounded in a chronic evasion of emotional experience. And if today there is no principle of integrity at work in any department of our life, if religion competes with advertising, art competes with trade, and trade gives itself out as philanthropy, if we present to the world at large the spectacle of a vast undifferentiated

herd of good-humored animals, it is because we have passively surrendered our human values at the demand of circumstance.

III

How then can our literature be anything but impotent?
It is inevitably so, for it springs from a national mind that has
been standardized in another sphere than that of experience.

How true this is can be seen from almost any of its enunci-
ations of principle, especially on the popular, that is to say
the frankest, level. I open, for instance, one of our so-called
better-class magazines and fall upon a character sketch of
William Gillette.[4] "What a word! *Forget!* What a feat! What
a faculty! Lucky the man who can himself forget. How gifted
the one who can make others forget. It is the triumph of the
art of William Gillette that in the magic of his spell an
audience forgets." Opening another magazine I turn to a
reported interview in which a well-known popular poet ex-
patiates on his craft. "Modern life," he tells us, "is full of
problems, complex and difficult, and the man who concentrates
his mind on his problems all day doesn't want to concentrate
it on tediously obscure poetry at night. The newspaper poets
are forever preaching the sanest optimism, designed for the
people who really need the influence of optimism—the bread-
winners, the weary, the heavy-laden. That's the kind of poetry
the people want, and the fact that they want it shows that
their hearts and heads are all right."

Here are two typical pronouncements of the American
mind, one on the art of acting, one on the art of poetry, and
they unite in expressing a perfectly coherent doctrine. This
doctrine is that the function of art is to turn aside the problems of life from the current of emotional experience and
create in its audience a condition of cheerfulness that is not
organically sprung from experience but added from the outside. It assumes, in short, what we in general assume, that

---

[4] William Gillette (1853-1937). A popular playwright who wrote comedies
and farces like *All the Comforts of Home* (1890) and *Mr. Wilkinson's Widows*
(1891) and romances like *Secret Service: A Romance of the Southern Con-
federacy* (1898).

experience is not the stuff of life but something essentially meaningless; and not merely meaningless but an obstruction which retards and complicates our real business of getting on in the world and getting up in the world, and which must therefore be ignored and forgotten and evaded and beaten down by every means in our power.

What is true on the popular level is not less true on the level of serious literature, in spite of everything our conscientious artists have been able to do. Thirty years ago an acute foreign critic remarked, apropos of a novel by Mr. Howells, that our novelists seemed to regard the Civil War as an occurrence that separated lovers, not as something that ought normally to have colored men's whole thoughts on life. And it is true that if we did not know how much our literature has to be discounted we could hardly escape the impression, for all the documents which have come down to us, that our grandfathers really did pass through the war without undergoing the purgation of soul that is said to justify the workings of tragic mischance in human affairs. Mr. Howells has himself given us the *Comédie humaine* of our post-bellum society, Mr. Howells whose whole aim was to measure the human scope of that society and who certainly far less than any other novelist of his time falsified his vision of reality in the interests of mere story-telling. Well, we know what sort of society Mr. Howells pictured and how he pictured it. He has himself explicitly stated in connection with certain Russian novels that Americans in general do not undergo the varieties of experience that Russian fiction records, that "the more smiling aspects of life" are "the more American," and that in being true to our "well-to-do actualities" the American novelist does all that can be expected of him.

In making this statement Mr. Howells virtually declared the bankruptcy of our literature. For in the name of the American people he denied the fundamental fact of artistic creation: that the reality of the artist's vision is something quite different from the apparent reality of the world about him. The great artist floats that reality on the sea of his own imagination and measures it not according to its own scale of values but according to the values that he has himself derived from his own descent into the abysses of life. The sketchiest, the most immature, the most trivial society is just as susceptible as any other of the most profound artistic reconstruction. All that is required is an artist capable of penetrating beneath it.

The fact is that our writers are themselves victims of the universal taboo the ideal of material success has placed upon experience. It matters nothing that they themselves have no part or lot in this ideal, that they are men of the finest artistic conscience. In the first place, from their earliest childhood they are taught to repress everything that conflicts with the material welfare of their environment, in the second place their environment is itself so denatured, so stripped of everything that might nourish the imagination, that they do not so much mature at all as externalize themselves in a world of externalities. Unable to achieve a sufficiently active consciousness of themselves to return upon their environment and overthrow it and dissolve it and recreate it in the terms of a personal vision, they gradually come to accept it on its own terms. If Boston is their theme they become Bostonian; if it is the Yukon they become "abysmal brutes;" if it is nature, nature itself becomes the hero of their work; and if it is machinery the machines themselves become vocal and express their natural contempt for a humanity that is incapable, either morally or artistically, of putting them in their place and keeping them there.

Thus, for example, in Mr. Howells' *A Modern Instance,* the whole tragedy is viewed not from the angle of an experience that is wider and deeper, as the experience of a great novelist always is, than that of any character the novelist's imagination is able to conceive, but from the angle of Ben Halleck, the best that Boston has to offer. Boston passes judgment and Mr. Howells concurs; and you close the book feeling that you have seen life not through the eyes of a free personality but of a certain social convention, at a certain epoch, in a certain place. It is exactly the same, to ignore a thousand incidental distinctions, in the work of Jack London. Between the superman of certain European writers and Jack London's superman there is all the difference that separates an ideal achieved in the mind of the writer and a fact accepted from the world outside him; all the difference, in short, that separates the truth of art from the appearance of life.

If these two talents, perhaps the freshest and most original our indigenous fiction has known since Hawthorne's day, have thus been absorbed in an atmosphere which no one has ever been able to condense, is it remarkable that the rank and file have slipped and fallen, that they have never learned to stand upright and possess themselves? Is it remarkable that they sell themselves out at the first bid, that they dress out their souls in the ready-made clothes the world offers them? So great is the deficiency of personal impulse in America, so overwhelming the demand laid upon Americans to serve ulterior and impersonal ends, that it is as if the springs of spiritual action had altogether evaporated. Launched in a society where individuals and their faculties appear only to pass away, almost wholly apart from and without acting upon one another, our writers find themselves enveloped in an impalpable atmosphere that acts as a perpetual dissolvent to the whole field of reality both within and without themselves, an atmosphere that invades every sphere of life and takes its discount from everything that they can do, an atmosphere that prevents the formation of oases of reality in the universal chaos. Is it remarkable that they take refuge in the abstract, the non-human, the impersonal, in the "bigness" of the phenomenal world, in the surface values of "local color," and in the "social conscience," which enables them to do so much good by writing badly that they come to think of artistic truth itself as an enemy of progress?

This is the tale of our past and of the present our past has made for us. We know now that all the fresh enthusiasm in the world cannot produce an American literature. To create that our writers have to create the life that literature springs from; they have to create a respect for experience, a profound sense both in their audience and in themselves of the significance and value of just those things of which literature is the expression.

Will they be able to do this? Yes. That is our categorical imperative.

4. Toward a National Culture

"When first hatched they are free-swimming, microscopic creatures, but in a few hours they fall to the bottom and are lost unless they can adhere to a firm, clean surface while making their shells and undergoing development."

—Report on the Oyster Industry.

WHY IS IT," asks the author[1] of *Jude the Obscure,* "that these preternaturally old boys always come out of young countries?" It was the spectacle of Jude himself, transplanted from Australia into the midst of the ancient peasantry of southern England that prompted the question, and I remember with what force it came into my mind once, during a brief visit in Oxford, when, accustomed as my eyes for the moment were to the jocund aspect of young England in flannels, I came upon a company of Rhodes scholars from across the Atlantic. Pallid and wizened, little old men they seemed, rather stale and flat and dry; and I said to myself, It is a barren soil these men have sprung from,—plainly they have never known a day of good growing weather.

They might not have been typical Rhodes scholars, these men—I don't pretend to any wide knowledge of the species. But I know that, as often happens abroad when we encounter the things of home in unfamiliar surroundings, they brought to a head certain obscure impressions that had long been working in my imagination. I remembered, for instance, the "young instructors" I had encountered between Boston and San Francisco; I remembered the sad, sapless air of so many of them and their sepulchral voices, the notes of that essential priggishness the characteristic of which, according to Chester-

SOURCE: I (March 1917), 535-547.

[1] Thomas Hardy.

ton,[2] is to have more pride in the possession of one's intellect than joy in the use of it. I fell to thinking about this professor and that I had known at home, and about our intellectual and artistic life in general. How anaemic it seemed, how thin, how deficient in the tang and buoyancy of youth, in personal conviction and impassioned fancy, how lacking in the richer notes! And at last there arose in my mind the memory of a concert at which all the accepted American composers had appeared on the stage one after another, grave, earnest, high-minded, and tinkled out their little intellectual harmonies.

Am I wrong in my impression that our "serious" people really are like leaves prematurely detached from the great tree of life? As a class they seem never to have been young, and they seem never to grow mellow and wise. Take our earnest popular novelists off guard; read their occasional comments on society, on the war, even on their own art. How dull, how mechanical, how utterly wanting in fresh insight their minds in general are! Mr. Winston Churchill,[3] expatiating on citizenship, talks in one breath with all the puzzled gravity of a child and some of the weary flatulence of a retired evangelist. Even when they are not evangelical but writers merely they still seem somehow uprooted from the friendly soil. Something infinitely old and disillusioned peers out between the rays of George Ade's wit;[4] Robert Herrick[5] writes like a man stricken with palsy, and Mrs. Wharton's intellectuality positively freezes the fingers with which one turns her page. And it is the same in our other arts, the plastic arts alone perhaps excepted. Think of that one little vibrant chord, like

[2] Gilbert Keith Chesterton (1874-1936). English wit, essayist and novelist, known as the "prince of paradox."

[3] Winston Churchill (1871-1947). Primarily known for his extremely popular historical epics; in his later life he became interested in social problems.

[4] George Ade (1866-1944). One of the many regional humorists of the period, Ade is known for his use of slang. Works like *Fables in Slang* (1900) were highly popular.

[5] Robert Herrick (1868-1938). Realistic novelist whose novels examine and indict the competition and materialism of his day. He was concerned, like Brooks, with the conflict between creativeness and acquisition. In *Memoirs of an American Citizen* (1905) he depicts the rise of a self-made capitalist.

a naked nerve perpetually harped on, that constitutes the theatrical art of Mrs. Fiske![6] Think of the arctic frigidity of Mr. Paul Elmer More's[7] criticism! That little seed of the spirit a wayward and unlucky wind has planted in them, why has it never been able to take on flesh and blood, why has it so dried up the springs of animal impulse? It is as if, driven in upon themselves, their life were a constant strain, as if their emotional natures had run dry and they had come to exist solely in their intellects and their nerves, as if in fact they had gone grey and bloodless precisely in the measure that an inflexible conscience had enabled them in spite of all to trim the little lamp that flickered in them.

Grow they certainly do not. With immense difficulty our intellectual types forge for themselves a point of view with which they confront the world, but like a suit of armor it permits no further expansion. They do not move easily within it; they are chafed and irritated by it; in order to breathe freely they are obliged to hold themselves rigidly to the posture they have at first adopted; and far from being able to develop spontaneously beyond this original posture they have to submit to its cramping limitations until the inevitable shrinkage of their mental tissues brings them release and relief.

Whatever the reason may be it is certain that the long-fermented mind, the wise old man of letters, the counsellor, is a type our civilization utterly fails to produce. Our thinking class quickly reaches middle age and after a somewhat prolonged period during which it seems to be incapable of assimil-

---

[6] Minnie Maddern Fiske (1865-1932). The leading American actress for a generation, especially known for her Shakespeare and Ibsen roles. She opened her own theater in Manhattan in 1901 to combat the theatrical syndicate of the 90s.

[7] Paul Elmer More (1865-1937). Dispensing judgment from his retreat in Shelburne, New Hampshire, More has been called a "secular monk." He also inhabited the editorial offices of the *Independent* and the New York *Evening Post* and was an editor of *The Nation* (1901-1914). The fourteen volumes of his *Shelburne Essays* (1904-1935) reflect a development from sympathy for the individual writer to an organized attack on modern literature. Deeply influenced by his contemporary and friend at Harvard, Irving Babbitt, both men are considered founders of the neo-humanist movement in American criticism. Brooks attacks More and others as old guard critics in "Our Critics," *Seven Arts,* II (May 1917), 103-116.

ating any fresh experiences it begins to decay. The rest of
our people meanwhile never even grow up. For if our old men
of thought come to a standstill at middle age, our old men of
action, as one sees them in offices, in the streets, in public
positions, everywhere! are typically not old men at all but old
boys. Greybeards of sixty or seventy, mentally and spiritually
indistinguishable from their sons and grandsons, existing on
a level of reflection and emotion in no way deeper or richer
than that of their own childhood, they seem to have miraculously passed through life without undergoing any of life's
maturing influences.

II

In short, I think we are driven to the conclusion that our
life is, on all its levels, in a state of arrested development, that
it has lost, if indeed it has ever possessed, the principle of
growth. To the general sense of this many of the main documents in our recent literature bear witness. The immense and
legitimate vogue of the "Spoon River Anthology," for example, is due to its unerring diagnosis of what we all recognize, when we are confronted with it, as the inner life of the
typical American community when the criterion of humane
values is brought to bear upon it in place of the criterion of
material values with which we have traditionally pulled the
wool over our eyes. It is quite likely of course that Mr.
Masters,[8] with a reasonable pessimism, has exaggerated the
suicidal and murderous tendencies of the Spoon Riverites.
But I know that he conveys an extraordinarily just and logical
impression. He pictures a community of some thousands of
souls every one of whom lives in a spiritual isolation as absolute as that of any lone farmer on the barren prairie, a community that has been utterly unable to spin any sort of
spiritual fabric common to all, which has for so many generations cherished and cultivated its animosity toward all those
non-utilitarian elements in the human heart that retard the

---

[8] Edgar Lee Masters (1869-1950). His *Spoon River Anthology,* published
anonymously in 1915, critically annotates small town life in free verse epitaphs
about Spoon River citizens.

successful pursuit of the main chance that it has reduced itself
to a spiritual desert in which nothing humane is able to find
rootage and grow at all. And yet all the types that shed
glory on humankind have existed in that, as in every community! They have existed, or at least they have been born.
They have put forth one green shoot only to wither and decay
because all the moisture has evaporated out of the atmosphere that envelops them. Poets, painters, philosophers, men
of science and religion, are all to be found, stunted, starved,
thwarted, embittered, prevented from taking even the first
step in self-development, in this amazing microcosm of our
society, a society that stagnates for want of leadership, and at
the same time, incurably suspicious of the very idea of leadership, saps away all those vital elements that produce the
leader.

For that is the vicious circle in which we revolve. We who
above all peoples need great men and great ideals have been
unable to develop the latent greatness we possess and have
lost an incalculable measure of greatness that has, in spite of
all, succeeded in developing itself. For one thing we have lost
an army of gifted minds, of whom Henry James and Whistler
and Sargent are only the most notorious examples, minds many
of them about which our intellectual life could have rallied to
its infinite advantage, as it always does when born leaders are
in the field, and which would have given far more to the
world as well had they been able to strike root among the
essential things of life. But the loss, great and continuing as it
is, of so many talents that we have repelled and poured out,
talents that have been driven to an exotic development in
other countries, is really nothing beside what we have lost in
less obvious ways.

In the absence both of an intellectual tradition and a sympathetic soil, in the absence above all of that peculiar intensive
knowledge of art that inoculates the artist against commercialism, a disproportionate amount of our talent has been seduced
from its right path, in comparison with other countries. And
of the talents we have been able to preserve in their integrity
there is hardly one, I believe, but would shine out with ten
times its actual power if literature and society in America bore

an organic relationship to one another. It is quite plain that there is nothing inherently "greater" in many of the writers whose work we import (and rightly import) from abroad than in writers of a corresponding order at home. The former simply have been able to make a better use of their talents owing largely to the complicated system of critical and traditional forces perpetually at play about them.

Indeed the more one thinks of our social history and of our present state the more one feels that for generations there has been going on in this country a systematic process of inverse selection so far as the civilizing elements in the American nature are concerned. Our ancestral faith in the individual and what he is able to accomplish (or, in modern parlance, to "put over") as the measure of all things has despoiled us of that instinctive human reverence for those divine reservoirs of collective experience, religion, science, art, philosophy, the self-subordinating service of which is almost the measure of the highest happiness. In consequence of this our natural capacities have been dissipated; they have become egocentric and socially centrifugal and they have hardened and become fixed in the most anomalous forms. The religious energy of the race, instead of being distilled and quintessentialized into the finer inspirations of human conduct, has escaped in a vast vapor that is known under a hundred names. So also our scientific energy has been diverted from the study of life to the immediacies of practical invention, our philosophy, quite forgetting that its function is to create values of life, has oscillated between a static idealism and a justification of all the anaemic tendencies of an anaemic age, and our art and literature, oblivious of the soul of man, have established themselves on a superficial and barren technique.

Of all this individualism is at once the cause and the result. For it has prevented the formation of a collective spiritual life in the absence of which the individual, having nothing greater than himself to subordinate himself to, is either driven into the blind alley of his appetites or rides some hobby of his own invention until it falls to pieces from sheer craziness. Think of the cranks we have produced! Not the mere anonymous cranks one meets, six to a block, in every American village, but the eminent cranks, and even the *preëminent* cranks, the Thoreaus and Henry Georges, men that might so immensely more have enriched our spiritual heritage had we been capable of assimilating their minds, nurturing and disciplining them out of their aberrant individualism. For every member of the vast army of American cranks has been the graveyard of some "happy thought," some thought happier than his neighbors have had and which has turned sour in his brain because the only world he has known has had no use for it.

It is this chaotic, unmotivated world, a world of things, an essentially prehistoric world that knows nothing of the compensations of an animal destiny to which we are all entitled as heirs of our human past, that Mr. Theodore Dreiser has memorialized in those vast literary pyramids of his, those prodigious piles of language built of the commonest rubble and cohering, in the absence of any architectural design, by sheer virtue of their weight and size. Mr. Dreiser's Titans and Financiers and Geniuses are not even the approximations of men in a world of men,—they are monsters, blindly effectuating themselves, or failing to effectuate themselves, in a primeval chaos; and the world wears them and wearies them as it wears and wearies the beasts of the field, leaving them as immature in age as it found them in youth. Cowperwood, the Financier, put in prison as a result of his piratical machinations, weaves chair-bottoms and marks time spiritually against the day of his release, when he snaps back into his old self absolutely unaltered by reflection: and of Eugene Witla, after he has passed through seven hundred and thirty-four pages of soul-searing adventure, Mr. Dreiser is able to inquire: "Was he not changed then? Not much, no. Only hardened intellectually and emotionally, tempered for life and work." Puppets as they are of an insensate force which has never been transmuted into those finer initiatives that shed light on human destiny, they are insulated against human values; love and art pass into and out of their lives like things of so little meaning that any glimmer of material opportunity outshines them; and therefore they are able to speak to us only of the vacuity of life, telling us that human beings are as the flies of summer.

One readily shares the objection commonly raised against Mr. Dreiser that his philosophy is a barren one, and that it is the business of literature to project those radiant attitudes by which life is filled with honor and dignity. Nevertheless one ought not to demand too much; it is a great thing to be enabled to see our life as it at present is, so completely industrialized that the capacity for spiritual initiative has been all but bred out of it. Ideals are healthily born midway in the evolution of a people; they spring from a certain level of experience that has been attained by all in common; and without this general touchstone they soon turn into vapor as our American ideals have done in the past.

III

Now it is the absence of this platform as it were of collective experience that we have suddenly come to realize. The balloon of material success, to which our people have attached the frail basket of their spirits, has begun to flap in the wind; we feel that we are falling, and that we are falling into a void. We are like explorers who, in the morning of their lives, have deserted the hearthstone of the human tradition and have set out for a distant treasure that has turned to dust in their hands; but having on their way neglected to mark their track they no longer know in which direction their home lies, nor how to reach it, and so they wander in the wilderness, consumed with a double consciousness of waste and impotence. I think this fairly describes the frame of mind of a vast number of Americans of the younger generation. They find themselves born into a race that has drained away all its spiritual resources in the struggle to survive and that continues to struggle in the midst of plenty because life itself no longer possesses any other meaning. Meanwhile, the gradual commercialization of all the professions has all but entirely destroyed the possibility of personal growth along the lines that our society provides and, having provided, sanctions. Brought up as they have been to associate actively almost solely with material ends and unable in this overwhelmingly prosperous age to feel any powerful incentive to seek these ends, acutely conscious of their spiritual unemployment and impoverished in will and impulse, they drift almost inevitably into a state of internal anarchism that finds outlet, where it finds outlet at all, in a hundred unproductive forms.

Our society, in fact, which does everything by wholesale, is rapidly breeding a race of Hamlets the like of which has hardly been seen before, except perhaps in nineteenth-century Russia. Nothing is more remarkable than the similarity in this respect between the two immense inchoate populations that flank Europe on east and west. To be sure, the Oblomovs[9] and Bazarovs[10] and Levins[11] and Dmitri Rudins[12] of Russian fiction are in many ways, like Hamlet himself, universal characters. But for one Hamlet in an organized society which, according to the measure of its organization, provides an outlet for every talent, there are twenty in a society which, as we say, has no use for its more highly developed types. And that is the situation both in Russia and in the United States: the social fabric is too simple to be able to cope with the complicated strain that has been suddenly put upon it by a radical change in the conditions of life. Yet in each case the complexities are developing along just the lines most necessary for the rounded well-being of society. The Hamlets of Russian fiction, generally speaking, are social idealists, wrapped up in dreams of agricultural and educational reform; they long to revolutionize their country estates and ameliorate the lot of their peasantry, and

[9] Oblomov, the indolent, passive gentleman who spends his life in bed, is the creation of Ivan Goncharov (1812-1891). He gives to the Russian language the term Oblomovism. The novel *Oblomov,* written in 1858, did not appear in English until 1915.

[10] Bazarov is the nihilist doctor-hero of Ivan Turgenev's (1818-1883) *Fathers and Sons* (1861) whose interest in scientific experiment gives him some fixed point of interest. His death by infection is accidental and ironic.

[11] Levin is the idealist in search of a proper relationship to the soil, to man, and to God in Leo Tolstoy's *Anna Karenina* (1875-1877). He retreats, finally, to his garden.

[12] Dmitri Rudin is the hero of Turgenev's *Rudin* (1855). A man of incomplete projects, he dies on the barricades in the revolution of 1848; the strength of this act is diluted when the French soldiers who find his corpse take him for a Pole. These four characters may represent a Russian version of what Brooks had earlier called "the malady of the ideal."

they lose their will and their vision because there is no social machinery they can avail themselves of: thrown as they are upon their own unaided resources, their task overwhelms them at the outset with a sense of futility. Turn the tables about and you have the situation of the corresponding class in America. They find the machinery of education and social welfare in a state as highly developed as the life of the spirit is in Russia; it is the spiritual technique, if I may so express myself, that is wanting, a living culture, a complicated scheme of ideal objectives, upheld by society at large, enabling them to submerge their liberties in their loyalties and to unite in the task of building up a civilization.

For only where art and thought and science organically share in the vital essential program of life can the artist and the thinker and the scientist find the preliminary foothold that enables them to undertake this task. To state the case in its lowest terms, only under these conditions are they able to receive an adequate, intensive training along non-utilitarian lines without hopelessly crippling their chances of self-preservation; for under these conditions they know that the social fabric is complicated enough to employ all the faculties of their minds and that in following non-utilitarian lines they are fulfilling a recognized need of society. It is this which breeds in them the sense that they are serving something great, something so generally felt to be great that society rewards them with a pride calling forth their own pride, taking delight in setting up the sort of obstacles that constantly put them on their mettle. Everywhere in Europe, in spite of the industrialization of society, that is still in some degree the case. It is because the social fabric is complicated enough for art and music and thought to have an organic share in it that artists and musicians and thinkers develop as richly and beneficently as they do, relatively speaking. It is because of the simplicity of our social fabric, in which bread and butter alone plays any organic part, that our effectual types narrow down to the captains of industry. The rest, in so far as they are liberated from this motive, are all but lost to society. Either, like the *émigrés* of France under Napoleon, they turn inward and lose themselves in introspection, or else they waste upon the desert air energies that ought to be conserved and sublimated in the interests of the whole race.

IV

And that is what is happening today. The miraculous rapidity and efficiency with which we have been able to effect the material conquest of the continent has resulted in throwing out of employment a prodigious amount of energy that our society is unable to receive and set to work. All the innate spirituality of the American nature, dammed up, stagnant from disuse, ineluctably romantic, has begun to pour itself out in a vast flood of undisciplined emotionalism that goes to waste largely because the scope of our "useful" objectives is so restricted; and because, inheriting as we do an ingrained individualism, an ingrained belief in quick returns, we are all but unable to retain these treacherous elements, of which we have had so little practical experience in the past, until they have reached a sufficient maturity to take shape in lasting forms.

But this new individualism, which finds its gospel in self-expression, is totally different in content from the individualism of the past. The old spiritual individualism was blood-brother to the old materialistic individualism: it throve in the same soil and produced a cognate type of mind. It was hard, stiff-necked, combative, opinionative, sectarian, self-willed; it gave birth to the crank, the shrill, high-strung propounder of strange religions, the self-important monopolist of truth. In short, it was essentially competitive. The new individualism, on the other hand, is individualistic only by default; its individualistic character, so to say, is only an inherited bad habit, a bad habit that is perpetuated by the want of objectives in the truly vacuous world with which it finds itself confronted. It has, I think, no desire to vaunt itself; it tends, instead of this, to lavish itself; it is not combative, it is coöperative, not opinionative but groping, not sectarian but filled with an intense, confused eagerness to identify itself with the life of the whole people. If it remains confused, if it is unable to discipline itself, if it is often lazy and wilful, if its smoke is only at intervals illuminated by flame—well, was it not the same with the Oblomovs of Russia? I can't conceive that anyone *wants* to be confused and lazy, especially if he has no material motives to console him in other ways. People who do not "burn with a hard, gem-like flame" are simply people who are not being employed by civilization.

Undoubtedly the gospel of self-expression, makeshift as it is, is leaving its deposit over the quicksand of our life. Isolated, secretive, bottled up as we have been in the past, how could we ever have guessed what aims and hopes we have in common had they not been brought to light, even in the crudest and most inadequate ways? To many people, I think, these last few years, during which the "lid" has been lifted with a vengeance, have been years of inspiring discovery as regards America. I don't say that the desert has blossomed like the rose; I should say rather, to mix metaphors, that an appalling number of skeletons had been pulled out of the closet. But somehow America has become under our eyes a living entity, visibly in process of developing a third dimension. It used to be a map, it has become a swarm; it used to be a bare place we moved about in, it has become a jungle of shoots. Americans, north, south, east, and west, have ceased to be "simply folks"; they have ceased to be merely Texans and Kentuckians and Californians and New Englanders, satisfied, so far as the art of writing is concerned, with the dialect and local color of a "Kentucky literature," or what not. They have become, to our imagination, human beings, and human beings faintly flushed with that desire for a higher life that implies a life in common. They have *manifested* themselves; but will they get any further? Only, it seems to me, if we are able to build up, to adapt a phrase from the slang of politics, a program for the conservation of our spiritual resources.

If this leads into the idea of a "national culture" to come it is only in order that America may be able in the future to give something to the rest of the world that is better than what the rest of the world at present calls "Americanism." For two generations the most sensitive minds in Europe— Renan, Ruskin, Nietzsche, to name none more recent—have summed up their mistrust of the future in that one word; and it is because, altogether externalized ourselves, we have typified the universally externalizing influences of modern industrialism. The shame of this is a national shame, and one that the war, with all the wealth it has brought us, has infinitely accentuated. And it covers a national problem—the problem of creating objects of loyalty within the nation by virtue of which the springs of our creative energy are not only touched into play but so economized as to be able to irrigate the entire subsoil of our national life.

How is this problem to be met? In many ways. But of the challenge it offers to criticism there can be no doubt whatever, if, as Matthew Arnold said, it is the business of criticism to make a situation of which the creative power can profitably avail itself.

5. The Culture of Industrialism [1]

IF WE ARE dreaming of a "national culture" today it is because our inherited culture has so utterly failed to meet the exigencies of our life, to seize and fertilize its roots. It is amazing how that fabric of ideas and assumptions, of sentiments and memories and attitudes which made up the civilization of our fathers has melted away like snow uncovering the sordid facts of a society that seems to us now so near the lowest rung of the ladder of spiritual evolution. The older generation does not recognize its offspring in the crude chaotic manifestations of the present day, but I wonder if it ever considers this universal lapse from grace in the light of cause and effect? I wonder

SOURCE: I (April 1917), 655-666.

[1] Thomas Carlyle coined the term industrialism. See Raymond Williams, *Culture and Society* (New York, 1958), p. 72, who also discusses the broadening meaning of the term culture; Brooks played a role in that broadening process, as the title of this essay indicates.

if it ever suspects that there must have been some inherent weakness in a culture that has so lost control of a really well-disposed younger generation, a culture which, after being dominant for so long, has left in its wake a society so little civilized? What is the secret of its decay? And how does it happen that we, whose minds are gradually opening to so many living influences of the past, can feel nothing but the chill of the grave as we look back over the spiritual history of our own race?

It was the culture of an age of pioneering, the reflex of the spirit of material enterprise—that is the obvious fact; and with the gradual decay of the impulse of enterprise it has itself disintegrated like a mummy at the touch of sunlight. Why? Because it was never a living, active culture, releasing the creative energies of men. Its function was rather to divert these energies, to prevent the anarchical, skeptical, extravagant, dynamic forces of the spirit from taking the wind out of the myth of "progress," that myth imposed by destiny upon the imagination of our forbears in order that a great uncharted continent might be subdued to the service of the race.

For the creative impulses of men are always at war with their possessive impulses, and poetry, as we know, springs from brooding on just those aspects of experience that most retard the swift advance of the practical mind. The spirit of a living culture, which ever has within it some of the virus of Pascal's phrase: "Caesar was too old to go about conquering the world; he ought to have been more mature"—how could this ever have been permitted to grow up, even supposing that it might have been able to grow up, in a people confronted with forests and prairies and impelled by the necessities of the race to keep their hearts whole and their minds on their task? No, it was essential that everything in men should be repressed and denied that would have slackened their manual energy and made their ingenuity a thing of naught, that would have put questions into their minds, that would have made them static materially and dynamic spiritually, that would have led them to feel too much the disparity between the inherited civilization they had left behind and the environment in which they had placed themselves, that would have neutralized the allure of the exterior ambition which led them on.

Puritanism was a complete philosophy for the pioneer and by making human nature contemptible and putting to shame the charms of life it unleashed the possessive instincts of men, disembarrassing those instincts by creating the belief that man's true life is altogether within him and that the imagination ought never to conflict with the law of the tribe. It was this that determined the character of our old culture, which cleared the decks for practical action by draining away all the irreconcilable elements of the American nature into a transcendental upper sphere.

European critics have never been able to understand why a "young nation," living a vigorous, primitive life, should not have expressed itself artistically in a cognate form; and because Whitman did so they accepted him as the representative poet of America. So he was; but it is only now, long after the pioneer epoch has passed and the "free note" has begun to make itself heard, that he has come to seem a typical figure to his own countrypeople. In his own time Whitman was regarded with distrust and even hatred because, by releasing, or tending to release, the creative faculties of the American mind, by exacting a poetical coöperation from his readers, he broke the pioneer law of self-preservation. By awakening people to their environment, by turning democracy from a fact into a principle, his influence ran directly counter to the necessities of the age, and his fellow-writers justly shunned him for hitting in this way below the belt. In fact had Whitman continued to develop along the path he originally marked out for himself he might have seriously interfered with the logical process of the country's material evolution. But there was in Whitman himself a large share of the naïve pioneer nature, which made it impossible for him to take experience very seriously or to develop beyond a certain point. As he grew older, the sensuality of his nature led him astray in a vast satisfaction with material facts, before which he purred like a cat by the warm fire. This accounts for the reconciliation which occurred in later years between Whitman and his literary contemporaries. They saw that he had become harmless; they accepted him as a man of talent; and making the most of his more conventional verse, they at last crowned him provisionally as the "good gray poet."

For the orthodox writers of the old school had a serious duty to perform in speeding the pioneers on their way; and they performed it with an efficiency that won them the gratitude of all their contemporaries. Longfellow with his lullabies, crooning to sleep the insatiable creative appetites of the soul, Lowell, with his "weak-wing'd song" exalting "the deed"—how invaluable their literature was to the "tired pioneer," forerunner of the "tired business man" of the present day and only a loftier type because, like the tired soldier of the trenches, it was in response to the necessities of the race that he had dammed at their source the rejuvenating springs of the spirit! Yes, it was a great service those old writers rendered to the progress of this country's primitive development, for by unconsciously taking in charge, as it were, all the difficult elements of human nature and putting them under chloroform, they provided a free channel for the *élan* of their age.

But in so doing they shelved our spiritual life, conventionalizing it in a sphere above the sphere of action. In consequence of this our orthodox literature has remained an exercise rather than an expression and has been totally unable either to release the creative impulses of the individual or to stimulate a reaction in the individual against his environment. Itself denied the principle of life or the power of giving life, it has made up for its failure to motivate the American scene and impregnate it with meaning by concentrating all its forces in the exterior field of aesthetic form. Gilding and idealizing everything it has touched and frequently attaining a high level of imaginative style, it has thrown veils over the barrenness and emptiness of our life, putting us in extremely good conceit with ourselves while actually doing nothing either to liberate our minds or to enlighten us as to the real nature of our civilization. Hence we have the meticulous technique of our contemporary "high-class" magazines, a technique which, as we know, can be acquired as a trick, and which, artistic as it appears, is the concomitant of a complete spiritual conventionality and deceives no sensible person into supposing that our general cleverness is the index of a really civilized society.

II

This total absence of any organic native culture has determined our response to the culture of the outer world. There are no vital relationships that are not reciprocal and only in the measure that we undergo a cognate experience ourselves can we share in the experience of others. To the Catholic, Dante, to the aristocrat, Nietzsche, to the democrat, Whitman, inevitably means more than any of them can mean to the scholar who merely receives them all through his intellect without the palpitant response of conviction and a sympathetic experience. Not that this "experience" has to be identical in the literal sense; no, the very essence of being cultivated is to have developed a capacity for sharing points of view other than our own. But there is all the difference between being actively and passively cultivated that there is between living actively or passively emotional lives. Only the creative mind can really apprehend the expressions of the creative mind. And it is because our field of action has been preëmpted by our possessive instincts, because in short we have no national fabric of spiritual experience, that we are so unable today to think and feel in international terms. Having ever considered it our prerogative to pluck the fruits of the spirit without undergoing the travail of generating them, having ever given to the tragi-comedy of the creative life a notional rather than a real assent, to quote Newman's famous phrase,[2] we have been able to feed ourselves with the sugar-coating of all the bitter pills of the rest of mankind, accepting the achievements of their creative life as effects which presuppose in us no casual relationships. That is why we are so terribly at ease in the Zion of world culture.

All this explains the ascendancy among our fathers of the Arnoldian doctrine about "knowing the best that has been thought and said in the world." For, wrapped up as they were

---

[2] See Chapter IV, "Notional and Real Assent" in *An Essay in Aid of a Grammar of Assent* (1870). Notional assent issues from the mind's contemplation of its own creations; real assent issues from the contemplation of things. The work analyzes the means by which educated minds may find rational grounds for Christian belief.

in their material tasks, it enabled them to share vicariously
in the heritage of civilization, endowing them, as it were, with
all the pearls of the oyster while neatly evading in their behalf
the sad responsibility of the oyster itself. It upholstered their
lives with everything that is best in history, with all mankind's
most sumptuous effects quite sanitarily purged of their ugly
and awkward organic relationships. It set side by side in the
Elysian calm of their bookshelves all the warring works of the
mighty ones of the past. It made the creative life synonymous
in their minds with finished things, things that repeat their
message over and over and "stay put." In short, it conven
tionalized for them the spiritual experience of humanity,
pigeon-holing it, as it were, and leaving them fancy-free to
live "for practical purposes."

I remember that when as children we first read Carlyle and
Ruskin we were extremely puzzled by their notes of exasperated indignation. "What are they so angry about?" we wondered, and we decided that England must be a very wicked
country. Presently, however, even this idea passed out of our
heads, and we came to the conclusion that anger and indignation must be simply normal properties of the literary mind
(as they are, in a measure) and that we ought to be grateful
for this because they produce so many engaging grotesqueries
of style. Our own life was so obviously ship-shape and water-
tight—was it possible that people in other countries could have
allowed their life to become less so? Unable as we were to
decide this point, we were quite willing to give the prophets
the benefit of the doubt, as regards their own people. But
it was inconceivable that for us they meant any more by their
contorting rages than the prophets of the Bible meant, whose
admirably intoned objurgations we drank in with perfect com-
posure on Sundays.

Consequently, those very European writers who might,
under normal circumstances, have done the most to shake us
out of our complacency have only served the more to confirm
us in it. Our immediate sphere of action being sealed against
them, their influence has been deflected into "mere literature,"
where it has not been actually inverted. For in so far as our
spiritual appetites have been awake, it has only gone to con-

vince us, not that we are unenlightened ourselves, but that other people are wicked. This incidentally explains the charge of hypocrisy that has been brought against the Anglo-Saxon mind in general ever since the industrial epoch began, a charge that has followed Puritanism as inevitably as trade has followed the flag; and it explains also the double paradox that while our reformers never consider it necessary to take themselves in hand before they set out to improve the world, our orthodox literary men, no matter what models they place before themselves, cannot rise above the tribal view of literature as either an amusement or a soporific.

How natural, then, that the greatest, the most "difficult" European writers should have had, as Carlyle and Browning and Meredith had, their first vogue in America! How natural that we should have flocked about Ibsen, patronized Nietzsche, found something entertaining in every kind of revolutionist, and welcomed the strangest philosophies (the true quite as readily as the false)! For having ourselves undergone no kindred creative experience for them to corroborate and extend, we have ever been able to escape their slings and arrows with a whole skin. They have said nothing real to us because there has been nothing in our own field of reality to make their messages real.

III

As a result of this immemorial inhibition of our humane impulses, this deliberate obliviousness to the facts of life, personal and social alike, the younger generation find themselves in a very peculiar position. For having, unlike Europeans of any class, no fund of general experience in their blood, as it were, to balance the various parts of their natures, they are incapable of coördinating themselves in a free world. So long as their creative and their possessive, their spiritual and their material, instincts frankly face in opposite directions they are able to make some sort of "go" of life, as their fathers did before them. But the whole spirit of our age tends to make this dualism more and more difficult. When, therefore, their instincts face about and confront one another and attempt to make some sort of compact, the material instinct inevitably comes out on top, because the material instinct alone is acquainted with the life of action. Their inherited and acquired culture drops away from them like a dream in the dawn and their consciousness immediately contracts into a field of reality that is restricted almost solely to the primary biological facts. This accounts for the brutality of so much of our contemporary realism; it accounts for the general poverty and chaos of our spiritual life.

Not that we only have suffered in this way, but that we have suffered more completely in certain respects than other countries. The world over the industrial process has devitalized men and produced a poor quality of human nature. By virtue of this process the orthodox culture of the world fell, during the nineteenth century, into the hands of the prig and the aesthete, those two sick blossoms of the same sapless stalk, whose roots have been for so long unwatered by the convictions of the race. But in Europe the great traditional culture, the culture that has ever held up the flame of the human spirit, has never been gutted out. The industrialism that bowled us over, because for generations our powers of resistance had been undermined by Puritanism, was no sooner well under way in Europe than human nature began to get its back up; and a long line of great rebels reacted violently against its desiccating influences. Philologists like Nietzsche and Renan, digging among the roots of Greek and Semitic thought, artists like Morris and Rodin, rediscovering the beautiful and happy art of the Middle Ages, economists like Marx and Mill, revolting against the facts of their environment, kept alive the tradition of a great society and great ways of living and thus were able to assimilate for human uses the positive by-products of industrialism itself, science and democracy. They made it impossible for men to forget the degradation of society and the poverty of their lives and built a bridge between the greatness of the few in the past and the greatness of the many, perhaps, in the future. Thus the democracies of Europe are richer than ours in self-knowledge, possessing ideals grounded in their own field of reality and so providing them with a constant stimulus to rise above their dead selves, never doubting that experience itself is worth having lived for even if it leads to nothing else. And thus, however slowly they advance, they advance on firm ground.

For us, individually and socially, nothing of this kind has been possible. It has been the very law of our life that our ways should be kept dark, that we should not be awakened to the hideousness of our civilization, that the principles in the light of which we are supposed to stand should remain abstract and impersonal. It seems to me wonderfully symbolic of our society that the only son of Lincoln should have become the president of the Pullman Company, that the son of the man who liberated the slaves politically should have done more than any other, as *The Nation* pointed out not long ago, to exploit them industrially. Our disbelief in experience, our habitual repression of the creative instinct with its consequent overstimulation of the possessive instinct, has made it impossible for us to take advantage of the treasures our own life has yielded. Democracy and science have *happened to* us abundantly, more abundantly than to others because they have had less inertia to encounter; but like children presented with shining gold pieces we have not known how to use them. Either we have been unable to distinguish them from copper pennies, or else we have spent them in foolish ways that have made us ill. Our personal life has in no way contributed to the enriching of our environment; our environment, in turn, has given us personally no sense of the significance of life.

IV

Thus we see today, emerging from his illusions, the American as he really is: obscure to himself and to others, a peasant, and yet not a peasant, an animal, but full of gentleness and humor, physically sane but neurotic from the denial of his impulses, a ragbag of inherited memories and unassimilated facts, a strange, awkward, unprecedented creature, snared by his environment, helplessly incapable of self-determination in a free world—in a word, "low-brow," and aware of it. As I visualize him, rather dimly, he has "made his pile" or has otherwise "fixed things" more or less so that he has time to come out into the open and look around a little. He is rather jocose about this because he is not used to it. Things in general puzzle him so much that he cannot work up very much interest in them. The wheels of his natural self are too rusty to generate any friction. Presently, therefore, reminded that he is wasting time, he turns back again to his old habits—only to find that they in turn no longer appeal to him as they formerly did. *Things,* in short, repel him now instead of engaging him; they have worked up a momentum of their own; they scarcely require his coöperation even. And so he has to turn about once more and face that blank within himself where a world of meaning ought to be.

Now is it possible that all the poets and artists of history, whose function it has been to create and manifest these meanings, are unable to fill up this blank in his mind? Our industrial conception of culture assumes that they can do so, out of hand, and that by a process of injection from the outside, by means of indiscriminate lecturing and the like, the fact that life is a miraculous and beautiful thing can be somehow pumped into the middle of his soul. But how does he himself feel about the matter? He knows that by this process only the upper levels of his brain are touched, and that they are touched only by minds in which the true fires of life have never been lighted.

That is why we feel today that it is the real work of criticism in this country to begin *low.* For the American mind will never be able to recapture the wisdom of the world except by earning it, and it can only earn this wisdom through its own ascent upward on the basis of these primitive facts to which it has been gradually awakened. Between the apparently civilized vision of life of our best conventional story-writers and the really civilized vision of writers like Anatole France[3] there yearns a gulf that is wide and deep, and we shall have to descend to the bottom of that gulf before we can begin the exhilarating climb to our own true heights. There are plenty of writers, of course, who imagine that they can get across from peak to peak by aeroplane, as it were, by dazzling flights of sophistication; but they do not achieve their aim and something within them tells them that they do not. They

[3] Anatole France (1844-1924). Pseudonym of Jacques Anatole Thibault, French writer who abandoned his spectator role during the Dreyfus affair for active support of liberal social and political issues.

divine, as we all divine, that the only strictly organic literature of which at the moment this country is capable is a literature that is being produced by certain minds which seem, artistically speaking, scarcely to have emerged from the protozoa. That our life contains a thousand elements to which these writers just now fail to do justice is quite beside the point.

Not that we are Hottentots, or even peasants, although our arrested development somewhat resembles that of peasants. No, we are simply at the beginning of our true national existence and we shall remain there, stock still, as we have already remained for a century and a half, until we have candidly accepted our own lowest common denominator. But once we have done that, we shall begin to grow, and having begun to grow we shall grow quickly. For we already possess elements that belong to every level of development, even the highest— some even that are higher than the highest and put heaven to shame. There are all there, but they are not grouped in the right order; and so they have no cumulative effect. As soon as the foundations of our life have been reconstructed and made solid on the basis of our own experience, all these extraneous, ill-regulated forces will rally about their newly found center; they will fit in, each where it belongs, contributing to the essential architecture of our life. Then, and only then, shall we cease to be a blind, selfish, disorderly people; we shall become a luminous people, dwelling in the light and sharing our light.

6. Our Awakeners

"HUMANITY," wrote mazzini in 1858, "is a great army marching to the conquest of unknown lands, against enemies both strong and cunning. The peoples are its corps, each with its special operation to carry out, and the common victory depends on the exactness with which they execute the different

Source: II (June 1917), 235-248.

operations." The world in general has, I think, accepted Mazzini's conception of this Occidental "division of labor"; but our intellects, stimulated by science, have rushed so far ahead of the rest of our natures that it is very difficult for us to retrace our steps and touch anew from time to time the home base of our fondest assumptions. . . . What, precisely, was Mazzini's idea? That nationalities are the workshops of humanity, that each nationality has a special duty to perform, a special genius to exert, a special gift to contribute to the general stock of civilization, and that each, in consequence, growing by the trust that other nationalities place in it, must be a living, homogeneous entity, with its own faith and consciousness of self.

We accept this doctrine in principle,—it has become one of the commonplaces of modern society; but that we have not risen to its implications is evident in the vague sense of humiliation that oppresses the American people. For what does this doctrine assume? That the capacity of a nation to unite in the general comity is to be measured by the degree to which it has attained this consciousness of its own gift, of its own task. We feel that the war has called every people to show its hand and that with all our prodigal endowments we are helplessly unable to visualize the faith the world expects of us, or to assemble our forces in pursuit of that faith. Now faith cannot be manhandled, it cannot be put together out of whole cloth, but it can be fostered, it can be fertilized, it can be developed; and it is certainly the business of criticism and philosophy to foster and develop it. Our critics have failed to do so because, while they have always upheld the view of life out of which faith springs, they have never related it to our own field of reality. But, after all, our critics do not set up to be national awakeners, nor do they pretend to be on terms of intimacy with modern conditions; they know, in fact, in their own hearts that they cannot suggest any feasible way out of our difficulties. Who, then, are, or who purport to be, our real awakeners? The sociologists, the environmentalists, the hygienists, and the pragmatic and realistic philosophers who stand behind them. For twenty years and more now they have occupied the center of our life. They have not only accepted reality, they have claimed reality; they have said that they alone apprehend reality, and that reality has been taken out of the hands of the muddlers and put in their special charge because they alone are able to do something with it. Well, and here we are. They have asked us to judge them by their fruits. What are we to say?

For the influence of these awakeners of ours has been, directly or indirectly, universal; their philosophy has been the formulation, the rationalization of the whole spirit of American life at least since the Spanish war. And observe the condition in which we now are: sultry, flaccid, hesitant, not knowing what we want and incapable of wanting anything very much, certainly not in love with our life, certainly not at home in this field of reality that our awakeners have bidden us to be at home in, inclined as ever to substitute monetary for real values, to resort to theories and abstractions of every kind, and to stand in mortal fear of letting loose the spiritual appetites that impede our pursuit of a neat, hygienic, and sterile success. . . . What, in fact, *is* the note of our society today? A universal tepidity, it seems to me, the faded offspring of the Puritan hatred of human nature, which makes perhaps a majority of our kindly and gentle fellow-countrymen seem quite incapable of living, loving, thinking, dreaming, or hoping with any degree of passion or intensity, pacifistic at bottom not from any specific realization of war but from a distaste for the militant life *in toto*. We know this only too well; it is the secret of our humiliation, and it explains the desire of so many people to see this country rudely jolted and shaken up; it explains the pathological hopes that so many people lavish upon the war, hopes that have been bred by the morbid state into which we are fallen. . . . What can our awakeners say to all this? It is not their fault, certainly, that things are so; but so things are, and it is in the days of their consulate that things have become so. That is why, when the young heroes of pragmatism observe, with just that complacent finality which characterized the young heroes of rationalism in the days of Darwin, "Pragmatism has won," the innocent bystander suddenly feels himself endowed with a little of the wisdom of the serpent.

II

Faith is an offspring of the poetic view of life, and a national faith is the outgrowth of a national poetry. . . . Does anyone imagine that we are the only people that has been reduced to the pulp-like, inelastic state in which we find ourselves today? Have we forgotten what Germany was like at the beginning of the nineteenth century, disjointed, vague and sentimental, for all the sporadic flames of her music and philosophy? And have we forgotten how Germany in a generation reached the wonderful maturity that preceded that plunge into imperialism which the bad old ways of the nineteenth century alone rendered inevitable? Our localists, our individualists, our American decentralizers may, if they choose, regard that process as an evil one, but if so they deny Goethe, the poet who, coöperating as it were with the Napoleonic wars, brought its dynamic unity to the German people. How did he do this? By projecting in *Faust* a personification of spiritual energy anchored by a long chain of specific incidents in the concrete experience of the German people and thereby infusing into that experience the leaven of development, impelling the individual to form himself into a peculiar being ever in search also of a conception of what men are collectively. By thus laying more and ever more demands upon human nature, by compelling men to accept that spirit of restless striving which gives them a leverage over things, he not only electrified the German people but obligated it to create an environment worthy of itself.

Now it is of no importance at the moment that we have no Goethe in America and that we have no reason to suppose we are going to get one; it is of no importance that we cannot count on a messianic solution of our troubles, any more than we can count on the rude jolt which the war may, or may not, give us. What is important is for us to see that the really effective approach to life is the poetic approach, the approach that Goethe summed up in his phrase "from within outward," and that it is the effective approach because it envisages method in terms of value, every ounce of pressure that is put upon value registering itself with a tenfold intensity, so to speak, in the sphere of application.

This has been the European approach from time immemorial. Since the days of the cathedral builders everything
that we call the environment has come as a natural result of
the demands that human nature has laid upon itself. Is this
less true of the present day than of the past? Has not the
whole impetus toward social reform in modern England come
about through that intensification of the poetic view of life
which began with Carlyle's terrific restatement of the spiritual
principle, which passed over into the economic sphere with
Ruskin and William Morris, and through which English
liberalism has since learned gradually but effectively to assimilate science and use it as a ship uses a search-light? Can
any of our awakeners take exception to the following passage
in which Morris, actuated by his own lusty, creative joy in
life and by his hatred, his vivid, compelling hatred of the
ugliness of modern society, pointed out the path to reform
from within outward?

It was my good luck only that has put me on this side of the
window among delightful books and lovely works of art, and not on
the other side, in the empty street, the drink-steeped liquor shops,
the foul and degraded lodgings. *I know by my own feelings and
desires* what these men want, what could have saved them from this
lowest depth of savagery: employment which would foster their self-
respect, and win the praise and sympathy of their fellows, and
dwellings which they would come to with pleasure, surroundings
which would soothe and elevate them, reasonable labor, reasonable
rest. There is only one thing that can give them this—Art.

Thus Morris, with his conception of "joy in labor," threw
out in the midst of a machine age a palpitant standard of
living that will in the end, especially now that it has come to
light again in the minds of English reconstructionists, serve to
de-limit the essential function of the machine in English
society. And he did this, precisely, by the "unrealistic" method
of projecting a Utopia, by seeing life in terms of that imagination which knows how important the intelligence is and is able
to impel it in the direction of a deeply desired goal. That
Morris knew little of science and cared little for it is beside the

point; by laying demands upon life, by insisting that human nature must be creative, he obligated his contemporaries and his successors to frame *through* science an environment that would make that consummation possible. That is why the English liberalism represented in various ways by Shaw and Wells and Graham Wallas[1] is so much more effective than the liberalism of our awakeners, who, while they have assimilated the ideas of all these men, have been unable to share their impulse. Shaw and Wells and Wallas, all of whom are as much the heirs of Morris's peculiar socialism as they are of science, have ever envisaged evolution in terms of a more stringent demand upon life; not in terms of fine thinking merely, but of "love and fine thinking," not in terms of man merely, but of self-surpassing man, not in terms of efficiency merely, but of happiness,—and all the other things have been added unto them. Is it not a sufficient comment on our awakeners, the environmentalists, that, possessing no infectious ideal of "joy in labor," the best they can do is to publish unleavened studies on the control of fatigue?

III

"I know by my own feelings and desires." Why has no one been able to embrace our American life in those dynamic personal terms with which Morris embraced the life of England? Why has it been impossible for us to compass the poetic view of life that has proved itself in other countries capable of so many wonderful things? It is because we have never been able to make any complicated imaginative demand upon life. Our field of reality has required such an over-development of our possessive instincts that our creative instincts have had no scope at all; and consequently we have never been able to rise above those two equally uncreative conceptions of human nature, the total depravity of Puritanism and that optimistic self-complacency which is Puritanism's

[1] Graham Wallas (1858-1932). A professor of political science at the University of London and a Fabian leader for twenty years, Wallas was probably more provocative and influential as a lecturer than as a writer. His most influential work, *Human Nature in Politics* (1908), is an essay on the political psychology of the common man.

obverse and twin brother. Instead of a Carlyle we have had an Emerson, instead of a Morris we have had a Whitman— that is the whole story.

For Emerson's private perfectibility, based as it was on the idea that all we have to do to attain our majority is to look within ourselves and cast off the swaddling-clothes of tradition, led by an easy transition, our society being what it was in the nineteenth century, into that conception of the "spontaneous man" which our political democracy had inherited from Rousseau and which, splendidly amplified by Walt Whitman, has weathered all the vicissitudes of our thinking to the present day. "Time," said Emerson, in words that might well be applied to himself, "melts to shining ether the solid angularity of facts"; is it remarkable that his own subjective idealism went by default? Not that one means to disparage Walt Whitman, who has taught us all to accept life and rejoice in it, but that Whitman's great work is to be measured in terms not of general human experience but of a special situation: one has only to recall that up to a generation ago our entire race was conceived in the holy shame of a reluctant wedlock to realize the extent of our national obligation to Whitman's robust animal humors. But greater as Whitman was than William Morris, he fulfilled a more primitive need, a need that would never have existed had it not been for our exclusively Puritan past; he was unable to carry us a step forward as Morris carried England, because, having embraced life, he was unable really to make anything of it. Where Morris, with his conception of "joy in labor," not only released the creative energies of men but held out before them a vision of excellence in labor that mobilized those energies and impelled men to reconstruct their environment in order to give them full play, Whitman merely universalized the miraculous animality that summed up his own experience. He knew nothing of what has been made of life, he was unable to imagine what can be made of life, over and above this miraculous animality. "Glad to be alive" simply, however intensely, he established a point of departure for the creative spirit—and there he left us. And there, so far as our poetical tradition is concerned, we have remained.

Now, this is the real background of pragmatism, with which, in its primitive aspect, we are all in cordial agreement. And moreover pragmatism was formulated by two thinkers who, in their feeling for reality, in their acceptance of a human nature that calls nothing common or unclean, and in their desire to make human nature more conscious of itself, might well be called rather poets than philosophers. They were poets, yes; but they were not *sufficiently* poets to intensify the conception of human nature that they had inherited from our tradition—their own vein of poetry, golden in Professor James, silver in Professor Dewey, ran too thin for that; and besides, their whole training had gone to make them students of the existing fact. Unable to alter the level of human vision, all they could do was to take men on the level where they found them and release their latent capacities on that level—an immensely valuable thing, of course, but not the vital thing for us, because it is the level itself that is at fault in America. Had our existing fact, had the core of our life been rich, as it is, for example, in Russia, then their programme of liberation and control would have been as adequate for the nation in general as it now is for the few qualified individuals. What it actually did was to unfold, for the most part, a human nature that was either detached from the sources of life or contented with a very primitive range of needs and desires. That is where pragmatism has "practically" failed us, and worse.

For not content with remaining a method, it has, owing to the impotence of our poetical tradition and the extra-scientific sympathies of its founders, attempted to fill the place which poetry alone can fill adequately, and which our poetry, in its complacent animalism, on the one hand, and its complicated escape from reality, on the other, has left vacant. That is to say, it has assumed the right to formulate the aims of life and the values by which those aims are tested, aims and values which, we are led by history to believe, can be effectively formulated only by individual minds not in harmony with the existing fact but in revolt against it. Social efficiency is the ideal posited by Professor Dewey; yes, but has not the *scope* of social efficiency ever been determined by individuals who from time to time repudiate the social organism altogether and, rising themselves to a fresh level, drag mankind after them? Since life proceeds not by the burnishing up of existent ideals, but by the discovery of new and more vital ones, thanks to the imagination, which reaches out into an unknown whither the intelligence is able to follow only by a long second, does not pragmatism turn the natural order of things inside out when it accepts the intelligence instead of the imagination as the value-creating entity? It does, virtually if not absolutely, and in so doing crowds out and replaces the essential factor from which all dynamic creativity springs. It becomes, in a word, the dog in the manger of our creative life. What if it is an amiable, friendly dog with none of the other disagreeable proclivities of the dog in the fable? The main thing is that it makes its bed where the winged horse of poetry ought to lie. And would we have any right to object were the winged horse suddenly to open his mouth and remark in the words of Æsop: "What a miserable cur! He cannot eat corn himself, nor will he allow others to eat it who can"?

Does it matter that the founders of pragmatism, like certain of its English congeners, H. G. Wells, for example, have passed outside it in order to meet the critical issues of life? The mercurial pilgrim soul of Professor James had passed on to a strange polytheistic mysticism long before he died; H. G. Wells, under the stress of the war, has redoubled his quest of "God, the Invisible King"; and Professor Dewey has not denied the need of a national faith in this country, to attain which we shall certainly have not merely to do something other than we normally do, but to be something other than we normally are. Creators themselves, and essentially poets, they have been free of their own creations, they have shown that they are members of the elect company of the "older and bolder"; nevertheless, they have justified a multitude of their followers in that complacent, mechanistic view of life to which everything else in our mock-efficient, success-loving society predisposes them. Establishing, as they have, the seeing-relation in place of the feeling-relation, they have "practically" sanctioned the type of mind whose emotional needs are so limited that the efficient pursuit of some special object is all that it demands of life.

IV

Such is the philosophy that actuates our awakeners. It is not because they lack a dynamic faith that one criticizes them, it is because, lacking a dynamic faith, their treatment of society is itself ineffective. And it is in this that they betray their unbroken descent from our old reformers, in this that they prove that pragmatism has not been the vital departure in our life that we have all been looking for. For what does it matter that our old reformers, ignorant of science, took for granted a "normal" human nature that was domestic and acquisitive while our awakeners of the present day, equipped with a consummate scientific knowledge of mankind, take for granted a normal human nature that is efficient and sophisticated? At bottom they are all chips of the same block. Whittier, having risen to the heights of passion over the question of slavery relapsed as soon as the war was over into a normal scale of values that enabled him to write that epic of satisfaction with things as they are, "Snow-bound." The muck-rakers of a later day having, at the rate of ten cents a word, abolished Peruna out of the world, passed on to that finer allopathic sphere in which Mr. Ray Stannard Baker[2] now writes his "Adventures in Contentment." And so it has been with the social workers and the big brothers of the settlement-house. Impelled to "give the other fellow a chance" to rise to the tepid status which life has portioned out to them and which they regard as highly fortunate and satisfactory, they have carried things to such a pass that immigrant sociologists, under the stimulus of a middle-class journalism, have been known to regard it as the highest dream of their hearts to be able to "lift" to the level of some ordinary American neighborhood into which they themselves have gained admittance men and women who are often immeasurably above it in the scale of the spirit.

Does it matter that our advanced sociologists have passed

---

[2] Ray Stannard Baker (1870-1946). American muckraking journalist, connected with *McClure's* magazine, whose *Adventures in Contentment*, a book of essays, appeared in 1907; Baker was later an associate of Woodrow Wilson and his biographer.

far beyond these crude, haphazard illusions? Incapable of
the poetic view of life and repudiating it, they are able only
to codify our society, to rearrange the allegiances that already
exist, and to impose upon the American people programmes
which have sprung from the poetic vision of other countries
and which they have assimilated through their intelligence
alone. Self-sufficient as they are, committed by the weakness
of their imagination and by the analytical habitude of their
minds to a mechanistic view of human nature, they are unable
to fuse and unify our wills, they are unable to communicate
any of those vital incentives which are the austere fruits not of
"interest" but of love. Did I say that, possessing no infectious
ideal of "joy in labor," the best they can do is to concentrate
their minds on the control of fatigue? No, they can do one
thing better; they can evade reality altogether and say with
Mr. Henry Ford that "no man can take pride in his work until
he gets something for it, until he has leisure to enjoy life."
In this way, throwing up the sponge altogether, accepting
machinery and more machinery and still more machinery as a
fait accompli, and giving up all hope of determining the rational place of machinery in life, they can tell everyone except
the favored few whose sophistication enables them to glut their
intelligence on that strange freak the American soul, to seek
reality in anything else than their work—riding about the
country in Ford cars, on Sundays, for example, with their
mouths open. Such is the destiny of the working class, as our
young pragmatic intellectuals see it. As to the middle class,
they can in time, by consummating their freedom and capping
it with control, attain the more discreet paradise that the
Pierce-Arrow Company is at last able to place at their dis-
posal.

Could there be a better proof that our awakeners have traduced us, our awakeners, who are always cutting off the heads
of the hydra which has us all in its grasp? They have traduced
us because our hydra is, and always has been, self-complacency,
satisfaction, that is to say, with a primitive scale of human
values; and self-complacency, as a spiritual fact, is proof
against all the arrows of the intelligence. Our awakeners
accept themselves as a norm and by so doing become them-

selves a part of the very hydra that they attack. Assuming the intelligence as a final court of appeal, they are sealed against those impulses that give birth to self-criticism and the principle of growth; all they can do, therefore, is to unfold the existing fact in themselves, and in the world about them. Why should it surprise us, then that *The New Republic,* having long since abandoned the hope of assuming that leadership the essence of which is to share sympathetically the desires of people in general and then to formulate them into a conscious programme, should have formulated only its own desires and imposed them on a muddle-headed public as "the deliberate choice of a limited but influential class" who know? It ought not to surprise us, for it is the voice of our old friend Barnum that speaks to us in this unexpected phrase. That human nature likes to be fooled has been the prime axiom of our leadership for a generation or more. Lincoln held another opinion, to be sure, but then Lincoln understood the nature of genuine leadership; he had learned by his own capacity for spiritual experience that mankind has latent forces which are capable of being drawn upon and developed, if we do but enter deeply enough into ourselves to perceive them.

V

* * *

Let no one imagine then that we have outgrown the poetic view of life; we have simply not grown up to it, we have not yet reached that full consciousness where faith and purpose, the hallmarks of the mature kind, are able to subjugate to their own ends the machinery of existence. "For life to be fruitful," said George Sand, "life must be felt as a blessing." But to love life, to perceive the miraculous beauty of life, and to seek for life, swiftly and effectively, a setting worthy of its beauty— this is the acme of civilization, to be attained, whether by individuals or by nations, only through a long and arduous process. But it is not true that human nature, at bottom the same the world over and at all times, irresistibly desires life and growth? And is it not true that human nature, in its infinite complexity, responds now with one set of faculties, now with another, according to circumstances and the quality of its leadership? If our poetic life is at present in the most rudimentary state and beset with fallacies of every kind, consider what our circumstances have been, and remember that our awakeners have not only not encouraged it, have not only averted their eyes from it, but have systematically over-stimulated those very elements in our make-up that most retard its development. If now they find that they are unable to imagine any vital future for America, is this not perhaps the natural penalty for their having repudiated the *life* of the imagination? But who is to blame for this, life, or America— or our awakeners themselves?

V

The Dial Essays

(1917-1918)

EDITORIAL NOTE: The original Transcendental *Dial* (it died in 1844) was revived in 1860 by Moncure Conway and again in 1880 by Francis Browne. The magazine passed to Martyn Johnson's direction in 1916. Under Johnson's editorship (1916-1919), *The Dial* was closer to *The Nation* and *The New Republic* than to a literary magazine. Both Brooks and Randolph Bourne were contributing editors from 1917 to 1918; another friend and colleague, Lewis Mumford, was an associate editor during the last months of the Martyn Johnson *Dial*. The magazine's manifesto of 1917 is characteristic of the expectant spirit of the pre-war years:

It will try to meet the challenge of the new time by reflecting and interpreting its spirit—a spirit freely experimental, skeptical of inherited values, ready to examine old dogmas and to subject afresh its sanctions to the test of experience.[1]

[1] *The Dial,* LXII (January 25, 1917), 45.

The fourth avatar of *The Dial* under Scofield Thayer's direction from 1920 to 1929 was more literary. It published, for example, T. S. Eliot's *The Waste Land* in 1922. Eliot received *The Dial* prize for that year. The battle-lines of the period were not so rigid as they were to become, for in 1923 *The Dial* prize was awarded to Van Wyck Brooks. The announcement of the award contained the following estimate of Brooks's role:

Our own award is for an American writer and goes this year to a critic whose chief interest it is that American writers should occur, should be able, in the American society, to exist and to create. One can recognize the supreme importance of such a figure even if one fails to accept the whole body of his doctrine. For there is in a critic as far removed as Mr. Brooks from the purely aesthetic attitude one assertion which underlies all others; it is that the creative life is the only life tolerable to intelligent men and women, that the life which is not creative, and more or less fully creative, is spoiled and stunted and unworthy.[2]

[2] *The Dial*, LXXVI (January 24, 1924), 96.

---

1. An American Oblomov[1]

THE UNWELCOME MAN. By Waldo Frank.[2] (Little, Brown and Co.; $1.50.)

Sixty years ago Goncharov created in the hero of a famous novel one of those archetypical characters that add so to the weight of Russian literature. What is the theme of *Oblomov*? The incapacity of a quite healthy, whole-hearted, good-natured young man to make connections with the world about him.

SOURCE: LXII (March 22, 1917), 244-245.
[1] See footnote 9, p. 188.
[2] Waldo Frank (1889-1967). Novelist, critic and a founder and editor of *The Seven Arts*.

Endowed with a normal variety of gifts, Oblomov finds himself thrown into a society whose immemorial inertia has prevented it from developing a rich fabric of objective life. He
himself, as a natural, average man, might easily have made
a career for himself in a more complex society. As it is, precisely because he is only a natural, average man, he cannot
create the conditions that are necessarily antecedent to such
a career. And so he personally falls a victim to that very inertia
which has made Russian society incapable of employing so
many of its talents and the virus of which he has himself
inherited.

Mr. Frank's Quincy Burt is a sort of American Oblomov, a
character which is quite as typical in his own time and place,
but of which all the terms are seen, as it were, in reverse. For
America is simply Russia turned inside out. Russia is the
richest of nations in spiritual energy, we are the poorest;
Russia is the poorest of nations in social machinery, we are
the richest. The problem of the Quincy Burts, therefore, is not
to find an external career or the incentive that makes an
external career seem desirable; the real trouble is not that
their material instincts are unable to find any scope, but that
their spiritual instincts are unable to develop sufficient intensity
to give them a survival value even under the best conditions,
while the conditions themselves, far from being the best, are
almost the worst that the world has known. It is this that is
creating a vast army of young men whose minds are filled, if
not with thoughts of war and suicide, at least with a sense of
the futility of living. The primitive, material, national job has
so largely been done that they are thrown out of the only
employment they are bred for into a world that has not been
interpreted and made ready for them. These are the "unwelcome men" of whom Mr. Frank has drawn a highly individual-
ized, but still composite, portrait.

Nine readers out of ten who are not "in the know" will
probably imagine that Mr. Frank has attempted to draw a
mute, inglorious Milton. This conception simply shows how
all but incapable we Americans are of apprehending the simp-
lest human values. We demand so little of life that we cannot
understand why any ordinary person should even desire to

develop and express more than one or two strands of his nature. But Quincy, like his obscure brothers in misfortune, is simply a boy all the sides of whose nature have unfolded themselves tentatively to the sunlight—and the sunlight isn't there! His father, on the upward swing materially, scents an enemy in all these impulses of his son, a superfluous son, any-way, whose untimely arrival has already branded him as an extra, leaden weight in an ascent all too difficult at best. His mother's affection, sapped at the roots, the cynicism, the blind-ness, the helplessness, and the inner poverty of his brothers and sisters are so many ever-present negations of the signifi-cance of life, a significance which he alone is totally unable to grasp if only because he is the offshoot of a stock that has immemorially denied it.

The vitality of Mr. Frank's conception is shown by the fact that it provides a concrete touchstone for most of the problems of our contemporary civilization. All the movements that are working themselves out in the thin, pragmatic way character-istic of the American mind at present refer back to just these "unwelcome men" in whom almost alone lies the promise of a richer and more rounded society in the future. Birth control, the free school, the socialization of industry,—what is the object of all these causes except to stimulate and fertilize the long-forgotten, ignored, neglected impulses which give life its meaning and which have been bled and trampled upon by the steam-roller of industrialism? It is just as John Stuart Mill predicted half a century ago: industrialism has carried out its threat; it has led to an appalling deficiency of human preferences. But half the ineffectualness of our reformers springs from the fact that they have never visualized in the concrete the human demands they are striving to fulfill. It is this that largely constitutes the social value of fiction. Russia, without her novelists, might have become conscious of the vacuity of her life; but it was the novelists nevertheless that made her actively conscious of it, conscious enough to seek values and create them. *The Unwelcome Man* belongs to the small group of American novels that promise to play the same part in our life.

Is it a successful work of art? Rather an extremely interesting than a successful one. The human material is perhaps not sufficiently thrown into relief; there is not enough of an air chamber, as it were, between the animate foreground and the inanimate background. The author is so much interested in life that his own mind becomes at moments a part of its flow; we are brought so close to Quincy Burt that we can't see him. But of how many first novels are we able to say that they are too full of curiosity to yield up any one secret completely?

2. On Creating A Usable Past

There is a kind of anarchy that fosters growth and there is another anarchy that prevents growth, because it lays too great a strain upon the individual—and all our contemporary literature in America cries out of this latter kind of anarchy. Now, anarchy is never the sheer wantonness of mind that academic people so often think it; it results from the sudden unbottling of elements that have had no opportunity to develop freely in the open; it signifies, among other things, the lack of any sense of inherited resources. English and French writers, European writers in general, never quite separate themselves from the family tree that nourishes and sustains them and assures their growth. Would American writers have done so, plainly against their best interests, if they had had any choice in the matter? I doubt it, and that is why it seems to me significant that our professors continue to pour out a stream of historical works repeating the same points of view to such an astonishing degree that they have placed a sort of Talmudic seal upon the American tradition. I suspect that the past experience of our people is not so much without elements that might be made to contribute to some common understanding

SOURCE: LXIV (April 11, 1918), 337-341.

in the present, as that the interpreters of that past experience have put a gloss upon it which renders it sterile for the living mind.

I am aware, of course, that we have had no cumulative culture, and that consequently the professors who guard the past and the writers who voice the present inevitably have less in common in this country than anywhere in the Old World. The professors of American literature can, after all, offer very little to the creators of it. But there is a vendetta between the two generations, and the older generation seems to delight in cutting off the supplies of the younger. What actuates the old guard in our criticism and their energetic following in the university world is apparently no sort of desire to fertilize the present, but rather to shame the present with the example of the past. There is in their note an almost pathological vindictiveness when they compare the "poetasters of today" with certain august figures of the age of pioneering who have long since fallen into oblivion in the minds of men and women of the world. Almost pathological, I say, their vindictiveness appears to be; but why not actually so? I think it is; and therefore it seems to me important, as a preliminary step to the reinterpretation of our literature, that we should have the reinterpretation of our professors that now goes merrily forward.

For the spiritual past has no objective reality; it yields only what we are able to look for in it. And what people find in literature corresponds precisely with what they find in life. Now it is obvious that professors who accommodate themselves without effort to an academic world based like ours upon the exigencies of the commercial mind cannot see anything in the past that conflicts with a commercial philosophy. Thanks to his training and environment and the typically non-creative habit of his mind, the American professor by instinct interprets his whole field of learning with reference to the ideal not of the creative, but of the practical life. He does this very often by default, but not less conclusively for that. The teaching of literature stimulates the creative faculty but it also and far more effectually thwarts it, so that the professor turns against himself. He passively plays into the hands that underfeed his own imaginative life and permits the whole weight of his meticulous knowledge of the past to tip the beam against the living present. He gradually comes to fulfill himself in the vicarious world of the dead and returns to the actual world of struggling and miseducated mortals in the majestic raiment of borrowed immortalities. And he pours out upon that world his own contempt for the starveling poet in himself. That is why the histories of our literature so often end with a deprecating gesture at about the year 1890, why they stumble and hesitate when they discuss Whitman, why they disparage almost everything that comes out of the contemporary mind.

Now it is this that differentiates the accepted canon of American literature from those of the literatures of Europe, and invalidates it. The European professor is relatively free from these inhibitions; he views the past through the spectacles of his own intellectual freedom; consequently the corpus of inherited experience which he lays before the practicing author is not only infinitely richer and more inspiring than ours, but also more usable. The European writer, whatever his personal education may be, has his racial past, in the first place, and then he has his racial past *made available* for him. The American writer, on the other hand, not only has the most meager of birthrights but is cheated out of that. For the professorial mind, as I have said, puts a gloss upon the past that renders it sterile for the living mind. Instead of reflecting the creative impulse in American history, it reaffirms the values established by the commercial tradition; it crowns everything that has passed the censorship of the commercial and moralistic mind. And it appears to be justified because on the whole, only those American writers who have passed that censorship have undergone a reasonably complete development and in this way entered what is often considered the purview of literary criticism.

What kind of literature it is that has passed that censorship and "succeeded" in this bustling commercial democracy of ours, we all know very well. It has been chiefly a literature of exploitation, the counterpart of our American life. From Irving and Longfellow and Cooper and Bryant, who exploited the legendary and scenic environment of our grandfathers, through the local colorists, who dominated our fiction during the intermediate age and to whom the American people accounted for artistic righteousness their own provincial quaintnesses, down to such living authors, congenial to the academic mind, as Winston Churchill, who exploits one after another the "problems" of modern society, the literature that has been allowed to live in this country, that has been imaginatively nourished, has been not only a literature acceptable to the mind that is bent upon turning the tangible world to account but a literature produced by a cognate process. Emerson, Thoreau, Whitman—there you have the exceptions, the *successful* exceptions; but they have survived not because of what they still offer us, but because they were hybrids, with enough pioneer instinct to pay their way among their contemporaries.

There is nothing to resent in this; it has been a plain matter of historic destiny. And historically predestined also is the professorial mind of today. But so is the revolt of the younger generation against the professorial mind. Aside from any personal considerations, we have the clearest sort of evidence that exploitation is alien to the true method of literature, if only because it produces the most lamentable effect on the exploiter. Look at the local colorists! They have all come to a bad end, artistically speaking. Is it necessary to recall the later work of Bret Harte after he had squeezed the orange of California?[1] Or the lachrymosity of Mr. James Lane Allen's ghost revisiting the Kentucky apple tree from which he shook down all the fruit a generation ago? That is the sort of spectacle you have to accept complacently if you take the word of the professors that the American tradition in literature is sound and true; and the public in general does accept it complacently, because it is not averse to lachrymosity and cares nothing about the ethics of personal growth. But the conscientious writer turns aside in disgust. Seeing nothing in the past but an oblivion of all things that have meaning to the creative mood, he decides to paddle his own course, even if it leads to shipwreck.

[1] In a later *Freeman* column Brooks discusses Bret Harte and false local color. See "A Reviewer's Note-book," *Freeman* I (August 25, 1920), 574-575.

Unhappily, the spiritual welfare of this country depends altogether upon the fate of its creative minds. If they cannot grow and ripen, where are we going to get the new ideals, the finer attitudes, that we must get if we are ever to emerge from our existing travesty of a civilization? From this point of view our contemporary literature could hardly be in a graver state. We want bold ideas, and we have nuances. We want courage, and we have universal fear. We want individuality, and we have idiosyncrasy. We want vitality, and we have intellectualism. We want emblems of desire, and we have Niagaras of emotionality. We want expansion of soul, and we have an elephantiasis of the vocal organs. Why? Because we have no cultural economy, no abiding sense of spiritual values, no body of critical understanding? Of course; that is the burden of all our criticism. But these conditions result largely, I think, from another condition that is, in part at least, remediable. The present is a void, and the American writer floats in that void because the past that survives in the common mind of the present is a past without living value. But is this the only possible past? If we need another past so badly, is it inconceivable that we might discover one, that we might even invent one?

Discover, invent a usable past we certainly can, and that is what a vital criticism always does. The past that Carlyle put together for England would never have existed if Carlyle had been an American professor. And what about the past that Michelet,[2] groping about in the depths of his own temperament, picked out for the France of his generation? We have had our historians, too, and they have held over the dark backward of time the divining-rods of their imagination and conjured out of it what they wanted and what their contemporaries wanted—Motley's great epic of the self-made man, for instance, which he called *The Rise of the Dutch Republic*. The past is an inexhaustible storehouse of apt attitudes and adaptable ideals; it opens of itself at the touch of

[2] Jules Michelet (1798-1874). The great historian of the romantic school whose major work is the *Histoire de France* (1833-1867). He lost his post as professor of history as a result of his refusal to take the oath of allegiance to Louis Napoleon.

desire; it yields up, now this treasure, now that, to anyone who comes to it armed with a capacity for personal choices. If, then, we cannot use the past our professors offer us, is there any reason why we should not create others of our own? The grey conventional mind casts its shadow backward. But why should not the creative mind dispel that shadow with shafts of light?

So far as our literature is concerned, the slightest acquaintance with other national points of view than our own is enough to show how many conceptions of it are not only possible but already exist as commonplaces in the mind of the world. Every people selects from the experience of every other people whatever contributes most vitally to its own development. The history of France that survives in the mind of Italy is totally different from the history of France that survives in the mind of England, and from this point of view there are just as many histories of America as there are nations to possess them. Go to England and you will discover that in English eyes "American literature" has become, while quite as complete an entity as it is with us, an altogether different one. You will find that an entire scheme of ideas and tendencies has survived there out of the American past to which the American academic point of view is wholly irrelevant. This, I say, is a commonplace to anyone whose mind has wandered even the shortest way from home, and to travel in one's imagination from country to country, from decade to decade, is to have this experience indefinitely multiplied. Englishmen will ask you why we Americans have so neglected Herman Melville that there is no biography of him.[3] Russians will tell you that we never really understood the temperament of Jack London. And so on and so on, through all the ramifications of national psychology. By which I do not mean at all that we ought to cut our cloth to fit other people. I mean simply that we have every precedent for cutting it to fit ourselves. Presumably the orthodox interpreters of our literature imagine that they speak for the common reason of humankind. But evidently as regards modern literature that common reason is

[3] Raymond Weaver's *Herman Melville: Mariner and Mystic* (New York 1921), generally accepted as initiating the Melville revival, had not yet been published.

a very subtle and precarious thing, by no means in the possession of minds that consider it a moral duty to impose upon
the world notions that have long since lost their sap. The
world is far too rich to tolerate this. When Matthew Arnold
once objected to Sainte-Beuve that he did not consider La-
martine an important writer, Sainte-Beuve replied, "Perhaps
not, but he is important *for us*." Only by the exercise of a
little pragmatism of that kind, I think, can the past experience
of our people be placed at the service of the future.

What is important for us? What, out of all the multifarious
achievements and impulses and desires of the American liter
ary mind, ought we to elect to remember? The more personally
we answer this question, it seems to me, the more likely we
are to get a vital order out of the anarchy of the present. For
the impersonal way of answering it has been at least in part
responsible for this anarchy, by severing the warm artery that
ought to lead from the present back into the past. To approach our literature from the point of view not of the successful fact but of the creative impulse, is to throw it into an
entirely new focus. What emerges then is the desire, the
aspiration, the struggle, the tentative endeavor, and the appalling obstacles our life has placed before them. Which
immediately casts over the spiritual history of America a
significance that, for us, it has never had before.

Now it is impossible to make this approach without having
some poignant experience of the shortcomings, the needs, and
the difficulties of our literary life as it is now conditioned. Its
anarchy is merely a compound of these, all of which are to be
explained not so much by the absence of a cultural past as by
the presence of a practical one. In particular, as I have said,
this anarchy results from the sudden unbottling of elements
that have had no opportunity to develop freely in the open.
Why not trace those elements back, analyzing them on the
way, and showing how they first manifested themselves, and
why, and what repelled them? How many of Theodore
Dreiser's defects, for example, are due to an environment that
failed to produce the naturalistic mind until the rest of the
world had outgrown it and given birth to a more advanced set
of needs? And there is Vachel Lindsay. If he runs to sound

and color in excess and for their sake voids himself within, how much is that because the life of a Middle Western town sets upon those things an altogether scandalous premium? Well, there you have two of the notorious difficulties of contemporary authorship; and for all that our successful tradition may say, difficulties like those have been the death of our creative life in the past. The point for us is that they have never prevented the creative impulse from being born. Look back and you will see, drifting in and out of the books of history, appearing and vanishing in the memoirs of more aggressive and more acceptable minds, all manner of queer geniuses, wraith-like personalities that have left behind them sometimes a fragment or so that has meaning for us now, more often a mere eccentric name. The creative past of this country is a limbo of the non-elect, the fathers and grandfathers of the talent of today. If they had had a little of the sun and rain that fell so abundantly upon the Goliaths of nineteenth-century philistinism, how much better conditioned would their descendants be!

The real task for the American literary historian, then, is not to seek for masterpieces—the few masterpieces are all too obvious—but for tendencies. Why did Ambrose Bierce go wrong? Why did Stephen Crane fail to acclimatize the modern method in American fiction twenty years ago? What became of Herman Melville? How did it happen that a mind capable of writing *The Story of a Country Town* should have turned up thirty years later with a book like *Success Easier Than Failure?* If we were able to answer the hundred and one questions of this sort that present themselves to every curious mind, we might throw an entirely new face not only over the past but over the present and the future also. Knowing that others have desired the things we desire and have encountered the same obstacles, and that in some degree time has begun to face those obstacles down and make the way straight for us, would not the creative forces of this country lose a little of the hectic individualism that keeps them from uniting against their common enemies? And would this not bring about, for the first time, that sense of brotherhood in effort and in aspiration which is the best promise of a national culture?

VI

The Freeman Essays

(1920-1924)

EDITORIAL NOTE: The Scofield Thayer *Dial* had not even published a flaming manifesto, preferring to allow its contents to speak more than its occasional editorial stands. *The Freeman* manifesto spoke diffidently, with the qualifying tone more usual in academicians and in the conservative diction a prewar little magazine would have avoided. The prospectus, presumably written by the editors, Francis Neilson and Albert Jay Nock, was fully aware of its diffident tone:

If in its announcements, *The Freeman* has seemed overcautious and less assertive of its ability to achieve its aims than is commonly expected of new enterprises, it is because it prefers directing its energy toward creating a good paper than to making large claims.[1]

In fact, its diffidence disappears. *The Freeman,* appearing weekly for its four year lifetime (1920-1924), makes its ver-

[1] *The Freeman,* I (March 17, 1920), p. 24.

sion of radicalism clear. A radical, the editors explain, "regards all projects of political reform as visionary" since the object of government is the "economic exploitation of one class by another."[2] This class view of society distinguishes *The Freeman* from *The Nation* or *The New Republic*. The magazine's tone stays serious and sober; its primary concern political rather than literary.

As Sherwood Anderson put it, neither *The Freeman,* nor *The Nation,* nor *The New Republic* "give a damn for literature really. They seem to feel that creative writing has nothing to do with revolution."[3] In his autobiography Brooks describes *The Dial* editors as "aesthetic or nothing" and Nock as "something more than anti-aesthetic." Yet *The Freeman* could surprise its literary oriented readers: in one issue Alexander Blok's "The Twelve" appeared, perhaps because it joined literary experimentalism with political radicalism. *The Freeman* also had Van Wyck Brooks, a charter associate editor, responsible for the book section, for short notes and for an article a week. The weekly article developed into the unsigned column, "A Reviewer's Note-book," which appeared quite regularly until the spring of 1922 and, after a break of nearly a year (when Nock took over the column), only sporadically during 1923 and 1924. The frequent deadlines, the limits of the book review form, his other manuscript reading commitments for B. W. Huebsch (the publisher of *The Freeman*) and his desire to give more time to *The Pilgrimage of Henry James* (1925), then in progress, did not allow for a level of excellence comparable to his *Seven Arts* essays.

[2] *The Freeman,* I (March 31, 1920), 52.

[3] Anderson to Brooks [Before August 22, 1920], *The Letters of Sherwood Anderson,* ed. Howard Mumford Jones (Boston 1953), p. 59.

1. A Reviewer's Note-book: Ezra Pound's Instigations

IT IS QUITE astonishing to find young and intelligent persons who cannot forgive Ezra Pound for living in England and sticking out his tongue at his native land. It seems to me that if American literature is ever to be really roused it will be largely through the *Instigations* (to use the apt title of Mr. Pound's new book, published by Boni and Liveright) of a band of impenitent gadflies who have nothing to lose and who have got their country into the sort of perspective that comes best from living outside of it. Do you remember in Ibsen's letters how he describes the sensations with which he sailed up the fjord after a ten years' absence from home?—"A feeling of weight settled down on my breast, a feeling of actual physical oppression. And this feeling lasted all the time I was at home; I was not myself under the gaze of all those cold, uncomprehending Norwegian eyes at the windows and in the streets." That abyss of the exile between Ibsen and his countrymen was indispensable to the growth of a vision that revolutionized in time the whole spiritual life of Norway. I am not suggesting that Ezra Pound is another Ibsen, or that one can not maintain this abyss of exile without crossing the ocean. What I mean is that Ezra Pound has very much at heart the civilization of these United States. And I am sure he has done more for the new literature in this country than many of those who claim a proprietary right over it.

Horace Brodzky's clever caricature on the paper wrapper of *Instigations* precisely recalls an evening when I dined with Ezra Pound in a little Soho restaurant. I forget whether or not he wore his turquoise ear-rings on that occasion, but the velvet jacket and the protective falsetto voice were enough to impress

SOURCE: I (June 16, 1920), 334-335.

me. Behind the Struwwelpeter[1] pompadour and the little transparent yellow goat's-beard (in the manner of Watts's[2] Swinburne and the traditional troubadour), one discerned—it was the freckles, perhaps—the Idaho farmer's boy who had cast the skin without losing the spots. Most of Mr. Pound's little expatriate coterie hails from the Valley of Democracy: Mr. John Gould Fletcher is a product of Kansas and Mr. T. S. Eliot of some other quarter in the corn belt. This quite explains their impudence, for there is no sophistication so insolent where it isn't frigid as the sophistication of the exotic Middle Westerner. It was evident that Ezra Pound was on his guard and that his rather insufferable air covered the most familiar of the complexes, but I loved his talk; and while I couldn't at that time make head or tail of his verse, and can't today, I was prepared to believe him a very distinguished man of letters. That was seven or eight years ago. Since then he has emerged from the rather dark and dubious role of the mystagogue, fulfilling the bright and ample promise of his first book, *The Spirit of Romance*.

Mr. Pound is still impudent, he still throws dust in our eyes; in certain characteristics he will probably follow in Whistler's tracks to the end. One has many legitimate causes of complaint against him, not the least of these being that he has all the animus of an outmoded generation in the matter of shocking the grocers. It is really Mr. Pound's loss that he hasn't been able to ally himself with the most vigorous creative forces of our day, on the side, I mean, of the intellectual-proletarian movement. For the first time in generations the aristocrat of the spirit has an opportunity to share, without abating a whit of his artistic conscience, in a great constructive effort of humanity. Because Mr. Pound does not feel this and is consequently obliged to regard humanity as inimical, he

---

[1] Struwwelpeter, literally Tousled or Dishevelled Peter, the main character in Heinrich Hoffman-Donner's famous children's book named for its hero. Its many editions since its original appearance in 1845 includes one translated and illustrated by Mark Twain.

[2] George Frederic Watts (1817-1904). English painter and sculptor well known for his allegories and portraits; his Swinburne hangs in the National Portrait Gallery, London.

expends a good deal of spleen in a manner that strikes us as rather tiresomely out-of-date. He is finical, too, as well as fastidious, as if he wanted to prove his fastidiousness; and he is quite incapable of developing an idea. When he downs a victim he stabs him; he can not abolish his prey by a systematic process of reason or ridicule. Nor, on the other hand, can he build up a coherent critique when he most desires the effect of one: witness, in the present volume, the long and brilliant essay on Henry James, a veritable "chaos of clear ideas." Finally, he is the most unblushing logroller on record. Ezra's little pound is full of queer stray animals who have become famous because he talks about them so much. He has a way of referring to Eliot and Gaudier-Brzeska[3] as if not to know of them were to inhabit perpetual night.

People used to tell of the extraordinary transformation that took place in Whistler when he set about his work. Off went the tile and the monocle and the swagger-stick and the wasp-waisted frockcoat; the paraphernalia of the mountebank vanished; nothing remained but the absorbed gravity of the devoted artist. Ezra Pound's impossibilities are trivial enough beside the conviction that emanates from every one of his pages: of the profound seriousness, I mean, of the business of literature. In this country even the priesthood is a rather pragmatic affair: how can we expect to have the monk of letters? Ezra Pound could hardly have won this conviction even in England where, with few exceptions, the truly devoted writer is devoted because of some extra-artistic element in his work: it is an effect of his association with Paris and the half-legendary example of such men as Mallarmé and Rémy de Gourmont. Grant that his range of sympathies is decidedly narrow, that he makes a perhaps unnecessary parade of his scholarship; you have still to admit that in his atmosphere literature becomes a high, difficult and austere pursuit and that he is within his rights when he speaks to "the twenty-three students of Provençal and the seven people seriously interested in the technic and aesthetic of verse." One can not imagine an atti-

---

[3] Henri Gaudier-Brzeska (1891-1915). Pound wrote a study of this French sculptor and exponent of vorticism who died prematurely during the war. See *Gaudier-Brzeska: A Memoir* (1916).

tude more vitally important for our literature at the present
time than that—not for the generality of writers, but for a
few, enough to raise the self-respect of the profession. In one
of the obituary notices of Mr. Howells the other day I noticed
a quotation from one of his books in which he observed that
his early reading gave him, naturally enough, no standing
among the other boys. "I have since found," Mr. Howells
went on, "that literature gives one no more certain station in
the world of men's activities, either idle or useful. We literary
folk try to believe that it does, but that is all nonsense. At
every period of life among boys or men we are accepted when
they are at leisure and want to be amused, and at best we are
tolerated rather than accepted." It was that pusillanimous
attitude we found it so hard to forgive in a man of whom we
should so gladly have said nothing that is not good, for it
vitiated the whole atmosphere of American literature. When
I say that Ezra Pound has done us a great service I have in
mind the pride with which he upholds the vocation of letters.

Let us also admit that he is an incomparable *causeur*, that
he understands the art of literary talk. His criticism is just
that. "Honest criticism, as I conceive it," he says in the paper
on Henry James, "can not get much further than saying to
one's reader exactly what one would say to the friend who
approaches one's bookshelf asking: 'What the deuce shall I
read?'" Criticism of this kind exacts everything in the way of
perception, and Ezra Pound, who is often so extraordinarily
clever, is often extraordinarily perceptive too:

If one sought, not perhaps to exonerate, but to explain the Victorian
era one might find some contributory cause in Napoleon. That is to
say, the Napoleonic wars had made Europe unpleasant, England
was sensibly glad to be insular. Emotions to Henry James were more
or less things that other people had and that one didn't go into; at
any rate not in drawing-rooms.

Most good prose arises, perhaps, from an instinct of negation; is
the detailed, convincing analysis of something detestable; of something which one wants to eliminate. Poetry is the assertion of a positive, *i.e.*, of desire, and endures for a longer period. Poetic satire is
only an assertion of this positive, inversely, *i.e.*, as of an opposite
hatred.

The "Henry James" exhibits the finest discernment; so does the somewhat arbitrary *Study of French Poets*, which occupies a hundred pages and offers, with certain rather wayward omissions, a whole anthology of the last forty years; so do the essay on Rémy de Gourmont and some of the reprinted reviews, especially those of James Joyce and Lytton Strachey. There are other pieces in the book that illustrate Ezra Pound's erudition and virtuosity: it is a glittering jumble—"a dance of the intelligence," to quote a phrase of his own, "among words and ideas." A fresh wind of the spirit blows through it from cover to cover, and one has but a single fundamental misgiving. Ezra Pound has inhabited for a long time a universe that consists mainly of Wyndham Lewis, Chinese characters, Provençal prosody, Rémy de Gourmont, Blast and the vortex. These are, quite peculiarly, themes of that limited sort which, if they are pursued too long, turn the best of talkers into a bore. In the name of literature, what can be done to prevent Ezra Pound from becoming a bore?

2. A Question of Honesty

THERE IS MUCH resentment in the heavenly and unheavenly breasts of American authors over the unending invasion of this country by lecturing novelists and poets and essayists from England. From stars of the first contemporary magnitude to stars of the sixth and seventh, they are all coming, it appears, these English writers, actuated by a dozen motives, worthy and unworthy; and they are all received with open arms by the public. Meanwhile, one hears it said that Englishmen, just because they are Englishmen, and even when their talents are of the slenderest, win a measure of respect and popular success such as never falls to the lot of conscientious native writers.

SOURCE: II (February 2, 1921), 486-487.

There is at least enough truth in this to justify Randolph Bourne's remarks on "our cultural humility."[1] And the question is, how are we going to meet this unhappy situation? The only coherent answer we have thus far heard has been that of our nationalist critics.

These nationalist critics answer with no uncertain voice. Cry up our native writers, they say, and without too scrupulous a regard for the actual merits of these writers. Boom them, boost them, praise them in season and out of season. What does it matter if one indulges in a few exaggerations? At least it will focus the attention of the country on its own talent. We have been too humble; now is the time to be proud. Down with all these foreign mediocrities! Up with Messrs. Dreiser and Cabell!

Now there are certain objections to this method of procedure. In the first place, it is difficult to draw the line between such an Americanism and that other unsavoury variety, measured by percentages, of which we have had more than too much during these latter years. If, without making superfine distinctions, we are going to cry up Messrs. Dreiser and Cabell because they are Americans, we shall soon find ourselves in a rather embarrassing proximity to those who cry up Messrs. Tarkington and Churchill because they are Americans also. In the second place, we run the risk of overshooting the mark; for while many of our writers may compare favourably with certain English writers who are justly preferred to them, there are few indeed who can live up to the highest praise and will not in fact, be rendered ridiculous by it. Thirdly, this method defeats its own ends by debasing the literary coinage; for while an acceptance of inferior English writers is due to a frankly uncritical attitude, this advocacy of our native writers purports to be critical while actually disregarding all the values of criticism. But the most serious of all objections to this method is that it ignores a fact of our literary history which, if we gave it proper consideration, might solve our whole problem.

[1] See Bourne's "Our Cultural Humility," *Atlantic*, CXIV (October 1914), 503-507.

Our nationalist critics complain that American writers do not receive their just deserts, that inferior English writers are preferred to them, that this is because America is still colonial, and that the way to improve matters is to cry up American writers because they are American. They ignore the significant fact that, during a period when America was still more distinctly colonial than it is now, American writers had all the prestige in America that English writers have at present. That period was the generation before the Civil War. It is true that Poe was defamed in that generation, as Whitman was defamed in the generation that followed it: on the other hand, there were no European writers (and it was an age of great writers in Europe) who were held in higher esteem in this country than Emerson, Hawthorne, Prescott, and half a dozen others almost equally eminent, as well from the European as from the American point of view; there were few, if any, European writers who, in fact, were esteemed in this country as highly as they. In that generation, America, colonial as it was, and narrow as it was, was also, in literature, proudly and frankly self-expressive and revolved on its own literary axis. This is a fact that can not be disputed; it is also a fact our nationalist critics are obliged to take into account.

How can we explain it? How can we explain why, at a time when America, in every other department of life, was more distinctly colonial than it is now, American literature commanded the full respect of Americans, while in these days, when the colonial tradition is vanishing all about us, American literature so little commands the respect of Americans that they go after any strange god from England? There is only one explanation. It is because in that period America produced indisputably great writers, writers who had been able to build up a public confidence in American literature, while in our generation . . . But no, it is not quite so simple as that.

Our generation, if one is not mistaken, has begun to witness the emergence, if not of great, at least of distinguished writers also. But the writers of our generation are not only still in the formative stage, they also have to live down the recent past of their profession. American literature has not, since the Civil War, been respected by Americans because it has not been respected by itself. Mr. Howells, writing of the American drama of the last few decades, once remarked that "mainly it has been gay as our prevalent mood is; mainly it has been honest as our habit is, in cases where we believe we can afford it; mainly it has been decent and clean and sweet as our average life is." *Mainly it has been honest as our habit is, in cases where we believe we can afford it;* that is a fair description not only of our recent American drama but of our whole literature during the last half century. How many times that honesty exacted too high a price! Was Mr. Howells himself honest, artistically speaking, when, to arrive at the doctrine that "the more smiling aspects of life are the more American," he deliberately, as he has told us, averted his eyes from the darker side of life? Was Mark Twain honest, artistically speaking, when he suppressed his real beliefs about man and the universe? Was Henry Adams honest, artistically speaking, when he refused to sign the novels that revealed what he considered to be the truth about American society? These were the men whose character and talent rendered them responsible for the literature of their generation. They were dishonest, artistically speaking, and therefore the literature of their generation was dishonest also. Did the public know this? The public certainly felt it, and in consequence the whole stock of American literature fell. Yes, we know it; the American people lost confidence in its literature; and not one of our nationalist critics can assert that, renascent as we believe our literature is, it has yet made adequate amends for this fiasco.

Does not this difficulty explain why the American public, once so respectful of its own writers, insists today, a little cynically, upon being "shown"? It has a certain excuse for imagining that no good thing can come out of Nazareth. If, therefore, our writers wish to win their public back, there is only one thing for them to do, and that is what their predecessors did who won the public in former times. They can win it only by sheer merit; by sheer merit they can not fail to win it; and, in fact, by sheer merit, they have already begun to win it. Let them forget the invading hosts, and leave nationalism to the politicians.

3. Our Lost Intransigents

As WE OBSERVE the latest American generation of "young intellectuals" shading off into the majority, losing its contour, its colour, its character, its tang, we ask ourselves why it is that not so many as a handful of our fellow-countrymen seem to be able to withstand the solicitations of the mob-existence. Without this remnant and its leaders, a remnant insulated against the common life and its common values, no real development can ever take place in society. "The power and salvation of a people," as Chekhov was only the last to say, "lie in its intelligentsia, in the intellectuals who think honestly, feel and can work." That is understood in other countries, and in other countries the remnant stands firm and only reconstitutes itself from decade to decade. We have, it is true, if not this remnant,[1] at least the impulse toward it, the feeling for it, the intention of it, but with us, instead of taking form, it is, so to speak, permanently in process of dissolution. One standard-bearer after another emerges from the mist, group follows group, and there is a great pother about a new heaven and a new earth. As nothing ever happens, however, one at last concludes that, upon a closer examination, our malcontents find the old earth good enough; they seem, for the most part, to have so little difficulty in making friends with it. Thus it appears that American society is like a wheel without any cogs,

SOURCE: III (August 10, 1921), 510-511.

[1] The doctrine of the saving remnant derives from Isaiah who speaks of the remnant without whom Israel would have been lost and from Plato who speaks of the very small remnant of honest followers of wisdom. Matthew Arnold gave the idea contemporary relevance in one of his *Discourses in America* (1885), "Numbers; or the Majority and the Remnant," which he delivered in New York. Despite the existence of the remnant, both the Hebrew kingdoms and democratic Athens fell. Arnold concludes that the remnant can save us today only if its numbers (paradoxically) increase.

and that, in spite of all its malcontents,[2] it is destined to turn round for ever in its own unbroken beatitude.

* * *

Evidently, then, it is our American philosophers and poets who are at fault for the stagnancy of our life; and indeed to explain the lapse, the defection, the fatuity of the most recent generation of intellectuals one need go no further back than their acknowledged master, William James. To trust a spontaneous self that has not been leavened with new values, not to seek new values but to turn those one has into "cash," to live the life not of thought but of will, such is the virtual fiat of the Jamesian pragmatism; but as thought scarcely exists in America, and our present values are as musty and stale as they can possibly be, this, for us, is simply to beg the whole question of philosophy. James, by giving a fresh ethical *cachet* to the ordinary working creed of our practical civilization, led his disciples back into the wilderness from which they had emerged, and left them there, with the result that their impulses trickled away into the sand.

As we read James's recently published letters we see that his philosophy of self-adaptation, for that is what it comes to, was the expression of his own life. He was unable to create values because he had never transcended his environment; and his failure to do so is perhaps typical of the failures of all those other men who might have deepened and strengthened the character of our society. He was, as he said, and like so many other sensitive Americans of his generation, a "victim of neurasthenia"; and that he did not "like" the society in which he lived, that he liked it no better than his brother Henry, that its values in no way corresponded with those he had instinctively absorbed from his father and from the European associations of his childhood, we can see from his lifelong desire to escape from it, "back to nature," back to the woods. "I am a badly mixed critter," he writes in 1895,

---

[2] Brooks's intransigents are Bourne's malcontents and Frank's unwelcome men. See Bourne's "Twilight of Idols," *The Seven Arts*, II (October, 1917), 688-702, for his discussion of the need for malcontents in American society.

"and I experience a certain organic need for simplification and solitude that is quite imperious." His whole life was thus an effort to reconcile himself, to bring himself into rapport with an industrialized world, an effort in which, in order to "play the game," he gradually and unconsciously surrendered his apprehension of any values superior to those that were current in the American society of his day. It was with reason that Henry James told him he would be "humiliated" if his brother liked a certain book of his and thereby lumped it, in his affection, "with things of the current age," as Henry James put it, "that I have heard you express admiration for and that I would sooner descend to a dishonoured grave than have written." The impairment our philosopher's aesthetic taste had suffered may be gauged by his remark at the age of sixty-six that the architecture of Stanford University was "purer and more lovely than aught that Italy can show." Indeed he reveals, in his comments on books, men and public affairs, an immaturity of judgment, a want of real discrimination, a levity of conviction that remind one of Mark Twain and Theodore Roosevelt. What shall one say of a man who considered Mr. Balfour[3] "great," who, anti-militarist that he was, thought it would be only poetic justice if England's volunteer army were defeated by a conscript army from the Continent, who, opposed as he was to the annexation of the Philippines, expressed himself as willing, once the annexation was a *fait accompli,* to be convinced that he was in error? There is nothing peculiar in these reactions, but that is just the point; they were typical of James's reactions, they were also the typical reactions of the everyday, liberal-minded citizen; they show how successfully James's self-adaptation had taken place. This philosopher, with his "genius for being frustrated and interrupted," who, regretting that he had not completed the arch of his thought, permitted himself, in the culminating years of his life, and with his conscience always nagging him, to be drawn off by every invitation to popularize his ideas, this philosopher was simply, in essence, a "normal," engaging,

[3] Arthur James Balfour (1848-1930). British Conservative statesman; framer of the Balfour Declaration which pledged British support for a Jewish homeland in Palestine.

spontaneous, impulsive member of the American tribe of his generation. As for his gospel of risk and adventure, how it suggests the bravado of R. L. Stevenson, how it suggests Roosevelt's "strenuous life"! These victims of neurasthenia, these lovers of the "simplification" of the wilderness and the woods, how well we know, when they express themselves *fortissimo,* that they are not attempting to surpass life, that they merely wish to live it on equal terms with their contemporaries!

It is not perhaps for the philosophers to legislate for the remnant alone; but unless they do legislate for the remnant, the remnant loses itself in the majority, and all movement comes to a stop. If those who should have been our creators of values have been, on the whole, men of insufficient strength, we have to remember the immense handicaps they have had to encounter, the fact that our mechanistic life overstrains the nerves of every sensitive man, the unique nature, at once gigantic and chaotic, of our society, which reduces the strongest to a sort of fatalism, the absence of any artistic or aristocratic tradition that might have mitigated, in this country, the predominance of purely tribal standards. It remains true that the vicious circle of "good customs that corrupt the world" will never be broken in this country till we produce a few men who are able to stand up to our life, and look it in the face, and then deliberately reject it, not through any need to escape, but at the command of a profound personal vision. Such a man was Randolph Bourne, the toughest and most intransigent mind the younger generation has produced, and one who might well have convinced us that we have had too many cheerful meliorists, too many apostles of the "glad hand." How much we should enjoy the spectacle of a sour-faced American Schopenhauer, an indigestible American Tolstoy, an insufferable American Ibsen, an incredible American Nietzsche—just one true-blue solitary rhinoceros!

4. A Reviewer's Note-book: Pamphleteering Today

MUCH HAS BEEN said lately about the possibilities of pamphleteering in this country. It is quite natural that people should speak of pamphlets at a time like the present, when so many parties and organizations devoted to change and reform have broken down, and our social life is engulfed in apathy and cynicism; the historic role of the pamphleteer has been to blow on the embers of the popular faith, with a success of which we are aware if we remember the various careers, for instance, of Voltaire and Lamennais,[1] of Cardinal Newman and Thomas Paine. There are periods of indifference and of a sort of brutalization when the social man falls into a stupor; then it is only the gadflies that are able to sting him back into consciousness. What a difference it might make in the sultry contemporary air if we had a brisk pamphlet-literature! That is a notion many people appear to share; but, on the one hand, the publishers say that they can not distribute pamphlets and, on the other, the pamphleteers we have (always excepting Mr. Upton Sinclair) complain that the public will not buy their wares. The prospects of American pamphleteering would thus be sorry indeed were it not for certain facts that seem to have been overlooked.

For the failure of pamphlet-literature in this country the publishers, it seems to me, are not greatly to blame. I say this in spite of the repulsive appearance of most American pam-

SOURCE: IV (September 28, 1921), 71.

[1] Félicité Robert de Lamennais (1782-1854). He denounced in his *Essai sur l'indifférence en matière de religion* (1817-1823) the spiritual inertia of his contemporaries and defended the Church, in which he had taken orders in 1818, as the repository of truth. *L'Avenir,* the newspaper he founded during the Revolution of 1830, upheld a liberal Catholic view. When the Church condemned his attempt to make democratic liberalism a part of Catholic orthodoxy in his *Paroles d'un croyant* (1834), he broke with it.

phlets. To judge how mean, how unreadable from this point of view they generally are, one has only to compare a lapful of them with such typical English publications as those of the Fabian Society. Most of them look like testimonials of cough medicines; their covers are designed without taste, their type-pages are to small and so crowded that the eye recoils from them, the abuse of italics and bold-faced capitals sets one's head aching, the titles attempt to out-scream the din of the subway. "GOUGED: or the National Crisis"—this is the sort of label that meets the expectant glance; it is like the noisy slamming of a door in one's face, and for all such errors of judgment the publishers are largely responsible. How can the written word win a hearing when it is clothed in this fashion, especially at a time when the cheapest magazines are cunningly designed to attract the eye? It is not these physical questions of which one chiefly thinks, however, as one concludes that the possibilities of the pamphlet have not been explored in this country. The real trouble lies with the form, the style, the quality of the contents. Our pamphleteers have not begun to learn their trade.

One can divide them roughly into two classes: the patient gatherers of facts and the stump-orators who have resorted to the printed page. Strictly speaking, neither of these types of mind fulfills the requirements of the pamphleteer. To write a good pamphlet it is not enough to be emotionally possessed; it is not enough to be a master of statistics. Facts in mass belong in books; only the few can ever wish to obtain them. Oratory belongs to the ear, not to the eye. The office of pamphlets is to pique the mind, to arouse the imagination, to stimulate the intellectual and moral appetite; and that is just what most of ours fail to do. There must be thousands of people in this country who remember Mr. Wells's little tract, "This Misery of Boots";[2] the radical movement in the English-speaking world has had no more effective literary aid. It is indeed an example of the pamphlet at its best; and it shows,

---

[2] "This Misery of Boots," written for the *Independent Review* in 1907, was reprinted in pamphlet form by the Fabian Society. Wells proceeds from the particularized misery of boots to larger social miseries and concludes with an argument for the socialized production and distribution of goods.

in this connexion, how greatly the literary faculty outweighs every other. Mr. Wells fixes the reader's attention on the problem of footgear, a problem, it is true, that has never been as acute in America as in England; before he has reached the fourth page he has made the reader groan with all the accumulated memories of the aches and pains he has suffered from inadequate, shoddy shoes; then into the problem of shoes he reads the problem of the existing social system; till the full force of one's indignation, drawn gradually away from the lesser problem, directs itself toward the greater, and one rises at last a radical for life. What torrents of exhortation could ever accomplish this result? What cataracts of statistics? One fact skillfully handled has aroused one's desire for all the other facts.

The conclusion one draws from this comparison is that our pamphleteers are not primarily concerned with awakening either desire or thought. They expose abuses, they stir the emotions; they never enter the sphere of discussion at all. There exist today immense numbers of people in this country who have been fed with the unhappy facts of our social life, whose emotions have been so worked upon that they have lost all sense of allegiance to the civilization we know. Very well; but they have no notion what to do about it, they have no plans of action, no ideas that are strictly germane to the conditions, they have nothing in fact but a confused feeling that whatever is up ought to be down and whatever is down ought to be up. If this is the case, it is largely because the ideas that have been generated in this country have not been rendered accessible; they are locked up in the tomes of thinkers whose fashion of writing is more formidable than the hieroglyphics of the Rosetta Stone. If these ideas were seized upon and placed in relation, one by one, ingeniously, tactfully, with the very facts our journalistic investigators have made so familiar to us, we might begin to form our programmes and overcome the inertia that besets us all. That is one task for our pamphleteers; to popularize, with as much wit as they can command, the findings of the dismal scientists. "The young radical today," said Randolph Bourne, "is not asked to be a martyr, but he is asked to be a thinker, an intellectual leader. The

labor movement in this country needs a philosophy, a literature. Labour will scarcely do this thinking for itself. Unless
middle-class radicalism threshes out its categories and interpre-
tations and undertakes this constructive thought it will not be
done."[3] Exactly; but enough ideas already exist to carry us
more than halfway to Utopia: what is wanting is the relation
of the ideas to the facts and the emotions. That is what the
"middle-class radicals" ought to undertake; and surely the
pamphlet is the appropriate vehicle for this work.

More important than everything else at present, however,
is a general harrowing of the American soil. Satire, controversy,
the smoking out of prejudice, the challenging of assumption,
the cross-firing of a lively intellectual warfare can alone rouse
us out of the lethargy which at present seems to block every
sort of social movement. Two or three dozen writers most
readily called to mind, whose work is scattered through the
reviews, might, if they set their pens to work, each on a subject that called forth all his powers, produce the nucleus of a
pamphlet-literature that would soon have its effect upon our
lifeless atmosphere. Effective as they so often are in their
shorter articles, how much more effective they would be if,
aside from their more ambitious undertakings, they plunged
into some subject either dear or hateful to their hearts and
explored it, with all the wit, the penetration, the good temper
at their command! A raking fire turned upon our popular
illusions, our literature, our stage, our political and economic
life! With such a start the pamphlet might soon come into its
own again. The question of distribution will never solve itself
as long as the pamphleteers have to seek the public. It can
only be solved when a portion of the public seeks the pamphleteers. And certainly to a portion of the public the pamphleteers, if they study their art, have it in their power to
make themselves indispensable.[4]

---

[3] "The Price of Radicalism," *New Republic,* VI (March 11, 1916), 161.

[4] In another *Freeman* essay, Brooks warns: "That is the great danger in
polemical criticism: it tends to establish an orthodoxy of rebellion as complacent and stagnant as the established orthodoxy against which it rebels." See
"A Reviewer's Note-book," *The Freeman,* II (November 24, 1920), 262-263.

VII

The Ordeal
of Mark Twain

New York, 1920

EDITORIAL NOTE: When war forced Brooks to return home from Europe in 1914, he encountered a climate of "arctic loneliness for American writers" (*Autobiography* 240). The pessimism of Twain's *The Mysterious Stranger*, posthumously published in 1916, was a shock to readers, but it did suit the tone of the war years, as did another work Brooks connected with the temper of the times, *The Education of Henry Adams*, published in 1918 (*Autobiography* 418), the year he began to work on his first biography of an American writer. The opening line of *The Ordeal of Mark Twain* speaks to Brooks's conviction that the private malaise of a great writer has national meaning and consequences: "To those who are interested in American life and letters there has been no question of greater significance during the last few years than the pessimism of Mark Twain."[1]

Brooks worked away in Carmel (where he also wrote his *Pilgrimage of Henry James*) into 1919, when he completed the book. An advance from Dutton helped to ease his financial insecurities (as did Eleanor Brooks's translation of five novels in ten months [Hoopes 129]), but not his psychological ones, for with the completion of *Ordeal* Brooks fell into the severe depression that was to trouble and sometimes disable him for the next ten years.

Despite the use of terms like dual personality, it is hard to call Brooks's study Freudian. For one thing, the book is as much an attack on the Gilded Age as on Mark Twain. Furthermore, Twain's repression of his artist self is not related to psychic or sexual causes. As has been pointed out, Brooks found more moral support than method in Bernard Hart (Hoopes 137). His emphasis on the will (plain "will," "free will," "creative will," even "soul") shows his continuing location in nineteenth-century formulations. Vitelli argues that "the real source of his method" lies with "the romantics' concern for the psyche, not the psychoanalysts' concern for the id" (93).

Nonetheless, the impact of *Ordeal* served to strengthen the credibility of psychoanalysis as a literary tool. The biography was controversial: it tore down a national idol; it turned Twain's mother and wife into villains (see Vitelli 94). It attacked, as Brooks had always done, the myth of the West and the business ideal.

Rebuttals, reevaluations, amplifications—and a great deal of research—followed, but doubling and division continue to remain the starting point of Twain criticism (see the foreword and accompanying notes). Brooks was also the first to recognize how crucial his early life on the Mississippi was to Twain's self-construction. The Brooks biography has been immensely fruitful and usable for American scholarship. Without it we doubtless would have had articles like "The Case for Mark

---

[1] See Ferguson. The article is reprinted in Lewis Leary's casebook for students, which opens with Brooks's "Charges," follows with sections headed "Reactions," "Anticipations," "The Countercharge," "Reactions," and concludes with "Wounded—but an Artist."

Twain's Wife," but they were bound to have come later and to have had a different slant.

His outlook and his temperament conjoined to make Brooks call out for a satirist. He had to devalue humor, especially western humor, and think of Twain as a failed satirist. In a revised 1933 *Ordeal*, he softened his language in parts, but did not subvert his thesis. His 1957 apology for his undervaluation of Twain ("I had fallen short"), strong as it was, did not represent a withdrawal from his earliest convictions: "I still felt [Twain] had made the great refusal and that *The Ordeal of Mark Twain* was substantially just" (*Autobiography* 426). On this issue Brooks stopped short of his own "great refusal."

Chapter VIII

THOSE EXTRAORDINARY TWINS

"Joy with us is the monopoly of disreputable characters."
ALEXANDER HARVEY.

AT THE CIRCUS, no doubt, you have watched some trained lion going through the sad motions of a career to which the tyrannical curiosity of men has constrained him. At times he seems to be playing his part with a certain zest; he has acquired a new set of superficial habits, and you would say that he finds them easy and pleasant. Under the surface, however, he remains the wild, exuberant creature of the jungle. It is only thanks to the eternal vigilance of his trainers and the guiding-lines they provide for him in the shape of

the ring, the rack and all the zest of the circus-paraphernalia
that he continues to enact this parody of his true life. Have
his instincts been modified by the imposition of these new
habits? Look at him at the moment when the trainer ceases
to crack his whip and turns his back. In a flash another self
has possessed him: in his glance, in his furtive gesture you
perceive the king of beasts once more. The sawdust of the
circus has become the sand of the desert; twenty thousand
years have rolled back in the twinkling of an eye.

So it was with Mark Twain. "We have no *real* morals," he
wrote in one of his later letters, "but only artificial ones, morals
created and preserved by the forced suppression of natural and
healthy instincts." Now that is not true of the man who is
master of himself. The morality of the free man is not based
upon the suppression of his instincts but upon the discreet
employment of them: it is a real and not an artificial morality,
therefore, because the whole man subscribes to it. Mark
Twain, as we have seen, had conformed to a moral régime in
which the profoundest of his instincts could not function: the
artist had been submerged in the bourgeois gentleman, the man
of business, the respectable Presbyterian citizen. To play his
part, therefore, he had to depend upon the cues his wife and
his friends gave him. Here we have the explanation of his
statement: "Outside influences, outside circumstances, wind the
man and regulate him. Left to himself, he wouldn't get regu-
lated at all, and the sort of time he would keep would not be
valuable." We can see from this how completely his conscious
self had accepted the point of view of his trainers, how fully
he had concurred in their desire to repress that unmanageable
creative instinct of his, how ashamed, in short, he was of it.
Nevertheless, that instinct, while repressed, while unconscious,
continued to live and manifest itself just the same. We shall
see that in the end, never having been able to develop, to
express itself, to fulfill itself, to air itself in the sun and the
wind of the world, it turned as it were black and malignant,
like some monstrous, morbid inner growth, poisoning Mark
Twain's whole spiritual system. We have now to note its constant blind efforts to break through the censorship that had
been imposed on it, to cross the threshold of the unconscious

and play its part in the conscious life of this man whose will was always enlisted against it.

First of all, a few instances from his everyday life. We know that he was always chafing against the scheme of values, the whole social régime, that was represented by his wife and his friends. His conscious self urged him to maintain these values and this régime. His unconscious self strove against them, vetoed the force behind his will, pushed him in just the opposite direction. We find this conflict revealed in his story, "Those Extraordinary Twins," about an Italian counterpart of the famous Siamese monstrosity. "Whenever Luigi had posses sion of the legs, he carried Angelo to balls, rumshops, Sons of Liberty parades, horse races, campaign riots, and everywhere else that could damage him with his party and his church; and when it was Angelo's week he carried Luigi diligently to all manner of moral and religious gatherings, doing his best to regain the ground he had lost." This story of the two incompatible spirits bound together in one flesh is, as we can see, the symbol of Mark Twain himself.

Glance at his business life. He pursued it with frantic eagerness, urged on by the self that loved success, popularity, prestige. Yet he was always in revolt against it. There were years during which he walked the floor at night, "over-wrought and unsettled," as he said, "by apprehensions—badgered, harassed"—and let us add Mr. Paine's adjectives—"worried, impatient, rash, frenzied and altogether upset," till he had to beg the fates for mercy, till he had to send his agent the pathetic, imploring appeal, "Get me out of business!" Why did he always fail in those spectacular ventures of his? Was it not because his will, which was enlisted in business, was not supported by a constant, fundamental desire to succeed in it, because, in fact, his fundamental desire pointed him just the other way?

Then there was his conventional domestic and social life. He had submerged himself in the rôle of the husband, the father, the neighbor, the citizen. At once he became the most absent-minded of men! His absent-mindedness, Mr. Paine assures us, was "by no means a development of old age," and he mentions two typical instances of it when Mark Twain was "in the very heyday of his mental strength." Once, when the house was being cleaned, he failed to recognize the pictures in his own drawing-room when he found them on the floor, and accused an innocent caller of having brought them there to sell. Plainly the eye of the householder was not confirmed by the instinctive love that makes one observant. The vagrant artist in him, in fact, was always protesting against the lot his other self had so fully accepted, the lot of being "bullyragged," as he said, by builders and architects and tapestry-devils and carpet-idiots and billiard-table-scoundrels and wildcat gardeners when what was really needed was "an incendiary." Moreover, "he was always forgetting engagements," we are told, "or getting them wrong." And this absent-mindedness had its tragic results too, for because of it, to his own everlasting remorse, Mark Twain became the innocent cause of the death of one of his children and only just escaped being the cause of the death of another. On one occasion, he was driving with his year-old son on a snowy day and was so extraordinarily negligent that he let him catch a severe cold which developed into a fatal pneumonia; on the other, when he was out with one of his little daughters, he inadvertently let go of the perambulator and the baby, after a frightful slide down a steep hill, tumbled out, with her heading bleeding, among the stones by the roadside. "I should not have been permitted to do it," he said of this first misadventure. "I was not qualified for any such responsibility as that. Some one should have gone who had at least the rudiments of a mind. Necessarily I would lose myself dreaming." Yes, Mark Twain was day-dreaming: that mind in which the filial and paternal instincts had almost supplanted every other caught itself wandering at the critical hour! And in that hour the "old Adam," the natural man, the suppressed poet, registered its tragic protest, took its revenge, against a life that had left no room for it. Truth comes out in the end. The most significant comment on Mark Twain's constant absent-mindedness as regards domestic matters is to be found in Mr. Paine's record that in his dictations in old age he was extremely inaccurate on every subject except the genesis and writing of his books. We can see from this that although his conscious life had been overwhelmingly occupied with non-artistic and anti-artistic interests, his "heart," as we say, had always been, not in them, but in literature.

And how can we explain the fervor with which this comrade of Presbyterian ministers and pillars of society, this husband of that "heavenly whiteness," Mrs. Clemens, jots in his note-book observations like the following: "We may not doubt that society in heaven consists mainly of undesirable persons"? How can we explain that intemperate, that vehement, that furious obsession of animosity against the novels of Jane Austen except as an indirect venting of his hatred of the primness and prig-gishness of his own *entourage?* I should go even further, I should be even more specific, than this. Mr. Howells had been Mark Twain's literary mentor; Mr. Howells had "licked him into shape," had regenerated him artistically as his wife had regenerated him socially; Mr. Howells had set his pace for him, and Mark Twain, the candidate for gentility, had been over-flowingly grateful. "Possibly," he had written to this father confessor, "possibly you will not be a fully accepted classic until you have been dead one hundred years—it is the fate of the Shakespeares of all genuine professions—but then your books will be as common as Bibles, I believe. In that day, I shall be in the encyclopedias too, thus: 'Mark Twain, history and occupation unknown; but he was personally acquainted with Howells.'" We know, as a matter of fact, that he delighted in the delicacy of Howells's mind and language. But this taste was wholly unrelated to anything else in Mark Twain's literary horizon. We can say, with all the more certainty because he "detested" novels in general, that if Howells's novels had been written by any one else than his friend and his mentor he would have ignored them as he ignored all other "artistic" writing, he would even have despised them as he despised all insipid writing. In short, this taste was a product of personal affection and gratitude; it was precisely on a par with his attitude toward the provincial social daintinesses of his wife. And in both cases, just in the measure that his conscious self had accepted these alien standards that had been imposed upon him, his unconscious self revolted against them. "I never saw a woman so hard to please," he writes in 1875, "about things she doesn't know anything about." Mr. Paine hastens to assure us that "the reference to his wife's criticism in this is tenderly playful, as always." But what a multitude of dark secrets that tender playfulness covers! Mark Twain's unconscious self barely discloses its claws in phrases like that, enough to show how strict was the censorship he had accepted. It cannot express itself directly; consequently, like a child who, desiring to strike its teacher, stamps upon the floor instead, it pours out its accumulated bitterness obliquely. When Mark Twain utters such characteristic aphorisms as "Heaven for climate, hell for society," we see the repressed artist in him striking out at Mrs. Clemens and the Reverend Joseph Twitchell, whose companionship the dominant Mark Twain called, and with reason, for he seems to have been the most lovable of men, "a companionship which to me stands first after Livy's." Similarly, when he roars and rages against the novels of Jane Austen we can see the buried self taking vengeance upon Mr. Howells, with whom Jane Austen was a prime passion, who had even taken Jane Austen as a model.

We know the constraint to which he submitted as regards religious observances. "And once or twice," he writes, "I smouched a Sunday when the boss wasn't looking. Nothing is half as good as literature hooked on Sunday, on the sly." Does it not explain the bitter animus that lies behind his comical complaint of George W. Cable, when the two were together on a lecture tour?—"You will never, never know, never divine, guess, imagine, how loathsome a thing the Christian religion can be made until you come to know and study Cable daily and hourly. . . . He has taught me to abhor and detest the Sabbath-day and hunt up new and troublesome ways to dishonor it." Habitually, as we have seen, he spoke of himself in public as a Presbyterian, as "Twitchell's parishioner." His buried self redressed the balance in a passionate admiration for Robert Ingersoll, the atheist. "Thank you most heartily for the books," he writes to Ingersoll in 1879. "I am devouring them— they have found a hungry place, and they content it and satisfy it to a miracle." What, in fact, were the books he loved best? We find him reading Andrew D. White's "Science and Religion," Lecky's "European Morals" and similar books of a rationalistic tendency. But his favorite authors—after Voltaire, whom he had read as a pilot—were Pepys, Suetonius and Saint-Simon. Saint-Simon's "Memoirs" he said he had read twenty times, and we gather that he almost learned by heart Suetonius's record of "the cruelties and licentiousness of imperial Rome." Why did he take such passionate pleasure in books of this kind, in writers who had so freely "spoken out"? Hear what he says in 1904 regarding his own book, "What Is Man?"—"Am I honest? I give you my word of honor (privately) I am not. For seven years I have suppressed a book which my conscience tells me I ought to publish. I hold it a duty to publish it. There are other difficult tasks I am equal to, but I am not equal to that one." And when at last he did publish it, anonymously, it was with this foreword: "Every thought in them [these papers] has been thought (and accepted as unassailable truth) by millions upon millions of men—and concealed, kept private. Why did they not speak out? Because they dreaded (*and could not bear*) the disapproval of the people around them. Why have not I published? The same reason has restrained me, I think. I can find no other." There we see, in all its absolutism, the censorship under which his creative self was laboring. One can easily understand his love for Saint-Simon and Casanova and why, in private, he was perpetually praising their "unrestrained frankness."

And is there any other explanation of his "Elizabethan breadth of parlance"? Mr. Howells confesses that he sometimes blushed over Mark Twain's letters, that there were some which, to the very day when he wrote his eulogy on his dead friend, he could not bear to reread. Perhaps if he had not so insisted, in former years, while going over Mark Twain's proofs, upon "having that swearing out in an instant," he would never have had cause to suffer from his having "loosed his bold fancy to stoop on rank suggestion." Mark Twain's verbal Rabelaisianism was obviously the expression of that vital sap which, not having been permitted to inform his work, had been driven inward and left there to ferment. No wonder he was always indulging in orgies of forbidden words. Consider the famous book, "1601," that "fireside conversation in the time of Queen Elizabeth": is there any obsolete verbal indecency in the English language that Mark Twain has not painstakingly resurrected and assembled there? He, whose blood was in constant ferment and who could not contain within the narrow bonds that had been set for him the riotous exuberance of his nature, had to have an escape-valve, and he poured through it a fetid stream of meaningless obscenity—the waste of a priceless psychic material! Mr. Paine speaks of an address he made at a certain "Stomach Club" in Paris which has "obtained a wide celebrity among the clubs of the world, though no line of it, or even its title, has ever found its way into published literature." And who has not heard one or two of the innumerable Mark Twain anecdotes in the same vein that are current in every New York publishing house?

In all these ways, I say, these blind, indirect, extravagant, wasteful ways, the creative self in Mark Twain constantly strove to break through the censorship his own will had accepted, to cross the threshold of the unconscious. "A literary imp," says Mr. Paine, "was always lying in wait for Mark Twain, the imp of the burlesque, tempting him to do the *outré*, the outlandish, the shocking thing. It was this that Olivia Clemens had to labor hardest against." Well she labored, and well Mark Twain labored with her! It was the spirit of the artist, bent upon upsetting the whole apple-cart of bourgeois conventions. They could, and they did, keep it in check; they arrested it and manhandled it, and thrust it back; they shamed it and heaped scorn upon it and prevented it from interfering too much with the respectable tenor of their daily search for prestige and success. They could baffle it and distort it and oblige it to assume ever more complicated and grotesque disguises in order to elude them, but they could not kill it. In ways of which they were unaware it escaped their vigilance and registered itself in a sort of cipher, for us of another generation who have eyes to read, upon the texture of Mark Twain's writings.

For is it not perfectly plain that Mark Twain's books are shot through with all sorts of unconscious revelations of this internal conflict? In the Freudian psychology the dream is an expression of a suppressed wish. In dreams we do what our inner selves desire to do but have been prevented from doing

either by the exigencies of our daily routine, or by the obstacles
of convention, or by some other form of censorship which has
been imposed upon us, or which we ourselves, actuated by
some contrary desire, have willingly accepted. Many other
dreams, however, are not so simple: they are often incoherent,
nonsensical, absurd. In such cases it is because two opposed
wishes, neither of which is fully satisfied, have met one another
and resulted in a "compromise"—a compromise that is often as
apparently chaotic as the collision of two railway trains running
at full speed. These mechanisms, the mechanisms of the "wish-
fulfillment" and the "wish-conflict," are evident, as Freud has
shown, in many of the phenomena of everyday life. Whenever,
for any reason, the censorship is relaxed, the censor is off
guard, whenever we are day-dreaming and give way to our
idle thoughts, then the unconscious bestirs itself and rises to
the surface, gives utterance to those embarrassing slips of the
tongue, those "tender playfulnesses," that express our covert
intentions, slays our adversaries, sets our fancies wandering in
pursuit of all the ideals and all the satisfactions upon which
our customary life has stamped its veto. In Mark Twain's
books, or rather in a certain group of them, his "fantasies," we
can see this process at work. Certain significant obsessions
reveal themselves there, certain fixed ideas; the same themes
recur again and again. "I am writing from the grave," he notes
in later life, regarding some manuscripts that are not to be
published until after his death. "On these terms only can a
man be approximately frank. He cannot be straightly and un-
qualifiedly frank either in the grave or out of it." When he
wrote "Captain Stormfield's Visit to Heaven," "Pudd'nhead
Wilson," "The American Claimant," "Those Extraordinary
Twins," he was frank without knowing it. He, the unconscious
artist, who, when he wrote his Autobiography, found that he
was unable to tell the truth about himself, has conducted us
unawares in these writings into the penetralia of his soul.

Let us note, prefatorily, that in each case Mark Twain was
peculiarly, for the time being, free of his censorship. That he
wrote at least the first draft of "Captain Stormfield" in reckless
disregard of it is proved by the fact that for forty years he did
not dare to publish the book at all but kept it locked away in

his safe. As for "The American Claimant," "Pudd'nhead Wilson," and "Those Extraordinary Twins," he wrote them at the time of the failure of the Paige Typesetting Machine. Shortly before, he had been on the dizziest pinnacle of worldly expectation. Calculating what his returns from the machine were going to be, he had "covered pages," according to Mr. Paine, "with figures that never ran short of millions, and frequently approached the billion mark." Then, suddenly, reduced to virtual bankruptcy, he found himself once more dependent upon authorship for a living. He had passed, in short, through a profound nervous and emotional cataclysm: "so disturbed were his affairs, so disordered was everything," we are told, "that sometimes he felt himself as one walking amid unrealities." At such times, we know, the bars of the spirit fall down; people commit all sorts of aberrations, "go off the handle," as we say; the moral habits of a lifetime give way and man becomes more or less an irresponsible animal. In Mark Twain's case, at least, the result was a violent effort on the part of his suppressed self to assert its supremacy in a propitious moment when that other self, the businessman, had proved abysmally weak. That is why these books that marked his return to literature appear to have the quality of nightmares. He has told us in the preface to "Those Extraordinary Twins" that the story had originally been a part of "Pudd'nhead Wilson": he had seen a picture of an Italian monstrosity like the Siamese Twins and had meant to write an extravagant farce about them; but, he adds, "the story changed itself from a farce to a tragedy while I was going along with it—a most embarrassing circumstance." Eventually, he realized that it was "not one story but two stories tangled together" that he was trying to tell, so he removed the twins from "Pudd'nhead Wilson" and printed the two tales separately. That alone shows us the confusion of his mind, the confusion revealed further in "The American Claimant" and in "Pudd'nhead Wilson" as it stands. They are, I say, like nightmares, these books: full of passionate conviction that turns into a burlesque of itself, angry satire, hysterical humor. They are triple-headed chimeras, in short, that leave the reader's mind in tumult and dismay. The censor has so far relaxed its hold that the unconscious has risen up to the surface: the battle of the two Mark Twains takes place almost in the open, under our very eyes.

Glance now, among these dreams, at a simple example of "wish-fulfillment." When Captain Stormfield arrives in heaven, he is surprised to find that all sorts of people are esteemed among the celestials who have had no esteem at all on earth. Among them is Edward J. Billings of Tennessee. He was a poet during his lifetime, but the Tennessee village folk scoffed at him; they would have none of him, they made cruel sport of him. In heaven things are different; there the celestials recognize the divinity of his spirit, and in token of this Shake speare and Homer walk backward before him.

Here, as we see, Mark Twain is unconsciously describing the actual fate of his own spirit and that ample other fate his spirit desires. It is the story of Cinderella, the despised step-sister who is vindicated by the prince's favor, rewritten in terms personal to the author. We note the significant parallel that the Tennessee village where the unappreciated poet lived to the scornful amusement of his neighbors is a duplicate of the village in which Mark Twain had grown up, the milieu of Huck Finn and Tom Sawyer.

This inference is corroborated by the similar plight of Pudd'nhead Wilson, the sardonic philosopher whom we should have identified with Mark Twain even if the latter had not repeatedly assured us that an author draws himself in all his characters, even if we did not know that Pudd'nhead's "cal endar" was so far Mark Twain's own calendar that he contin- ued it in two later books, "Following the Equator" and "A Double-Barrelled Detective Story." Pudd'nhead, in short, is simply another Edward J. Billings and the village folk treat him in just the same fashion. "For some years," says the author, "Wilson had been privately at work on a whimsical almanac, for his amusement—a calendar, with a little dab of obstensible philosophy, usually in ironical form, appended to each date, and the Judge thought that these quips and fancies of Wilson's were neatly turned and cute; so he carried a handful of them around one day, and read them to some of the chief citizens. But irony was not for those people; their mental vision was not focussed for it. They read those playful trifles in the solidest

earnest and decided without hesitancy that if there ever had
been any doubt that Dave Wilson was a pudd'nhead—which
there hadn't—this revelation removed that doubt for good and
all." And hear how the half-breed Tom Driscoll baits him
before all the people in the square: "Dave's just an all-round
genius—a genius of the first water, gentlemen; a great scientist
running to seed here in this village, a prophet with the kind
of honor that prophets generally get at home—for here they
don't give shucks for his scientifics, and they call his skull a
notion-factory—hey, Dave, ain't it so? . . . Come, Dave, show
the gentlemen what an inspired Jack-at-all-science we've got
in this town and don't know it." Is it possible to doubt that
here, more than half consciously, Mark Twain was picturing
the fate that had, in so real a sense, made a buffoon of him?
Hardly, when we consider the vindictive delight with which
he pictures Pudd'nhead outmanœuvring the village folk and
triumphing over them in the end.

Observe, now, the deadly temperamental earnestness of "The
Man That Corrupted Hadleyburg," a story written late in life
when his great fame and position enabled him to override the
censorship and speak with more or less candor. "The temptation and the downfall of a whole town," says Mr. Paine, "was
a colossal idea, a sardonic idea, and it is colossally and sar-
donically worked out. Human weakness and rotten moral force
were never stripped so bare or so mercilessly jeered at in the
market-place. For once Mark Twain could hug himself with
glee in derision of self-righteousness, knowing that the world
would laugh with him, and that none would be so bold as to
gainsay his mockery. Probably no one but Mark Twain ever
conceived the idea of demoralizing a whole community—of
making its 'nineteen leading citizens' ridiculous by leading them
into a cheap, glittering temptation, and having them yield and
openly perjure themselves at the very moment when their
boasted incorruptibility was to amaze the world." It was the
"leading citizens," the pillars of society Mark Twain had himself been hobnobbing with all those years, the very people in
deference to whom he had suppressed his true opinions, his
real desires, who despised him for what he was and admired

him only for the success he had attained in spite of it—it was
these people, his friends, who had, in so actual a sense, imposed upon him, that he attacks in this terrible story of the
passing stranger who took such a vitriolic joy in exposing their
pretensions and their hypocrisy. "I passed through your town
at a certain time, and received a deep offense which I had not
earned. . . . I wanted to damage every man in the place, and
every woman." Is not that the unmistakable voice of the mis-
prized poet and philosopher in Mark Twain, the worm that
has turned, the angel that has grown diabolic in a world that
has refused to recognize its divinity?

Here, I say, in these two or three instances, we have the
"wish-fulfillment" in its clearest form. Elsewhere we find the
wish, the desire of the suppressed poet for self-effectuation,
expressing itself in many vague hopes and vague regrets. It is
the sentiment of the suppressed poet in all of us that he voices
in his letter to Howells about the latter's novel, "Indian Summer"—saying that it gives a body "a cloudy sense of his having
been a prince, once, in some enchanted, far-off land, and of
being an exile now, and desolate—and Lord, no chance ever
to get back there again!" And consider the unfinished tale of
"The Mysterious Chamber," "the story," as Mr. Paine describes
it, "of a young lover who is accidentally locked behind a secret
door in an old castle and cannot announce himself. He wanders
at last down into subterranean passages beneath the castle, and
he lives in this isolation for twenty years." There is something
inescapably personal about that. As for the character of the
Colonel Sellers of "The American Claimant"—so different from
the Colonel Sellers of "The Gilded Age," who is supposed to
be the same man and whom Mark Twain had drawn after one
of his uncles—every one has noted that it is a burlesque upon
his own preposterous business life. Isn't it more than this? That
rightful claimant to the great title of nobility, living in exile
among those fantastic dreams of wealth that always deceive
him—isn't he the obscure projection of the lost heir in Mark
Twain himself, inept in the business life he is living, incapable
of substantiating his claim, and yet forever beguiled by the
hope that some day he is going to win his true rank and live

the life he was intended for? The shadowy claim of Mark Twain's mother's family to an English earldom is not sufficient to account for his constant preoccupation with this idea.

Just before Mark Twain's death, he recalled, says Mr. Paine, "one of his old subjects, Dual Personality, and discussed various instances that flitted through his mind—Jekyll and Hyde phases in literature and fact." One of his old subjects, Dual Personality! Could he ever have been aware of the extent to which his writings revealed that conflict in himself? Why was he so obsessed by journalistic facts like the Siamese Twins and the Tichborne case, with its theme of the lost heir and the usurper? Why is it that the idea of changelings in the cradle perpetually haunted his mind, as we can see from "Pudd'nhead Wilson" and "The Gilded Age" and the variation of it that constitutes "The Prince and the Pauper"? The prince who has submerged himself in the rôle of the beggar-boy—Mark Twain has drawn himself there, just as he has drawn himself in the "William Wilson" theme of "The Facts Concerning the Recent Carnival of Crime in Connecticut," where he ends by dramatically slaying the conscience that torments him. And as for that pair of incompatibles bound together in one flesh—the Extraordinary Twins, the "good" boy who has followed the injunctions of his mother and the "bad" boy of whom society disapproves—how many of Mark Twain's stories and anecdotes turn upon that same theme, that same juxtaposition!—does he not reveal there, in all its nakedness, as I have said, the true history of his life?

We have observed that in Pudd'nhead's aphorisms Mark Twain was expressing his true opinions, the opinions of the cynic he had become owing to the suppression and the constant curdling as it were of the poet in him. While his pioneer self was singing the praises of American progress and writing "A Connecticut Yankee at the Court of King Arthur," the disappointed poet kept up a refrain like this: "October 12, the discovery. It was wonderful to find America, but it would have been more wonderful to lose it." In all this group of writings we have been discussing, however, we can see that while the censorship had been sufficiently relaxed in the general confusion of his life to permit his unconscious to rise to the surface, it was still vigilant enough to cloak its real intentions. It is in secret that Pudd'nhead jots down his saturnine philosophy; it is only in secret, in a private diary like Pudd'nhead's, that young Lord Berkeley, in "The American Claimant," thinks of recording his views of this fraudulent democracy where "prosperity and position constitute rank." Here, as in the malevolent, Mephistophelian "passing stranger" of "The Man That Corrupted Hadleyburg," Mark Twain frankly images himself. But he does so, we perceive, only by taking cover behind a device that enables him to save his face and make good his retreat. Pudd'nhead is only a crack brained fool about things in general, even if he is pretty clever with his finger-print invention— otherwise he would find something better to do than to spend his time writing nonsense; and as for Lord Berkeley, how could you expect a young English snob to know anything about democracy? That was the reaction upon which Mark Twain could safely count in his readers; they would only be fooling themselves, of course, they would know that they were fooling themselves: but in order to keep up the great American game of bluff they would have to forgive *him*! As long as he never hit below the belt by speaking in his own person, in short, he was perfectly secure. And Mark Twain, the humorist, who held the public in the hollow of his hand, knew it.

It is only after some such explanation as this that we can understand the supremacy among all Mark Twain's writings of "Huckleberry Finn." Through the character of Huck, the disreputable, illiterate little boy, as Mrs. Clemens no doubt thought him, he was licensed to let himself go. We have seen how indifferent his sponsors were to the writing and the fate of this book: "nobody," says Mr. Paine, "appears to have been especially concerned about Huck, except, possibly, the publisher." The more indifferent they were, the freer was Mark Twain! Anything that little vagabond said might be safely trusted to pass the censor, just because he was a little vagabond, just because, as an irresponsible boy, he could not, in the eyes of the mighty ones of this world, know anything in any case about life, morals and civilization. That Mark Twain was almost, if not quite, conscious of his opportunity we can see from his introductory note to the book: "Persons attempting to find a motive in this narrative will be prosecuted; persons attempting to find a moral in it will be banished; persons attempting to find a plot in it will be shot." He feels so secure of himself that he can actually challenge the censor to accuse him of having a motive! Huck's illiteracy, Huck's disreputableness and general outrageousness are so many shields behind which Mark Twain can let all the cats out of the bag with impunity. He must, I say, have had a certain sense of his unusual security when he wrote some of the more cynically satirical passages of the book, when he permitted Colonel Sherburn to taunt the mob, when he drew that picture of the audience who had been taken in by the Duke proceeding to sell the rest of their townspeople, when he has the King put up the notice "Ladies and Children not Admitted," and add: "There, if that line don't fetch them, I don't know Arkansaw!" The withering contempt for humankind expressed in these episodes was of the sort that Mark Twain expressed more and more openly, as time went on, in his own person; but he was not indulging in that costly kind of cynicism in the days when he wrote "Huckleberry Finn." He must, therefore, have appreciated the license that little vagabond, like the puppet on the lap of a ventriloquist, afforded him. This, however, was only a trivial detail in his general sense of happy expansion, of ecstatic liberation. "Other places do seem so cramped up and smothery, but a raft don't," says Huck, on the river; "you feel mighty free and easy and comfortable on a raft." Mark Twain himself was free at last!—that raft and that river to him were something more than mere material facts. His whole unconscious life, the pent-up river of his own soul, had burst its bonds and rushed forth, a joyous torrent! Do we need any other explanation of the abandon, the beauty, the eternal freshness of "Huckleberry Finn"? Perhaps we can say that a lifetime of moral slavery and repression was not too much to pay for it. Certainly, if it flies like a gay, bright, shining arrow through the tepid atmosphere of American literature, it is because of the straining of the bow, the tautness of the string, that gave it its momentum.

Yes, if we did not know, if we did not feel, that Mark

Twain was intended for a vastly greater destiny, for the rôle of a demiurge, in fact, we might have been glad of all those petty restrictions and misprisions he had undergone, restrictions that had prepared the way for this joyous release. No smoking on Sundays! No "swearing" allowed! Neckties having to be bothered over! That everlasting diet of Ps and Qs, petty Ps and pettier Qs, to which Mark Twain had had to submit, the domestic diet of Mrs. Clemens, the literary diet of Mr. Howells, those second parents who had taken the place of his first—we have to thank it, after all, for the vengeful solace we find in the promiscuous and general revolt of Huckleberry Finn:

"Don't talk about it, Tom. I've tried it and it don't work; it don't work Tom. It ain't for me; I ain't used to it. The widder's good to me, and friendly; but I can't stand them ways. She makes me git up just at the same time every morning; she makes me wash, they comb me all to thunder; she won't let me sleep in the woodshed; I got to wear them blamed clothes that just smothers me, Tom; they don't seem to any air git through 'em, somehow; and they're so rotten nice that I can't set down, nor lay down, nor roll around anywher's; I hain't slid on a cellar door for—well, it 'pears to be years; I got to go to church and sweat and sweat—I hate them ornery sermons! I can't ketch a fly in there, I can't chaw, I got to wear shoes all Sunday. The widder eats by a bell; she goes to bed by a bell; she gits up by a bell—everything's so awful reg'lar a body can't stand it."

"Well, everybody does that way, Huck."

"Tom, it don't make no difference. I ain't everybody, and I can't *stand* it. It's awful to be tied up so. And grub comes too easy. I don't take no interest in vittles, that way. I got to ask to go a-fishing; I got to ask to go in a-swimming—dern'd if I hain't got to ask to do everything. Well, I'd got to talk so nice it wasn't no comfort—I'd got to go up in the attic and rip out a while, every day, to git a taste in my mouth, or I'd a died, Tom. The widder wouldn't let me smoke; she wouldn't let me yell, she wouldn't let me gape, nor stretch, nor scratch, before folks. . . . I *had* to shove, Tom—I just had to. . . . Now these clothes suits me, and this bar'l suits me, and I ain't ever going to shake 'em any more. . . ."

This chapter began with the analogy of the lion in the circus. You see what happens with Mark Twain when the trainer turns his back.

Chapter X

LET SOMEBODY ELSE BEGIN

"No real gentleman will tell the naked truth in
the presence of ladies."
A Double-Barrelled Detective Story.

"I AM PERSUADED that the future historian of America will find your works as indispensable to him as a French historian finds the political tracts of Voltaire." In these words, which he addressed to Mark Twain himself, Bernard Shaw suggested what was undoubtedly the dominant intention of Mark Twain's genius, the rôle which he was, if one may say so, pledged by nature to fulfill. "He will be remembered," says Mr. Howells, "with the great humorists of all time, with Cervantes, with Swift, or with any others worthy of his company." Voltaire, Cervantes, Swift! It was as a satirist, we perceive, as a spiritual emancipator, that those of his contemporaries who most generously realized him thought of Mark Twain. Did they not, under the spell of that extraordinary personal presence of his, in the magnetism, the radiance of what might be called his temperamental will-to-satire, mistake the wish for the deed?

What is a satirist? A satirist, if I am not mistaken, is one who holds up to the measure of some more or less permanently admirable ideal the inadequacies and the deformities of the society in which he lives. It is Rabelais holding up to the measure of healthy-mindedness the obscurantism of the Middle Ages; it is Molière holding up to the measure of an excellent sociality everything that is eccentric, inelastic, intemperate; it is Voltaire holding up to the measure of the intelligence the forces of darkness and superstition: it is a criticism of the spirit of one's age, and of the facts in so far as the spirit is embodied in them, dictated by some powerful, personal and supremely conscious reaction against that spirit. If this is true, Mark Twain cannot be called a satirist. Certain of the facts of American life he did undoubtedly satirize. "The state of American society and government his stories and articles present," says Miss Edith Wyatt, "is, broadly speaking, truthfully characteristic of the state of society and government we find now in Chicago, the most murderous and lawless civil community in the world. What is exceptional in our great humorist's view of our national life is not the ruffianism of the existence he describes for us on the Mississippi and elsewhere in the United States, but the fact that he writes the truth about it." Who will deny that this is so? Mark Twain satirizes the facts, or some of the facts, of our social life, he satirizes them vehemently. But when it comes to the spirit of our social life, that is quite another matter. Let us take his own humorous testimony: "The silent, colossal National Lie that is the support and confederate of all the tyrannies and shams and inequalities and unfairnesses that afflict the peoples—that is the one to throw bricks and sermons at. But let us be judicious and let somebody else begin."

It has often been said that Mark Twain "lost his nerve." It ought to be sufficiently clear by this time, however, that he did not lose his nerve, simply because, in reality, he had never found it. He had never, despite Mr. Howells, "come into his intellectual consciousness" at all, he had never come into the consciousness of any ideal that could stand for him as a measure of the society about him. Moreover, he had so involved himself in the whole popular complex of the Gilded Age that he could not strike out in any direction without wounding his wife or his friends, without contravening some loyalty that had become sacred to him, without destroying the very basis of his happiness. We have seen that he had never risen to the conception of literature as a great impersonal social instrument. An irresponsible child himself, he could not even feel that he had a right to exercise a will-to-satire that violated the wishes of those to whom he had subjected himself. Consequently, instead of satirizing the spirit of his age, he outwardly acquiesced in it and even flattered it.

If anything is certain, however, it is that Mark Twain was intended to be a sort of American Rabelais who would have done, as regards the puritanical commercialism of the Gilded Age, very much what the author of "Pantagruel" did as regards the obsolescent mediævalism of sixteenth-century France. Reading his books and his life one seems to divine his proper character and career embedded in the life of his generation as the bones of a dinosaur are embedded in a prehistoric claybank: many of the vertebræ are missing, other parts have crumbled away, we cannot with final certainty identify the portentous creature. But the dimensions help us, the skull, the thigh, the major members are beyond dispute; we feel that we are justified from the evidence in assuming what sort of being we have before us, and our imagination fills out in detail what its appearance must, or rather would, have been.

When we consider how many of Mark Twain's yarns and anecdotes, the small change as it were of his literary life, had for their butt the petty aspects of the tribal morality of America—Sabbath-breaking, the taboos of the Sunday School, the saws of Poor Richard's Almanac, we can see that his birthright was of our age rather than of his own. Hear what he says of "the late Benjamin Franklin": "His maxims were full of animosity toward boys. Nowadays a boy cannot follow out a single natural instinct without tumbling over some of those everlasting aphorisms and hearing from Franklin on the spot. If he buys two cents' worth of peanuts, his father says, 'Remember what Franklin has said, my son, "A groat a day's a penny a year."' and the comfort is all gone out of those peanuts." He delights in turning the inherited wisdom of the pioneers into such forms as this: "Never put off till to-morrow what you can do day after to-morrow, just as well." Here we have the note of Huckleberry Finn, who is not so much at war with the tribal morality as impervious to it, as impervious as a child of another epoch. He visits a certain house at night and describes the books he finds piled on the parlor table: "One was 'Pilgrim's Progress,' about a man that left his family, it didn't say why. I read considerable in it now and then. The statements was interesting, but tough." And again, speaking of a family dinner: "Uncle Silas he asked a pretty long blessing over it, but it was worth it; and it didn't cool it a bit, neither, the way I've seen them kind of interruptions do lots of times." One may say that a man in whom the continuity of racial experience is cut as sharply as these passages indicate it was cut in Mark Twain is headed straight for an inferior cynicism; but what is almost destiny for the ordinary man is the satirist's opportunity: if he can recover himself quickly, if he can substitute a new and personal ideal for the racial ideal he has abandoned, that solution of continuity is the making of him. For Mark Twain this was impossible. I have already given many instances of his instinctive revolt against the spirit of his time, moral, religious, political, economic. "My idea of our civilization," he said, freely, in private, "is that it is a shabby poor thing and full of cruelties, vanities, arrogancies, meannesses and hypocrisies. As for the word, I hate the sound of it, for it conveys a lie; and as for the thing itself, I wish it was in hell, where it belongs." And consider this grave conclusion in one of his later letters: "Well, the 19th century made progress—the first progress in 'ages and ages'—colossal progress. In what? Materialities. Prodigious acquisitions were made in things which add to the comfort of many and make life harder for as many more. But the addition to righteousness? Is that discoverable? I think not. The materialities were not invented in the interest of righteousness; that there is more righteousness in the world because of them than there was before, is hardly demonstrable, I think. In Europe and America there is a vast change (due to them) in ideals—do you admire it? All Europe and all America are feverishly scrambling for money. Money is the supreme ideal—all others take tenth place with the great bulk of the nations named. Money-lust has always existed, but not in the history of the world was it ever a craze, a madness, until your time and mine. This lust has rotted these nations; it has made them hard, sordid, ungentle, dishonest, oppressive." Who can fail to see that the whole tendency of Mark Twain's spirit ran precisely counter to the spirit of his age, that he belonged as naturally in the Opposition, as I have said, as all the great European writers of his time? Can we not also see, accordingly, that in stultifying him, in keeping him a child, his wife and his friends were the unconscious agents of the business régime, bent upon deflecting and restraining a force which, if it had matured, would have seriously interfered with the enterprise of industrial pioneering?

Far from having any stimulus to satire, therefore, Mark Twain was perpetually driven back by the innumerable obligations he had assumed into the rôle that gave him, as he said, comfort and peace. And to what did he not have to submit? "We shall have bloody work in this country some of these days when the lazy *canaille* get organized. They are the spawn of Santerre and Fouquier-Tinville," we find Thomas Bailey Aldrich writing to Professor Woodberry in 1894. There was the attitude of Mark Twain's intimates toward social and economic questions: the literary confraternity of the generation was almost a solid block behind the financial confraternity. In the moral and religious departments the path of the candidate for gentility was no less strait and narrow. "It took a brave man before the Civil War," says Mr. Paine, "to confess he had read 'The Age of Reason' ": Mark Twain observed once that he had read it as a cub pilot "with fear and hesitation." A man whose life had been staked on the pursuit of prestige, in short, could take no chances in those days! The most fearful warnings followed Mark Twain to the end. In 1880 or thereabouts he saw his brother Orion, in the Middle West, excommunicated, after a series of infidel lectures, and "condemned to eternal flames" by his own Church, the Presbyterian Church. "Huckleberry Finn" and "Tom Sawyer" were constantly being suppressed as immoral by the public libraries, and not in rural districts merely but in great centers: in Denver and Omaha in 1903, in godly Brooklyn as late as 1906. If the morals of those boys were considered heretical, what would have been thought of Mark Twain's other opinions? Even the title he suggested for his first important book–"The New Pilgrim's Progress"–

was regarded in Hartford as a sacrilege. The trustees of the American Publishing Company flatly refused to have anything to do with it, and it was only when the money-charmer Bliss threatened to resign if he was not allowed to publish the book that these pious gentlemen, who abhorred heresy, but loved money more than they abhorred heresy, gave in. It was these same gentlemen who later became Mark Twain's neighbors and daily associates: it was with them he shared that happy Hartford society upon whose "community of interests" and "unity of ideals" the loyal Mr. Paine is obliged to dwell in his biography. Was Mark Twain to be expected to attack them?

His spirit was indeed quiescent during the middle years of his life: it is only in his early work, and only in his minor work, his "Sketches," that we find, smuggled in as it were among so many other notes, the frank note of the satirist. One recalls the promise he had made, as a sort of oblique acknowledgment of his father-in-law's loan, to the readers of his Buffalo paper: "I only want to assure parties having a friendly interest in the prosperity of the journal that I am not going to hurt the paper deliberately and intentionally at any time. I am not going to introduce any startling reforms, nor in any way attempt to make trouble." He, that "rough Western miner" on probation, knew that he could not be too circumspect. And yet among those early sketches a risky note now and then intrudes itself: "A Mysterious Visit," for example, that very telling animadversion upon a society in which "thousands of the richest and proudest, the most respected, honored and courted men" lie about their income to the tax-collector "every year." Is it not the case, however, that as time went on he got into the habit of somehow not noticing these little spots on the American sun?

In "The Gilded Age," it is true, his first and only novel, he seems frank enough. One remembers the preface of that book: "It will be seen that it deals with an entirely ideal state of society; and the chief embarrassment of the writers in this realm of the imagination has been the want of illustration. In a state where there is no fever of speculation, no inflamed desire for sudden wealth, where the poor are all simple-minded and contented, and the rich are all honest and generous, where society is in a condition of primitive purity, and politics is the occupation of only the capable and the patriotic, there are necessarily no materials for such a history as we have constructed out of an ideal commonwealth." That is fairly explicit and fairly animated, even if it is only a paragraph from a preface; and in fact the whole background of the story, from the capital city, that "grand old benevolent national asylum for the Helpless," down, with its devasting irony about every American institution save family life—Congress, the law, trial by jury, journalism, business, education and the Church, East and West alike, almost prepares us for Mark Twain's final verdict regarding the "Blessings-of-Civilization Trust." And yet the total effect of the book is idyllic; the mirage of the America Myth lies over it like a rosy veil. Mark Twain might permit himself a certain number of acid glances at the actual face of reality; but he had to redeem himself, he wished to redeem himself for doing so—for the story was written to meet the challenge of certain ladies in Hartford—by making the main thread the happy domestic tale of a well brought up young man who finds in this very stubbly field the amplest and the softest straw for the snug family nest he builds in the end. Would he, for that matter, have presumed to say his say at all if he had not had the moral support of the collaboration of Charles Dudley Warner? "Clemens," we are told, "had the beginning of a story in his mind, but had been unwilling to undertake an extended work of fiction alone. He welcomed only too eagerly, therefore, the proposition of joint authorship." Mark Twain, the darling of the masses, brought Warner a return in money such as he probably never experienced again in his life; Warner, the respected Connecticut man of letters, gave Mark Twain the sanction of his name. An admirable combination! A model indeed, one might have thought it, for all New Englanders in their dealings with the West.

Am I exaggerating the significance of what might be taken for an accident? In any case, it was not until that latter period when he was too old and too secure in his seat to fear public opinion quite in this earlier way that he had his revenge in "The Man That Corrupted Hadleyburg"—not till then, and then only in a measure did he ever again, openly and on a large scale, attack the spiritual integrity of industrial America.

Occasionally, in some little sketch like "The Great Revolution in Pitcairn," where the Presbyterian Yankee is described as "a doubtful acquisition," he ventures a pinprick in the dark; and we know that he sent his "1601" anonymously to a magazine editor who had once remarked, "O that we had a Rabelais!": "I judged," said Mark Twain, "that I could furnish him one." But he had had his fingers burnt too often: he had no intention of persisting. It is notable, therefore, that having begun with contemporary society in "The Gilded Age," he travels backward into the past for his subsequent pseudo-satirical themes: he feels free to express his social indignation only in terms of the seventh century England of the "Connecticut Yankee," the fifteenth century England of "The Prince and the Pauper," the fourteenth century France of "Joan of Arc," the sixteenth century Austria of "The Mysterious Stranger." Never again America, one observes, and never again the present, for the first of these books alone contains anything like a contemporary social implication and that, the implication of the "Connecticut Yankee," is a flattering one. But I am exaggerating. Mark Twain does attack the present in the persons of the Czar and King Leopold, whom all good Americans abhorred. As for his attacks on corruption in domestic politics, on the missionaries in China, was he not, when he at last "spoke out," supported by the leading citizens who are always ready to back the right sort of prophet? Turn to Mr. Paine's biography: you will find Mr. Carnegie, whom he called Saint Andrew, begging Saint Mark for permission to print and distribute in proper form that "sacred message" about the missionaries. Mark Twain knew how to estimate the sanctity of his own moral courage. "Do right," he notes, in his private memoranda—"do right and you will be conspicuous."

Let us take one more instance, the supreme instance, of Mark Twain's intention and failure in his predestined rôle, the "Connecticut Yankee" itself. This was his largest canvas, his greatest creative effort, the most ambitious and in certain respects the most powerful of his works. Nothing could be more illuminating than a glance at his motives in writing it.

What, in the first place, was his ostensible motive? "The book," he says, in a letter to his English publisher, "was not

written for America; it was written for England. So many
Englishmen have done their sincerest best to teach us something for our betterment that it seems to me high time that
some of us should substantially recognize the good intent by
trying to pry up the English nation to a little higher level of
manhood in turn."

No doubt, if Mark Twain had read this over in cold blood
he would have blushed for his own momentary priggishness;
it was not characteristic of him to talk about "higher levels of
manhood." But he was in a pet. Matthew Arnold had been
wandering among us, with many deprecating gestures of those
superangelic hands of his. Matthew Arnold must always have
been slightly irritating—he was irritating even at home, and
how much more irritating when, having visited this country,
he chose to dwell upon the rudimentary language of General
Grant! Mark Twain saw red. An animadversion upon General
Grant's grammar was an attack upon General Grant, an attack
upon General Grant was an attack upon America, an attack
upon America *and* upon General Grant was an attack upon
Mark Twain, upon his heart as a friend of General Grant,
upon his pocket-book as the publisher of General Grant, upon
his *amour-propre* as the countryman of General Grant. The
pioneer in him rose to the assault like a bull-buffalo in defense
of the herd. Mark Twain relapsed into a typical Huck Finn
attitude: he doubled his fists and said, "You're another!"—just
as he did a few years later in his reply to Paul Bourget. Then,
longing for "a pen warmed-up in hell," he set to work to put
those redcoats, Matthew Arnold, King George III, General
Cornwallis and all the rest of them, for by this time he was in
the full furore of the myth of the American Revolution, in their
place. He even began a frantic defense of American newspa-
pers, which at other times he could not revile enough, and
filled his note-books with red-hot absurdities like this: "Show
me a lord and I will show you a man whom you couldn't tell
from a journeyman shoemaker if he were stripped, and who,
in all that is worth being, is the shoemaker's inferior." In short,
he covered both shoulders with chips and defied any and every
Englishman, the whole English race, indeed, to come and
knock them off.

Now here, I say, is the crucial instance of Mark Twain's failure as a satirist. In the moment of crisis the individual in him loses itself in the herd; the intellect is submerged in a blind emotion that leads him, unconsciously, into a sort of *bouleversement* of all his actual personal intentions. Against his instinct, against his purpose he finds himself doing, not the thing he really desires to do, i.e., to pry up the American nation, if the phrase must be used, "to a little higher level of manhood," which is the true office of an American satirist, but to flatter the American nation and lull its conscience to sleep. In short, instead of doing the unpopular thing, which he really wanted to do, he does the most popular thing of all: he glorifies the Yankee mechanic, already, in his own country, surfeited with glory, and pours ridicule upon the two things that least needed ridicule for the good of the Yankee mechanic's soul, if only because in his eyes they were sufficiently ridiculous already—England and the Middle Ages.

Could we have a better illustration of the betrayal of Mark Twain's genius? If any country ever needed satire it is, and was, America. Did not Mark Twain feel this himself in those rare moments of his middle years when he saw things truly with his own eyes? Let us take from his letters a comment on American society that proves it: "There was absolutely nothing in the morning papers," he writes in 1873: "you can see for yourself what the telegraphic headings were: BY TELEGRAPH— A Father Killed by His Son, A Bloody Fight in Kentucky, An Eight-Year-Old Murderer, A Town in a State of General Riot, A Court House Fired and Three Negroes Therein Shot While Escaping, A Louisiana Massacre, Two to Three Hundred Men Roasted Alive, A Lively Skirmish in Indiana (and thirty other similar headings). The items under those headings all bear date yesterday, April 16 (refer to your own paper)—and I give you my word of honor that that string of commonplace stuff was everything there was in the telegraphic columns that a body could call news. Well, said I to myself, this is getting pretty dull; this is getting pretty dry; there don't appear to be anything going on anywhere; has this progressive nation gone to sleep?" Knowing as we do the significance of Mark Twain's humor, we divine from the tone of these final comments that he already considers it none of his business, that as a writer he proposes to do nothing about it. But his eye is exceedingly wide open to those things! Would not any one say, therefore, that there is something rather singular in the spectacle of a human being living alertly in a land where such incidents were the staple of news and yet being possessed with an exclusive public passion to "pry the English nation up to a little higher level of manhood"? Isn't it strange to see the inhabitant of a country where negroes were being lynched at an average rate of one every four days filled with "a holy fire of righteous wrath," as Mr. Paine says, because people were unjustly hanged in the seventh century? Mark Twain was sincerely angry, there is no doubt about that. But isn't it curious how automatically his anger was deflected from all its natural and immediate objects, from all those objects it might have altered, and turned like an aircraft gun upon the vacuity of space itself? "Perhaps," he says, in "What Is Man?" defining what he calls the master passion, the hunger for self-approval, "perhaps there is something that (man) loves more than he loves peace—*the approval of his neighbors and the public*. And perhaps there is something which he dreads more than he dreads pain—the *disapproval* of his neighbors and the public." Mark Twain ate his cake and had it too. He avoided the disapproval of his neighbors by not attacking America; he won their approval by attacking England. then, as we can see from his famous letter to Andrew Lang, he tried to win the approval of England also by deprecating the opinion of cultivated readers and saying that he only wanted to be taken as a popular entertainer! "I have never tried, in even one single little instance, to help cultivate the cultivated classes. . . . And I never had any ambition in that direction, but always hunted for bigger game—the masses. I have seldom deliberately tried to instruct them, but I have done my best to entertain them, for they can get instruction elsewhere." That was what became of his noble purpose to "pry up the English nation" when the English nation manifested its objection to being pried up by virtually boycotting the book. The wiles of simple folk! They are the most successful of all.

The ironical part of this story—for it is worth pursuing—is

that Mark Twain, the sober individual, had for England an exaggerated affection and admiration. His "first hour in England was an hour of delight," he records; "of rapture and ecstacy." "I would a good deal rather live here if I could get the rest of you over," he writes frankly in 1872; and Mr. Paine adds that, "taking the snug island as a whole, its people, its institutions"—its institutions, observe—"its fair rural aspects, he had found in it only delight." That was true to the end of his days; against a powerful instinct he defended even the Boer War because he so admired the genius of English administration. He had personal reasons for this, indeed, in the affection with which England always welcomed him. "On no occasion in his own country," we are told, of his first English lecture tour, "had he won such a complete triumph"; and how many of those triumphs there were! "As a rule," says Mr. Paine, "English readers of culture, critical readers, rose to an understanding of Mark Twain's literary value with greater promptness than did the same class of readers at home." "Indeed," says Mr. Howells, "it was in England that Mark Twain was first made to feel that he had come into his rightful heritage." Did his feeling for England spring from this? Who can say? But certainly it was intense and profound. Early in his life he planned, as we have seen, a book on England and gave it up because he was afraid its inevitable humor would "offend those who had taken him into their hearts and homes." Why, then, safely enthroned in America, did he, merely because he was annoyed with Matthew Arnold, so passionately desire to "pry" the English nation up? One key to this question we have already found, but it requires a deeper explanation; and the incident of this earlier book suggests it. Mark Twain's literary motives, and it was this, as I have said, that made him the typical pioneer, were purely personal. Emerson wrote his "English Traits" before the Civil War: in reporting his conversation with Walter Savage Landor, he made a remark that could not fail to hurt the feelings of Robert Southey. What was his reason, what was his excuse? That Southey and Landor were public figures and that their values were values of public importance. Emerson, in short, instinctively regarded his function, his loyalties and his responsibilities as those of the man

of letters, the servant of humanity. Mark Twain, no less typical
of his own half-century, took with him to England the pioneer
system of values in which everything was measured by the
ideal of neighborliness. If he couldn't write without hurting
people's feelings, he wouldn't write at all, for always, likc the
good Westerner, he thought of his audience as the group of
people immediately surrounding him. In America, on the other
hand, the situation was precisely reversed. What would please
his Hartford neighbors, who had taken him into *their* hearts
and homes?—that was the point now; and they, or the less
cultivated majority of them, could not see England, through
the eyes of a Connecticut Yankee, damned enough! Something,
Mark Twain knew, he wanted to satirize—he was boiling with
satirical emotion; and while the artist in him wished to satirize
not England but America, the pioneer in him wished to satirize
not America but England. And as usual the pioneer won.

Another motive corroborated this decision. "He had published," Mr. Paine tells us, "nothing since the 'Huck Finn' story,
and his company was badly in need of a new book by an
author of distinction. Also, it was highly desirable to earn
money for himself." Elsewhere we read that the "Connecticut
Yankee" "was a book badly needed by his publishing business
with which to maintain its prestige and profit." Mark Twain,
the author, we see, had to serve the prestige and profit of Mark
Twain, the publisher; he was obliged, in short, to write something that would be popular with the American massses. How
happy that publisher must have been for the provocation Matthew Arnold offered him! Mark Twain, on the top-wave of his
own capitalistic undertakings, was simply expressing the exuberance of his own character not as an artist but as an industrial pioneer in the person of that East Hartford Yankee who
sets out to make King Arthur's England a "going concern."
Who can mistake this animus?—"Look at the opportunities
here for a man of knowledge, brains, pluck and enterprise to
sail in and grow up with the country. The grandest field that
ever was; and all my own, not a competitor." Prying up the
English nation ends, as we see, with a decided general effect
of patting the American nation on the back. The satirist has
joined forces with the great popular flood of his generation; he

has become that flood; he asks neither the why nor the whither of his going; he knows only that he wants to be in the swim. If, at that moment, the artist in Mark Twain had had only the tail of one eye awake, he would have laughed at the spectacle of himself drawing in dollars in proportion to the magnificence of his noble and patriotic defense of what every-body else, less nobly perhaps, but no less patriotically, was defending also.

"Frankness is a jewel," said Mark Twain; "only the young can afford it." Precisely at that moment when he was writing to Robert Ingersoll that remarkable letter which displayed a thirst for crude atheism comparable only to the thirst for crude alcohol of a man who has been too long deprived of his normal ration of simple beer, he was at work on "Tom Sawyer." "It is not a boys' book, at all," he says. "It will only be read by adults. It is only written for adults." Six months later we find him adding: "I finally concluded to cut the Sunday School speech down to the first two sentences, leaving no suggestion of satire, since the book is to be for boys and girls." Tell the truth or trump—but get the trick!

Almost incredible, in fact, to any one who is familiar with the normal processes of the literary mind, was Mark Twain's fear of public opinion, that fear which was the complement of his prevailing desire for success and prestige. In later life it was his regular habit to write two letters, one of which he suppressed, when he was addressing any one who was not an intimate friend upon any subject about which his instinctive feelings clashed with the popular view. These unmailed letters in which, as Mr. Paine says, "he had let himself go merely to relieve his feelings and to restore his spiritual balance," accu-mulated in such a remarkable way that finally, as if he were about to publish them, Mark Twain for his own amusement wrote an introduction to the collection. "Will anybody con-tend," he says, "that a man can say to such masterful anger as that, Go, and be obeyed? . . . He is not to *mail* this letter; he understands that, and so he can turn on the whole volume of his wrath; there is no harm. He is only writing it to get the bile out. So to speak, he is a volcano; imagining himself erupt-ing does no good; he must open up his crater and pour out in

reality his intolerable charge of lava if he would get relief. . . .
Sometimes the load is so hot and so great that one writes as
many as three letters before he gets down to a mailable one; a
very angry one, a less angry one, and an argumentative one
with hot embers in it here and there."

Tragic Mark Twain! Irresponsible child that he is, he does
not even ask himself whether he is doing right or wrong, so
unquestioningly has he accepted the code of his wife and his
friends. That superb passion, the priceless passion of the satirist, is simply being wasted, like the accumulated steam from
an engine whose machinery has broken down and cannot employ it.

Turn to one of these occasions when the charge of lava boiled
up in Mark Twain; compare the two unsent messages he wrote
and the message he finally sent to Colonel George Harvey when
the latter invited him to dine with the Russian emissaries to
the Portsmouth Conference in 1905. To understand them we
must recall Mark Twain's opinion that the premature end of
the Russo-Japanese War was "entitled to rank as the most
conspicuous disaster in political history." Feeling, as he did,
what if the war had lasted a month longer the Russian autoc-
racy would have fallen, he was bitterly opposed to the conference that had been arranged by Roosevelt. Here are the two
telegrams he did not send:

> To COLONEL HARVEY.—I am still a cripple, otherwise I should
> be more than glad of this opportunity to meet those illustrious
> magicians who with the pen have annulled, obliterated and abol-
> ished every high achievement of the Japanese sword and turned
> the tragedy of a tremendous war into a gay and blithesome comedy.
> If I may, let me in all respect and honor salute them as my fellow-
> humorists, I taking third place, as becomes one who was not born
> to modesty, but by diligence and hard work is acquiring it.
>
> MARK.

> DEAR COLONEL—No, this is a love-feast; when you call a lodge
> of sorrow send for me.   MARK.

And this is the telegram he sent, which pleased Count Witte
so much that he announced he was going to show it to the
Czar:

To Colonel Harvey.—I am still a cripple, otherwise I should
be more than glad of this opportunity to meet the illustrious ma-
gicians who came here equipped with nothing but a pen, and with
it have divided the honors of the war with the sword. It is fair to
presume that in thirty centuries history will not get done admiring
these men who attempted what the world regarded as impossible
and achieved it.   Mark Twain.

Another example. In 1905 he wrote a "War Prayer," a bitterly
powerful fragment of concentrated satire. Hear what Mr. Paine
says about it: "To Dan Beard, who dropped in to see him,
Clemens read the 'War Prayer,' stating that he had read it to
his daughter Jean, and others, who had told him he must not
print it, for it would be regarded as sacrilege. 'Still you are
going to publish it, are you not?' Clemens, pacing up and down
the room in his dressing-gown and slippers, shook his head.
'No,' he said. 'I have told the whole truth in that, and only
dead men can tell the truth in this world. It can be published
after I am dead.' He did not care," adds Mr. Paine, "to invite
the public verdict that he was a lunatic, or even a fanatic with
a mission to destroy the illusions and traditions and conclusions
of mankind." The conclusions of mankind! And Mark Twain
was a contemporary of William James! There was nothing in
this prayer that any European writer would have hesitated for
a moment to print. Well, "I have a family to support," wrote
this incorrigible playboy, who was always ready to blow thirty
or forty thousand dollars up the chimney to some new mechanical invention. "I have a family to support, and I can't
afford this kind of dissipation."

Finally, there was the famous episode of the Gorky dinner.
Mark Twain was always solicitous for the Russian people; he
wrote stinging rebukes to the Czar, rebukes in the Swinburnian
manner but informed with a far more genuine passion; he
dreamed of a great revolution in Russia; he was always ready
to work for it. When, therefore, Maxim Gorky came to America to collect funds for this purpose, Mark Twain gladly offered
his aid. Presently, however, it became known that Gorky had
brought with him a woman without benefit of clergy: hotel
after hotel, with all the pious wrath that is so admirably characteristic of Broadway, turned them into the street. Did Mark

Twain hesitate even for a moment? Did anything stir in his conscience? Did it occur to him that great fame and position carry with them a certain obligation, that it is the business of leaders to prevent great public issues from being swamped in petty, personal ones? Apparently not. The authors' dinner, organized in Gorky's honor, was hastily, and with Mark Twain's consent, abandoned. "An army of reporters," says Mr. Paine, "was chasing Clemens and Howells," who appear on that page for all the world like a pair of terrified children. "The Russian revolution was entirely forgotten in this more lively, more intimate domestic interest." What was Mark Twain's own comment on the affair? "Laws," he wrote, in a private memorandum, "can be evaded and punishment escaped, but an openly transgressed custom brings sure punishment. The penalty may be unfair, unrighteous, illogical, and a cruelty; no matter, it will be inflicted just the same. . . . The efforts which have been made in Gorky's justification are entitled to all respect because of the magnanimity of the motive back of them, but I think that the ink was wasted. Custom is custom; it is built of brass, boiler-iron, granite; facts, reasonings, arguments have no more effect upon it than the idle winds have upon Gibraltar." What would Emerson or Thoreau have said, fifty years before, of such an argument, such an assertion of the futility of the individual reason in the face of "brass, boiler-iron, granite" and mob-emotion? It is perhaps the most pitifully abject confession ever written by a famous writer.

This is what became of the great American satirist, the Voltaire, the Swift, the Rabelais of the Gilded Age. If the real prophet is he who attacks the stultifying illusions of mankind, nothing, on the other hand, makes one so popular as to be the moral denouncer of what everybody else denounces. Of the real and difficult evils of society Mark Twain, to be sure, knew little. He attacked monarchy, yes; but monarchy was already an absolescent evil, and in any case this man who took such delight in "walking with kings," as the advertisements say, in actual life, never attacked the one monarch who really was, as it appeared, secure in his seat, the Kaiser. He attacked monarchy because, as he said, it was an eternal denial of "the numerical mass of the nation." He had become, in fact, the incarnation of that numerical mass, the majority, which, in the face of all his personal impulses, he could not consider as anything but invariably right. He could not be the spokesman of the immensities and the eternities, as Carlyle had been, for he knew them not; he could not be, like Anatole France, the spokesman of justice, for indeed he had no ideal. His only criterion was personal, and that was determined by his friends. "On the whole," as Mr. Paine says, "Clemens wrote his strictures more for relief than to print," and when he printed them it was because he had public opinion behind him. Revolt as he might, and he never ceased to revolt, he was the same man who, at the psychological moment, in "The Innocents Abroad," by disparaging Europe and its art and its glamorous past, by disparaging, in short, the history of the human spirit, had flattered the expanding impulse of industrial America. In the face of his own genius, in the face of his own essential desire, he had pampered for a whole generation that national self-complacency which Matthew Arnold quite accurately described as vulgar, and not only vulgar but retarding.

Glance at those last melancholy satirical fragments he wrote in his old age, those fragments which he never published, which he never even cared to finish, but a few paragraphs of which appear in Mr. Paine's biography. We note in them all the gestures of the great unfulfilled satirist he was meant to be; but they are empty gestures; only an impotent anger informs them; Mark Twain's preoccupations are those merely of a bitter and disillusioned child. He wishes to take vengeance upon the Jehovah of the Presbyterians to whom his wife has obliged him to pay homage; but the Jehovah of the Presbyterians, alas! no longer interests humanity. He is beset by all the theological obsessions of his childhood in Missouri; he has never even read "Literature and Dogma"; he does not know that the morbid fears of that old Western village of his have ceased to trouble the moral conscience of the world; he imagines that he can still horrify us with his antiquated blasphemies. He has lived completely insulated from all the real currents of thought in his generation. "The human being," he says, in one of his notes, "needs to revise his ideas again about God. Most of the scientists have done it already, but most of them don't care to say so." He imagines, we see, that all the scientists have, like himself, lived in Hartford and Elmira and married ladies like Mrs. Clemens; and as, according to Mr. Paine, nobody ever dared to contradict him or tell him anything, he never, dazzled as he was by his own fame, discovered his mistake. "The religious folly you were born in you will die in." he wrote once: he meant that he had never himself faced anything out. Was he, or wasn't he, a Presbyterian? He really never knew. If he had matured, those theological preoccupations, constantly imaged in his jokes and anecdotes about heaven, hell and St. Peter, would have simply dropped away from his mind: his inability to express them had fixed them there and his environment kept him constantly reacting against them to the end. Think of those chapters in his Autobiography which he said were "going to make people's hair curl." Several of them, at least, we are told, dealt with infant damnation; but whose hair, in this twentieth century, is going to curl over infant damnation? How little he had observed the real changes in public opinion, this man who lived, instinctively, all his life long, in the atmosphere of the Western Sunday School! "To-morrow," he tells Mr. Paine, in 1906, "I mean to dictate a chapter which will get my heirs and assigns burnt alive if they venture to print it this side of A.D. 2006—which I judge they won't"; and what he dictates is an indictment of the orthodox God. He often spoke of "the edition of A.D. 2006," saying that it would "make a stir when it comes out," and even went so far, as we have seen, as to negotiate for the publication of his memoirs one hundred years after his death. He might have spared himself the trepidation. It is probable that by 1975 those memoirs will seem to the publishing world a very doubtful commercial risk.

Mark Twain's view of man, in short, was quite rudimentary. He considered life a mistake and the human animal the contemptible machine he had found him: that argues the profundity of his own temperament, the depth and magnitude of his own tragedy, but it argues little else. The absurdity of man consisted, in Mark Twain's eyes, in his ridiculous conception of heaven and his conceit in believing himself the Creator's pet. But surely those are not the significant absurdities. "His

heaven is like himself: strange, interesting, astonishing, grotesque," he wrote in one of those pseudo-Swiftian "Letters from
the Earth," which he dictated with such fervor to Mr. Paine.
"I give you my word it has not a single feature in it that he
actually values. It consists—utterly and entirely—of diversions
which he cares next to nothing about here on the earth, yet he
is quite sure he will like in heaven. . . . Most men do not sing,
most men cannot sing, most men will not stay where others
are singing if it be continued more than two hours. Note that.
Only about two men in a hundred can play upon a musical
instrument, and not four in a hundred have any wish to learn
how. Set that down. Many men pray, not many of them like
to do it. . . . All people, sane or insane, like to have variety
in their lives. Monotony quickly wearies them. Now, then, you
have the facts. You know what men don't enjoy. Well, they
have invented a heaven, out of their own heads, all by themselves; guess what it is like?" How far does that satirical gesture
carry us? It is too rustically simple in its animus, and its
presuppositions about the tastes of humanity are quite erro-
neous: to sing, to play and to pray, in some fashion or other,
are universal, admirable and permanent impulses in man.
What is the moral even of that marvelous Odyssey of "Huckleberry Finn"? That all civilization is inevitably a hateful error,
something that stands in the way of life and thwarts it as the
civilization of the Gilded Age had thwarted Mark Twain. But
that is the illusion, or the disillusion, of a man who has never
really known what civilization is, who, in "The Stolen White
Elephant," like H. G. Wells in his early tales, delights in the
spectacle of a general smash-up of a world which he cannot
imagine as worth saving because he has only seen it as a fool's
paradise. What is the philosophy of "The Man That Corrupted
Hadleyburg"? "That every man is strong," as Mr. Paine says,
"until his price is named." But that is not true, to the discrim-
inating sense, at all. It is an army of fifty-two boys that the
Connecticut Yankee collects in order to start the English republic: in childhood, and childhood alone, in short, had Mark
Twain ever perceived the vaunted nobility of the race. The
victim of an arrested development, the victim of a social order
which had given him no general sense of the facts of life and

no sense whatever of its possibilities, he poured vitriol promiscuously over the whole human scene. But that is not satire: that is pathology.

Mark Twain's imagination was gigantesque: his eye, in later life, was always looking through the small end or the large end of a telescope; he oscillated between the posture of Gulliver in Lilliput and the posture of Gulliver in Brobdingnag. That natural tendency toward a magnification or a minification of things human is one of the ear-marks of the satirist. In order to be effectual, however, it requires a measure, an ideal norm, which Mark Twain, with his rudimentary sense of proportion, never attained. It was not fear alone then, but an artistic sense also that led him to suppress, and indeed to leave incomplete, most of the works in which this tendency manifested itself. One recalls his "3000 Years Among the Microbes," passages of which have been published by Mr. Paine. Glance at another example. "I have imagined," he said once, "a man three thousand miles high picking up a ball like the earth and looking at it and holding it in his hand. It would be about like a billiard-ball to him, and he would turn it over in his hand and rub it with his thumb, and where he rubbed over the mountain ranges he might say, 'There seems to be some slight roughness here, but I can't detect it with my eye; it seems perfectly smooth to look at.' " There we have the Swiftian, the Rabelaisian note, the Rabelaisian frame for the picture that fails to emerge. The fancy exists in his mind, but he is able to do nothing with it: all he can do is to express a simple contempt, to rule human life as it were out of court. Mark Twain never completed these fancies precisely, one can only suppose, because they invariably led into this *cul-de-sac*. If life is really futile, then writing is futile also. The true satirist, however futile he may make life seem, never really believes in futile: his interest in its futility is itself a desperate registration of some instinctive belief that it might be, that it could be, full of significance, that, in fact, it *is* full of significance: to him what makes things petty is an ever-present sense of their latent grandeur. That sense Mark Twain had never attained: in consequence, his satirical gestures remained mere passes in the air.

VIII

The Pilgrimage
of Henry James

(New York, 1925)

EDITORIAL NOTE: The composition of *The Pilgrimage of Henry James* was difficult; it was attended by doubts and depression.[1] The availability of James's letters, which Brooks reviewed in 1920 for the *Freeman*, may have precipitated his decision to undertake the biography. The book was interrupted by the need to earn money. This need was in part assuaged by Brooks's usual editorial hack work, then more positively by the *Dial*'s purchase of three James essays, which were to be-

---

[1]In a September 13, 1925, letter, Brooks writes to Mumford of his emergence from a two-year breakdown (*Letters* 33). Much later, he believed his doubts about his expatriation thesis brought him to a "state of irresolution" that "carried me into a formidable nervous breakdown" (*Autobiography* 432).

come chapters in the book. Brooks put the book aside in 1924 hoping to return to it. This seems not to have happened and Brooks fretted that the book was published in an unfinished state.

Brooks had also come to seem an old critic new style as even some supporters—Frank, Rosenfeld, Munson, Wilson, for example—became critical of his positions and his methods. The *Dial* prize in 1924 (Eliot had received it in 1923 for *The Waste Land*) was an alloyed pleasure, as it came with qualified praise from a magazine more "esthetic" than cultural.[2] Although Brooks chafed under writing commitments for the *Freeman*, its demise in 1924 was another blow. By May 1924 he had decided on his next project, a life of Emerson that would represent synthesis to the antitheses of Twain and James (*Autobiography* 425).

Pilgrimage never generated the same excitement or controversy or long-lasting critical impact that *The Ordeal of Mark Twain* had. Critics have not seen James as "an intimidated or sidetracked artist" (Wilson, *Shores* 227) or expatriation as artistically debilitating for him.[3] Quite the reverse. Whatever ambivalence or private pain James suffered as a result of his presumed alienated state, the America-Europe conflict and interaction are usually seen as the source of his greatest fiction.

As noted in the foreword to the 1993 Edition of this volume, Brooks arrives, with *Pilgrimage*, at the pastiche method associated with his later work. Hyman (109) and other critics have pointed out that the habit of reworking quotes or sources without attribution probably derives from Léon Bazalgette's *Henry Thoreau, Sauvage* (1914), which Brooks translated in 1924.

Brooks's desire to have his works read like novels lies behind the questionable methodological shift he announces in his prefactory Note:

[2] Nelson comments that by the time of the *Dial* award, "Brooks's public and private experience had . . . gone hopelessly out of phase" (172).

[3] Some of the biographical gaps in *Pilgrimage* are astonishing. Henry has no mother, only one brother, William, and no sister. The book opens with part of a letter from Henry Sr. about his "four stout boys" (1). Neither the other brothers, Garth and Robertson, nor Alice, nor the mother, Mary Walsh, is ever referred to or named in the text proper.

Readers who are familiar with Henry James will observe that many phrases and even longer passages from his writings have been incorporated in the text of this book, usually without any indication of their source. The author has resorted to this expedient because he knows of no other means of conveying with strict accuracy at moments what he conceives to have been James's thoughts and feelings (v).

Chapter V

THE SACRED FOUNT

IN THE STORY called *The Private Life* the author Clarence Vawdrey is represented as carrying on a double existence. He has indeed, like Dr. Jekyll, two characters, the character that writes and the character that appears in society. "One goes out," says the narrator of the story, "the other stays at home. One is the genius, the other's the bourgeois, and it's only the bourgeois whom we personally know." Here again James describes himself. "Much as he always delighted in sociable communion," says Mr. Lubbock, "all his friends must have felt that at heart he lived in solitude and that few were ever admitted into the inner shrine of his labor."

"There it was nevertheless," Mr. Lubbock continues, "that he lived most intensely and most serenely." And there we must observe him now. He had published in 1875 *A Passionate Pilgrim and Other Tales*; he had written *Watch and Ward* and *Roderick Hudson* in Italy and Cambridge; *The American* had been a fruit of his year in Paris. At the moment of his arrival in England (1876) he had scarcely begun to gather in the

harvest of the experience of his childhood and youth. That was
to be his task for a decade to come: he was to produce in
London chiefly the long series of his American and international
novels and tales, *The Europeans*, *Daisy Miller*, *An International Episode*, *Washington Square*, *The Portrait of a Lady*,
The Siege of London, *Four Meetings*, *The Bostonians*, *The
Aspern Papers*, and it was not till 1890, with the publication
of *The Tragic Muse*, in which for the first time, as he says, he
attacked "a purely English subject on a large scale," that his
first phase was to reach a definite climax. We cannot hope to
characterize all these works. We cannot attempt to trace the
astonishing development of a creative faculty which, in the
course of a dozen years, transcended the simple plot-maker's
art of *The American*, the factitious local-colorism of *Roderick
Hudson*, and rendered itself capable of the serene beauty of
The Portrait of a Lady, the masterly assurance of *The Bostonians*, the mature perfection of *Washington Square*. Least of all
can we penetrate to the heart of this genius, account for it,
apprehend its secret. The most we can do is to endeavor to
describe certain of its qualities, to grasp a few of its aspects,
to perceive it as it were in operation. For the rest, can we
draw out Leviathan with a hook, or his tongue with a cord
which we let down? I will not conceal his parts, said the Lord
to Job, nor his power, nor his comely proportion. But who can
open the doors of his face? His scales are his pride, shut up
together as with a close seal.

As the Lord abashed Job, so genius abashes the critic. Who
can enter into the springs of the sea of personality? Let us seek
merely to observe our author at his writing-table, to experience
a few of the sensations that animate him, to share some of the
thoughts that ascend from the obscure regions of his inner
being. What images, what central vision do we perceive cours-
ing through his brain as he sits, a "bearded Buddha," pen in
hand, amid the flooding daylight of his Kensington flat, as he
walks, the stockiest of apparitions, but with something vague
in the bushiness of his head—an apparition indeed!—as he
saunters, with his devouring eye, through the darkening
streets? A world has come to birth in his soul, a world no
other mind has contemplated. Who are these people that rise

before him in a blazing actuality, rise like flowers, like bitter herbs, in the fat soil of a well-nurtured garden? They are the citizens of a domain of which he is the Prospero. Christopher Newman, Daisy Miller, Isabel Archer, Olive Chancellor, Ralph Touchett, Catherine Sloper, Gilbert Osmond, Verena Tarrant: are they parts of himself, these marvellous creatures? Are they selves that he has dreamed of being, longed to be or feared to be, selves to which he is on the point of giving the *coup de grâce* by endowing them with an external existence? They are his, at least, his in their individuality, his in their community, for innumerable ties unite them. He is their master, their principle of life, the force that moves them all.

"Who is Madame Bovary?" said Flaubert. "She is myself." Shall we insist that all the vital characters in the world of fiction are projections of the "selves" of their authors, of aspects of that Protean creature which every creative personality is? How can we know this? How can we say it? But we are justified perhaps in asserting with Maupassant that a writer cannot explain the springs of action of anyone who is remote in character from himself, in believing with Vernon Lee that the most convincing figures in fiction are those which "to all appearance have never been previously analyzed or rationally understood by the author" but rather, "connected always by a similar emotional atmosphere, have come to him as realities, realities emotionally borne in upon his innermost sense." To this is due that intimacy of presentation, that freedom and spontaneity, that zest in treatment which are characteristic of all the master novelists and appear so markedly in this early world of James. He has inherited Washington Square, he has grown up with the Bostonians, he has shared from his infancy the dreams of the "European" American! Catherine Sloper is the cousin of his own cousins, if not by blood at least by the associations of the little circle of his childhood. But glance at these other characters: are they not all related to him in a similar fashion—as facets, so to speak, of his own multiple psyche, the psyche that has been formed by his heredity, by his environment, by his desires, his fears, his sympathies, his antipathies, by everything which, whatever its source, has lodged in the secret places of his being? Olive Chancellor is

the quintessence of the dry, predacious Boston that he has
watched with the horrified fascination of a young man who
feels that his right to live his own life has been menaced—the
Boston that insists upon subjecting the impulses of the free
individual to the reign of its own provincial law. And how
many of his "selves" have escaped to Europe! Roderick Hudson
is the artist who has come to fill his pitcher at the fountain.
Christopher Newman is the man who has dreamed of entering
the great world and who has been somehow rebuffed. Gilbert
Osmond is the "sterile dilettante" from whom James has taken
warning, the dilettante of whom he has felt the germs in his
own being. Who that has crossed the threshold of this world
and stood in the presence of its inhabitants would ever ask for
the credentials of its creator or question the degree of his
saturation? It is his by a sort of divine right, by the right of
instinctive perception, personal experience, absolute knowledge. He has taken notes indefatigably, but these notes have
served merely to establish in his consciousness facts that have
already existed as it were in the depths of himself. People, his
own people—they crowd, they jostle one another in his imagination. Each person has a story, but the story comes to him
as a consequence of the qualities of the person: he has no
interest in preconceived situations. To give, as Turgenev gave
it, the impression of life itself, and not of an arrangement a
réchauffé of life: that is his desire. And "the form," he feels,
"is to be appreciated after the fact."

The fact. He is a historian, a historian of manners. He is
never to relinquish this rôle which is that of all the novelists
he admires; he is never to relinquish his belief that "the novel
is history" and that "the air of reality (solidity of specification)
is the merit on which all its other merits helplessly and sub-
missively depend." The fact obsesses him: it has called into
play all his knowledge of form. With what grace, what light-
ness and purity he has learned to transmit his impressions!
Turgenev has shown him how to deal with small groups of
characters, isolated and analyzed; Flaubert has taught him the
art of achieving a certain unity of tone; Daudet has helped him
to render the most delicate shades of the actual. But behind
these secrets of the trade there is always life; and he regards

it as the task of the novelist to find out, to know, to see. He
has himself found out, he has known, he has seen: but what
does he know? He knows as no one else has known it one of
the two or three capital phases of the civilization of his country.
Do not ask him if he knows the America that is rooted in the
soil, the sober, laborious America of the pioneers, the dim,
unconscious, Titanic America that is taking shape in the darkness of the hinterland. His America, no less real, is that of the
great towns of the Atlantic seaboard; it is, in particular, the
America that lives in the thought, the memory, the expectation
of the European world from which it has sprung. The nostalgia
for the home of his ancestors of the American who has been
liberated from the bondage of necessity, the romantic vision of
the Old World that exists in the American heart, the drama of
the *émigré* in search of the arts of life—this is his natural
domain. He possesses it as truly as Balzac possessed the Paris
of the Restoration.

He invented it—he discovered it, that is, for literature. He
was the first to become conscious of an actual historic drama
that has played its part in countless lives on the stage of two
continents. He seized upon this drama, traversed and penetrated it in all its aspects; he distinguished the principal types
that were involved in it; he found in it themes for tragedy,
comedy, satire. The American business man who, having made
his fortune, sets out in quest of the fortune he has missed; the
village artist for whom his own country is too immature to
provide a school; the ambitious wife of the captain of industry
who is so anxious to discover "the best"; the schoolmistress
whose parched imagination has been nourished on photographs
of castles and cathedrals; the young girl for whom the idea of
Europe is interchangeable with the idea of culture; the colonists, the wanderers, the dilettanti, the lovers of the past—
such are these beguiled, unsatisfied, imaginative, aspiring, or
merely avid souls whose individual development has outshot
in some fashion or other the general development of the civilization to which they belong. "Our people," said Emerson,
"have their intellectual culture from one country and their
duties from another." This defines the phase of American life
of which James is the historian and the poet. An America that

is actually simple and primitive is inhabited by Americans who inherit the desires, the social and spiritual needs of a civilization that is complex and mature. Release these people from the compulsions of poverty and custom: they read, they dream, they become aware of a thousand requirements for which the world about them affords no scope. There is little in the past of their own country to give shape to these errant fancies that emerge in their minds already clothed as it were in European forms. And accordingly they set forth, as pilgrims to Zion, seekers of the shrine of culture.

Tragedy, satire, comedy are inherent in the situation. Tragedy. The crusade is a children's crusaders are, in our author's phrase, "almost incredibly unaware of life, as the European order expresses life." They are themselves the creatures of another order; they know nothing of the traditions of the Old World, they are unconscious of the fund of evil that runs in the blood of ancient societies, and they take it for granted that the Europeans among whom they are thrown are as ingenuous as themselves. Thus they expose themselves to the direst misunderstandings or they fall into traps and are victimized. To the end of his life, in various forms, James is to repeat this story: for Isabel Archer is only a lovelier Daisy Miller, and Milly Theale is the shadow of Isabel Archer. But comedy and satire spring from these roots as well. The lady correspondent who is so anxious to rifle the secrets of the aristocracy, the American colonists in Paris who are so certain that the French people should be "kept down," Mrs. Touchett, with her "investments," who has lived abroad so long that she has lost her native tact in matters of etiquette, Mr. Flack, the society reporter—they have only to cross the stage to leave in our minds ineffaceable images. They people the Continent with their wit, their vivacity, their absurdity, their vulgarity, their beauty, their avidity.

We are at Geneva, in the 'seventies, in the days of Baron Tauchnitz, on the terrace of the hotel overlooking the lake. There is a flitting hither and thither of stylish young ladies, a rustling of muslim flounces, a rattle of dance-music, a sound of high-pitched voices. Daisy Miller emerges from the open French window, but the youthful Randolph has preceded her.

He has just asked Winterbourne if they have candy in Italy. Rome. The sky is a blaze of blue and the fountains are plashing in their mossy niches. Roderick Hudson has just arrived: he saunters forth into the streets, his brain the theatre of all the emotions of the young artist who has entered Italy for the first time. Venice, and Miss Bordereau hiding away in the depths of her chamber in the old palazzo the letters of the great poet who was her lover in the dim past. Venice, and little Morgan Moreen, the "pupil," dragged about from city to city by his blowsy and sinister family. The café at Havre, and the little schoolmistress of *Four Meetings*, tricked out of her hard earned savings at the very gate of this dear old Europe. Florence, and Gilbert Osmond and Pansy, "the ideal *jeune fille* of foreign fiction," an edifying blank, and the Countess Gemini who has been written over in a variety of hands. Paris, and the C. P. Hatches and Mrs. Tristram, and Christopher Newman looking up at the towering wall of the Carmelite convent and deciding that revenge is "really not his game." But what eye can embrace at a glance this incomparable community, more real and coherent than any that exists in the world? It lives and moves and breathes in all its members, lives and moves with the poignancy of actual life.

It has been observed from above, as Lilliput is observed by Gulliver. This mind sees everything as in itself it really is; nothing escapes it, nothing deludes it.

> Mrs. Luce had been living in Paris since the days of Louis-Philippe; she used to say jocosely that she was one of the generation of 1830—a joke of which the point was not always taken. When it failed Mrs. Luce used always to explain—"Oh, yes, I am one of the romantics"; her French had never become very perfect.

In two sentences we have the germ of a character-study in full length; we know Mrs. Luce as well as if we had been for years one of her visitors on Sunday afternoons.

> The train presently arrived, and Miss Stackpole, promptly descending, proved to be, as Isabel had said, decidedly pretty. She was a fair, plump person, of medium stature, with a round face,

a small mouth, a delicate complexion, a bunch of light brown
ringlets at the back of her head, and a peculiarly open, surprised-
looking eye. The most striking point in her appearance was the
remarkable fixedness of this organ, which rested without impudence
or defiance, but as if in conscientious exercise of a natural right,
upon any object it happened to encounter. It rested in this manner
upon Ralph himself, who was somewhat disconcerted by Miss
Stackpole's gracious and comfortable aspect, which seemed to indicate that it would not be so easy as he had assumed to disapprove
of her. . . . "I don't suppose that you are going to undertake to
persuade me that *you* are an American," she said.

Do we need to be told that Miss Stackpole is a militant patriot,
a resolute woman of action, a resourceful journalist whom
nothing daunts, upon whom nothing is lost, and that in spite
of her disregard of certain fine shades we are going to like her?

[Mrs. Farrinder] was a copious, handsome woman, in whom
angularity had been corrected by the air of success. . . . You . . .
had to feel that Mrs. Farrinder imposed herself. There was a
lithographic smoothness about her, and a mixture of the American
matron and the public character. There was something public in
her eye, which was large, cold, and quiet; it had acquired a sort
of exposed reticence from the habit of looking down from a lecture-
desk, over a sea of heads, while its distinguished owner was eu-
logized by a leading citizen. Mrs. Farrinder, at almost any time,
had the air of being introduced by a few remarks. She talked with
great slowness and distinctness, and evidently a high sense of responsibility; she pronounced every syllable of every word and insisted on being explicit. If, in conversation with her, you attempted
to take anything for granted, or to jump two or three steps at a
time, she paused, looking at you with a cold patience, as if she
knew that trick, and then went on at her own measured pace. She
lectured on temperance and the rights of women; the ends she
labored for were to give the ballot to every woman in the country
and to take the flowing bowl from every man.

[Selah Tarrant] looked like the priest of a religion that was
passing through the stage of miracles; he carried his responsibility
in the general elongation of his person, of his gestures (his hands
were now always in the air, as if he were being photographed in
postures), of his words and sentences, as well as in his smile, as

noiseless as a patent hinge, and in the folds of his eternal waterproof. . . . [He] and his companion had strange adventures; she found herself completely enrolled in the great irregular army of nostrum-mongers, domiciled in humanitary Bohemia. It absorbed her like a social swamp; she sank into it a little more every day, without measuring the inches of her descent. . . . She had lived with long-haired men and short-haired women, she had contributed a fleixble faith and an irremediable want of funds to a dozen socal experiments, she had partaken of the comfort of a hundred religions, had followed innumerable dietary reforms, chiefly of the negative order, and had gone of an evening to a *séance* or a lecture as regularly as she had eaten her supper. Her husband always had tickets for lectures; in moments of irritation at the want of a certain sequence in their career, she had remarked to him that it was the only thing he did have. The memory of all the winter nights they had tramped through the slush (the tickets, alas! were not car-tickets) to hear Mrs. Ada T. P. Foat discourse on the "Summerland," came back to her with bitterness. . . . She had blinked and compromised and shuffled; she asked herself whether, after all, it was any more than natural that she should have wanted to help her husband, in those exciting days of his mediumship, when the table, sometimes, wouldn't rise from the ground, the sofa wouldn't float through the air, and the soft hand of a loved lost one was not so alert as it might have been to visit the circle. Mrs. Tarrant's hand was soft enough for the most supernatural effect, and she consoled her conscience on such occasions by reflecting that she ministered to a belief in immortality.

These are the guardians of the exquisite Andromeda, chained to the rock of the Philistines, about whom the battles rage, in *The Bostonians*—the same Verena Tarrant who, in her fantastic costume, appears, springs up, before the astonished eyes of Basil Ransom, as if it were the necessity of her nature "to emit those charming notes of her voice, to stand in those free young attitudes, to shake her braided locks like a naiad rising from the waves, to please everyong who came near her, and to be happy that she pleased." James's young girls are always his happiest creations; it is as if they alone, of all his compatriots, filled him with frank satisfaction. Here again he resembles Turgenev, and like Turgenev, when he writes of them, he abandons his irony. Glance at this first sketch of Isabel Archer.

A dozen words are enough to engage our affection; we are prepared to follow her, if the author wills it, through ten volumes, and we are aware from the first sentence that her destiny is not to be a happy one.

> Her thoughts were a tangle of vague outlines, which had never been corrected by the judgment of people who seemed to her to speak with authority. In matters of opinion she had had her own way, and it had led her into a thousand ridiculous zigzags. Every now and then she found out she was wrong, and then she treated herself to a week of passionate humility. After this she held her head higher than ever again; for it was of no use, she had an unquenchable desire to think well of herself. She had a theory that it was only on this condition that life was worth living; that one should be one of the best, should be conscious of a fine organization (she could not help knowing her organization was fine), should move in a realm of light, of natural wisdom, of happy impulse, of inspiration gracefully chronic. . . . She spent half her time in thinking of beauty, and bravery, and magnanimity; she had a fixed determination to regard the world as a place of brightness, of free expansion, of irresistible action; she thought it would be detestable to be afraid or ashamed. . . . Altogether, with her meagre knowledge, her inflated ideals, her confidence at once innocent and dogmatic, her temper at once exacting and indulgent, her mixture of curiosity and fastidiousness, of vivacity and indifference, her desire to look very well and to be if possible even better; her determination to see, to try, to know; her combination of the delicate, desultory, flame-like spirit and the eager and personal young girl, she would be an easy victim of scientific criticism, if she were not intended to awaken on the reader's part an impulse more tender and more purely expectant.

Such is the population of this little world, this *piccolo mondo antico* that is yet so modern. And mingling with these Americans are the Europeans who cross their path, lightly sketched but closely observed, filling the middle distance. Lord Warburton, the Misses Molyneux, the dilapidated *cavaliere* in *Roderick Hudson*, Mr. Vetch, the old fiddler in *The Princess Casamassima*, M. Poupin, the exiled Communard, Miss Pynsent—how clearly they have been seen, how fairly judged! And who can forget Millicent Henning, daughter of the London streets, or the death of Hyacinth's mother in Millbank Prison? Such had been the result of James's first impressions in the London air, of the "assault," as he calls it somewhere, "directly made by the great city upon an imagination quick to react." He had seen England in relief against the world that he intimately knew. Faces at the window, figures in the doorway— the harvest of an ever-burning eye.

Yes, to this eye pensions and hotels and ocean liners and the streets and the theatres of the Old World have given up their secrets. "I have always thought the observant faculty a windy impostor," our author says in one of his early stories, "so long as it refuses to pocket pride and doff its bravery and crawl on all-fours, if need be, into the unillumined corners and crannies of life." And again, in his essay on Du Maurier: "There are certain protensions [the thorough-going artist] can never take seriously; in the artist there is of necessity, as it appears to us, a touch of the democrat. . . . Du Maurier possesses in perfection the independence of the genuine artist in the presence of a hundred worldly superstitions and absurdities." James is to forget this truth as the years pass, but not for nothing has he prowled about in the days of his obscurity. His mind has retained its independence; he has, if not the universalized, at least the generalized consciousness of the authentic realist. Life judges itself through his perceptions, and behind what is he sees what ought to be. For he is by nature a social critic, a satirist, in the line of his adored Thackeray, Balzac and Turgenev.

A historian of manners, a critic of manners, a mind at home with itself, alert, witty, instructed, in its own familiar domain. Yes, and in the foreground of life, the ground of the typical, the general. Turgenev said of Flaubert's Monsieur Homais that the great strength of such a portrait consisted in its being at once an individual, of the most concrete sort, and a type. James creates these types again and again: they are not universal but they are national—there are scarcely half a dozen figures in American fiction to be placed beside them. Christopher Newman remains for all time the wistful American businessman who spends his life hankering after the fine things he has missed. Daisy Miller's character, predicament, life, and death are the story of a whole phase of the social history of America. Dr. Sloper, that perfect embodiment of the respectability of old New York; Miss Birdseye, the symbol of the aftermath of the heroic age of New England; Mrs. Burrage, the eternal New York hostess; Gilbert Osmond, the Italianate American—these are all veritable creations: indeed one has only to recall Winterbourne, in *Daisy Miller*, the American who has lived abroad so long that he has ceased to understand the behavior of his fellow-countrywoman, to perceive with what an unfailing resourcefulness James infuses into the least of his characters the element of the typical. It goes without saying that all this, together with the tenderness and the benevolent humor that bathe the primitive Jamesian scene, indicates the sort of understanding that is born only of race. These novels are the work of a man who was so sure of his world that he could play with it as all the great novelists have played with their worlds. The significant theme came to him with a natural inevitability, for he shared some of the deepest and most characteristic desires of his compatriots. And this relation, as long as he maintained it, endowed him with the notes of the great tellers of tales, the note of the satirist, the note of the idyllist, the note of the tragedian.

And "how does he feel about life? What, in the last analysis, is his philosophy? When vigorous writers have reached maturity," James remarks in *Partial Portraits*, "we are at liberty to look in their works for some expression of a total view of the world they have been so actively observing." Nothing could be clearer than his own view, the point, as it might be called, of these gathered novels and tales. Mr. Hueffer says that James's chief mission was to civilize America; and if by civilizing one means the development of individuality, the development of consciousness, one can hardly find a happier phrase. He is the friend of all those who are endeavoring to clarify their own minds, to know their own reasons, to discover their real natures, to make the most of their faculties, to escape from the lot of mere passive victims of fate. His tragedies are all the tragedies of *not knowing*; and those against whom he directs his shafts are the representatives and advocates of mass-opinion and of movements that mechanize the individual. He was the first novelist in the distinctively American line of our day: the first to challenge the herd-instinct, to reveal the inadequacy of our social life, to present the plight of the highly personalized human being in the primitive community. And James succeeds, where so many later novelists have failed, succeeds in present-ing the struggle for the rights of personality—the central theme of all modern American fiction, because he is able to conceive personalities of transcendent value.

Yes, his own race, even his own soil—the soil to which he had remained for so long uneasily attached, the soil in which, in response to his own desire, he was brought back to be buried at last—was for James, in spite of all, the Sacred Fount. It was the spring of his own unconscious being; and the world to which it gave birth in his mind was a world that he saw with a level eye, as it was, as it should be, that he loved, hated, possessed, caressed, and judged. Judged it humanely, in the light of essential standards, of the "scale of mankind," in Dos-toevsky's phrase, and by so doing created values for it. . . . As long as he retained a vital connection with it. But later? . . . "The world," says Mr. Lubbock, referring to his life in England, "is not used to such deference from a rare critical talent, and it certainly has much less respect for its own stan-dards than Henry James had, or seemed to have. His respect was of course very freely mingled with irony, and yet it would be rash to say that his irony preponderated. He probably felt that this, in his condition, was a luxury which he could only afford within limits." That is discreetly put, but what it was to mean we can divine from one of his own early letters from London: "You will have read the second part [of *An Interna-tional Episode*] by this time," he writes to his mother, "and I hope that you won't, like many of my friends here (as I partly know and partly suspect) take it ill of me as against my 'British entertainers.' It seems to me myself that I have been very delicate; but I shall keep off dangerous ground in future. It is an entirely new sensation for them (the people here) to be (at all delicately) *ironized* or satirized, from the American point of view, and they don't at all relish it." That is also discreetly put; nevertheless, it marks the beginning of the gradual meta-morphosis of James's mind. He had seen life, in his own way, as all the great novelists have seen it, *sub specie æternitatis*; he was to see it henceforth, increasingly, *sub specie mundi*— for had he not subscribed, as only a probationer can subscribe, to the codes and scruples, the conventions and prejudices, the standards (held so lightly by everyone else) of the world he longed to possess? In adapting himself to this world he was to lose his instinctive judgment of men and things; and this explains his "virtuosity of vision," as Mr. Brownell describes it, the gradual decomposition, more and more marked the more his talent grew, of his sense of human values.

Bibliography

SPECIAL MATERIALS

Van Wyck Brooks Papers, Special Collections, Van Pelt Library, University of Pennsylvania.

WORKS (arranged chronologically)

(with John Hall Wheelock) *Verses by Two Undergraduates*. Cambridge, Mass., 1905.

The Wine of the Puritans. London, 1908.

The Soul. San Francisco, 1910.

The Malady of the Ideal. London, 1913.

John Addington Symonds: A Biographical Study. New York, 1914.

The World of H. G. Wells. New York, 1915.

America's Coming-of-Age. New York, 1915.

Letters and Leadership. New York, 1918. Collects *The Seven Arts* essays.

The Ordeal of Mark Twain. New York, 1920.

The Pilgrimage of Henry James. New York, 1925.

Emerson and Others. New York, 1927. Collects previously published material, especially from *The Freeman*.

The Life of Emerson. New York, 1932.

Sketches in Criticism. New York, 1932. Collects previously published material, especially from *The Freeman*.

Three Essays on America. New York, 1934. Republishes, with revisions, *America's Coming-of-Age, Letters and Leadership* and *The Literary Life in America*.

Makers and Finders: A History of the Writer in America, 1880-1915. The Flowering of New England. New York, 1936.

New England: Indian Summer. New York, 1940.

The World of Washington Irving. New York, 1944.

The Times of Melville and Whitman. New York, 1947.

The Confident Years: 1885-1915. New York, 1952.

On Literature Today. New York, 1941.

The Opinions of Oliver Allston. New York, 1941.

A Chilmark Miscellany. New York, 1948.

The Writer in America. New York, 1953.

John Sloan: A Painter's Life. New York, 1955.

From a Writer's Notebook. Worcester, Mass., 1955.

Helen Keller: Sketch for a Portrait. New York, 1955.

The Dream of Arcadia: American Writers and Artists in Italy, 1760-1915. New York, 1958.

Howells: His Life and Work. New York, 1959.

Fenollosa and His Circle. New York, 1962.

An Autobiography. New York, 1965. Contains the three previously published volumes:
Scenes and Portraits. New York, 1954.
Days of the Phoenix. New York, 1957.
From the Shadow of the Mountain. New York, 1961.

EDITIONS AND TRANSLATIONS: A SELECTED LIST

Malherbe, Henri. *The Flame That Is France*, trans. Van Wyck Brooks. New York, 1918.

Bourne, Randolph. *The History of a Literary Radical*, ed. with an introduction by Van Wyck Brooks. New York, 1920.

Berguer, Georges. *Some Aspects of the Life of Jesus from the Psychological and Psychoanalytic Point of View*, trans. Eleanor Stimson Brooks and Van Wyck Brooks. New York, 1923.

Columbus, Christopher. *Journal of the First Voyage to America*, intro. Van Wyck Brooks. New York, 1924.

Bazalgette, Léon. *Henry Thoreau: Bachelor of Nature*, trans. Van Wyck Brooks. New York, 1924.

Rourke, Constance. *The Roots of American Culture,* ed. with a preface by Van Wyck Brooks. New York, 1942.

MISCELLANEOUS

Brooks, Van Wyck. "The Literary Life," in *Civilization in the United States: An Inquiry by Thirty Americans,* ed. Harold Stearns. New York, 1922. This essay was published as *The Literary Life in America,* New York, 1927, and republished under the same title in *Three Essays on America.*

Brooks, Van Wyck. "Recollections of Plainfield: An Informal Talk Delivered at the 70th Anniversary Celebration of the Plainfield Public Library, November 11, 1951." Plainfield, 1952.

Van Wyck Brooks, 1886–1963: Materials for a Biography, Publication No. 224, American Academy of Arts and Letters, 1965.

Brooks, Van Wyck, and Lewis Mumford. *Letters: The Record of a Literary Friendship, 1921–1963.* Ed. Robert E. Spiller. New York, Dutton, 1963.

ARTICLES

Forum

"Vernon Lee," XLV (April 1911), 447-456.

"Maurice de Guérin," XLVII (May 1912), 621-628.

"Amiel," XLVIII (July 1912), 120-128. The articles on de Guérin and Amiel were incorporated into *The Malady of the Ideal.*

"Platitude," XLVIII (November 1912), 608-611.

"John Addington Symonds," XLIX (April 1913), 489-500. Incorporated into the biography of Symonds.

"The World of H. G. Wells," LII (July-September 1914), 128-142; 278-298; 451-462. Incorporated into the biography of Wells.

"Highbrow and Lowbrow," LIII (April 1915), 481-492. Incorporated into *America's Coming-of-Age.*

The Seven Arts

"Enterprise," I (November 1916), 57-60.

See *Letters and Leadership,* Chapter I, pp. 1-7. All references to *Letters and Leadership* are only approximate; Brooks transposed and edited these essays and one *Dial* essay to form that book.

"Young America," I (December 1916), 144-151.

"The Splinter of Ice," I (January 1917), 270-280.
See *Letters and Leadership,* Chapter II.

"Toward A National Culture," I (March 1917), 535-547.
See *Letters and Leadership,* Chapter I and III.

"The Culture of Industrialism," I (April 1917), 655-666.
See *Letters and Leadership,* Chapters II, III, VI.

"Our Critics," II (May 1917), 103-116.
See *Letters and Leadership,* Chapter IV. *Letters and Leadership* omits the discussion of Phelps and adds a discussion of Sherman. The version of *Letters and Leadership* in *Three Essays on America* entirely omits the sections on Phelps, Sherman and Spingarn.

"Sinclair Lewis and Others," II (May 1917), 121-122.

"Our Awakeners," II (June 1917), 235-248.
See *Letters and Leadership,* Chapters III, V.

The Dial (under Martyn Johnson)

"Ireland, 1916," LXI (November 30, 1916), 458-460.

"An American Oblomov," LXIII (March 22, 1917), 244-245.

"War's Heritage to Youth," LXIV (January 17, 1918), 47-50.
Revised to become Chapter VI, "Towards the Future," in *Letters and Leadership.*

"On Creating a Usable Past," LXIV (April 11, 1918), 337-341.

The Dial (under Scofield Thayer)

"Mark Twain's Humour," LXVII (March 1920), 275-291.

"Mark Twain's Satire," LXVIII (April 1920), 424-443.
Both articles on Twain were incorporated into *The Ordeal of Mark Twain.*

"Henry James: The First Phase," LXXIV (May 1923), 433-450.

"Henry James: The American Scene," LXXV (July 1923) 29-42.

"Henry James: An International Episode," LXXV (September 1923), 225-238.

The James articles were incorporated into *The Pilgrimage of Henry James*.

The Freeman

The listing is not complete since many *Freeman* articles are anonymous.

A "A Reviewer's Note-book."

For identification of Van Wyck Brooks as the "Reviewer" see footnote announcements, *Freeman*, V (May 24, 1922), 262; VI (Jan. 10, 1923), 166. See also Van Wyck Brooks to Sherwood Anderson, March 1, 1920. Unpublished letter; Sherwood Anderson Collection, Newberry Library, and Helen Swift Neilson's copy of *The Freeman*. Volume and page numbers are listed for simplification.

I (1920), 47, 70-71, 95, 118-119, 143, 166-167, 190-191, 214-215, 238-239, 262-263, 286-287, 310-311, 334-335, 358-359, 382-383, 407, 430-431, 454-455, 478-479, 501-503, 526-527, 550-551, 574-575, 598-599, 622-623.

II (1920-1921) 22-23, 46-47, 70-71, 94-95, 118-119, 142-143, 166-167, 190-191, 214-215, 238-239, 262-263, 286-287, 311, 334-335, 358-359, 383, 406-407, 431, 455, 479, 502-503, 526-527.

III (1921), 22-23, 47, 71, 94-95, 118-119, 142-143, 166-167, 190-191, 214-215, 238-239, 262-263, 286-287, 310-311, 334-335, 358-359, 382-383, 406-407, 478-479, 526-527, 574-575, 598-599, 622-623.

IV (1921-1922), 22-23, 46-47, 71, 118-119, 166-167, 190-191, 214-215, 262-263, 286-287, 310-311, 334-335, 358-359, 382-383, 407, 430-431, 455, 478-479, 502-503, 526-527, 550-551, 598-599, 622-623.

V (1922), 22-23, 47, 70-71, 94-95, 118-119, 142-143, 166-167, 191, 214-215, 238-239.

VI (1923), 454-455, 478-479, 502-503, 526-527, 550-551, 598-599, 622-623.

VII (1923), 47-214-215, 238-239, 262-263, 286-287, 334-335, 358-359, 431, 378-379, 502-503, 527, 574-575.

VIII (1924), 527, 550-551, 574-575, 598-599, 622-623.

B. Separate articles.

Brooks has been identified as the author of the anonymous articles marked below with an asterisk by Helen Swift Neilson in her copy of *The Freeman*, now part of the Helen Swift Neilson Collection, the Newberry Library.

"A Lost Prophet," I (March 24, 1920), 46-47.

"The Genesis of Huck Finn," I (March 31, 1920), 59-62.

"A French View of Whitman," I (March 31, 1920), 68-69.

"Chekhov in His Letters," I (April 7, 1920), 93-95.

"An Heir of Patrick Henry," I (April 14, 1920), 118.

"Spanish-American Literature," I (April 21, 1920), 141-143.

"Our Illustrious Expatriate," I (April 28, 1920), 164-165.

*"French Literature in the War," I (June 9, 1920), 309-310.

*"Thomas Hardy," I (June 23, 1920), 344.

*"A Moral Hobbledehoy," I (July 14, 1920), 427-428.

*"A Creative Traveller and Others," I (July 14, 1920), 429-430.

*"A Vindication of Literature," I (July 21, 1920), 437-439.

*"The Limbo of the Magazine," I (Jcly 28, 1920), 461-63.

*"Back to the Woods," II (Sept. 15, 1920), 7-8.

*"Professor Sherman's Tradition," II (Oct. 27, 1920), 151-154.

*"The Loneliness of American Life," II (Oct. 6, 1920), 79-80.

*"Mr. Mencken and the Prophets," II (Oct. 13, 1920), 103-104.

*"The Integrity of Individuality," II (Nov. 24, 1920), 247.

*"Enemies of the People," II (Jan. 19, 1921), 437-439.

*"A Question of Honesty," II (Feb. 2, 1921), 486-487.

*"The Migratory Artist," II (March 9, 1921), 607-608.

*"Under a Leaden Sky," III (July 20, 1921), 438-440.

*"Our Lost Intransigents," III (Aug. 10, 1921), 510-511.

*"The Key of Liberty," VII (May 2, 1923), 173-174.

SELECTED SECONDARY SOURCES

Abrahams, Edward. *The Lyrical Left: Randolph Bourne and Alfred Stieglitz and the Origins of Cultural Radicalism in America*. Charlottesville: University Press of Virginia, 1986.

Biel, Steven. *Independent Intellectuals in the United States: 1910–1945*. New York: New York University Press, 1992.

Blake, Casey Nelson. *Beloved Community: The Cultural Criticism of Randolph Bourne, Van Wyck Brooks, Waldo Frank, and Lewis Mumford*. Chapel Hill: University of North Carolina Press, 1990.

Bourne, Randolph. *The Letters of Randolph Bourne*. Ed. Eric J. Sandeen. Troy, N.Y.: Whitston, 1981.

———. "The Puritan's Will to Power." *Seven Arts* I (April 1917): 631–627.

———. "Seeing We See Not." In *Youth and Life*. 1913; rpt. New York: Franklin, 1971, 217–224.

———. "Trans-National America." *Atlantic* 118 (July 1916): 86–97. Rpt. in *The History of A Literary Radical*. Ed. Van Wyck Brooks. New York: Russell, 1956: 260–284.

———. *The World of Randolph Bourne*. Ed. Lillian Schlissel. New York: Dutton, 1965.

Brooks, Gladys. *If Strangers Meet: A Memory*. New York: Harcourt, 1967.

De Voto, Bernard. *Mark Twain's America*. Cambridge: Houghton Mifflin, 1932.

Dewey, John. "The Principle of Nationality." *Menorah Journal* 3 (October 1917). Quoted in Abrahams, 65.

Dickstein, Morris. *Double Agent: The Critic and Society*. New York: Oxford University Press, 1992.

Douglas, Ann. *Feminization and American Culture*. New York: Avon, 1978.

Dow, Eddy. "Van Wyck Brooks and Lewis Mumford: A Confluence in the 'Twenties.'" *American Literature* 45 (November 1973): 407–422. Rpt. in Wasserstrom, 1979, 239–251.

Dupee, F. W. "The Americanism of Van Wyck Brooks." In *Partisan Reader*. Ed. William Phillips and Philip Rahv. New York: Dial Press, 1946, 363–377. Rpt. in Wasserstrom, 1979, 117–128.

Ferguson, DeLancey. "The Case for Mark Twain's Wife." *U of Toronto Q* 9 (October 1939): 9–21.

Frank, Waldo. *Memoirs of Waldo Frank.* Ed. Alan Trachtenberg. Introduction by Lewis Mumford. Amherst: University of Massachusetts Press, 1973.

Frank, Waldo, Lewis Mumford, Dorothy Norman, Paul Rosenfeld, and Harold Rugg, eds. *America and Alfred Stieglitz.* New York: Doubleday, 1934.

Gates, Henry Louis, Jr. *Loose Canons: Notes on the Culture Wars.* New York: Oxford University Press, 1992.

Gordon, Robert. *John Butler Yeats and John Sloan: The Records of a Friendship.* New Yeats Papers XIV. Dublin: Dolmen Press, 1978.

Hoffman, Andrew Jay. *Twain's Heroes, Twain's Wounds.* Philadelphia: University of Pennsylvania Press, 1988.

Hoffman, Frederick, Charles Allen, and Carolyn F. Ulrich. *The Little Magazine.* Princeton: Princeton University Press, 1946.

"Homage to Van Wyck Brooks." *Proceedings of the American Academy of Arts & Letters and The National Institute of Arts and Letters.* 2d Ser., no. 12 (1962): 142–168. Rpt. in Wasserstrom, 1979, 169–185.

Hoopes, James. *Van Wyck Brooks: In Search of American Culture.* Amherst: University of Massachusetts Press, 1977.

Hyman, Stanley Edgar. "Van Wyck Brooks and Biographical Criticism." In *The Armed Vision.* New York: Knopf, 1948, 106–126.

Jackson, Holbrook. *The Eighteen Nineties.* New York: Putnam's, 1966.

James, William. *A Pluralistic Universe.* London: Longmans, Green, 1909.

Kaplan, Justin. *Mr. Clemens and Mark Twain.* New York: Simon & Schuster, 1966.

Krupnick, Mark. *Lionel Trilling and the Fate of Cultural Criticism.* Evanston, Ill.: Northwestern University Press, 1986.

Lears, T. J. Jackson. *No Place of Grace: Antimodernism and the Transformation of American Culture 1880–1920.* New York: Pantheon, 1981.

Leary, Lewis, ed. *A Casebook on Mark Twain's Wound.* New York: Crowell, 1962.

Mencken, H. L. "Puritanism as a Literary Force." *A Book of Prefaces*. 1917; rpt. Garden City, N.Y.: Doubleday, 1927, 197–283.

Mumford, Lewis. *The Golden Day*. 1926; rpt. Boston: Beacon Press, 1957.

———. *The Story of Utopias*. 1922; rpt. New York: Viking, 1962.

Munson, Gorham B. "Van Wyck Brooks: His Sphere and His Encroachments." *Dial* 78 (1925): 28–42. Rpt. in Wasserstrom, 1979, 44–55.

Nelson, Raymond. *Van Wyck Brooks: A Writer's Life*. New York: Dutton, 1981.

Paul, Sherman. "The Ordeal and the Pilgrimage." *New Leader* (February 15, 1965): 19–20. Rpt. in Wasserstrom, 1979.

Rahv, Philip. "De Voto and Kulturbolschewismus." In *Image and Idea*. Norfolk, Conn.: New Directions, 1949, 161–164.

———. "Paleface and Redskin." In *Image and Idea*. Norfolk, Conn.: New Directions, 1949, 1–5.

Reising, Russell J. *The Unusable Past: Theory and the Study of American Literature*. New York & London: Methuen, 1986.

Rosenfeld, Paul. "Van Wyck Brooks." In *Port of New York*. 1924; rpt. Champaign: University of Illinois Press, 1961, 11–32.

Slotkin, Richard. *The Fatal Environment: The Myth of the Frontier and the Age of Industrialism: 1800–1890*. New York: Athenaeum, 1985.

Spiller, Robert E. "The Battle of the Books." In *Literary History of the United States*. New York: Macmillan, 1946, 1953, 1135–1156.

Stoneley, Peter. *Mark Twain and the Feminine Aesthetic*. Cambridge: Cambridge University Press, 1992.

Thomas, John L. "The Uses of Catastrophism: Lewis Mumford, Vernon L. Parrington, Van Wyck Brooks, and the End of American Regionalism." *American Q* 42:2 (June 1990): 223–251.

Tompkins, Jane. *Sensational Designs: The Cultural Work of American Fiction, 1790–1860*. New York: Oxford University Press, 1985.

Trilling, Lionel. "Reality in America." In *The Liberal Imagination*. Garden City, N.Y.: Doubleday, 1950, 15–32.

Vitelli, James R. *Van Wyck Brooks*. New York: Twayne, 1969.

Wasserstrom, William. *The Legacy of Van Wyck Brooks: A Study of Maladies and Motives.* Carbondale: Southern Illinois University Press, 1971.

———. "Van Wyck Brooks." University of Minnesota Pamphlets on American Writers No. 71. Minneapolis: University of Minnesota Press, 1968. Rpt. in Wasserstrom, 1979, 212–237.

———. *Van Wyck Brooks: The Critic and His Critics.* Port Washington, N.Y.: Kennikat, 1979.

Wescott, Glenway. "Van Wyck Brooks." *New York Times Book Review* (December 13, 1964): 2. Rpt. in Wasserstrom, 1979, 202–205.

Williams, Raymond. *Keywords: A Vocabulary of Culture and Society.* New York: Oxford University Press, 1976.

Wilson, Edmund. "Ezra Pound's Patchwork." *New Republic* (April 19, 1922). Rpt. in *The Shores of Light.* New York: Farrar, Straus & Young, 1952, 44–48.

———. "A Picture to Hang in the Library: Brooks's Age of Irving." *New Yorker* (October 7, 1944). Rpt. in *Classics and Commericals.* New York: Farrar, Straus, 1950, 224–230.

———. "*The Pilgrimage of Henry James.*" *New Republic* (May 6, 1925). Rpt. in *The Shores of Light,* 217–228.

———. "Van Wyck Brooks's Second Phase." *New Republic* (Sept. 30, 1940). Rpt. in *Classics and Commercials,* 10–18.

INDEX